FROM MUTUAL AID TO THE WELFARE STATE

DAVID T. BEITO

From Mutual Aid
to the Welfare State

Fraternal Societies and Social Services,

1890–1967

The University of North Carolina Press

Chapel Hill and London

The paper in this book meets the guidelines for permanence and
durability of the Committee on Production Guidelines for Book
Longevity of the Council on Library Resources.

Library of Congress Cataloging-in-Publication Data

Beito, David T.   From mutual aid to the welfare state : fraternal
societies and social services, 1890–1967 / David Beito.
p. cm.   Includes bibliographical references and index.
ISBN 0-8078-2531-x (cloth : alk. paper)
ISBN 0-8078-4841-7 (pbk. : alk. paper)
1. Friendly societies—United States—History.   2. Insurance,
Fraternal—United States—History.   3. Mutualism—United States
—History.   I. Title.
HS61.A17 2000   334'.7'0973—dc21   99-41895 CIP
04 03 02 01 00   5 4 3 2 1

To Linda, my beautiful wife.

My scholarship is inspired by her

never-failing love and encouragement.

CONTENTS

TABLES

ACKNOWLEDGMENTS

U nfortunately, I do not have enough space to properly thank everyone who contributed to this book. My interest in this topic was first sparked by Tom G. Palmer and Walter Grinder, who recommended that I read the works of David G. Green and Lawrence Cromwell, especially *Mutual Aid or Welfare State? Australia's Friendly Societies* (Sydney: Allen and Unwin, 1984).

I received financial support for research and writing from several organizations: the John M. Olin Foundation, the Social Philosophy and Policy Center at Bowling Green State University, the Institute for Humane Studies at George Mason University, and the Earhart Foundation. Without the help of these organizations, I would never have completed this book.

A few individuals deserve special recognition for their editorial comments on manuscript drafts. The unparalleled editing skills of Ellen McDonald helped bring the length to a manageable size. Carrie-Ann Biondi, Richard Keenam, and my mother, Doris Beito, devoted much time to reading drafts, and their advice vastly improved the final version. My good friend T. J. Olson not only carefully read all drafts but was a source of moral support and good humor.

Parts of this book appeared in the *Journal of Policy History*, the *Journal of Urban History*, the *Journal of Interdisciplinary History*, and the *Journal of Southern History*. I would like to thank the editors for their cooperation.

Many others contributed in various capacities to the completion of this book, including David M. Anderson, William Beach, Jonathan Bean, David Bernstein, Bradley Birzer, David D. Boaz, John B. Boles, Stephen Borrelli, Donald J. Boudreaux, Lawrence W. Boyd, Mark Brady, Kay Branyon, Bryan Caplan, John Chodes, Robert H. Cihak, Richard Cornuelle, Jay Coughtry, Stephen Cox, Donald T. Critchlow, Milburn Crowe, Stephen Davies, Mary Dilsaver, John Dittmer, Harold Dolan, Minneola Dixon, Steven Eagle, John S. Evans, David M. Fahey, David Fitzsimons, Edward M. Freedman, Anne Freer, Tony Freyer, Jeffrey Friedman, Loretta Fuller, David R. Goldfield, Charles Hamilton, John Hasnas, Howard Husock, Howard Jones, Daniel Klein, Alan M. Kraut, Gail Ann Levis, Bronwen Lichtenstein, Leonard Liggio, John McClaughry, Deidre McCloskey, Forrest McDonald, Steven Macedo, R. Reid McKee, Ron Maner, Scott

Marler, Vernon Mattson, Adam Meyerson, Fred D. Miller Jr., Eugene Moehring, Julie Moore, Jennifer Morse, Charles Murray, Evelyn Nolen, Ellen Frankel Paul, Mavis Paull, Alan Petigny, Robert D. Putnam, Greg Rehmke, David K. Rosner, David Schmidtz, Daniel Shapiro, Tammara Sharp, Jeremy Shearmur, Leslie Siddeley, Theda Skocpol, Carol DeGroff Sook, Kory Swanson, Maarten Ultee, Terrie Weaver, Stephanie Wenzel, Charles A. Westin, Nancy Wingfield, Martin Wooster, and Keith L. Yates. Finally, I am delighted to once again have had the privilege of working with Lewis Bateman of the University of North Carolina Press.

ABBREVIATIONS USED IN THE TEXT

AALL	American Association for Labor Legislation
AFA	Associated Fraternities of America
AMA	American Medical Association
AOF	Ancient Order of Foresters
AOUW	Ancient Order of United Workmen
FOE	Fraternal Order of Eagles
GUOOF	Grand United Order of Odd Fellows
IESA	Insurance Economics Society of America
IFA	Insurance Federation of America
IOF	Independent Order of Foresters
IOOF	Independent Order of Odd Fellows
IOSL	Independent Order of Saint Luke
LOTM	Ladies of the Maccabees
MWA	Modern Woodmen of America
NAACP	National Association for the Advancement of Colored People
NCF	National Civic Federation
NFC	National Fraternal Congress
NFCA	National Fraternal Congress of America
NMA	National Medical Association
OEO	Office of Economic Opportunity
RCNL	Regional Council of Negro Leadership
SBA	Security Benefit Association
UOTR	United Order of True Reformers
WBA	Woman's Benefit Association
WC	Workmen's Circle

INTRODUCTION

The tendency to join fraternal organizations for the purpose of obtaining care
and relief in the event of sickness and insurance for the family in case of death
is well-nigh universal. To the laboring classes and those of moderate
means they offer many advantages not to be had elsewhere.
—New Hampshire Bureau of Labor, *Report* (1894)

Nineteen thirty-four was one of the worst years of the Great Depression in the United States. Unrelenting hard times had devastated the incomes of millions and exhausted their savings. Many others teetered on the edge. For these men and women, an unanticipated family emergency, such as a hospital stay, could have dire economic consequences. Unlike many Americans, Ruth Papon of Olathe, Kansas, was prepared. She was a member of the Security Benefit Association (SBA), a fraternal society. The SBA's hospital in Topeka provided care to members at reduced cost. In February 1934 Papon checked in for a "4-in-1 major operation." Although the surgery was successful, she contracted a severe case of lobar pneumonia a week after her release. She returned to the hospital in March and was released again after a short stay. Four months later Papon reflected on her experiences: "I know I owe my life to the care the doctors and nurses gave me. . . . They seem to take a personal interest and there is such a homey air. No other hospital seems like ours."[1]

Ruth Papon was not alone. During the late nineteenth and early twentieth centuries, millions of Americans received social welfare benefits from their fraternal societies. The defining characteristics of these organizations usually included the following: an autonomous system of lodges, a democratic form of internal government, a ritual, and the provision of mutual aid for members and their families. An organization of females that also met these criteria generally embraced the label of "fraternal" rather than "sororal."[2]

By the late nineteenth century three fraternal types dominated: secret societies, sick and funeral benefit societies, and life insurance societies. The first emphasized ritualism and eschewed uniform payment schedules. The second and

third types devoted somewhat less attention to rituals but openly solicited recruits with the lure of health and life insurance protection. These distinctions
were not hard and fast, however, and all three varieties shared a common emphasis on mutual aid and reciprocity. As a spokesman for the Modern Woodmen of America (MWA) (which called its members "neighbors" and its lodges
"camps") wrote in 1934, a "few dollars given here, a small sum there to help a
stricken member back on his feet or keep his protection in force during a crisis
in his financial affairs; a sick Neighbor's wheat harvested, his grain hauled to
market, his winter's fuel cut or a home built to replace one destroyed by a midnight fire—thus has fraternity been at work among a million members in 14,000
camps." [3]

The provision of insurance was the most visible manifestation of fraternal
mutual aid. By 1920 members of societies carried over $9 billion worth of life
insurance. During the same period lodges dominated the field of health insurance. They offered two basic varieties of protection: cash payments to compensate for income from working days lost and the care of a doctor. Some societies, such as the SBA and the MWA, founded tuberculosis sanitariums, specialist
clinics, and hospitals. Many others established orphanages and homes for the
elderly. [4]

More Americans belonged to fraternal societies than any other kind of voluntary association, with the possible exception of churches. A conservative
estimate would be that one of three adult males was a member in 1920, including a large segment of the working class. Lodges achieved a formidable presence among blacks and immigrant groups from Eastern and Southern Europe.
Lizabeth Cohen points out that in the 1920s, ethnic social welfare organizations,
most notably fraternal societies, "provided more assistance than other institutions, public or private, which were only viewed as a last resort." Along the same
lines, August Meier observes that lodges among blacks during this period reflected "the thinking of the inarticulate majority better than any other organizations or the statements of editors and other publicists." [5]

The perspective of this book differs from the two best-known general studies
on the subject, Mark C. Carnes, *Secret Ritual and Manhood in Victorian America*, and Mary Ann Clawson, *Constructing Brotherhood: Class, Gender, and Fraternalism*. Carnes identifies changing conceptions of gender and masculinity as
the keys to explaining the rise and fall of lodges. He asserts that ritualistic societies appealed to the psychological needs of white, male Victorians who sought
masculine substitutes for their emotionally distant fathers. Clawson approaches
these issues from a different angle. She also highlights the influence of gender

but puts greater stress on the role of class: "Fraternalism is a valuable subject precisely because it is so difficult to understand it *except* in terms of class, gender, and the complex interaction between them."[6]

Analytical frameworks based on race, class, and gender, at least as currently conceived, have shown limited value as explanatory tools. Often, advocates of these perspectives seem to forget that fraternalism was considerably more than a white male phenomenon. Its influence extended to such disparate groups as blacks, immigrants, and women. Just as importantly, the preoccupation of historians with race, class, and gender has done little to answer the overriding question of why these widespread societies invested so much money in social welfare.

The fraternal society was far more than another device to address deep-seated cultural, psychological, and gender needs. It allowed Americans to provide social welfare services that could be had in no other way. The aid dispensed through governments and organized charities during the late nineteenth and early twentieth centuries was not only minimal but carried great a stigma. In contrast to the hierarchical methods of public and private charity, fraternal aid rested on an ethical principle of reciprocity. Donors and recipients often came from the same, or nearly the same, walks of life; today's recipient could be tomorrow's donor, and vice versa.[7]

This book examines only a small portion of fraternal social welfare services. The sheer diversity of fraternalism and the vastness of the sources involved make it hard to do otherwise. Because of constraints such as time, money, and language skills, for example, the discussion of immigrant-based societies will not include much original research. Instead it relies primarily on secondary works about these organizations. Hopefully, a future historian will undertake the arduous task of writing a general study of immigrant fraternalism.

At the beginning of the twenty-first century, fraternal societies may seem far removed from the concerns of most Americans. They have declined in influence since the depression, especially as providers of mutual aid and philanthropy. Many are now almost wholly convivial organizations. Even so, an examination of the past fraternal record has much to offer modern Americans. Societies accomplished important goals that still elude politicians, specialists in public policy, social reformers, and philanthropists. They successfully created vast social and mutual aid networks among the poor that are now almost entirely absent in many atomistic inner cities. Americans can also learn from studying the contrast between voluntary fraternal medical care and third-party payment systems such as private insurance and Medicaid.

It would be foolish, and probably impossible, to try to recreate the fraternal social welfare world of Ruth Papon and those who came before her. Ritualistic societies thrived in specific historical contexts that have long since disappeared. Nevertheless, it would be equally foolish to dismiss societies as the quaint curiosities of a bygone era. Despite continuing efforts, Americans have yet to find a successful modern analogue to the lodge, either as a provider of services, such as low-cost medical care, or as a means to impart such survival values as thrift, mutualism, and individual responsibility.

CHAPTER ONE

This Enormous Army

Any study of the origins of American fraternal societies cannot ignore the work of Alexis de Tocqueville. His discussion of voluntary associations from the 1830s has become a classic: "Americans of all ages, all conditions, and all dispositions constantly form associations. . . . The Americans make associations to give entertainment, to found seminaries, to build inns, to construct churches, to diffuse books. . . . Wherever at the end of some new undertaking you see the government in France, or a man of rank in England, in the United States, you will be sure to find an association." [1]

Fraternal societies had appeared in the American colonies long before Tocqueville wrote. The most prestigious was Freemasonry. Despite many fanciful legends about great antiquity, scholars generally trace Masonic origins to either England or Scotland in the late seventeenth century. A common theory holds that it arose in some way from stone (or operative) masonry. At some point the operatives began to admit nonoperatives (or "accepted masons") as members. In any case, by the first decade of the eighteenth century, nonoperatives controlled a network of lodges in both England and Scotland. [2]

The first official lodge of Freemasonry in the thirteen colonies opened in Boston in 1733, only seventeen years after the founding of the British Masonic grand lodge. Early growth was slow and largely confined to coastal cities such as Boston and Philadelphia. As in Great Britain, lodges drew membership primarily from the higher social, political, and economic ranks of society. [3]

The Revolution marked a turning point in American Freemasonry. The presence of prominent members, such as George Washington, John Hancock, and Paul Revere, greatly widened the fraternity's popular appeal in the new nation. Initiates flocked to special traveling lodges chartered for the troops. The war served to "Americanize" Freemasonry. The colonial "brethren" reacted to changing events by staging their own war of separation. They organized grand lodges for each state that were independent of the British structure. American Freemasonry expanded in size and numbers as well as in membership diversity. The Revolution speeded a trend, already under way by the 1750s, to broaden the ranks beyond a narrow upper crust. By the end of the eighteenth century, artisans and skilled workers formed important components of the membership, even a majority in some lodges. Although American Freemasonry still catered to an elite after the Revolution, it had become a less exclusive one.[4]

The Revolutionary Era also brought changes in the methods of Masonic social welfare assistance. In the colonial period barely a pretense of centralization had existed. Each lodge had enjoyed full authority to raise and disperse money and establish requirements for recipients. By the 1780s modifications began to be introduced. The state grand lodges established charity committees to supplement (although never supplant) the local lodges. In 1789 the Pennsylvania Grand Lodge created a fund financed through annual assessments of 65 cents per member. That same year the Connecticut Grand Lodge began to deposit a portion of each initiation fee into a state charity fund.[5]

Although the full extent of Masonic charity will probably never be known, fairly detailed figures exist for selected periods and locations. The Pennsylvania Grand Lodge assisted 129 individuals between 1792 and 1809. It allocated between $57 and $155 annually for this purpose. Such amounts were still negligible compared with the combined totals raised through local lodges. Between 1798 and 1800 (the years for which complete figures exist for both the state and local lodges), Masons in Pennsylvania disbursed more than $6,000. This amount was higher than the median annual spending of other private charities in Philadelphia.[6]

It is risky, however, to draw grand conclusions from these account book tallies. A sizable portion of Masonic mutual aid entailed intangibles such as employment information, temporary lodging, and character references. The famous evangelist Charles Finney recalled that when he first left home, his uncle recommended that he join because as "a Freemason I should find friends everywhere." The underlying premise was that brethren should favor their own in any social or economic situation. "You are not charged to do beyond your Ability," summarized an early Masonic document, "only to prefer a poor Brother that is a good Man and true, before any other poor people in the same Circumstances."[7]

American Freemasonry was not exclusively a white phenomenon. In 1775 a British army lodge in Boston initiated fifteen blacks. One of them was Prince Hall, a free black man from Barbados. The members of the new African Lodge

No. 1 petitioned the white Grand Lodge of Massachusetts for authorization, but the whites spurned them. They obtained a warrant from the Grand Lodge of England in 1787, but the American whites doggedly refused to grant them recognition as "legitimate." In response, the separate African Grand Lodge of Massachusetts (later renamed the Prince Hall Grand Lodge) officially came into existence in 1791. Growth was slow but steady. By the 1840s black Freemasonry had spread along much of the eastern seaboard, including New York, Pennsylvania, Maryland, and the District of Columbia. As would be true in the twentieth century, it represented the cream of black intellectual, social, political, and economic leadership, including Absalom Jones, Richard Allen, and James Forten.[8]

American sick and funeral benefit societies, much like American Masonic lodges, first developed from British sources. Many were influenced by precedents such as the friendly society or "box club." The first friendly societies appeared in Great Britain as early as the 1630s and 1640s. Freemasonry and friendly societies differed greatly in function and membership composition. The average Mason was either a merchant or a professional, but members of friendly societies were more likely to be wage earners or artisans. In addition, Masonic mutual aid tended to be informal, secretive, and geared to special cases, while friendly societies focused unabashedly on insurance.[9]

The early friendly societies were almost wholly local in character. "Affiliated societies" with multiple lodges did not emerge until the early 1810s. One of the largest was the Manchester Unity of Oddfellows. It arose in 1814 as a federation of previously independent lodges. The first of these Oddfellow lodges probably appeared in the 1730s or 1740s. The origins of this name elude historians. Like the Masons, the Oddfellows liked to claim an ancient pedigree and hoped to inspire awe through exotic symbols such as a terrestrial globe, the all-seeing-eye, the beehive, and the hourglass.[10]

Friendly societies enjoyed almost uninterrupted growth in the nineteenth century. Membership in Great Britain surged from at least 600,000 in 1793 to as many as 4 million by 1874. A rising demand for funeral insurance by the working and lower middle classes fueled much of this expansion. "A pauper funeral," notes E. P. Thompson, "was the ultimate social disgrace. And ceremony bulked large in folk-lore, and preoccupied dying men."[11]

A close parallel between the United States and Great Britain was the early primacy of localism. During the colonial and early national periods, an American "society" rarely encompassed more than a single lodge. Not until the 1820s did national sick and funeral benefit orders of any consequence appear. The Ameri-

cans also lagged behind the British in numbers of organizations. Forty-one mutual insurance societies (including Masonic lodges) existed in Massachusetts
at the beginning of the nineteenth century, compared with just nineteen three
decades earlier. This growth, while impressive, still left Americans behind the
British total of 9,000 friendly societies.[12]

One possible explanation for this contrast is the differing impact of industrialization and urbanization in each country. Fraternal orders developed first, and
most successfully, in towns and cities. The migration to cities, combined with
increases in disposable income, created a niche for the formation of these and
other formal associations. In Massachusetts during the early national period,
for example, voluntary associations generally arose after communities reached
population thresholds of between 1,000 and 2,000. Another precondition for
the emergence of associations was that one-fourth or more of adult males be
employed in nonagricultural pursuits. More recent research for New England
as a whole bolsters the importance of an urban threshold for voluntarism.[13]

For many who joined, a lodge affiliation was a means to enhance older and
more stable forms of mutual aid based on blood ties, geography, and religion.
Hence, according to Don Harrison Doyle, fraternal orders "acted to reinforce,
rather than to supplant, the family as a social institution. They also supplemented the extended kinship networks that supported the nuclear family." Similarly, Mary Ann Clawson stresses that "fraternal association provided the ritu-
alized means by which their members could define one another as brothers;
biologically unrelated individuals thus used kinship to construct the solidarity
necessary to accomplish a variety of tasks." Much like the older kin and geographical networks, the earliest mutual aid organizations were loose and informal in their methods. A survey of the bylaws and constitutions of six leading
societies in Boston during the eighteenth century shows a reluctance to guarantee specific cash benefits for working days lost or funerals. Only one, the Massachusetts Charitable Mechanic Association, named an exact sum ($40.00) for
burial.[14]

The usual practice of these societies was to consider applications for aid on a
case-by-case basis. The Scots' Charitable Society, for instance, allocated funds
for such diverse purposes as ship passage, prison bail, and an old-age pension.
All of these organizations showed little regard for consistency in the spending
levels for each situation. Extant records invariably classified any cash dispersals
as "charity" and "relief" rather than "benefits."[15]

Americans may have been informal in matters of money, but they were models of clarity in formulating sanctions for misconduct. The Boston Marine Soci-

ety imposed fines and other punishments for a multitude of offenses, including failure to attend members' funerals, blaspheming "the Name of Almighty GOD," and promoting at monthly meetings "the playing of any Cards, Dice, or other Gaming whatsoever." It provided the ultimate punishment of expulsion for the "common Drunkard." [16]

The exactitude of the American societies in the punishment of infractions and their ambiguity on guarantees of benefits made economic sense. Actuarial science was in an embryonic stage. Promises to pay uniform sick and death benefits entailed greater risk than levying fines. The emphasis on behavioral restrictions also helped to weed out the poorer risks and heighten feelings of solidarity. Many American societies, after all, had not advanced beyond the formative stage of groping for an identity. It was not a time for reckless departures.

Some historians contend that American fraternal societies were more likely than their British counterparts to recruit members from all economic classes. Clawson notes that "the American multi-class fraternal order, with its large membership and popularity among male wage-earners, represents a phenomenon for which there is no exact equivalent in European societies." This view may be only half right. It was true that fraternal orders in the United States rarely discriminated, at least as official policy, on the basis of economic class. Even in the colonial period the most prominent groups in Boston, such as the Massachusetts Charitable Society, the Boston Marine Society, and the Hartford Charitable Society, attracted both skilled workers and merchants. As historian Conrad Edick Wright has concluded, lodges in New England "tended to reflect the communities they served." Wage earners, primarily from skilled occupations, often represented one-third or more of all members. [17]

The problem with Clawson's characterization is that it understates the multi-class basis of British friendly societies. Business owners constituted a majority of more than 100 principal leaders of the Manchester Unity of Oddfellows and the Ancient Order of Foresters (AOF), the two leading affiliated orders in Great Britain during the nineteenth century. It may be that British wage earners were more prevalent in the rank and file than their American counterparts, but even this remains unproven. [18]

The Odd Fellows: The First Affiliated Order

In 1819 an immigrant opened a Baltimore lodge of the Manchester Unity of Oddfellows. It was the first affiliated order in the United States. Eleven years later, lodges of the Oddfellows had appeared in four states and increased to more than 6,000 members. The Americans seceded in 1842 and formed a separate organization called the Independent Order of Odd Fellows (IOOF). Although other British friendly societies, such as the Foresters, Rechabites, and Druids, had entered the fray by this time, they had a limited impact by comparison.[19]

The commonalities in the characteristics of American affiliated orders and the older localized sick and funeral benefit societies are obvious. Historical studies of Albany, Providence, and Kingston, New York, confirm that American Odd Fellowship, much like its colonial predecessors, drew liberally from all economic classes. Moreover, a substantial segment of skilled workers in Albany and perhaps elsewhere obtained leadership positions. According to Stuart Blumin, Odd Fellowship in the United States during these years was "a distinctively working-class movement" that only later began to appeal to the middle and professional ranks.[20]

The IOOF was an American fraternal trendsetter. It initiated the first major departure from the often haphazard grants of previous societies by using a clear schedule of guaranteed benefits. Each member when taken sick could claim a regular stipend per week (usually $3.00 to $6.00) to compensate for working days lost. In addition, the Odd Fellows helped to revise the language of American fraternalism. Most earlier societies had favored the words "charity" and "relief" to describe their aid, but the Odd Fellows preferred "benefit" and "right." Hence, as one member declared, money was "not paid or received as charity: it is every Brother's right, and paid to every one when sick, whether he be high or low, rich or poor." This was not a philosophy of unconditional entitlement, however. The Odd Fellows followed in the footsteps of colonial fraternal societies in vowing to withhold aid for habitual drunkenness, profanity, adultery, or disruptive behavior.[21]

The decades before and just after the Civil War were a time of sustained expansion for the IOOF. From 1830 to 1877 the membership rose from about 3,000 to 465,000. Total aid dispensed during these years topped $69 million. Sick and funeral benefits accounted for a majority of this spending, but lodges devoted substantial sums to other purposes. In 1855, for example, the Grand Lodge of Maryland provided aid to 900 orphans of deceased members.[22]

The geographically extended structure of the Odd Fellows allowed mobile members to retain benefits. It also facilitated a kind of coinsurance to mitigate local crises such as natural disasters or epidemics. In 1855 members in Massachusetts contributed more than $800 to relieve lodges in Pittsburgh that had exhausted their funds because of a fire. Ten years later they provided $400 to lodges in Virginia during an outbreak of yellow fever.[23]

The greater reliance on national systems, however, opened the door to abuse and fraud. By the antebellum period, publications of American Odd Fellowship began to warn of traveling impostors who filed false claims. This problem had been less prevalent among sick and funeral benefit orders during the eighteenth century, which could more readily rely on local knowledge to expose suspicious characters. To cope with these new risks the national organization required that members who moved first obtain transfer or "clearance" cards. At the state levels, grand lodges established boards of relief to investigate itinerants who petitioned for aid. According to the *Emblem*, a leading voice of American Odd Fellowship, each state board was a "sort of detective police force" and "scarecrow" to frighten off impostors.[24]

Another device used by the Odd Fellows to short-circuit fraud was the ritual itself. "Pass-words and signs," asserted G. W. Clinton, a past grand president, "the later common to the whole Order, and the former ever-changing and ever-circulating, guard us against the impositions of the unworthy, assure us our rights, and open the hearts of our brethren to us." The increasingly elaborate amalgam of grips, regalia, uniforms, and pageantry was a world apart from the comparatively Spartan rituals of eighteenth-century societies. It became all the rage to lengthen and embellish rituals and add to the number of degrees. A goal of each degree was to teach valuable moral and practical lessons. The ceremony in the eighth and final degree of Odd Fellowship, for example, warned the member against "lust, intemperance and sensuality" as well as falling prey to "a sad display of worldly glory."[25]

In certain respects the successful climb up the degree ladder was the antebellum equivalent of building a good credit rating. With each new degree a member achieved greater influence in the organization and expanded his network of trust. As a corollary, of course, the attention to degrees served to reinforce those fraternal bonds of trust and solidarity that cut across community, class, or ethnic ties.

Blacks also founded a separate version of the Odd Fellows during the antebellum period. The origins of this organization were similar to those of Prince Hall Freemasonry. The founder was Peter Ogden, an American free black man who had been admitted to a Liverpool lodge. When he returned to New York City, Ogden joined forces with two local black literary societies and petitioned the IOOF for an official warrant. After receiving an almost inevitable rebuff, he traveled to Great Britain in 1842 and applied for a charter from the Grand United Order of Odd Fellows (GUOOF). The British, who were more tolerant than their American lodge brothers, granted the request. Like its white counterpart, the black GUOOF specialized in the payment of sick and funeral benefits. In 1867 there were 3,358 members in over fifty lodges. The amount of benefits ($7,760 disbursed in 1867) was high for the small membership.[26]

The National Life Insurance Order

The formation of the Ancient Order of United Workmen (AOUW) in 1868 signaled the onset of a new phase in American fraternal development. The AOUW was the first major national life insurance order. The founder, John Jordan Upchurch, a master mechanic on a railroad in Pennsylvania and an ardent Mason, had not planned it that way. Originally he had envisioned the AOUW as a forum that would unite "through the medium of lodge affiliation employer and employee, and under solemn bond of helpful cooperation, adjust differences that might arise between them and thus avoid strikes." Had Upchurch achieved his original goal, the AOUW would have become a kind of conservative Knights of Labor.[27]

The AOUW's life insurance plan, which had started as an incidental feature to attract members, quickly moved to center stage. It guaranteed a death benefit of $1,000 (later, $2,000), which was funded through a $1.00 per capita assessment. It would have been beyond the capacity of antebellum societies to pay out this kind of money because no individual lodge had the necessary resource base. The AOUW dealt with the problem by spreading the burden. It centralized the dispersal of funds into state (and later national) organizations. As a result the membership expanded rapidly and crested at 450,000 in 1902.[28]

Before the Civil War, fraternal societies had focused on the payment of sick benefits. Individual lodges had paid funeral benefits, but the amount had rarely exceeded $150. The AOUW reversed these priorities. Although many lodges provided sick benefits, this feature was never more than a secondary concern.[29]

The next three decades brought a full flowering of national life insurance orders. Hundreds of organizations, such as the Royal Arcanum, the Knights of Honor, the Order of the Iron Hall, and the MWA, sprang up. Many older societies, which had specialized in sick and funeral benefits, such as the Knights of Pythias and the Improved Order of Redmen, followed suit with their own national life insurance plans. By 1908 the 200 leading societies had paid well over $1 billion in death benefits. Membership grew rapidly; according to *Everybody's Magazine* the ranks of fraternalism had become an "enormous army." The foot soldiers were "the middle-class workman, the salaried clerk, the farmer, the artisan, the country merchant, and the laborer," all attempting to "insure their

John Jordan Upchurch, ca. 1887, founder of the AOUW, the first
fraternal life insurance society. (Walter Basye, *History and
Operation of Fraternal Insurance* [Rochester, N.Y.:
Fraternal Monitor, 1919])

helpless broods against abject poverty. Rich men insure in the big companies to create an estate; poor men insure in fraternal orders to create bread and meat. It is an insurance against want, the poorhouse, charity, and degradation."[30]

The precise extent of fraternal organizations in the United States during this period will never be known. The fraternal life insurance societies had at least 1.3 million members by 1890, and by 1910 they had grown to 8.5 million. That year the combined membership of all types of fraternal societies was at least 13 million. The proportion of Americans who were lodge members is more difficult to gauge. Many individuals belonged to more than one society, and large segments of the fraternal population, such as blacks and immigrants, were often undercounted. A conservative estimate would be that one-third of all adult males over age nineteen were members in 1910.[31]

American fraternal life insurance societies had the good fortune to arrive on the scene at a time when commercial companies faced especially bad publicity. A spate of bankruptcies associated with financial panics in the 1870s had shaken consumer confidence. By one estimate the unrecovered losses suffered by policyholders in commercial companies totaled $35 million. In addition the assessment approach of fraternal organizations allowed rates low enough to undercut commercial insurance companies—at least initially. Most members paid a flat premium that did not vary on the basis of age or health. Many societies scrimped on the common commercial practice of accumulating a large reserve. Most fraternal orders eventually abandoned the crude assessment method as untenable, but it gave them a leg up in the market at first. By 1895 half the value of all life insurance policies in force was on the fraternal plan. The United States had entered an unprecedented "Golden Age of Fraternity."[32]

The interest shown by fraternal orders in life insurance, while certainly considerable, never became all encompassing. At the local level especially, sick and funeral benefit societies still predominated. In 1891 a detailed study conducted by the Connecticut Bureau of Labor Statistics found 126,613 members of fraternal insurance societies in the state. More than 60 percent belonged to sick and funeral benefit orders, compared with 28 percent in life insurance societies. Almost all the life insurance orders were affiliates of centralized national organizations, such as the Royal Arcanum and the Legion of Honor. About 70 percent of these societies entrusted the payment of death or funeral benefits to an office outside the state. By contrast, an amazing 99 percent of sick and funeral benefit societies assigned this responsibility to local or state lodges. Even the national sick and funeral orders, such as the AOF, the Ancient Order of Hibernians, the IOOF, the Grand United Order of Galilean Fishermen, and the Deutscher Orden

The drill team of Camp 566, MWA, Hutchinson, Kansas, ca. 1892. (Courtesy
of the Modern Woodmen of America, Archives, Rock Island, Ill.)

Harugari, relied almost wholly on local and state affiliates to raise and disperse
benefit money.[33]

This study by the Connecticut Bureau of Labor Statistics found that the membership of fraternal insurance orders relative to the general population (men,
women, and children) was 15 percent. It calculated that if "to the membership
reported should be added the number in the Masonic societies, the Elks, the Patrons of Husbandry, and other societies, not co-operative benefit, and therefore
not included herein, the total would be in excess of the total male adult population of the state." This figure, of course, included individuals who belonged to
more than one society.[34]

The period of greatest success for fraternal societies coincided with an intense
American fascination with ritualism. No class or ethnic group was immune.
Ritualistic trappings, including grips, degrees, and passwords, appeared in
groups as diverse as the Knights of Labor, the Ku Klux Klan, the Farmers Alliance, the Union League, the American Protective Association, Tammany Hall,
the Church of Jesus Christ of Latter-day Saints, and the Patrons of Husbandry.

Most were variants on the Masonic model. The linkage was especially close in the Knights of Labor, the Patrons of Husbandry, and the modern Ku Klux Klan, all founded by Masons.[35]

At the beginning of the twentieth century, fraternal societies seemed destined for a bright future. They had achieved a striking level of development. In 1800 the fraternal scene (with the possible exception of Freemasonry) was characterized by small and localized societies with meager budgets and haphazard schedules of benefits. By 1900 Americans had flocked to far-flung national organizations with multiple lodges and hefty death and sick benefits. Observers were optimistic about the prospects for fraternalism in the coming century. As Charles Moreau Harger commented in the *Atlantic Monthly*, so "rapidly does [the fraternal order] increase in popularity that it shows little indication of ever wielding less power over men's destinies than it does today." [36]

CHAPTER TWO

Teaching Habits of Thrift and Economy

T he United States at the turn of the century offered fertile soil for the continued flourishing of fraternal organizations. The most visible contrast with the past was not in the character of fraternalism but in the social context. This was the era of the "new immigration." More than 18 million individuals entered American ports between 1890 and 1920. Most were from Eastern and Southern Europe and were Catholic, Jewish, or Greek Orthodox in religion. They differed significantly from their predecessors, the mostly Protestant "old immigrants" from Western and Northern Europe. But the new immigrants were not the only ones to flock to American cities during this period. By 1930 1.2 million blacks had settled in the North. This movement, which began modestly at the end of the 1890s, crested in the first Great Migration during and after World War I.[1]

Never before had the United States experienced such an infusion of ethnic and cultural diversity in so short a time. By 1900 four in ten people in the largest cities were foreign born, while an additional two in ten were children of immigrants. John R. Commons, a leading labor economist, found the "variety of races" to be "astonishing. New York excels Babel." The newcomers often encountered hostility. Their relative lack of education, tendency to cluster in unskilled occupations, and peasant habits and superstitions inspired great fears among old-stock intellectuals. Robert Hunter wrote in his well-known treatise *Poverty* that the evils of immigration "if they are to be called evils, are not temporary. The direct descendants of the people who fought for and founded the Republic, and gave us a rich heritage of democratic institutions, are being displaced by the Slavic, Balkan and Mediterranean peoples."[2]

Hierarchical Relief and Reciprocal Relief

Regardless of where they came from, the members of nearly all ethnic and national groups erected formidable networks of individual and collective self-help for protection. These social welfare systems fell into two broad categories: hierarchical relief and reciprocal relief. Hierarchical relief was characterized by large, bureaucratic, and formalized institutions. The donors usually came from geographical, ethnic, and income backgrounds significantly different from those of the recipients. Reciprocal relief tended to be decentralized, spontaneous, and informal. The donors and recipients were likely to be from the same or nearly the same walks of life. Today's recipient could be tomorrow's donor. Leading examples of reciprocal relief included informal giving, church assistance at the congregational level, and donations from fraternal organizations.

When individuals resorted to hierarchical relief, it was generally with considerable reluctance. In ethnic communities a great stigma was attached to dependence on outsiders. This aversion was most intense against indoor relief, which helps explain why so few people ended up receiving it. In 1880, for example, 1 in 758 Americans was in an almshouse, and the ratio actually widened to 1 in 920 by 1903. The pattern of low dependence was not limited to almshouses. According to the U.S. Census in 1904, 1 in 150 Americans (excluding prisoners) lived in public and private institutions, including hospitals, orphanages, and insane asylums.[3]

Hierarchical relief also appeared in the guise of cash and in-kind assistance to people in their homes, called outdoor relief. The "charity society" best exemplified the direct private role. Nearly all large and many small cities had versions of groups such as the Associated Charities of Boston and the Charity Organization Society of Buffalo. These organizations relied on the services of volunteers, who were often middle-class college women. Many charity societies received subsidies from state and local governments. Governments played a diminished direct role in outdoor relief by the turn of the century. About half of all cities over 200,000 had nearly eliminated public outdoor relief, including New York, Philadelphia, Baltimore, New Orleans, and San Francisco. These cities were responding to complaints from social workers that aiding people in their homes fostered corruption, waste, and malingering.[4]

As an alternative to public and outdoor relief, states and local governments shifted to more indirect methods, such as subsidies to private charities. A variety of entities received public aid during the late nineteenth and early twentieth centuries, including orphanages, schools for the deaf, and insane asylums. By 1901 the annual amount of governmental subsidies topped $10 million. Even so, the combined federal, state, and local involvement in social welfare was Lilliputian by current standards. As late as the first decade in the twentieth century, combined governmental spending on public outdoor and indoor relief, charitable subsidies, and eleemosynary institutions was less than 1 percent of the gross national product.[5]

Governmental outdoor relief enjoyed a revival during the 1910s. The chief impetus was the introduction of mothers' (or widows') pensions at the state level. In 1931, 93,620 families (up from 45,825 in 1921) were on the pension rolls. The numbers were small; the combined caseload for mothers' pensions constituted less than 1 percent of the American population.[6]

The typical pension recipient could expect little better than a hand-to-mouth existence. In 1931 monthly grants ranged from a high of $69 in Massachusetts to only $4 in Arkansas. Recipients often had to earn income on the side to scrape by. Racial discrimination was rampant, especially in the South. The city of Houston, Texas, was one of the most egregious. Although blacks constituted 21 percent of the city's population in 1920, not one black family received a pension.[7]

Reciprocal relief was far more prevalent than either governmental or private hierarchical relief. Its most basic expression was informal giving, the countless and unrecorded acts of kindness from neighbors, fellow employees, relatives, and friends. The precise magnitude of informal giving can never be known, but it was undeniably vast. A study of 200 wage-earning families in New York City conducted in 1905 revealed that almost "every family of small income received some help or other from friends or relatives in the form of clothing for the children, money for the rent, or occasional gifts to carry the family over a tight place. In the entire number investigated there were over 60 instances discovered of this fraternal helpfulness." According to the study, informal giving aided so many that it was fallacious to classify families into distinct categories such as "dependent" or "independent." The assistance provided through church congregations included many elements of reciprocal relief. It often appeared in spontaneous and unrecorded guises. Help came from collection plates and via such monetary intangibles as job information, homes for orphans, barn raisings, and temporary housing.[8]

The self-help and informal neighborly arrangements created by the poor themselves dwarfed the efforts of formal social welfare agencies. In this regard Edward T. Devine, a prominent social worker, used an article in the *Survey* to warn his colleagues against the sin of self-importance. He reiterated that millions of poor people were able to survive and progress without recourse to organized charities and governmental aid: "We who are engaged in relief work . . . are apt to get very distorted impressions about the importance, in the social economy, of the funds which we are distributing or of the social schemes which we are promoting. . . . If there were no resources in times of exceptional distress except the provision which people would voluntarily make on their own account and the informal neighborly help which people would give to one another . . . most of the misfortunes would still be provided for." Similarly, Frederic Almy, in a much cited study of private and public outdoor relief in 1899, noted that he had been unable to tally "the vast amount of individual private charity" and relief dispensed through "masonic lodges and mutual benefit societies."[9]

Although fraternal societies had features of hierarchical relief, they were primarily institutions of reciprocal relief. Jane Addams marveled at how many such organizations "honeycombed" the slums of Chicago. Similarly, Peter Roberts observed that among the Italians the "number of societies passes computation," while according to John Daniels, the typical Jewish neighborhood on the Lower East Side of Manhattan "swarms with voluntary organizations of many kinds." Roberts was amazed at how rapidly Eastern Europeans formed lodges. He reasoned that the communal "tendency is in the blood of the Slav, and it finds expression in organizations in America." Another study noted that Boston's Polish "clubs, mutual benefit fraternities, patriotic societies and political organizations are legion. All belong to several insurance societies."[10]

Fraternal and other mutual aid societies also existed among groups not usually identified with the new immigration. To Paul S. Taylor they represented "the only continuous organized life among the Mexicans in which the initiative wholly comes from the Mexicans themselves." The tendency of Japanese Americans to join associations spurred Konrad Bercovici to conclude, probably with some exaggeration, that nearly "every Japanese belongs to one or more societies." Associationalism was pervasive among the Chinese. They established numerous societies, including the famous "Six Companies," which provided sick and funeral benefits and arbitrated disputes. In 1921 Robert E. Park and Herbert A. Miller wrote that "there is nothing mysterious about Chinese institutions. The more data we secure on them, the more we are impressed with their resemblance to our own."[11]

During the same period blacks developed a reputation as "joiners" that rivaled that of recent immigrants. "No racial type," John Daniels declared, "has a stronger craving to 'belong.' They have clubs and societies without number and of every description." Howard Odum wrote that lodges constituted "a vital part" of black life in the South and estimated that the membership, "paying and non-paying is nearly equal to the total church membership." Fannie Barrier Williams echoed this assessment, proclaiming that in "nothing does the col-

TABLE 2.1. Lodge Membership among Wage Earners
in New York City, by Income, 1909

Family Income	Number of Families	Percentage with Lodge Member
$600 to $699	72	36
$700 to $799	79	38
$800 to $899	73	37
$900 to $999	63	40
$1,000 and over	31	58

Source: Robert Coit Chapin, *The Standard of Living among Workingmen's Families in New York City* (New York: Charities Publication Committee, 1909), 209.

ored man live such a strenuous life as he does as a lodge man. The lodge, more than any other merely social organization, is a permanent and ever-increasing force." [12]

A recurrent theme was that blacks had a peculiar flair for the art of organization. They were, according to one writer, "more social in disposition and more absorbed in social life than white people." Even progressive reformer Isaac Rubinow, not usually prone to acknowledge fraternal achievements, declared that "outside of the immigrant groups, Negroes represent the only class of population where the habit of mutual insurance through voluntary association has developed to the highest degree in the United States." [13]

The Membership Profile

Information from empirical studies reinforces anecdotal evidence, indicating the popularity of fraternalism. In 1909 Robert Coit Chapin examined the budgets of 318 "workingmen's families" in New York City, most of whom earned less than $1,000 a year. Forty percent had at least one member in a lodge. Membership extended to the poorest of the poor. Of the families earning between $600 and $800, an income insufficient "to permit the maintenance of a normal standard," 37 percent had lodge members (table 2.1). Chapin's definition of a minimum standard was fairly close to that of other investigators. In 1907, for instance, Louise Bolard More arrived at a "conservative conclusion" that a "'fair living wage' for a workingman's family of average size in New York City should be *at least* $728 a year." [14]

TABLE 2.2. Lodge Membership among Wage Earners in New York City
with Family Incomes between $600 and $799, by Ethnicity, 1909

Ethnicity	Number of Families	Percentage with Lodge Member
Austrian	15	66.6
Black	17	35.2
Bohemian	7	71.4
Irish	11	9.0
Italian	30	30.0
Native white	30	30.0
Russian	17	76.4
Teutonic	11	27.2

Source: Robert Coit Chapin, *The Standard of Living among Workingmen's Families in New York City* (New York: Charities Publication Committee, 1909), 208.

Chapin found that ethnicity was more important than income in deter-mining fraternal affiliation (table 2.2). Certain nationalities, regardless of eco-nomic standing, were susceptible to the lure of the lodge. For Russians (most of whom were probably Jews) and Bohemians, seven of ten families earning be-tween $600 and $799 had a fraternal membership. The proportion for blacks was higher than that for native whites, Italians, or Irish. Clearly, blacks from the rural South kept their old fraternal affiliations in the new urban environment.[15]

An extensive study of wage earners and insurance in Chicago revealed the same patterns. In 1919 the Illinois Health Insurance Commission questioned some 2,700 wage-earning families. According to the commission, 38.8 percent carried life insurance through fraternal organizations. This figure was probably on the low side because respondents did not provide information about frater-nal membership per se; they only indicated whether they held life insurance in these organizations. This distinction was not trivial. Chapin found that of sixty-nine families who belonged to lodges, only thirty-five carried fraternal life in-surance. If an analogous situation existed in Chicago, a majority of wage earn-ers may have been members.[16]

Fraternal affiliation in Chicago reached down to the very poor. The commis-sion estimated that 32.6 percent in the lowest income group carried life or fu-neral benefits in fraternal societies. The authors considered the standard of liv-ing in this bracket to be "insufficient to provide for the subsistence budget." As in New York, ethnicity was the most reliable predictor of fraternal membership

TABLE 2.3. Fraternal Life Insurance among a Sample of Wage-Earning
Male Heads of Families in Chicago, by Ethnicity, 1919

Ethnicity	Number of Families	Percentage of Male Family Heads with Fraternal Life Insurance
Black	229	12.2
Bohemian	218	48.6
German	206	33.4
Irish	102	53.9
Italian	199	21.1
Jewish	203	40.3
Lithuanian	111	72.0
Native white	577	32.7
Polish	503	52.4
Scandinavian	198	48.9
Other	210	28.0

Source: Illinois Health Insurance Commission, *Report* (Springfield, 1919), 228.

(table 2.3). A notable point of contrast between the cities, and deserving of further study, was the showing of the Irish. In New York 9 percent of the male heads of Irish families belonged to fraternal organizations, while in Chicago 53.9 percent had such memberships. In the latter case this percentage was higher than that for Poles and Jews, two groups who, unlike the Irish, had reputations as joiners.[17]

Compared to New York and Chicago, societies were ubiquitous in Homestead, Pennsylvania. Margaret Byington estimated in 1910 that 57 percent of the male heads of families who worked in the steel mills were members. For families earning under $610 a year, less than "a living wage," 46.8 of the male breadwinners belonged to societies. Again there was wide variation in the frequency of fraternal affiliation based on ethnicity. For the male heads of Italian families membership was 57 percent; for Slavs it exceeded 90 percent.[18]

One factor in the popularity of lodges in Homestead was the mill workers' need for protection against physical risks. "Given the constant peril of accident or death and a community which takes little interest in the immigrant's welfare, the extent to which the lodge has been developed is not surprising." The social features of the lodge also had drawing power. Immigrants in Homestead experienced unusual ethnic isolation and had meager choices of social amenities, such as theaters and parks. As Byington put it, the "lodges seek to arouse the sense of fraternity and common interest which otherwise finds little stimulus in the town. . . . There are no unions to give a sense of common interest, and the political organizations are largely dominated by a few gangs. The lodges form really the only clubs."[19]

The Spread of Life Insurance

Studies during the period repeatedly point to the pervasiveness of life insurance ownership among the working class. The Illinois Health Insurance Commission found that 81.9 percent of wage-earning families in Chicago had at least one member with a life insurance policy. Although this tendency declined with income, 73.2 percent of the lowest income class still carried such policies. As with fraternal membership, there was a strong correlation between ethnicity and life insurance. The Slavs of Chicago and Homestead were not only accomplished fraternalists but more likely to purchase life insurance. The correlation between ethnicity and insurance was also high among blacks. In Chicago and Homestead nine in ten black families carried some life insurance, more than any other group, including native whites.[20]

Blacks in other cities demonstrated an equal readiness to purchase insurance. In Philadelphia a study of black migrant families in 1917 showed that 98 percent had policies. Of 348 family heads in Kansas City in 1913, according to Asa E. Martin, only 24 failed to carry insurance, "and in most of those cases the other members of the families held policies." By comparison, Chapin calculated that 7 in 10 black families in New York owned life insurance. This figure is conservative, however, because it apparently omitted fraternal policies.[21]

Fraternal hegemony in insurance did not go unchallenged. Commercial industrial insurance (small burial policies paid on a weekly basis) spread rapidly among the poor. Significantly, two of the three largest companies in this field, Prudential and Metropolitan Life, had evolved from fraternalism. Prudential was originally chartered as a friendly society, while Metropolitan Life initially relied on the Hildise Bund, a German mutual aid association, to collect its premiums.[22]

The rivalry between fraternal and commercial insurance was complicated. The competition was not a simple zero-sum game in which increases in the one led, perforce, to diminutions in the other. Wage earners did not necessarily think in terms of an either/or choice. Many carried some combination of both

TABLE 2.4. Life Insurance Ownership in a Sample of
Wage-Earning Families in Chicago, 1919

Ethnicity	Number of Families	Percentage with Policy
Black	274	93.8
Bohemian	243	88.9
German	240	85.0
Irish	129	88.4
Italian	204	57.8
Jewish	218	63.8
Lithuanian	117	79.5
Native white	644	85.2
Polish	522	88.5
Scandinavian	232	75.4
Other	225	75.1

Source: Illinois Health Insurance Commission, Report (Springfield, 1919), 223.

industrial and fraternal insurance. Black families were particularly noted for relying on private companies for industrial policies and fraternal societies for sick
benefits. In Chicago 9 of 10 black families had life insurance (table 2.4), but only
1 in 10 (table 2.3) had fraternal life policies. By the same token, more than 4 in
10 blacks in Chicago carried sick benefits. This ratio was higher than that of any
other group except Lithuanians, and twice that of native-born whites.[23]

Black families in other cities had similar insurance habits. In 1921 Sadie Tanner Mossell found that 100 black migrant families in Philadelphia, with "few exceptions," carried their life insurance in commercial companies. At the same
time, 4 of 10 of these families had either mothers or fathers in "lodges and sick
benefit assessment societies maintained entirely by Negroes." This profile also
applied to the smaller black population of Kansas City. Asa Martin concluded
that nearly "every adult of both sexes, even though he belongs to one or more
of the fraternal orders, carries [commercial] insurance also."[24]

The Dread of Dependence

For many poor people the sharing of risk, whether through fraternal or commercial insurance, was an essential precaution against the stigma of charity and

the poorhouse. Louise Bolard More concluded that "insurance fosters a pride which is to a certain degree creditable, a spirit of independence, and a commendable horror of pauperism."[25]

The "dread of charity," as settlement house leader Sophonisba Breckinridge phrased it, was almost universal among the poor. William I. Thomas and Florian Znaniecki commented that every "Pole who accepts the help of American institutions is . . . considered not only disgraced personally as a pauper, but as disgracing the whole Polish colony." According to Phyllis H. Williams, Italian immigrants showed a veritable "horror" of dependence: "In America as in Italy, Italians are no more willing to commit feeble-minded dependents to institutions than they are the aged." The head of the Federated Jewish Charities observed with pride that despite the rapid increase of Jews in New York, their dependence on charity had actually declined substantially between 1901 and 1916. He cited this as proof that "the Jews from eastern European countries are not willing dependents. On the contrary, they make every effort to care for themselves and thus remain self-respecting as well as self-supporting."[26]

The abhorrence of hierarchical relief also permeated the folkways of black communities. James Borchert argued that there was a relative absence of what might be called a psychology of dependence. Blacks in Washington, D.C., he asserted, "were not generally wards of the state. Rather than being indolent 'welfare cheaters,' they took responsibility for their own lives, demonstrating pride, independence, and strength. . . . Contrary to scholars' and reformers' descriptions of disorder and pathology," they were "able to maintain their old cultural patterns in the new environment, adapting and adjusting them when necessary."[27]

In *American Charities* Amos G. Warner emphasized that blacks shared a palpable "dread of being assisted, especially when they think an institution will be recommended." Similarly, John Daniels commented that "seldom does one find a Negro begging on the streets. The members of the race possess in high degree the quality of human kindness, and are ever ready to help their fellows in times of need." Pride in self-reliance was infectious. Black leaders peppered their speeches with versions of Booker T. Washington's famous boast that since Reconstruction, blacks had not asked "the national government to appropriate a single dollar to be used in providing us as a race, shelter, clothes, or food."[28]

Regardless of one's ethnic or national group, a primary motivation for taking out insurance was to avoid the humiliation of a pauper's grave. As Mary Willcox Brown of the Children's Aid Society of Baltimore expressed it, poor people looked on such a burial as "a degradation" and subscribed to the view "that to

allow the city to perform such an act would mean that a family deserved to become social outcasts." Similarly, Asa E. Martin regarded as typical the comments of a black citizen of Kansas City who, when confronted by the prospect
of a pauper's grave, declared, "Man I have just got to be buried if I should die."
Martin stated that despite the expense of insurance, "very few Negroes of Kansas City are buried at the expense of the city."[29]

Martin was taken aback by how many blacks lived in abject poverty yet regularly paid weekly premiums. He encountered an especially memorable case of
a man who resided in a saloon basement, a place "unfit for human habitation."
Martin observed with more than a hint of sarcasm that "his future was well provided for—he belonged to three fraternal orders and carried two [industrial]
insurance policies, all of which guaranteed him a $275 burial, concerning which
he spoke with much pride."[30]

Although it was obviously in the self-interest of industrial companies and fraternal societies to attribute their contributions to the low levels of dependence
among the poor, the evidence they cited was persuasive. Between 1871 and 1918
the rate of pauper burials per 100,000 population actually *fell* from 185 to 86.
This decline outpaced decreases in the death rate.[31]

A Shared Value System

Americans were attracted to fraternal societies for a variety of reasons. Some
wanted sick and death benefits. Others sought expanded social ties. Still others
hoped to find a source of entertainment and diversion. But there were motivations less easy to identify but perhaps more important. By joining a lodge, an
initiate adopted, at least implicitly, a set of values. Societies dedicated themselves
to the advancement of mutualism, self-reliance, business training, thrift, leadership skills, self-government, self-control, and good moral character. These
values reflected a fraternal consensus that cut across such seemingly intractable
divisions as race, gender, and income.

This sharing of a value system is clearly demonstrated by five societies that
thrived at or near the turn of the century. Each had a very different membership
base. Two of the societies, the Independent Order of Saint Luke (IOSL) and the
United Order of True Reformers (UOTR), were all black, while the others had
entirely white memberships. The Loyal Order of Moose was an exclusively male
society that emphasized sick and funeral benefits. The Security Benefit Association followed in the tradition of life insurance orders, but it broke from the
mainstream by allowing men and women to join on equal terms. The Ladies of

the Maccabees (LOTM) was a life insurance order that did not admit men as members.

The societies showed striking similarities in outlook. With perhaps a slight change in wording, the following statement, penned by a member of the SBA, was suitable to each: "Its prime object is to promote the brotherhood of man, teach fidelity to home and loved ones, loyalty to country and respect of law, to establish a system for the care of the widows and orphans, the aged and disabled, and enable every worthy member to protect himself from the ills of life and make substantial provision through co-operation with our members, for those who are nearest and dearest." [32]

To advertise its ideals, each society propagated a motto. The UOTR went on record in favor of "unity, temperance, and charity." The LOTM and the IOSL pledged, respectively, to advance "Faith, Hope and Charity" and "love, purity, and charity." The motto of the SBA emphasized mutual aid: "The mystic words of our Order are Wisdom, Protection, Security, Fraternity. But the greatest of these is Fraternity." Lodge brothers of the Loyal Order of Moose used the salutation "Howd'y Pap" for "Purity, Aid, Progress." The Junior Order of Moose did its bit with the slogan "Be good, do good, make good." [33]

All of these societies stressed that fraternity and mutualism created possibilities for individual and collective advancement. To drive home this point, the LOTM and the SBA incorporated versions of "Blest Be the Tie That Binds" in their rituals:

> Blest be the tie that binds
> Us in Fraternal love;
> The Fellowship of kindred minds
> Is like to that above. [34]

Through keeping this fraternal tie, societies defended members from a cruel world. The ritual of the LOTM proclaimed, "Stand Back, Grim Poverty! We Protect the Child." An official of the Loyal Order of Moose struck the same pose, declaring that when "the vicissitudes of life circumstances change a brother's condition from wealth to want . . . this Order comes to his relief and helps him tide across the unexpected happening." [35]

The theme of the loving and extended family found universal fraternal appeal. According to the ritual of the IOSL, all initiates were "members of the same family" pledged to "stand by one another at all hazards." It specified that what "[we] lack by the sacred ties of blood we make up by a solemn oath-bound obligation, declaring ourselves sisters and brothers, children of the same Father." The Loyal Order of Moose promoted its orphanage by vowing that "this Order comes as a Mother to her children to help them in their hour of trial."[36]

There were graphic reminders of the sad fate suffered by those who did not join the fraternal family. The SBA's newsletter printed a cartoon depicting a chance meeting between a boy and a disheveled bum. As he walked to the poorhouse, the man gestured to a recruiting sign for the SBA and counseled the boy to "do what that sign says and avoid my mistake!" Similarly, the initiation ceremony of the LOTM featured a slide show titled "The Unprotected Home" during hard times. "One by one," read the narration, "the household articles have found their way to the pawnbroker or the second hand man. What of the future now?"[37]

Rituals often relied on the Bible to impart lessons of fraternity. The IOSL took its name from the Luke of the gospels. An initiate vowed to "be true and faithful to the Christian religion" and devote leisure time to "searching the Holy Scriptures, so that I may become useful and true to all mankind." The ritual of the LOTM drew inspiration from the Old Testament: "Like the Maccabees of old we are marching forward, a mighty army, for the defense of our loved ones and the protection of our homes."[38]

All of the societies advocated self-reliance, a hallmark of fraternalism. This objective was a centerpiece of the initiation ceremony of the IOSL, which featured a symbolic journey to Jerusalem. To foster humility it required the candidate to wear a torn white robe. Prior to the journey a member foretold what lay ahead: "You may find the road rough and rugged, and you may meet with disappointment and mistrust. . . . You will find no friendly hand extended, or kind advice given you on which to lean." The meaning of the lesson was plain: "This is one of the times that self-reliance must be exerted. You must seek to find the emblem of the cross, with patience and unceasing energy as it is claimed Helena possessed in searching for the cross of Calvary."[39]

The value of thrift ranked high in the fraternal consensus. The LOTM repeatedly extolled the benefits of frugality. The *Ladies Review* identified the "ways of thrift" as the "ways of pleasantness" and endorsed the "noble" campaign of the American Society for Thrift headed by Simon W. Straus: "Our Order is proud to feel that its members have exercised thrift in the securing of protection for their homes in the best Order on earth. Its members are women willing to work."[40]

If self-reliance and thrift were fraternal watchwords, so too was individualism. The word did not entail Epicurean self-gratification or Emersonian contrariness; instead it was akin to a winnowing-out process for the improvement of character. Successful fraternal individualists were to be economically self-reliant as well as proficient in the arts of cooperation and leadership. Although this ideal entailed self-discipline, the ultimate goal was not purely, or even mainly, selfish. For this reason an official of the UOTR rejected any contradiction between opposition to "selfish individualism, intemperance and non-accumulativeness" and support for a program to enable "people to get homes and means upon which they may independently subsist."[41]

A key tenet of fraternal individualism was the need to exercise mastery over the self. As a promotional publication of the Loyal Order of Moose put it, the "kingship of self-control" was the "noblest royalty of a man. The self-control he is taught to observe is the highest and best use of all his faculties, the mastery of his desires, passions and appetites, and the power to withstand temptation to the illegitimate use or prostitution of any part of his being, body, mind, spirit, and will." Self-control meant the power to resist such vices as gluttony, "over-drinking, over-smoking, lack of exercise, bad air, bad conversation, fool books."[42]

But according to this pan-fraternal philosophy, such qualities were useless unless tempered with civility. Vigilant watch was maintained against those who endangered the harmony of the lodge by indulging in personal attacks. As Mary MacEachern Baird of the LOTM framed it, the "woman with a grievance is welcome—nowhere." The IOSL required that an initiate forswear "slandering a member of this Order or a family of a member." The ritual of the Order of the Rose, the youth group of the LOTM, taught the same basic lessons. The instructions stipulated that the queen of the court teach young members to avoid "envy and unkindness, selfishness and strife," which were "poisonous weeds that would destroy our lovely blossoms. Sow not their seeds within these walls, but pluck them out wherever you find them growing." The queen was to urge the new member to follow the credo, "Love is service. Love is giving."[43]

Nonpartisanship was another component of the fraternal value consensus. Typically, an official of the LOTM characterized the organization as "non-sectarian" and "non-political." Societies favored nonpartisanship to achieve harmony and to widen the applicant pool. It was standard practice for aspiring Republican and Democratic politicians to join all the leading societies in their community. Individuals who were bitter rivals politically could coexist under a common fraternal banner. The Loyal Order of Moose was not unique when it signed up prominent politicians from both parties—William Jennings Bryan, Theodore Roosevelt, and Champ Clark.[44]

All of the societies prohibited formal distinctions based on income and class.

The UOTR boasted that it "makes capital and labor friends"; the ritual of the LOTM called on the initiate to know "no selfish ambitions, no class distinctions." The better-off members were more often leaders, but it was not hard to find examples, such as that described by the publicity for the Loyal Order of Moose, of a "modest workingman" directing "the affairs of the lodge, while seated in the meeting is his employer."[45]

While fraternal ritual writers disdained partisanship, they zealously promoted patriotism. The *Security News* phrased the matter bluntly: "The Lodge System is the foe of the outlaw and the anarchist, inculcating patriotism and love for country and that to live for one's country is as essential as to die for it." The ritual of the LOTM required the initiate to "behold that glorious banner, our Nation's Flag" and featured a group rendition of "Flag of Our Nation." Fraternalists contended that patriotism and good moral character were part of one package. The official historian of the UOTR, for instance, defined as "good citizens" those who strived "to obey the laws of the government, and to practice virtue, morality, industry, and economy."[46]

Although the members of all five societies relied on nearly identical terminology, the interpretations and applications often diverged. As Louis Hartz once wrote, a consensus does not necessarily entail uniformity of thought; the fraternal consensus was a case in point. Societies found creative ways to customize ideals such as thrift, self-reliance, and self-government to suit the special needs and interests of members. This behavior reached fullest expression outside the white male fraternal mainstream. For example, societies that catered to blacks and women used the fraternal consensus to overcome disfranchisement, segregation, and discrimination. These issues can be explored in greater depth by focusing on the agendas of three of the five organizations: the LOTM, the UOTR, and the IOSL.[47]

The Ladies of the Maccabees

The LOTM was founded in 1892 as the auxiliary of the Knights of the Maccabees, a life insurance society. At the beginning it was similar to groups such as the Eastern Star of the Masons or the Rebekahs of the Odd Fellows. Within a decade, however, the LOTM had established a separate identity. A key figure in speeding this process was Bina West, a former assistant principal and school examiner from Capac, Michigan. West became supreme record keeper in 1892 and supreme grand commander in 1911, a position she held until her retirement in 1948. She was instrumental in building up the lodges (or "hives") during the

Bina M. West, 1892, Supreme Record Keeper (1892–1911) and Supreme Grand
Commander (1911–48) of the LOTM (later the WBA). (Edward J. Dunn, *Builders
of Fraternalism in America*, bk. 1 [Chicago: Fraternal Book Concern, 1924])

1890s by successfully pitching to women an attractive combination of low-cost
life insurance coverage, a forum in which to socialize, and opportunities to cultivate organizational and business skills. The LOTM eventually severed official
ties with the Knights of the Maccabees and changed its name to the Woman's
Benefit Association (WBA). Long before this time, however, it had become the
largest fraternal order controlled exclusively by women, with membership passing the 200,000 mark by 1920.[48]

Although the LOTM required that members keep politics from entering the
lodge portals, this did not preclude support for feminist causes. Many of its lead-
ers played prominent roles in suffrage and temperance organizations. Lillian
Hollister, the first grand commander, was parliamentarian for the Michigan
Woman's Christian Temperance Union. She also was active in club work and
served as the president of the National Council of Women in 1909. Alice B.
Locke, a supreme trustee of the LOTM, participated in the affairs of the National
American Woman Suffrage Association and the League of Women Voters.[49]

The women in these organizations regarded themselves as members of fraternal rather than sororal societies. For them, fraternity, much like liberty and
equality, was the common heritage of both men and women. "Fraternity in

these modern days," asserted Elizabeth E. Brown, the great record keeper for Pennsylvania, "has been wrested from its original significance and has come to mean a sisterhood, as well as a brotherhood, in the human family."[50]

The women of the LOTM belonged to a feminist tradition that emphasized individualism over group differences. They drew inspiration from doctrines of natural rights as expressed in the Declaration of Independence. In this respect they followed in the footsteps of the 1848 women's rights convention in Seneca Falls, New York. The delegates at that conference drafted a Declaration of Sentiments that held "these truths to be self evident: that all men and women are created equal; and that they are endowed by their Creator with certain inalienable rights; that among these are life, liberty and the pursuit of happiness." According to this conception of feminism, women deserved rights not because of their sex but because they were individuals. In her famous address of 1892, "The Solitude of Self," Elizabeth Cady Stanton, a veteran of Seneca Falls, restated this theory of natural rights. She argued that woman suffrage fulfilled "the individuality of each human soul. . . . In discussing the rights of woman, we are to consider, first, what belongs to her as an individual."[51]

Echoing Stanton, Emma E. Bower, the great record keeper of the Michigan Great Hive, looked forward to a day when "we shall hear no more of woman's sphere than we shall hear of woman's rights or any of the other outworn phrases of man's inventive brain." When this day arrived, the competition between the sexes would cease and the law would treat women as equal individuals. Bower showed little patience for traditionalists and, increasingly, feminists who trumpeted theories of female superiority. Practical experience had proved that women "were not created to be either man's inferior or his superior, but his equal."[52]

Even before the LOTM broke with the Knights of the Maccabees, it differed from other auxiliaries by enforcing a rule against male members. Female exclusivity was defended as essential to preserve the society's independence and credibility. In West's first recruiting address in 1891, she described with some amusement how several men from the Knights of the Maccabees had applied as honorary members. She responded that "L.O.T.M. which means Ladies of the Maccabees, may also be construed to mean, Leave out Those Men." But even for West this stance did not entail complete sex segregation. She wanted to create opportunities for men and women to meet as independent equals. Hence, the LOTM regularly held joint social and fraternal gatherings with the Knights of the Maccabees.[53]

The basis of the all-female policy fit comfortably within the fraternal value consensus: the promotion of self-reliance. Elizabeth B. McGowan stated that women who participated with the opposite sex in auxiliaries often became "timid in the presence of men of superior knowledge." As a result they "waive their rights and privileges and become reliant and dependent. . . . Thus, woman becomes irresponsible." McGowan concluded that such a woman was more likely to be "courageous and strong in her own meeting hall where only sisterly faces greet her and conscious that she must assume all the responsibilities." More bluntly, Emma Olds, the great commander of Ohio, argued that self-reliance was worthy of the name only if it came from the initiative of women. She approvingly quoted President James A. Garfield that the best lesson for a young man was to be "thrown overboard." For Olds, it "should be equally helpful to character building to women to be thrown upon their own business resources, to be allowed and even compelled to rely upon their own judgment and business sagacity." [54]

The all-female rule reinforced another cornerstone of fraternalism: training in self-government. Dr. Elsie Ada Faust, the district medical examiner for the West, praised this policy for enabling a woman "to associate with her kind in other ways than social pastimes. It teaches her many things that man has arrogated to himself: the business conduct of a meeting, parliamentary law, many details of money expenditure." Faust expressed boundless faith in the potential of women, given the right incentives and opportunities, to rise to any occasion. She predicted that "if all the work of man was wiped from the earth, women could reconstruct it and add to it." [55]

Another justification for male exclusion was that it would foster civility. In an all-female society, women of various incomes and social backgrounds had to cooperate. According to Bower this policy created "a bond which binds together people of all classes, of all languages; the educated and the uneducated; the rich and the poor." Through the lodge, West added, "the sharp corners of egotism and vanity are broken off, and the rough surfaces or inexperience are smoothed and polished." Another official wrote that the give-and-take of meetings exposed the "quarrelsome, sarcastic, meddlesome, woman" as a "weakling and her opinions are treated accordingly. Women *can* learn tolerance, and *are* learning it." [56]

A defining aim was to recast fraternalism through creating an organization that was "to the working woman what the woman's club is to her sister of the leisure class. Here she gets her first lessons in parliamentary law. . . . Here the working woman comes for relaxation from the drudgery of domestic life." In a direct sense, this language addressed the day-to-day concerns of the rank and file. An actuarial study indicated that 86.6 percent of the members were house-wives at the time of initiation. Among those with gainful employment, the most common occupations were sewing (mostly dressmaking) at 3.4 percent, office work at 1.6 percent, and professionals at 1.4 percent.[57]

The LOTM tailored its message to ordinary members by repeatedly stressing the glories of the home. An advertisement for the society touted its goal, "Pro-tect the Home: The Parental Hearth is the Rallying Place of the Affections," and characterized the *Ladies Review* as "a home magazine for the home woman." Other advertisements featured a husband, wife, and child gathered around a cozy fireplace. The theme of hearth and home pervaded the initiation cere-mony. The lodge commander gave a "lecture on protection," describing the home as "the most sacred word in the English language" and as the "woman's kingdom. It is her natural impulse to protect it." She delivered this speech to the accompaniment of members singing "Home, Sweet Home." The message to initiates was that only through the LOTM's death benefit could the financial se-curity of loved ones be best assured.[58]

According to the LOTM's message, a woman who failed to secure protection was just as guilty as the uninsured man of shirking family responsibilities. The fate of her dependents would not be pleasant. In 1913 the *Ladies Review* reprinted a letter from the commander of a hive in California to illustrate what could hap-pen. A woman had let her membership lapse through carelessness and died leaving her child "in destitute circumstances." The editor pointedly cited this story as an object lesson: "We *cannot* know our future. We can know, however, that the holding secure of our benefit certificates is the surest sign of our love and interest in those who are dependent upon us."[59]

In stating the case for female life insurance, the LOTM turned the interpreta-tion of the death benefit as used by male organizations on its head. Dr. Ella J. Fifield, the district medical examiner for the West, ridiculed the stereotype that the wife was less able to cope after the death of a spouse. On the contrary, the man was "often more helpless than a mother left in the same circumstances." For Fifield it was truly "one of the saddest sights in life to see a father left with his little group of helpless children." By contrast, a wife in the LOTM had "thrown a circle of sisterly care and protection around her children." The pro-vision of death benefits for women actually made good actuarial sense. An in-creasing number of statistical studies showed that women generally outlived men, thus confounding stereotypes of the "weaker vessel." Hollister credited this longer life span to healthful habits; women, unlike men, did "not stay out late at night, do not chew, smoke, or drink."[60]

The LOTM had few rivals, at least among native white societies, in the high priority it assigned to entrepreneurship. Though the organization did not own businesses or grant loans, it endeavored to teach managerial and financial skills. Fifield asserted that the lodge provided "business training which can be had in no other way" by showing "the ways of handling money, and ordinary business forms." It was also the teacher of more intangible skills. The work of the lodge, as the *Ladies Review* put it, necessitated the exercise of "patience, forbearance, perseverance, and practicability." Just as importantly, the LOTM hoped to advance entrepreneurship through participation in the "greatest business Association of women in the world." The LOTM's success gave the lie to the stereotype that women were inferior in finance and business. Citing statistics on membership and financial growth, an organizing manual concluded, "If you will compare the above figures with those of organizations that have men for their leaders, you will find that we stand second to none, in the matter of finance."[61]

The LOTM combined this promotion of female entrepreneurship with a confident faith in the liberating possibilities of the market. On more than one occasion Hollister favorably referred to the writings of Herbert Spencer, the most famous exponent of laissez-faire. In particular she cited Spencer's well-known dichotomy of "industrial" societies (characterized by contract and voluntary exchange) and "militant" societies (dominated by status and political coercion). Spencer had held that the rise of industrial societies served to elevate the status of women. Agreeing, Hollister paraphrased Spencer's assertion that "in the United States, where the degree of militancy had been so small, and the industrial type of social structure and action was predominant, women have reached a higher status than anywhere else, thus proving that where there is a degree of militancy, an increase in industrialism are [sic] generally concomitant of a rise in their position."[62]

The United Order of True Reformers

While the LOTM deployed fraternalism to advance women in business and politics, the UOTR used it to nurture entrepreneurship. The UOTR had been founded in 1872 in Kentucky as the semiofficial black affiliate of the all-white Independent Order of Good Templars. It languished during its first decade, and by the end of the 1870s most of the original state affiliates, or fountains, were defunct. The agenda of temperance and prohibition did not have enough drawing power. A sustained revival began in 1881 when William Washington Browne, a former slave from Georgia and a Union army veteran, took over as grand worthy master of the Virginia Grand Fountain. Browne succeeded because he shifted the organization's focus to practical concerns. Under his leadership the UOTR became the first black society to provide life insurance benefits above the costs of a funeral.[63]

The membership surged to 50,000 by the first decade of the twentieth century, and fountains spread to twenty states. While this growth was impressive, the membership was never as large as that of the black Masons, Odd Fellows, and Knights of Pythias. Even so, people began to take notice. The U.S. Bureau of Labor Statistics published a detailed and highly favorable report. In addition, Booker T. Washington and W. E. B. Du Bois, despite their other differences, praised the UOTR as an exemplar of black self-help and creativity.[64]

The UOTR was one of the minority of societies (black or white) to operate businesses on the side. Browne's aim was not just to "take care of the sick and bury the dead" but to create an organization "united in finance" as well as "united in brotherhood." The linchpin of the UOTR's business enterprises was the True Reformers' Savings Bank of Richmond, Virginia. Founded in 1889, it had a half-million dollars in assets by 1907. During the next two decades the UOTR established a 150-room hotel, a newspaper called the *Reformer*, several retail stores, and an old-age home. It also purchased lots for a settlement to be called Brownesville.[65]

The UOTR was well within the fraternal mainstream in its celebration of thrift. Following the slogan "Save the cents, and the dollars will take care of themselves," Browne predicted that great things would result from the frugality and resourcefulness of ordinary blacks. He boasted that the person who had toiled in the cotton field "can beat the plan laid by people that have been free all their lives" because "he is the best financier who can make money go the farthest."[66]

To instill these habits at an early age, the UOTR established a children's department in 1887, the Rosebud Nursery. By 1906 it had about 15,000 members. These children were assessed monthly dues and were eligible for sick and funeral benefits. The UOTR was an innovator. Not until the late 1910s did juvenile departments become common among fraternal societies, black or white. The goal of the Rosebud Nursery was to "discipline the young" and train them in "thrift and economy." The name reflected Browne's belief that the "children were to be the buds of the Order as well as of the race" and "a blessing to their communities if they [were] carefully nurtured and directed." In 1907 Mrs. M. A. Lane, the president of the Rosebud Nursery, underscored the broad educational

goals of the department. The intention was "not only to make and save a dollar, but how to form a character; the fundamental principle to permanent success in this life and the life to come."[67]

Although Browne's self-help ideals were similar to Booker T. Washington's,
Browne gave them a more radical edge. He declared a war of independence
against white financial control. Citing his unhappy experiences with insurance
regulators, he cautioned that "white men try to break up every plan the Negro
has. In order to split the log you must find the seam. White men find the seam
of our union, and unless we are strongly united, they will split us up." Mattie
Bowen of the Rosebuds depicted the UOTR as an economic self-defense league
in an era of Jim Crow. She did not "believe in brawls" but recommended that
"when the Race is assailed, stand up or step back." Many members of the UOTR
fought back with political action when the city of Richmond introduced Jim
Crow streetcars. They helped organize boycotts and offered meeting facilities
for protesters.[68]

But the primary focus was always on economic rather than political strategies. Browne complained that blacks were "throwing away money enough to
buy this country" on personal frills and the patronage of white businesses. He
and other leaders had great faith that the UOTR could marshal resources for self-
help. Despite the poverty of the current generation, he often said that there was
still a chance to leave a viable legacy for the next.[69]

In addition to collective improvement the UOTR stressed individual entrepreneurship. Browne touted the True Reformers' Savings Bank as a depository
for black businesses and a source for loans. Through the Rosebuds the young
generation would, as Bowen put it, learn to follow the adage "Roll up your
sleeves, go to work and make business for yourselves." The leaders of the UOTR
were much like those of the LOTM in their commitment to group business pride.
They wanted to spur individual successes by holding up an exemplar of "Afro-
American skill, energy and push." Browne supported wide dissemination of the
Reformer to publicize the achievements of blacks. His dream was to build it into
a black analogue of the highly successful *Irish World* of New York City.[70]

Long before the founding of the SBA, the UOTR allowed women to join as
equal members. In defending this policy Browne kept well within prevailing
stereotypes. "Ladies ought to be in societies where men are," he argued, "as they
act as moderators, and help the presiding officer keep order." Despite Browne's
careful words, women in the UOTR were far more than moderators. They were
critical to the success of the organization. Although men retained power,

women often held leadership positions at the local and state levels. The Rosebud Department in particular was a stronghold of female influence.[71]

Although the bank and other businesses failed during the 1910s, the UOTR left a lasting imprint on black economic and social life throughout the twentieth century. Because of the organization's activities, many future black entrepreneurs were introduced to finance, management, and actuarial principles. With only slight exaggeration, historian Walter B. Weare has observed that "virtually every insurance association founded in the Upper South during the late nineteenth and early twentieth centuries can be traced to ex–True Reformer agents who organized their own societies."[72]

The Independent Order of Saint Luke

For many years the IOSL languished in the shadow of its more prestigious neighbor in Richmond, the UOTR. The IOSL traced its origins to a factional dispute in the Grand United Order of Saint Luke. The Grand United Order, based in Baltimore, had been founded in 1867 by Mary Prout, an educator and reformer who had been free since birth. Like many black fraternal orders, the United Order emerged out of a church, in this case the Bethel African Methodist Episcopal Church. Prout initially restricted membership to women but soon opened the doors to men. In 1869, however, dissident members in Richmond split off to form the wholly separate IOSL, with William M. T. Forrester as grand secretary. Although the headquarters was in Richmond, it had lodges in several states.[73]

In 1899 Maggie L. Walker, who had once been a paid employee of the UOTR, replaced Forrester, who had resigned claiming that the IOSL was on its last legs. During Walker's tenure, which lasted until her death in 1934, membership and assets grew rapidly. Consciously emulating the strategy of the UOTR, she set up side businesses, the most durable being the Saint Luke Penny Savings Bank, founded in 1903. She was probably the first woman in American history who was a bank president in her own right and not chosen because of family connections. The IOSL also established a printing plant, a newspaper called the *Saint Luke Herald*, and for a brief time, a department store, the Saint Luke Emporium.[74]

Like the SBA and the UOTR, the IOSL incorporated women in the fraternal consensus by allowing them equal membership rights. In contrast to those organizations, however, the IOSL was more likely to entrust them with a leadership voice. Walker recalled that her "first work was to draw around me *women*." In elections for the executive board in 1901, women won six of the nine slots. Although Walker made sure that men participated in the leadership, she kept female concerns at the center. In 1913, for example, she praised God "that this is a *woman's* organization, broad enough, liberal enough, and unselfish enough to accord equal rights and equal opportunity to men."[75]

Walker probably never heard of Bina West, but it is not hard to identify similarities between the two and their organizations. Both used fraternalism to advance agendas of feminism and business ownership. Both participated in the national and local women's club movement. Walker was the vice-president of the National Association of Colored Women and a founder and vice-president of Richmond's Council of Colored Women. Like West, she wanted to broaden women's sphere beyond "the mere drudgery of domestic life, the house, the cook, the house-servant." The two women shared a vision of fraternalism as a means to teach business skills and the practical benefits of thrift. "Sisters," Walker implored, "let us combine our pennies, our nickels, our dimes and our dollars. Let us provide employment for our girls." She regarded providing job opportunities as essential to protect women from the "snares and traps of sin and satan."[76]

Like West and Browne, Walker often sang the praises of thrift. She established thrift clubs for the young and called on blacks to emulate "the wealthiest men" of Richmond, who accumulated vast bank accounts with "simply a dollar or two to which they constantly added." With a Franklinesque flourish Walker urged members "to save some part of every dollar you have, and the practice will become a habit—a habit which you will never regret, and of which you will never grow shame."[77]

Walker regarded the advancement of black women as a precondition for collective political and economic uplift, though she warned that women would never reach their potential so long as a husband could "lord it over, or dominate the wife." For Walker, business partnerships and marriages needed the same elements to be successful. Pointing out that business partners "consult, agree and act," she asked why "then should not the partners in the home and the children, do the things which have made all other partnerships a success?" Walker used this analogy for other reasons. She considered equal marriages to be the prerequisite for raising children, as well as for building entrepreneurship. As Walker put it, "What stronger combination could God make—than the partnership of a businessman and a businesswoman[?]"[78]

In Walker's view black women could only have genuine success if they formed

Members of the Juvenile Division of the IOSL, ca. 1927. (Wendell P. Dabney, *Maggie L. Walker and the I.O. of Saint Luke: The Woman and Her Work* [Cincinnati: Dabney Publishing, 1927])

common cause in an organization with its own businesses. She envisioned the banks and other enterprises of the IOSL as means not only to provide direct employment but also to advance start-up loans. Walker made some headway in achieving these goals. Elsa Barkley Brown has estimated that the IOSL employed one-third of the black female clerical workers in Richmond during the 1920s.[79]

The sentimental rhetoric about the home, a staple for the LOTM, rarely appeared in Walker's speeches. Such talk was removed from the economic and social realities of the lives of members. Many had no choice but to continue to work outside the home after marriage, usually in unskilled occupations. Brown's survey of the financial records of the Saint Luke Penny Savings Bank reveals that "its earliest and strongest supporters were washerwomen." Like it or not, Walker concluded that the "old doctrine that a man marries a woman to support her is pretty nearly thread-bare to-day."[80]

The IOSL, unlike other organizations, could not ignore the issue of race. Walker marshaled her resources, including the editorial pages of the *Saint Luke Herald*, against discriminatory legislation and lynching. From 1923 until her death she served on the board of the National Association for the Advancement of Colored People (NAACP) and formed common cause with the UOTR in protests against the Jim Crow streetcar law of 1904. Partly because of her efforts, by the 1920s about 80 percent of eligible black voters in Richmond were women.[81]

At the same time Walker argued that blacks could never achieve dignity and first-class citizenship without laying an economic foundation. She stressed the benefits that a black-owned store, such as the Saint Luke Emporium, would bring to women as consumers. There it would finally be possible for the black female to shop without fear of facing disrespectful treatment from white merchants. Walker underscored that this choice would never exist unless blacks created a clientele by kicking their habit of depositing their money in white banks and spending their paychecks in white stores.[82]

For Walker the advent of Jim Crow legislation made it all the more foolhardy for blacks to keep patronizing white stores. Such behavior encouraged the throttling of "Negro business enterprises, the refusal of employment to Negroes; the attempt to drive out Negro barbers." To illustrate the critical need for blacks to set up businesses, Walker cited the recent trend by white stores to hire white female clerks. She added that black consumers through their spending habits keep "*her* there, WHILE YOUR OWN WOMEN, FLESH OF YOUR FLESH, BLOOD OF YOUR BLOOD ARE LEFT TO SHIFT FOR THEMSELVES."[83]

After Walker's death, the IOSL suffered a period of slow and continual decline, but much like the UOTR, its legacies had broader ramifications. The most tangible was the Saint Luke Penny Savings Bank. Although this institution severed legal ties with the fraternal order in 1911 because of state laws, it continued to prosper as the renamed Consolidated Bank and Trust Company of Richmond, Virginia. According to *Black Enterprise* in 1998, it ranked as the thirteenth largest black-owned bank, with assets of over $100 million.[84]

Conclusion

During this period millions of Americans lived in a state of poverty that would be considered intolerable by today's "underclass." Many had to endure these conditions without the basic tools of literacy or, for that matter, knowledge of English. Moreover, there was no recourse to unemployment insurance, minimum wages, governmental job training, or the other institutional trappings of a modern welfare/regulatory state.

In short, the social and political environment left the poor and other members of the working class with little choice but to fend for themselves. As growing opportunities drew millions of immigrants from Europe and blacks from the rural South, the new residents responded by building networks of mutual assistance. Although insurance gave some protection, individuals who subscribed to fraternal societies gained access to services not easily guaranteed in a commercial contract. The lodge offered its members the formal and informal components of mutual aid and sought to educate them in a set of values.

Focusing on the ideals and strategies of particular societies illustrates the many variants of fraternalism and the breadth of the fraternal value consensus. The influence exerted by all five organizations extended beyond the narrow confines of their memberships and entailed economic, social, and political consequences for American society as a whole. The UOTR and the IOSL advanced programs of ethnic self-help; the LOTM wanted female political and economic emancipation. For the SBA and the Loyal Order of Moose, the key goals were to impart life skills and establish social welfare institutions.

There was considerable diversity in the economic profile of the memberships served by these organizations. These differences, however, should not obscure the commonalties. All of these societies drew from the same basic fraternal pantheon of self-help, individualism, self-government, civility, and mutualism.

CHAPTER THREE

Not as Gratuitous Charity

Selectivity was at the heart of fraternalism. Societies established extensive behavioral standards for joining. Moreover, even veteran members risked, at least in theory, losing benefits for failure to fulfill certain conditions. Fraternalists boasted that they enjoyed liberty and equality as birthrights, but almost all acknowledged that they had to earn the fruits of fraternity.

Many membership and benefit requirements stemmed from actuarial motivations. This consideration was especially strong for the life insurance orders. The constitution of the Nevada Jurisdiction of the AOUW, for instance, denied or restricted admission for anyone who manufactured explosives, worked as "an aeronaut," or played professional football; the Independent Order of Foresters (IOF) excluded miners. The SBA's prohibited list extended to chauffeurs, oil-well shooters, and soldiers in time of war. Policemen, firemen, electricians, sawyers, and railroad engineers could join but paid higher dues.[1]

In combination with these standards, societies enforced moral behavioral codes. The initiation ritual of the IOF warned against the unworthy. "Some, alas! have fallen in the scale of humanity," it cautioned, "and their depravity is so great, it is not expedient that we associate with them." At the same time, however, it urged that members extend a "helping hand" to such individuals so as to "raise them up and make them up, if possible."[2]

Most societies established similar guidelines. Typically, the SBA stipulated that a member be "of good moral character, able and competent to earn a livelihood, engaged in an honorable occupation, and a believer in a Supreme Being." A guidebook for deputies of the LOTM stated that the society would keep out "women of immoral or questionable behavior." Not surprisingly, the correlation between the fraternal standard of "good moral character" and the "middle class values" of the period was close. In 1892, for example, the Connecticut Bureau of Labor Statistics found that societies followed the "invariable rule" of denying benefits "for any sickness or other disability originating from intem-perance, vicious or immoral conduct." A study by the Illinois Health Insurance Commission twenty years later reported the same finding.[3]

Fraternalists had long emphasized temperance as a desirable moral trait, and by the turn of the century they had redoubled this commitment. By enforc-ing restrictions on alcohol and narcotics, they combined the advancement of moral values with the practical goal of maintaining health standards. Lodges of the AOUW, the SBA, the IOF, and the Knights of Columbus barred admission to participants in the liquor trade. The constitutions of these societies exem-plified the pre-Prohibition trend to cast a wide net to cover everyone involved in manufacture and sale.[4]

The regulation of sexual behavior also arose from a combination of health and actuarial motivations. The rules almost always denied benefits for venereal diseases or any ailment caused by "immoral conduct," but the specifics varied. The LOTM, for example, promised expulsion for any woman who attempted to "produce abortion, self-inflicted, or by any one else with her consent."[5]

Other common fraternal restrictions had little to do with health or moral concerns, at least in the traditional sense. The SBA expressed its commitment to law and order and patriotism not only in the ritual but in the method of deter-mining benefits. It refused payment for any injury caused during participation in "a mob, riot, or insurrection, or as a result of being engaged in committing any offense against the laws of any State or of the Nation." It suspended benefits for members serving prison time. Other societies enacted restrictions with a re-ligious basis. The constitution of the LOTM prohibited lodge meetings or enter-tainment events on Sunday.[6]

Almost all white fraternal societies scrupulously enforced the color line. Of 386 organizations in Connecticut in 1891, for example, 97.6 percent barred blacks. Nearly fifty years later the racial lines in the United States were still "tightly drawn." Nevertheless, some societies were more restrictive than others. To join the MWA, one had to be at least "seven eighths white blood and no strain of negro blood." The Loyal Order of Moose kept out individuals "married to some one of any other than the Caucasian race." The definition of "white" in the constitution of the LOTM was slightly less restrictive. It barred women with "more than one-quarter colored blood in their veins."[7]

While virtually all fraternalists excluded black applicants, a few showed flex-ibility toward American Indians. But even here restriction was still the norm. The policy of the Improved Order of Red Men was perhaps the most ironic. Al-though the ritual celebrated the culture and tribal structure of "the vanishing race," no actual Indians could join. Other predominantly white groups such as the Knights of the Pythias officially exempted Indians from their racial restrictions. Fraternal liberality toward Indians was often the result of either intentional or accidental omission. For example, the LOTM excluded blacks while remaining silent, and thus presumably allowing, people from other nonwhite ethnic groups to join. Even then, local lodges were generally free to discriminate against Indians through informal methods.[8]

A notable exception to this policy was the IOF. For twenty-six years Oronhyatekha, a Mohawk from Canada, led this overwhelmingly white organization. His background did not fit the usual fraternal profile. Oronhyatekha was born in 1841 on a reservation near Brantford, Ontario. His close relatives had served in tribal leadership positions; hence members of the IOF often referred to him as "chief." He attended a local industrial school and, later, Wesleyan Academy in Wilbraham, Massachusetts. In 1860 the chiefs of the Six Nations asked him to read an address in honor of Edward, the Prince of Wales, who was touring Canada. Oronhyatekha's presentation was so polished that the prince arranged for him to study medicine at Oxford University.[9]

After earning his M.D., Oronhyatekha opened a medical practice in Ontario, where he became quite active in the Independent Order of Good Templars, a predominantly white temperance organization. In 1878 Oronhyatekha applied for membership in the IOF, which recently had split from the AOF, a British friendly society. For reasons that are somewhat obscure, the supreme chief ranger of the IOF gave Oronhyatekha a special "dispensation" from the rule that members be "white males." In 1881, shortly after he returned to Canada, Oronhyatekha won election as chief supreme ranger, a position he held until his death in 1907. He proved an able and charismatic organizer. The membership rose dramatically during his years in office from 369 to about 248,000.[10]

Several factors may explain why the IOF was so receptive to Oronhyatekha. He was not considered an ordinary Indian applicant; he was a "Mohawk chief." Moreover, his educational and professional credentials impressed many members (including powerful sponsors). His individual profile, with the notable exception of race, made him a major "catch" for any fraternal organization. His quick and disarming wit was legendary. When opponents of his admission to membership first quoted to him the IOF's rule excluding Indians, Oronhyatekha quipped that the "law was intended to exclude from the Order only the races which were regarded as being inferior to the whites and therefore did not apply to the Mohawks." His rejoinder silenced the objectors and "brought down the Court."[11]

Oronhyatekha, ca. 1900, the Chief Supreme Ranger of the IOF (1881–1907).
Oronhyatekha was not only a physician but also a full-blooded Mohawk
from Canada. (Edward J. Dunn, *Builders of Fraternalism*, bk. 1
[Chicago: Fraternal Book Concern, 1924])

Members showed little embarrassment about the ancestry of their supreme
chief ranger; they rather reveled in it. The IOF's publications often pictured Oronhyatekha in native garb and noted that he spoke only Mohawk in his home.
Members were quick to rise to his defense in response to slurs from insurance
competitors and other detractors. According to an article in the *Forester*, "There
is not a Forester in the wide world but knows that this full-blooded Indian chief

is the one man to whom the Order should be thankful for its wonderful growth."
Oronhyatekha himself was not always so tolerant. Motivated by some combination of prejudice and expediency, he refused to have his picture taken with black
members of the Independent Order of Good Templars. He never challenged the
IOF's exclusion of blacks.[12]

The IOF was tolerant compared with most societies. The vast majority
of fraternal organizations kept careful guard against the admission of non-
Caucasians. One historian, concluding that fraternalism and racism were two
sides of the same coin, asserts that the egalitarianism of American fraternal orders was "made possible by the exclusion of women, blacks, and ethnic minor-
ities from the relevant social universe, a universe whose boundaries fraternal institutions helped to demarcate and guard."[13]

This characterization is not really fair or, at the very least, paints an incomplete picture. Fraternal societies were hardly alone in drawing the color line.
Other major institutions in American society, including labor unions, professional associations, suffrage organizations, and colleges, followed essentially the
same policy. Moreover, fraternal societies during this period were not unusually extreme on this issue. The theme of race rarely appeared in the rituals, with
the notable exceptions of organizations such as the Ku Klux Klan. Few societies
tried to link fraternalism explicitly to the doctrine of Anglo-Saxon superiority.
Instead, most skirted race issues. The argument that racism was endemic to fraternalism is also at odds with the readiness of so many black societies to adopt
the name, ritual, and themes of "white" societies such as the Odd Fellows, the
Knights of Pythias, and the Elks.

Neither Silks nor Rags

Societies relied on several methods to enforce selectivity. Most of the largest organizations and many smaller ones required that applicants receive the imprimatur of an investigative committee, which sought to verify worthiness. Hence,
according the rules of the LOTM, the "investigating committee shall make investigation of an application personally, or shall take up the matter by correspondence and obtain written references as to the social desirability of the
applicant."[14]

Even candidates who won the endorsement of the investigating committee
faced another obstacle: the blackball. The usual procedure was for members to
drop balls into a box when they voted on each application. A white ball showed
support; a black ball, rejection. A few societies, such as the Masons, required

total unanimity; most provided that two or three blackballs vetoed an application. The blackball epitomized the quest of societies to avoid the vagaries of ma-
joritarianism in favor of a more restrictive standard of unanimity or a super-
majority. Still, the blackball was controversial, and members who abused it were
admonished. The LOTM condemned any member who rejected initiates out of
spite, while the IOF enacted a rule to invalidate blackballs cast to "serve personal
ends." Most societies stipulated that the tally of blackballs be kept secret and
that members could not be asked how they voted.[15]

The obligation of members to follow the fraternal moral code of deserving
and undeserving did not cease upon initiation. Most societies required claimants for sick benefits to pass muster with a visiting committee. These committees, usually selected by rotation, did not just offer physical and moral support
to the sick. They also stood on guard against false claims. They could disqual-
ify claimants for malingering or trying to collect for afflictions regarded as immoral or self-destructive.[16]

These arrangements had much in common with the aid criteria and enforcement systems of public and private charities. Organized charities, like lodges,
invariably distinguished between "deserving" and "undeserving." They, too,
wanted to root out persons who were guilty of immoral or malingering behavior. Instead of using visiting committees, however, they relied on "friendly visitors." Caseworkers and fraternalists agreed on the need to cultivate values of
"thrift, self-dependence, industry, [and] virtue" in recipients.[17]

Many social welfare historians argue that the standard of deserving and undeserving was at odds with the values of the poor and working class. For one
historian the concept exemplifies a "strategy of class control" and "a convenient
but destructive fiction" that has steered discussion away from the social causes
of poverty. He argues that the use of these categories has cruelly consigned the
poor to be objects of pity and charity, thus depriving them of their just entitlement as equal members of the community.[18]

Other historians voice a less extreme but overlapping view. To varying degrees they associate the dichotomy of deserving and undeserving with efforts
to impose (or at least instill) attitudes of thrift, measured gain, decorum, sexual restraint, and sobriety. Frequently historians have grouped these values
under such rubrics as middle class, bourgeois, Social Darwinist, individualis-
tic, and Protestant. This labeling has had the effect of fostering the impression
that a wide chasm separated economic classes in their attitudes toward social
welfare.[19]

The extensive record left by fraternal societies calls into question these assumptions. I have focused on the aid criteria used by the Household of Ruth and the Workmen's Circle (wc). Each offers a window into the attitudes of two large but highly disparate segments of the working class during the early twentieth century. Neither organization seems a likely repository for "middle-class" values. For much the same reason, they offer better case studies than more mainstream white societies such as the IOF, the MWA, and the Loyal Order of Moose.

The Household of Ruth: Sojourna Lodge

The Household of Ruth was the women's affiliate of the all-black GUOOF. Like the black versions of the Elks, the Knights of Pythias, and the Masons, it owed its founding to the exclusionary racial restrictions of the parallel white organization. The GUOOF grew rapidly and had 304,000 members in 1916, making it by far the largest voluntary association of blacks in the country.[20]

The Household originated in 1857, fourteen years after the founding of the parent male society. Wives of the black Odd Fellows, as well as their female relatives, were eligible. The GUOOF's leaders depicted the Household as "part and parcel" of the overall organization and scorned labels such as "ladies auxiliary." These claims were somewhat overblown, but the Household did enjoy a high degree of independence, as indicated by the activities of the Sojourna Lodge of New York City. Moreover, the Household's popularity makes it difficult to dismiss it as a mere puppet of the male organization. By 1916 it had an impressive membership of 197,000 in nearly 5,000 lodges. It easily ranked as the single largest black female voluntary organization in the United States.[21]

In their economic class backgrounds, members of both the Household and the GUOOF fell somewhere in the middle rank of black fraternal organizations. They lacked the prestige of the Prince Hall Masons and its auxiliary, the Eastern Star, but probably could claim higher class status than societies without white namesakes, such as the IOSL. If Prince Hall Masonry spoke for an elite, however, it was an elite only in terms of the black community. Judged by the overall standards of American society, most Prince Hall Masons were either poor or at least lower income. Surveys of lodges in California and Nebraska during the early twentieth century reveal that the vast majority of members were unskilled. The elite in the organization were Pullman Porters.[22]

The records of the Sojourna Lodge are too scanty to provide a thorough occupational profile, but application forms for new members between 1921

and 1930 are available for the St. Paul Lodge in New York City. In the absence of
contradictory evidence, it seems safe to assume that members of the Sojourna
Lodge fit a similar occupational pattern. Of those new initiates who gave an occupation, seventeen listed "housework" (which could mean a number of different things) and three listed "housewife." The other fourteen worked in unskilled occupations, particularly domestic service. The members of the St. Paul
Lodge were slightly more likely than black women as a whole to have gainful
employment. Census figures from 1920 show that 32.5 percent of black women
had outside work, while 34.1 percent of those in the St. Paul Lodge had such
employment.[23]

In their tendency to be "joiners," the members of the St. Paul and Sojourna
Lodges typified black women in New York. According to a detailed block survey of the tenement area of the nineteenth assembly district in Manhattan conducted in 1897 by the Social Gospel-oriented Federation of Churches and Christian Workers, lower-class black women had a greater inclination than any other
ethnic group to join "economic clubs" such as fraternal societies. The study
found that 52 percent subscribed to economic clubs, a higher percentage than
belonged to a church. "The insurance of the colored women," it opined, "is
phenomenal. If the churches will work the colored people as industriously as
the insurance societies have done, it will be to the community's advantage." In
1909 Robert Coit Chapin's survey of wage earners in New York uncovered similar results. Ten of the twenty-eight black families questioned had at least one
member in a fraternal lodge.[24]

Like other affiliates of the Household, the Sojourna Lodge paid sick benefits.
The lodge's constitution outlined the obligations and responsibilities of members. It required monthly dues of 50 cents in addition to a $2.50 initiation fee.
This amount entitled members to a weekly payment of $6.00 for the first six
weeks of any disabling illness and $3.00 per week for the next six weeks.[25]

The Sojourna Lodge did not distribute aid as a blanket entitlement. The constitution laid out precautions against malingering that easily rivaled (and often
exceeded) those of the elite-controlled charity societies. The lodge could deny
support to members who "feign sickness or disability" or suffered from an illness caused by "immoral practice." It required an applicant to present a doctor's
certificate with a notarized seal for each week she was sick. To enforce these requirements it charged a committee to investigate suspect claims as well as to offer "support and comfort."[26]

Rules, of course, can be a deceptive guide to actual practice. By themselves they do not reveal how seriously the sick committee or the Sojourna Lodge as a whole viewed its responsibilities. Enough records exist for a two-year period, however, to answer part of this question. While they indicate great generosity to those in need, they also show little reluctance to revoke funds to the few deemed undeserving. The lodge dispensed weekly sick benefits more than fifty times between May 1914 and July 1916; the sick committee conducted more than seventy visits over the same period. The notations in the minute book (which probably underestimated amounts paid and numbers of beneficiaries) reveal that the lodge turned down at least four applicants.[27]

The minute book gives the reasons for rejection in two of the cases, both of which bespeak the Sojourna Lodge's willingness to deploy "middle-class standards" of morality. It dismissed the first summarily by announcing that "the Household does not pay for the illness the Sis. is suffering from and moreover the Sister has not being [sic] to meeting for quite some time." The lodge took more time to consider the other request. In April 1916 a member named Lottie Laster asked for benefits. She claimed that this money was due her because of four weeks spent in a Harlem hospital. From the outset the sick committee, as well as other members, was leery. Further investigation confirmed their suspicions. When a member reported that no one at the hospital had ever heard of Laster, the lodge rejected her application.[28]

The extent to which the Sojourna Lodge adopted middle-class morality might have been due to necessity. After all, it had to grapple with tight budgets and needed to draw the line somewhere. That general explanation, however, does not address the question of why the lodge used a middle-class standard instead of another, less morally laden rationing mechanism. The explanation of limited resources falls short in another respect. The lodge was quite ready to stretch scarce dollars to help certain members considered deserving but technically ineligible. For every case such as Laster's, the lodge bent over backward to advance charity to someone who had exhausted benefits or lapsed in dues. Indeed, the rules showed sensitivity to special hardships. Taking note of the sporadic nature of black employment, the constitution stipulated that members could continue to receive benefits even if they were up to six months behind in dues and allowed retention of membership standing if a member was less than one year in arrears.[29]

By no means was the Household of Ruth the only major black fraternal society to refuse aid to members perceived as undeserving. The Prince Hall Masons was typical in forbidding lodges to "receive or retain . . . any man who is a common profane swearer, a reputed libertine, an excessive drinker, or one who is

guilty of any crime involving moral turpitude or . . . any demoralizing practice."
William Muraskin excoriates these restrictive policies as a misguided strategy by
a black middle-class minority to conform to "bourgeois values." He concludes
that these distinctions have proved "detrimental to black unity" and have served
to exclude, and thus cast a stigma on, the majority of blacks not subscribing to
the dominant white value system.[30]

Such an evaluation cannot withstand close scrutiny. These bourgeois values
were not the exclusive domain of the more elite Prince Hall Masons and GUOOF.
They appeared across a wide spectrum of black fraternal societies regardless of
economic class, including such lower-status groups as the UOTR, the International Order of Twelve Knights and Daughters of Tabor, the IOSL, and the Mosaic Templars of America, Europe, Asia, and Africa. All enthusiastically embraced the full gamut of middle-class values. The UOTR restricted membership
to people of "sound bodily health and good moral character." The IOSL denied benefits for false statements, participation in mobs or riots, or illnesses
caused by intemperance or other "vicious or immoral" acts. The Mosaic Templars promised to "cause the doors of this or any other Chamber of this order
to be closed against unworthy sisters."[31]

A member of the Knights and Daughters of Tabor used a poem to summa-
rize the moral values and selectivity of her organization. Written in 1913, it re-
fers to the mythical goat ridden by all initiates:

> The fraternal part of this Order
> Should be practiced by every hand
> It protects the young members
> From the evils of our land
> Instead of roving around at night
> And gambling just for sport,
> They go to the Camp Forest,
> And see the new members ride the goat.
>
> This goat is very useful.
> He is wise, as well as good,
> He knows just what a man can do
> When he comes to this Order of Twelve
> He knows the good men from the bad,
> He scrambles o'er the floor
> If he comes in that isn't fit,
> He throws him out the door.[32]

Macon Drill Corps, International Order of Twelve Knights and Daughters of Tabor,
Macon, Georgia, 1921. (International Order of Twelve Sir Knights and Daughters
of Tabor, minutes, 1921; courtesy of Photographs and Prints Division,
Schomburg Center for Research in Black Culture, Astor, Lenox, and
Tilden Foundations, New York Public Library, New York, N.Y.)

For these societies, much as in white organizations, "good moral character"
was a defining feature of worthiness. The recommendations of an official of
the black Knights of Pythias on blackballs were virtually indistinguishable from
those offered by groups such as the Loyal Order of Moose. He warned that a
"black ball is not made to be cast against an applicant who wears better clothes
than I do; who lives in a better house than I do; who has more brains than I
have. . . . It was made to keep out members who are undesirable because of
their moral fitness to associate with good people. Neither silks nor rags indicate
character." [33]

In their willingness to invoke distinctions of deserving and undeserving,
the mostly working-class black women who joined fraternal societies differed
greatly from the more elite "black women's network" identified by Linda Gordon. Gordon compared the "visions of welfare" advocated by selected samples
of prominent black and white female social welfare activists between 1890 and
1940. "Among whites, a relatively large middle class encouraged reformers to
focus their helping efforts on others and kept alive and relatively uncriticized

the use of means and moral testing as a way of distributing help, continuing the division of the 'deserving' from the 'undeserving' poor. Among black reformers, despite their relatively elite position, welfare appeared more closely connected with legal entitlements, not so different from the right to vote or to ride the public transportation system."[34]

The examples presented in this book point to a possible divergence of values on social welfare held by elite and lower-class black females. The women in the Household (as expressed in their institutional behavior) apparently did not share the entitlement perspective embraced by the leading black activists in Gordon's survey.

The Workmen's Circle

On first inspection, the wc (Arbeiter Ring) did not have much in common with the Household of Ruth. It was a predominantly Jewish fraternal society pledged to uphold the principles of proletarian solidarity and socialism. Both the Household and the wc recruited primarily from the working class, but they attracted vastly different kinds of workers. Members of the Household were housewives or unskilled workers, while 80 percent of those in the wc were semiskilled or skilled. Despite these contrasts the Household of Ruth and the wc showed similar attitudes toward malingering. Although neither would seem a likely exemplar of exclusionary middle-class values, both diligently weeded out the deserving from the undeserving.[35]

The wc originated in 1891 as a Jewish fraternal society. By the early 1900s, proudly dubbing itself the "Red Cross of the Labor Movement," it had forged close links with the Socialist Party. During these years the wc counted Emma Goldman and Alexander Berkman as members. The membership expanded from about 8,000 in 1908 to 70,000 by the early 1930s, almost half of whom lived in New York City. The benefits included free burial and a small death benefit. Like the Household, the wc dispensed weekly cash payments to the sick.[36]

The motivating ideology of the wc was self-consciously working class, socialist, and egalitarian. Even so, it was an egalitarianism that, when push came to shove, was selective. Not unlike the Household, it guarded against false sick claims. The rules stipulated that no members could receive benefits unless they suffered disabling illnesses. Although individual lodges (branches) ruled on the validity of claims, members could appeal to the National Benefit Committee in New York. From 1926 to 1936 the committee heard hundreds of appeals but described only eight in detail in its reports. The Benefit Committee overturned the ruling of the individual branch in four cases and sustained it in four others. One branch had denied sick benefits because a member reported that the applicant had been out and about wearing his conductor's uniform. The committee ruled against the branch on the ground that the evidence of disability was insufficient. Two years later it heard a similar appeal. A lodge had refused sick benefits after the visiting committee had gone to the member's home and been told by his wife that "he could not be found home any evening after 5 P.M." This time the Benefit Committee upheld the branch's refusal to pay.[37]

In common with the Household, the Benefit Committee of the wc coupled strict restrictions against cheating with flexibility toward members who seemed worthy. It reinstated the membership of an individual with tuberculosis who had been expelled by the local branch for nonpayment of dues, and the committee ruled that he could receive free treatment in the wc's sanitarium. Additionally, during the depression the national office established a relief department to care for destitute members and advanced $100,000 to assist members who were unemployed or had fallen into arrears.[38]

The wc expected a good deal of its members. It rigorously enforced rules against false claims and laid out strict guidelines for personal, moral, and political behavior. Punishments for violations ranged from fines to outright expulsion. Throughout the 1920s the wc had a substantial yearly expulsion rate of between 7 and 15 percent of the total national membership. Punishable offenses included working during (or otherwise impeding) a strike, charging "usurious interest rates," or supporting candidates of the "capitalistic" parties, the Republicans or the Democrats. The fines averaged a staggering $99.00 per individual found guilty.[39]

The restrictions of the wc were not exceptional. The International Worker's Order, a fraternal society aligned closely with the Communist Party, denied benefits for disabilities caused by venereal disease, alcohol, and narcotics. The National Slovak Society, the United Societies of the U.S.A. (Russian Slovak), and the Croatian Fraternal Union added adultery and divorce to the list of unworthy behavior. The Greek Catholic Union voided benefits not only for adultery and profanity but also for failure to observe Easter confession. Among Jews many regional associations (or *landsmanshaftn*) and family circles expelled members who married gentiles. Fines for failure to attend funerals were common. Significantly, while only a handful of historians emphasize these exacting fraternal behavioral restrictions, many others castigate as moralistic analogous efforts by charity and welfare agencies to enforce (often less demanding) requirements.[40]

Despite sharing the dichotomy between deserving and undeserving, the social welfare policies of fraternal societies, governmental relief agencies, and organized charities were not of a piece. Historians raise valid issues when they stress the patronizing and degrading aspects of charity and welfare casework during the late nineteenth and early twentieth centuries. This inspires the question of why exhortations by charity and welfare officials against the undeserving often strike such a false note to modern ears. Perhaps the answer lies not so much in the specific content of the requirements but because they came from outsiders, most of whom had never been poor. Charity and welfare workers could never truly comprehend the conditions of recipients or entirely win their trust. Understandably, the poor resented and distrusted the impersonal and bureaucratic system that distributed alms.

Almost as a matter of course, charity and welfare aid restrictions revolved around adversarial donor and recipient relationships. Those of fraternal societies, on the other hand, more closely approximated principles of reciprocity. At bottom, adversarial relationships between donor and receiver seemed endemic to *any* impersonal poor relief system (public or private, entitlement based, or means-tested) controlled and funded by distant bureaucrats or other outsiders. Donor and recipient in the fraternal society were peers in the same organization. They often knew each other well on a personal level. Of course, the process of deciding aid eligibility was not without acrimony or oversimplification. Undoubtedly at least some members used the process to settle scores, and thus the "unworthy" had to pay a price and fend for themselves. Even so, fraternal aid rarely carried a patronizing stigma. It was, after all, frequently a matter of low-income people determining the aid worthiness or unworthiness of one another.

The fraternal concept of reciprocity entailed mutual obligations between members and the organization to which they belonged. It was wholly antagonistic to the idea that the donor should dole out one-way entitlements. To underline this point, Walter Basye, editor of the *Fraternal Monitor*, asserted that "fraternity, like religion or a savings bank, gives most to those who put in most. And the best deposit in the bank of fraternity is heart-felt interest and support."[41]

Lodge benefits may not have been unconditional obligations, but neither could they be properly classified as charity. The manual of the black Knights of Pythias, for example, declared that the "sick among our brethren are not left to the cold hand of public charity; they are visited, and their wants provided for out of the funds they themselves have contributed to raise, and which, in time of need, they honorably claim, without the humiliation of suing parochial or individual relief—from which the freeborn mind recoils with disdain." Similarly, Maximilian Hurwitz, member and chronicler of the wc, contrasted a recipient of fraternal medical services and "a charity patient, which is repugnant to the self-respecting man."[42]

Few lodge leaders stated this distinction more clearly than Bina West. In a speech to the National Fraternal Congress (NFC) in 1901, she characterized fraternity as "absolutely distinct from charity or philanthropy. It is liberalizing, self-sustaining, elevating, gives mutual rights and preserves independence of character." Philanthropy, on the other hand, "signifies condescension, a position of superiority on the part of the organization, and of dependency on the part of the recipient." Fraternalists, such as West, while conceding the need for public and private charity, depicted it as a necessary evil. The *Knights and Ladies of Security* editorialized that most individuals would contribute to "the relief of distress but what a tragedy it is for those who are forced to accept charity. And how needless."[43]

Fraternal benefits, if viewed from this angle, more closely resembled conditional entitlements than charity. As long as members kept their end of the contractual relationship, they could justly demand aid as their due. As an official of the *kehillah* (or Jewish community) said, "Mutual aid organizations were formed for the purpose of rendering aid to members, not as gratuitous charity, but as obligatory settlement of claims based on a mutual agreement as formulated in the constitution of the respective organizations or in the membership certificate."[44]

The aid restrictions of fraternal societies rested on an ethic of solidarity. By limiting benefits to those deemed deserving of this solidarity, they were not unlike labor unions. In unions, members who violated certain restrictions (by not paying dues or by strikebreaking, for example) lost their rights to help. For both types of organization, the full force of solidarity extended to those within the circle. Bernard J. Monaghan, the grand worthy president of the Fraternal Order of Eagles (FOE), stated a simple rule: "Charity to the outside world but to a brother anything we can give . . . is his due." This philosophy found expression in the rituals of numerous societies. Second-degree initiates of the IOSL pledged to extend aid to the distressed "wherever I find them, but particularly to a brother or sister." They also vowed to provide members with employment opportunities or business patronage in "preference to all other males or females."[45]

The Intangible Dimensions of Membership

The advantages of lodge membership did not end with formal insurance benefits. The initiate gained access to a larger social and financial network. In his comments on fraternal societies in the United States during a visit in 1904, Max Weber described lodge affiliation as a mark of "credit worthiness." He noted that membership was acquired "through balloting and a determination of moral worth. And hence the badge in the buttonhole meant 'I am a gentleman patented after investigation and probation and guaranteed by my membership.' . . . One could observe that business opportunities were often decisively influenced by such legitimation." [46]

Specific incidents clearly bear out Weber's claim. In 1908 the *Ladies Review* tried to illustrate the intangible benefits of fraternalism by recounting the experience of a member whose brother was injured in a railroad accident. After a lodge sister spotted her Maccabee pin, "members of the Order came to her from far and near in her trouble and made her feel that she was among friends." A better-known case in 1897 involved longtime Mason Samuel Gompers, the president of the American Federation of Labor. While walking down a street, he had exchanged Masonic signs with a stranger. The man confessed to Gompers that a mining company had hired him as a spy. He then handed over the negatives of pictures he had taken of Gompers. Years later Gompers recalled that he "frequently found that my affiliation to the Masonic order has been a protection to me." Fraternal membership often opened doors to employment opportunities. C. L. Dellums, the president of the Brotherhood of Sleeping Car Porters and a Prince Hall Mason, described how his fraternal affiliation even transcended ethnic differences on occasion. He obtained his first job on the railroad because a white Mason had noticed his Masonic pin. [47]

Societies gave nonmonetary help to members on a more systematic level. Organizations ranging from *landsmanshaftn* to the white Knights of Pythias functioned as "labor exchanges" to bring together workers and businesspeople who were members. For several decades the Irish owners of the Anaconda Copper Company entrusted authority for hiring in Butte, Montana, to "job committees" of the Ancient Order of Hibernians. The membership of the order comprised not only many ordinary miners but also the first four presidents of the company. [48]

Almost all societies recognized the need to help the worthy member who had fallen victim to extraordinary and unanticipated setbacks. Sociologist Peter

Roberts described how fraternal societies among the coal workers of Pennsylvania at the turn of the century regularly sponsored raffles to help members who exceeded the time limit of their benefits. During the relatively prosperous year of 1910 the national special committee of the Polish National Alliance aided 1,150 individuals, or 2.1 percent of the membership. This count was on the low side because it did not include the efforts of local lodges.[49]

Fraternal assistance was most in demand, of course, during hard times. During the early 1920s, for example, the Loyal Order of Moose adopted a program to aid unemployed members after 32,000 of them had fallen into arrears during a recession. It recommended carrying 22,000 of those members on the rolls "if fair extension of time could be arranged." Because of this help, the Supreme Lodge asserted that "we have been able to save many splendid members." Examples such as this moved insurance historian Terence O'Donnell to comment that the "*esprit de corps* of a fraternal beneficiary society is one of its most valuable assets, and is far out of proportion to the 'good will' a purely commercial company can claim."[50]

Many lodges were willing to bend or even break national rules when they conflicted with the perceived needs of local members. The actual practices of lodges in the mining community of Cripple Creek, Colorado, for example, showed intriguing contrasts to the seemingly inflexible uniform rules. The MWA was especially illustrative. Local lodges aggressively recruited miners in the Cripple Creek area despite the fact that the rules of the national organization listed mining as an "excluded" occupation.[51]

Informal fraternal assistance had limits, however. The official policy of most societies condemned members who joined for mercenary reasons. At the same time, the line between acceptable and unacceptable motivations was not always obvious. Consider the ambiguous comments of Edward Hearn, who became supreme knight of the Knights of Columbus in 1899. For Hearn the thought of a person joining "to advance his business interests is not to be entertained, but that our Order has for its object the advancement of the social and business interests of its members is true, for we are a body of Catholic men associated for our common good." The same ambiguity appeared in the comments of A. E. Partridge, the grand secretary of the FOE. He cautioned that "while no member will use his membership therein as a lever to obtain favors from any man, at the same time his membership therein is undoubtedly of mutual financial benefit."[52]

The informal financial side of fraternal assistance was most visible after nat-

ural and man-made disasters. During 1927, for example, the national office of
the Improved Benevolent and Protective Order of the Elks, a black organization,
donated more than $4,000 to members who had been victims of Mississippi
floods and Florida hurricanes. A wide range of societies responded to the San
Francisco earthquake of 1906. The hives of the LOTM contributed $6,000 in cash
and dozens of boxes of clothes. The much larger IOF also launched a campaign
for the earthquake victims. By July lodges in the United States and Canada had
raised $15,000 in special aid.[53]

A typical pattern was for the national organization to act as a clearinghouse
to collect and distribute funds. The SBA coordinated such a campaign after a fire
that had affected about 100 members. It issued a circular calling for contributions, noting that "most of our sister orders have issued a call to their membership." Many of the letters from contributing lodges survive, such as one from
Hugh Gowan, the secretary of a lodge in Mount Olive, Illinois. He apologized
for sending only a $5.00 contribution: "We as miners here are not in a very
Good shape to help any one at present as we have bin on strik bout 6 week and
don't now much longer or we might of bin in a shape to of don our duty in
more libery way."[54]

As Gowan's comments indicate, fraternalists generally gave priority to the
needs of the immediate circle of the local lodge. They gave help to beleaguered
members elsewhere, but recipients and donors took it for granted that local
lodges came first. In 1902 the SBA issued a national appeal for contributions
after a devastating flood in Topeka, Kansas. One lodge that provided assistance
was led by Mary J. Crum of Lyndon, Kansas. Crum apologized for the low total contribution of $10.00 but pointed out that "we have several very poor mem-
bers and they have to be helped often or we would lose them."[55]

Scholars have made much of the fraternal dedication to exclusivity and selectivity. As Mary Ann Clawson points out, "Fraternalism bases itself on a principle of exclusion, from which it derives much of its power." This characterization, although true, deserves qualification. While societies urged members to
show preferential treatment to brothers and sisters, they also called for more
general acts of charity and civic involvement. The evidence indicates that, on
the whole, these claims were sincere. Officials of the LOTM, for example, contributed much time and energy to feminism and temperance. The IOSL, Prince
Hall Masons, and black Elks worked to further civil rights. The FOE played an
important role in the campaign for mothers' pensions. Participation in lodges
served as a springboard for broader activism rather than as an excuse to isolate

initiates from noninitiates. This behavior was in line with the fraternal philoso-phy that the lodge equipped members with transferable leadership, business, social, and political skills.[56]

The experiences of a wide cross section of societies reveal some critical dis-tinctions between fraternal methods of assistance and the approaches of gov-ernments and organized charities. Most societies held to a philosophy that members had a right to assistance. This stand was in direct contrast to the offi-cial policies of organized charities and governments. At the same time, societies never provided unconditional aid. For this reason, one cannot automatically affix a middle-class label to the concept of deserving and undeserving. Frater-nal lodges subscribed to many stereotypical middle-class credos, such as tem-perance and fidelity, and piled on new requirements for achieving worthiness. Moreover, these were not just paper regulations. Like organized charities and governments, fraternal orders, such as the Household of Ruth and the wc, ag-gressively investigated eligibility.

CHAPTER FOUR

The Child City

V ivienne Cottingham began kindergarten in 1920, but her experience did not fit the norm. Her school was Mooseheart, the national orphanage of a fraternal society. The Loyal Order of Moose had established this institution to clothe, feed, and educate the children of deceased members.[1]

Vivienne's childhood had been punctuated by tragedy. She was born in Ponca City, Oklahoma, where her father, a member of a Moose lodge, worked in the oil fields. When Vivienne was four, her mother abandoned the family. Her grandmother took in the children while her father provided financial support. The family descended into a financial crisis, however, when he died in a car accident on New Year's Day 1919.[2]

Help came when her grandmother discovered that Vivienne was eligible for Mooseheart. The lodge made all the arrangements to send her to Illinois. Vivienne decided to make the most of the situation and excelled in activities such as Camp Fire Girls and basketball. As a teenager she earned money typing for her teachers. Thirteen years after she had arrived, Vivienne graduated with a high school diploma and a vocational degree.[3]

Thousands of children had similar stories. All manner of groups operated orphanages, including religious orders, immigrant organizations, and county and state governments. The orphanage population increased from 50,579 in 1880 to an all-time high of 142,971 in 1923. Fraternal societies founded seventy-one orphanages between 1890 and 1922, almost all without governmental subsidy. The array of sponsors included the IOF, the Knights of Pythias, B'nai B'rith, and the Sons of Italy. But two societies stood out: the IOOF and the Masons. Between them they operated sixty-four orphanages in 1933, accounting for more than half of the 9,409 children in fraternal orphanages.[4]

The origins of Mooseheart can be traced to 1910. That year the national convention of the Loyal Order of Moose authorized the building of a "Moose Na-

tional Industrial School for the orphans and children of members of the Order"
and appointed a board of trustees to carry out the task. From the outset the
founders envisioned the institute as an exemplar of vocational training and
pedagogical innovation. Edward J. Henning, a board member and a federal
judge from Pennsylvania, anticipated a slogan of Mooseheart when he wrote
that the public schools had made a great mistake of "training the boys and girls
for the university instead of training them for life." The early promotional literature promised to "give a thorough practical training in any one of the many
trades; to graduate pupils as skilled craftsmen who can earn a competence.
Agriculture will be taught in all its branches." [5]

The board, after a two-year search, purchased 1,014 acres just outside Aurora,
Illinois. The location allowed for expansion. Financing for the purchase and
early construction came through a mixture of voluntary contributions and the
proceeds of a weekly "tax" of 2 cents on each member. To underscore the cen-
trality of the orphanage to the fraternal members, the board named the enterprise Mooseheart.[6]

The opening ceremony in 1913 took place under less than ideal conditions.
The organizers had hastily thrown up a circus tent to shield the guests from the
blazing July sun. Present were the eleven children who were the first residents.
Thomas R. Marshall, the vice-president of the United States, delivered the dedication address. He touted Mooseheart as a solution for the "educational, the
social, and the economic problems of our times." The upbeat rhetoric hardly
corresponded to the threadbare appearance.[7]

Marshall had been reluctant to come. When asked to deliver the dedication,
he exclaimed, "I detest orphanages. . . . I won't help you to lay the cornerstone
of another one of them." Marshall relented, but only after a longtime friend,
one of the trustees, promised that Mooseheart would not "be an orphanage at
all. Technically, legally, yes, it will be an orphanage. Actually, it will be a home,
a home and school for the dependent children of our deceased members." [8]

By the end of the first year the Supreme Council of the Moose had selected a
board of governors to administer Mooseheart and appoint a superintendent.
The members included Henning; John J. Lentz, a former member of the U.S.
House of Representatives; and James J. Davis, the order's general director.
Davis, along with his allies in the fraternal leadership, exercised working control. Another influential member was Albert Bushnell Hart, the renowned historian from Harvard University. Hart would be a central figure in shaping the
pedagogical philosophy and character of Mooseheart. The two most famous

board members, Governor Hiram Johnson of California and Senator Arthur
Capper of Kansas, were little more than names on a letterhead.[9]

Growing Pains

Mooseheart grew rapidly. The student body had risen sixfold by the end of 1914.
Many of the children continued to live in circus tents until the 1920s. The tents
had stoves and wooden floors, but the conditions were embarrassingly primi-
tive. An employee remembered that "pranksters among the boys would get up
at night sometimes and jerk the tents down or open the flaps so that the snow
could get in." Mooseheart was on its way to becoming the largest fraternal orphanage in the United States. By 1919 it had 720 children; 17 arrived during one
day in March alone. The number of children passed the 1,000 mark in 1921 and
did not begin to decline until the 1940s. Mooseheart was truly a "child city."[10]

It was akin to a city in other ways as well. The physical infrastructure was
vast. Mooseheart had a power plant, a separate water supply, a small stream
and lake, a twenty-eight-bed hospital, a baby nursery, a large assembly hall, several buildings of classrooms, a department store, a post office, a bank, a radio
station, and miles of storm and sanitary sewers. The farm, which consisted of
800 acres, had 85 cows, 185 hogs, 1,000 chickens, and an apple orchard.[11]

Because Mooseheart had a school year of forty-eight weeks, it could offer an
intense and varied curriculum. The academic portion excluded esoteric subjects such as Latin and Greek in favor of civics, American history, English composition, and commercial history. Students who could not fulfill the academic
requirements graduated with vocational degrees. The vocational component
started in the eighth grade with optional "try out" courses of three months
each. The choices for boys included animal husbandry, carpentry, automobile
repair, and electrical work. Try-out courses for girls were shorthand, typing,
sewing, printing, and music. In the tenth grade the boys and girls selected a specialty. The fraternal membership appreciated this pedagogical approach. As
Davis pointed out, the "Moose are mostly working men, and so they equip their
wards for industrial life." The Mooseheart vision was "Industry first and literature afterward."[12]

Events proved that the initial reliance on voluntary contributions, while
sufficient to start the project, was no longer adequate. In 1914 the Supreme
Lodge instituted a compulsory annual membership fee of $1.00 dollar to sup-
port Mooseheart. It encouraged lodges to sponsor special projects; more than

one residence hall bears the name of the lodge that endowed it. One lodge in Philadelphia raised the funds for the hospital, which cost $125,000.[13]

An important innovation was the establishment of the Mooseheart Laboratory for Child Research in 1930 under the leadership of Dr. Martin L. Reymert, a child psychologist and former graduate student of G. Stanley Hall of Columbia University. Reymert was attracted by the "limitless possibilities for Research" offered by an environment of "about thirteen-hundred normal children" in "a complete and self-contained . . . community-embracing experimental laboratory." During the next two decades the laboratory made itself available to psychologists, anthropologists, sociologists, and other academics. Researchers studied topics such as anorexia, bed-wetting, childhood slang, and the effect of environment on IQ.[14]

Guarding against the Unworthy

The admission procedure for children was fairly straightforward. The local lodge helped fill out the paperwork. Each application had to provide confirmation that the child's father had been a member for five years before his death, a certificate of the child's good health from a doctor, a statement by a schoolteacher, and details about the family's economic condition. A final stipulation was that the guardian sign a contract ceding day-to-day control of the child. In exchange the board of governors provided free room and board, medical care, and education. This was a conditional promise. Mooseheart did not make a formal adoption and reserved the right to return the child at any time to the legal guardian.[15]

The children who lived at Mooseheart came overwhelmingly from working-class backgrounds. This reflected the claim that the Loyal Order of Moose represented "*common people*, the *average* American, men who largely work with their hands." Between 45 and 55 percent (table 4.1) of the fathers were unskilled or semiskilled. The children probably came disproportionately from families on the lower income rungs of the membership.[16]

The ever increasing number of applications pressured the board to act as gatekeeper against the "unworthy." For example, it often denied admission to children with criminal records, even if they were guilty of minor crimes, for fear that they would be carriers of antisocial behavior. It refused to admit children who were fourteen or older on the theory that they were less adaptable and more capable of self-support. The superintendent referred to the biographies of

TABLE 4.1. Occupations of the Fathers of Children at Mooseheart and
Adult Males in Illinois, Percentage of Group

Type of Occupation	Admissions (1925–27)	In Residence (October 1934)	Males in Illinois
Unskilled	19.6	24.4	8
Semiskilled	25.5	31.7	15
Skilled	39.9	31.1	39
Small business and clerical	14.4	11.6	35
Professional	.7	1.4	3

Source: Martin L. Reymert and John Frings, "Children's Intelligence in Relation to Occupation of Father," American Journal of Sociology 41 (November 1935): 352.

two board members who at age fourteen had been "thrown on their own resources and improved their minds between working hours. . . . It is hard to
make such men believe that a fourteen-year-old boy or girl is a dependent
child."[17]

The standards of worthiness applied to the guardians as well as the children.
A consistent concern was that guardians would exploit Mooseheart as a free
boarding school, withdrawing and readmitting children for short-term conve-
nience. The board warned that "Mooseheart is not intended to be a charity to
relieve comfortable people from their responsibilities." This attitude was not
surprising. Officials of many orphanages, fraternal or otherwise, expressed this
concern.[18]

Despite the formal rules, the final decision of the board of governors regarding the disposition of each application depended on individual circumstances.
Special situations and ambiguities demanded a measure of discernment and
flexibility. Between 1922 and 1924 the board considered applications for 472
children. It admitted almost 70 percent (table 4.2) without imposing further requirements, accepted 15 percent conditionally, and rejected 15 percent outright.
One measure of the board's flexibility was that it repeatedly set aside the rule
that the father have been a member in good standing for five years prior to his
death. Davis explained these exceptions as the result of the "utter destitution of
the cases."[19]

The board's most radical departure from the original standard of worthiness
involved the admission of children who had one parent living. The founders
had conceived Mooseheart as a haven for full orphans. By 1919 the annual re-

TABLE 4.2. Decisions by the Board of Governors on Applications for Admission to Mooseheart, 1922–1924, Percentage of Children Considered for Admission

Admitted (with no further requirements)	69.70
Admitted (if certain requirements met)	15.04
Must pass mental test	6.14
Mother must agree to come	4.02
Must be approved by caseworker	3.17
Guardian must provide contribution	1.48
Must pass physical examination	.21
Turned down for admission	15.25
No explanation given	11.44
No dependency	2.33
Odd Fellows will admit	1.05
Father committed suicide	.42

Source: Folders 1–2: Moose and Mooseheart, Board of Governors, Correspondence and Reports, 1922–24, box 14, Albert Bushnell Hart Papers, Harvard University Archives, Pusey Library, Harvard University, Cambridge, Mass.

port indicated a change, stating that if a mother was "ill or for any reason, not capable of taking care of her children, the Governors go beyond the letter to the spirit of the votes of the Order, the main issue being, are these children of a loyal Moose . . . who without Mooseheart would be thrown upon charity?" Between 1922 and 1924 half-orphans accounted for more than 75 percent (table 4.3) of admissions, while full orphans made up 22.3 percent.[20]

The vast majority of the half-orphans had mothers. As a matter of course the board discouraged widowed fathers from applying. When it made exceptions, it usually required the father to send contributions for the children's upkeep. This practice never really worked; the board's annual report complained that payments from fathers "are often slow or even cease."[21]

The board followed the opposite course with mothers, allowing them to come and live with their children. Indeed, it increasingly required them to do so. The board described the mothers as a key "factor in Mooseheart life." By 1929 110 mothers lived and worked there along with 1,274 children. They provided a cheap source of labor as cooks, secretaries, nurses, laundresses, and most importantly, dormitory housemothers. An obvious advantage of this policy was that indigent widows could be near their children. Just as importantly, the expectation that mothers would work deterred those who looked

TABLE 4.3. Status of Families Admitted to Mooseheart, 1922–1924

Status of Parents	Percentage of Families
Both dead	22.3
One living	76.1
Mother widowed and at home	71.2
Father widowed and at home	2.8
Father dead, mother insane	1.4
Father has tuberculosis, mother dead	.7
Both living	1.4
Father deserted child, mother at home	.7
Mother living, father insane	.7

Source: Folders 1–2: Moose and Mooseheart, Board of Governors, Correspondence and Reports, 1922–24, box 14, Albert Bushnell Hart Papers, Harvard University Archives, Pusey Library, Harvard University, Cambridge, Mass.

upon Mooseheart as a free boarding school or a place to abandon unwanted children.[22]

The Mooseheart Extension Service

Other admission requirements had little to do with moral worth. Most notably, the rules barred children who needed constant medical attention, carried communicable diseases, or were "mentally subnormal." The underlying premise for the last stipulation was that "the child shall have the mental ability to tell right from wrong, and to guide his own character." The board relied on IQ tests to make this judgment and admitted children too young for testing on a probationary basis. The Mooseheart Laboratory for Child Research administered the tests.[23]

Early criticism of Mooseheart centered on its use of the IQ test to exclude children. Neva R. Deardorff caustically stated that a policy "which classes dull children with imbeciles, is not scientifically defensible. But before a man joins the Moose, as a means of obtaining insurance, he would be prudent to find out the IQ of his offspring." Even some officials of Mooseheart privately expressed discomfort. Writing to James J. Davis, Hart agreed that Deardorff was "perfectly right in criticizing our present method of excluding children solely on an unfavorable IQ. It does not seem fair to the father." Although officials were generally sincere in following the slogan "Stop Separating Families," the rules sometimes encouraged that situation. Between 1922 and 1924 the board considered applications from 122 families. In more than 85 percent of the cases all the siblings were accepted, but for 14.9 percent only some of the children were admitted.[24]

In response to criticisms the Loyal Order of Moose enacted reforms. First, it lowered the minimum IQ (Stanford-Binet Test) for admission from 85 to 70. Another reform was the creation of the Mooseheart Extension Service in 1925. The name was somewhat misleading because it was organizationally separate from Mooseheart. Financial support for the extension service came from a portion of the membership dues levied by the Supreme Lodge. The goal was to help lodges care for those children who were otherwise ineligible for Mooseheart. The local lodges, which received funds, worked in cooperation with the child's church and school and sought additional support from charities and government.[25]

In 1929 alone the Mooseheart Extension Service helped 1,190 children at a per capita cost of $130. This amount compared favorably to that spent on mothers' pensions, the leading governmental aid program at the state level. In 1931 annual per capita spending on mothers' pensions was $136. Neither the Mooseheart Extension Service nor state mothers' pensions approximated the per child outlay of Mooseheart. Mooseheart spent more than $800 (including the cost of room, board, extracurricular offerings, education, and medical care) per child.[26]

Financing Mooseheart

The tremendous expense of maintaining Mooseheart, the Mooseheart Extension Service, and other activities spurred the Supreme Lodge to approve a dramatic overhaul in fund-raising methods in 1927. The system, dubbed the ABC Dollar (A Big Charity Dollar), included the following allocation from membership dues: $2.00 for Mooseheart, $1.00 to the Supreme Lodge, $1.00 divided between Moosehaven (the home for the elderly in Florida) and the extension service, and approximately $10.00 for services provided by the local lodge.[27]

The Supreme Lodge had also started to amass an endowment for Mooseheart. The money was raised primarily through the "Nine O'Clock" ceremony. The ceremony began at 9:00 P.M. to coincide with the nightly prayers at Mooseheart. As it proceeded, the head of the lodge appealed for contributions. Henning's description gives the flavor of the proceedings: "Here drama mounts al-

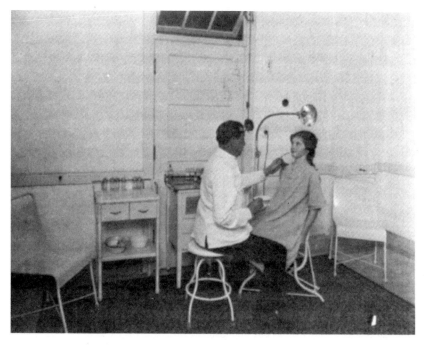

Examining room, Mooseheart Hospital, 1921. (Courtesy of
Moose International, Mooseheart, Ill.)

most to religious fervor. Here His words, 'Suffer the little children to come unto
Me,' are employed and supplication is made for the blessing of the Almighty on
our endeavors. 'God bless Mooseheart' is our fervent prayer." By 1930 the accumulated endowment was a half-million dollars.[28]

The Women of the Moose also contributed. The group came into its own after 1925 when Katherine Smith, a professional organizer, became grand re-
corder. She had risen to prominence as the campaign manager of the women's
division of the Republican National Committee for the 1924 election. Her talents so impressed James J. Davis, then the secretary of labor, that he asked
her to organize a ladies' auxiliary. Under Smith's leadership the Women of the
Moose established scholarships, paid the salary of the librarian, purchased
thousands of books, and raised money for the Mooseheart Hospital.[29]

A National School Home

Throughout its history Mooseheart represented a self-conscious rejection of
the orphanage stereotype as popularized in the writings of Charles Dickens. It

banished or radically modified such obvious badges of institutional life as uniforms, factory-like dormitories, corporal punishment, and military regimentation. In this way Mooseheart followed the model of the "anti-institution institution." Matthew P. Adams, superintendent from 1916 to 1927, drew a contrast between Mooseheart and the "cruel old-fashioned institution." In his view Mooseheart more closely approximated a loving family, or "National School Home," than an orphanage. Similarly, another official declared that "real homes, the genuine affection and the spirit of a home, can be found all over our Child City."[30]

The publicity for Mooseheart sometimes drew direct analogies with the extended fraternal family. An article in the *Mooseheart Magazine*, written by a student, recounted the life of two siblings, Mable Stone, age nine, and Charles Stone, age four. Their father had been a machinist in Syracuse, New York, and a Moose. An outbreak of influenza claimed both their parents, but because of their father's fraternal membership, the children could go to Mooseheart. Mable's playmates predicted a dire fate at this "school," which "would be a place with a high wall, where they whipped you with a paddle so hard that you had to eat your meals standing up, and fed you nothing but beans, milk, and mush." To Mable's surprise Mooseheart was like a comfortable home. Not only was she able to play in an orchestra, but the "eats are great." Mable summed it up: "Best of all, I'm not alone. I've got six hundred thousand daddies, all Moose. I'm glad my daddy was a Moose!"[31]

Mooseheart tried to find the middle way. Adams readily conceded that a "loving father and mother" were better than "any institution or school no matter how good," but he cautioned that "a good school home is better for children than some unfortunate homes." Officials made sincere efforts to foster a homelike atmosphere. When newcomers arrived, a "motherly woman" met them at the bus station. The entire family stayed for two weeks in a reception cottage. The goal was to ease the transition and guard against communicable diseases. Then the arrivals began daily life in a dorm or the "baby village." Each residence hall was under the authority of a houseparent charged with providing "real home love." The houseparents for the younger children were women; for the teenage boys, married couples often served. Three adults—a housemother, an assistant housemother, and a cook—lived in each hall.[32]

The home motif informed the design of the living quarters. Mooseheart was part of a nationwide trend to replace large barracks with a cottage, or modified cottage, arrangement. Each cottage had a kitchen, a dining room, and a living room. The goal was to foster a "normal home atmosphere" with "no central dining halls, no separate dormitories, in short, no institutional living." There was, however, crowding. It was common to have six children to a room and thirty to a hall. In some rooms up to nine residents slept on cots.[33]

The early practice was to mix old and young in the same residence hall, sometimes in the same room. This arrangement fostered "big brother and big sister" relationships. The older child had the duty of helping the younger to dress in the morning and be on time to class. The authorities reasoned that since an "ordinary family" usually had children from different age groups, "Why not in a large family such as we have at Mooseheart?" A related goal was to encourage the older children to act as guides and role models.[34]

Two former residents of Mooseheart, Vivienne Cottingham and Suzanne Kelly, speak highly of the arrangement. It helped accustom them to an unfamiliar environment and teach responsibility. "I had two sisters I had to keep track of," Cottingham recalls, "and they kept me on the straight road." Her greatest challenge was teaching English to a little Italian girl.[35]

Although age mixing served a useful purpose, it had lost its appeal by the early 1930s. Officials complained that it had become too unwieldy and did not allow them to cater to the individual emotional, educational, and physical needs of the children. Another charge against age mixing was that "seniority or size may permit 'one cock to rule the roost.'" The board, therefore, instituted an arrangement based on age cohorts. Henceforth, children moved from hall to hall along with their peers.[36]

Christmas presented a visible opportunity to display Mooseheart's dedication to the family spirit. Gala events were staged, topped off by a lighting ceremony at a giant tree. Cottingham remembers that the children "would go out and sing carols under the stars. I must have been easy to please or something, but I loved every bit of it." Each of the halls had separate celebrations with presents under a tree. Christmas was the only time when mothers and siblings came together for a meal. Adams wrote that "we agree on some hall where they are to eat and all of the brothers and sisters of that family, even including the babies in the nursery, are there to eat as one family."[37]

The holiday season brought a deluge of gifts. In 1922 alone, Mooseheart's post office delivered 4,000 packages and several thousand dollars. There was no guarantee, however, of gifts for all the children. Some who no longer had relatives or active home lodges received little or nothing. To ensure at least two gifts per child, the Loyal Order of Moose established a special Christmas fund. By the early 1920s, annual spending from the fund was about $4,000.[38]

By contrast, birthday celebrations received short shrift. They were not completely ignored, however; one day per month was set aside to observe the birthdays of children born in that month. These group celebrations included an exchange of gifts and sharing of birthday cake. But enforcement by housemothers was spotty, and some halls ignored birthdays entirely.[39]

Finding substitutes for the lost parental role in a large institutional context was difficult. The problem did not stem from a lack of adults per se. Hundreds of teachers, houseparents, deans, and support personnel were on campus. In 1940 the ratio of adults to children was 1 to 1.8, larger than the "average private home." But an adult worker in the course of a career might encounter hundreds, even thousands, of children. Giving individual attention was a hard task.[40]

The adults who mattered the most in the lives of the children were the houseparents and the cooks. Even the most critical child generally give them high marks. A former resident credits them with providing "a nice clean home for us. I can't say that I always liked them, but I think that they were always pretty fair." But because some residence halls had as many as forty children, the houseparents had difficulty keeping tabs on everyone. As a teenager Kari Reymert Morlock, a daughter of Martin Reymert, spent time with seven-year-olds. Although most children were "very peaceful," there were usually "one or two clingers" who craved attention.[41]

To their credit, authorities at Mooseheart tried to find substitutes for the parental role or at least promote active involvement by adults. One solution was a program of sunshine parents. The basic idea was for a lodge member to serve as a kind of surrogate parent by sponsoring a child. The results were mixed, but the system did enable children to establish ties based on affection. By all accounts sunshine parents regarded Christmases and birthdays as opportunities to shower their charges with presents. But the structure of the program did not encourage emotional intimacy. The rules generally limited contact to a few hours on weekends and did not permit trips away from campus. Some children viewed their sunshine parents as primarily "a sugar daddy type of thing. . . . I know that I must have had one of the best sunshine fathers in the whole place, but you just never did really get close."[42]

Another source of adult emotional support was the Mooseheart Laboratory for Child Research. The staff compiled psychological profiles of the children and monitored employees. Reymert's prized innovation was "play therapy." Preschool children were allowed free reign to act out their feelings under the supervision of a nonjudgmental therapist. Because of the small size of the staff, however, only the "problem children" could receive services. Most children encountered the laboratory as the "bug house" or as a place where they went to take tests.[43]

Ultimately the children established among themselves the most durable and emotionally satisfying relationships. They, rather than the adults, came closest to achieving the ideal of "real home love." The family analogy shows up repeatedly in the comments of former residents. "Everybody was your sister," remembers Cottingham. "You learned to function as a family," states Marie Smejkal, a student between 1937 and 1954; "everybody depended on everybody else."[44]

The environment of Mooseheart greatly intensified normal peer loyalties. As Cottingham states, "We had a moral attitude of our own. You just didn't snitch no matter what, even if you got in trouble. You trusted them. You didn't tell on them and you didn't lie." One measure of group cohesiveness was that the children coined their own "Mooseheart slang." Popular terms included "aggie" (to gossip), "walking tree" (night watchman), and "smutch" (to slip out without being noticed). Even a distinct accent took hold. Tellingly, the speech patterns of the mothers at Mooseheart and their offspring diverged sharply. The accents of the mothers retained their regional flavor, but those of the children were "unusually homogeneous . . . even in the case of the youngsters who come very little before high school age."[45]

Mooseheart Mothers

The children with the greatest likelihood to establish loving relationships with adults were those with mothers at Mooseheart. One alumnus who lost his mother during the 1930s describes them as "really the fortunate ones." These children "had some place to go, a sanctuary, and just get away from it all. The mothers supported them in their accomplishments and encouraged them in school." Mother and child could see each other every day and even leave the campus as long as they returned by curfew.[46]

In return mothers gave up a great deal, including virtually all control in matters of discipline and education. The authorities did not permit them to live in the same residence halls as their children lest they show favoritism. Rules prevented mothers from leaving the campus for more than one day except under special circumstances, such as attending a funeral. The weekly salary was $15.50 in 1924 and $75.00 by the 1950s. A Mooseheart mother faced obstacles in establishing romantic (much less marital) relationships. She could not keep a car or stay out past a "reasonable hour." She was free to date but not to have male visitors. "There was kind of a disapproval," comments Ralph Meister, who worked under Martin Reymert, "of those women who went into town and tried to have a personal post-widowhood life of their own."[47]

Some mothers chafed under these restrictions. In 1923 Adams reported to the board of governors on the subject. He cautioned that his comments applied to "a very few, perhaps five, six or seven out of the one hundred" mothers and that most were "efficient, loyal and fine in every way." Still, he recorded complaints by and about mothers guilty of such infractions as slackness, gossiping about "love affairs," or accepting gifts from men they had "only known for a few months." Some mothers complained of low pay. Others resented having to work in the laundry. One mother wrote an angry anonymous letter to a house-mother: "You give the kids beans and mush and make them help with the work. . . . I hope they throw it in your face and don't forget, they didn't come to this dump for work." Another regarded it as unfair that she was compelled to work at Mooseheart because "there are so many children here who do not have any mothers and many whose mothers have never been here."[48]

There were also more serious incidents. The authorities had transferred one housemother to the laundry because she had slapped a boy "on the shoulder, the mark of which was on for a day or two." Another mother had a reputation for making her hall "hell on earth," yelling "until she can be heard a thousand feet away. She is very vile mouthed." Pointing to such incidents, Adams asked the board to reconsider the requirement that mothers come to Mooseheart against their wishes. He concluded that if "they are the marrying kind, they will get married much quicker away from Mooseheart," thus relieving the financial burdens of the institution. These words fell on deaf ears. The board did not re-lax its expectations.[49]

Even with these problems there were compensations for a Mooseheart mother. She had free food, medical care, and lodging and, if she wished, job se-curity after her children graduated. Her free time off campus was her own, and a bus service to Chicago and nearby communities opened access to the outside. While some women felt socially deprived, others thrived. According to Helen Koepp, the mothers "had a ball" playing bingo, dancing, and drinking beer at the Moose lodge in nearby Batavia. In addition, many developed loving rela-tionships with the children they looked after.[50]

Although mothers gave up much parental authority, there were ways to ex-ercise indirect influence. Many built relationships of trust with other mothers to share information and exchange advice about child rearing. In a limited way these arrangements resembled an Israeli kibbutz. Helen Koepp, a housemother during the 1950s, appreciated the discipline enforced by the housemothers who looked after her children. "I was agreeable," she declares, "to anything they [the housemothers] did. I wanted them [her children] to mind."[51]

Their Precious Individuality

Officials of Mooseheart pointed with pride to their efforts to cultivate freedom of choice and the flowering of the individual personality. As Adams put it, "Children are not numbered and are not 'cases,'" and Mooseheart would strive to "conserve their precious individuality." He contrasted Mooseheart and the "cruel old-fashioned institution" where children were "sheep." Sympathetic observers echoed these views, declaring that Mooseheart promoted "social responsibility, individual initiative, and individual responsibility" and that the children had freedom "to express themselves, in speech, in dress, and in occupation."[52]

Mooseheart was exceptional in not censoring the mail of the older children except upon specific request of a guardian. According to the promotional literature, they had "the right to communicate to outside people anything that takes place in the institution." Within limits the children were free to decorate their rooms and select their clothes. For Rudolph Binder, a sociologist at Columbia University, it was a "pleasure to go through the cottages and note the color schemes of the different rooms, each presenting a different but always pleasant ensemble." The commitment to individualism was even applied to the toys and other possessions that children owned as their private property.[53]

Mooseheart offered many choices in extracurricular activities. It had a student newspaper, two debate teams, three theatrical organizations, and a small radio station. Two bands and an orchestra took part in state, regional, and national tours. The Camp Fire Girls and the Boy Scouts established several chapters. The Junior Order of Moose, with a campus membership of 153 children in 1933, served as a feeder organization into the Loyal Order of Moose. In 1931 John C. Meikle, a veteran of the Junior Order, became the first graduate of Mooseheart to win election to the board of governors.[54]

Mooseheart's team sports included football, swimming, basketball, and volleyball. During the 1920s and 1930s the track team won several state championships. Between 1919 and 1926 the football team scored fifty-one victories and suffered four loses, a record that favorably impressed Knute Rockne, a mem-

Members of a girls' band, Mooseheart, Illinois, the children's home of the Loyal Order of Moose, ca. 1921. (Courtesy of Moose International, Mooseheart, Ill.)

ber of the Loyal Order of Moose. In the movie *Knute Rockne, All-American*, Rockne postponed a vacation to stop at "Mooseheart to talk to my boys." The girls participated in intramural sports, including tennis, track, baseball, and swimming.[55]

Striking a Balance between Freedom and Control

The authorities sometimes had to walk a fine line between freedom and regulation. One example was the imbroglio over hair bobbing, which Mooseheart prohibited for girls as well as adult employees. Adams fought a rear-guard action against this policy, castigating the ban as unfair and an incitement to disorder. The girls were flouting the rule, and nearly all who graduated "bobbed their hair the day after they left." The board backed down and legalized bobbing after an assurance from Adams that "the hair is not to be curled by any means." It also reiterated that the board, not the mothers, exercised ultimate authority.[56]

Mooseheart's policy regarding gender further illustrated the tensions between freedom and control. It emphasized separation and required that boys and girls live on their own campuses and sit apart at assemblies, church services, and movies. But officials tempered separation by creating opportunities for teenagers to socialize. They acknowledged that complete segregation led to an "unhealthy atmosphere." For example, the authorities scheduled weekly dances for the sophomores.[57]

The board even showed a willingness to compromise on the thorny question of whether to tolerate kissing and holding hands. During the 1920s it partially lifted an earlier ban. Adams persuaded the board to compromise, arguing that it was entirely natural for teenagers to show physical affection and warning against the "danger in our fighting things at Mooseheart which are accepted by the general public outside." By the 1930s the board permitted the boys to visit the girls' campus on Sunday afternoons. Nevertheless, it made sure that chaperones were ubiquitous. By one measure Mooseheart's approach to gender relations was a success. Neither the available minutes of the board nor the recollections of former staff and alumni implies that any girl became pregnant.[58]

In matters of contact with the outside world, Mooseheart was less protective than the typical orphanage. Children were free to visit town on weekends, although overnight stays were forbidden. The outings were usually in small groups supervised by an adult. The reins of control gradually loosened with age. Teenagers, if they showed good behavior, could visit town unchaperoned on Sundays or Saturdays as long as they returned by 5:00 P.M. Many students, however, did not bother to leave. There was plenty to do on campus, including movies and dances. Mooseheart kids seemed to keep busy. Another factor that lessened the urge for shopping trips was the presence of stores on campus.[59]

Officials boasted that Mooseheart was receptive to visitors. Outsiders freely wandered the campus and struck up conversations with the children. "We could talk to anybody," Cottingham declares matter-of-factly, "who came along. No one told us that you couldn't say this and couldn't say that." Binder said that "every visitor [was] impressed by the cheerful, courteous behavior of these children." The authorities obviously took pride in the institution and staged special "state days" for members from particular states to visit.[60]

At the same time, the board was vigilant, sometimes overly so, against outside contagion. It prohibited female visitors from wearing knickers on campus because of "considerable excitement" among the boys, who "sort of hung around them, watched them and made comments on them." Mooseheart was equally protective of its public image. According to a former resident, the authorities enforced a ban on the crew-cut hairstyle because it made the boys look uncomfortably like prisoners rather than members of a happy family.[61]

Religious Education

Character building found a valued place in Mooseheart's pedagogical philosophy. The basic agenda included an emphasis on such virtues as politeness, thriftiness, religiosity, and proficiency in the arts of self-government. Mooseheart hoped to make children "independent, self-respecting, self-supporting, self-directing, God-fearing, law-abiding, country-loving and cheerful citizens." Not coincidentally, the Loyal Order of Moose had long embraced these values.[62]

The fraternal ideas of Mooseheart's founders clearly shaped the approach to religion. Like many societies, the Moose had followed a live-and-let-live rule of banishing organized religion from the lodge room. In 1915 Rodney Brandon, a member of the board of governors, had argued that this was the proper model for Mooseheart. "When you join the Loyal Order of Moose," he confidently declared, "you have to admit belief in a Supreme Being, and that is just the amount of religious practice there is at Mooseheart. Mooseheart is not in the religion business." Brandon's recommendation was to turn religious instruction over to the relevant local denomination. If, for example, the child came from a Brahman family, an official of Mooseheart would write to "the nearest Brahman church, and explain to the head of that church that it is up to him."[63]

Brandon's vision proved unrealistic over time, but Mooseheart achieved a fairly close approximation. A key requirement was that children be brought up in the faith of their fathers. This rule applied even if the mother or guardian objected. Mooseheart hired Catholic and Protestant chaplains to live on campus and conduct services. Attendance was compulsory. Older children from Mooseheart and volunteers from nearby communities served as the Sunday school teachers.[64]

Mooseheart took care to respect sectarian differences. Local ministers from various denominations visited on Saturday mornings to give special lessons and oversee baptisms and confirmations. During the week children attended fifteen minutes of mandatory Bible or catechism study in their halls. The authorities transported the few Mormon and Jewish children to Chicago for services and lessons.[65]

One touchstone of this policy was that "no arguments or discussions of religious questions are allowed." Mooseheart prohibited any behavior that could lead to religious conflict. A particularly hot issue was the format of Bible or catechism study. During the first decade the housemother of each hall had enjoyed considerable discretion concerning the details of religious instruction, but this system sparked controversy. Adams told of a Protestant housemother who had tried "to give instruction in the Catholic Catechism," a matter that could "only lead to trouble." Searching for a balance, he rejected as impractical proposals to separate the children for their daily religious instructions. Instead he persuaded the board to accept a compromise: silent study. According to the new requirement, "No one is to give any instruction or help any of the students with their religious study. In case a younger student should need someone to find the Bible lesson . . . an older student of the same religious faith is to look after the matter." [66]

At times the commitment to religious toleration and harmony led to almost comical results. In 1923 the Church of Jesus Christ of Latter-day Saints offered to send books on Mormonism to the library. The board accepted the gift but required that these books and all other sectarian publications be shelved in closed stacks. Furthermore, when a student of a particular faith borrowed a book, "the book MUST be in the student's locker. This book is not to be put in the Hall library or left on Hall tables. It is NOT to be loaned to or borrowed by other students." [67]

Use of Money, Discipline, and Self-Government

Mooseheart had much in common with another set of experiments during this period, the George Junior Republics. Beginning in the 1890s William R. George organized self-contained communities for dependent and delinquent youth in New York, Michigan, Illinois, and other states. Many of these institutions featured alternatives to corporal punishment, a greater element of personal choice, student-run banks, and some degree of self-government.[68]

Like the George Junior Republics, Mooseheart endeavored to promote economic self-reliance and thrift. The children were paid small regular allowances to cultivate habits of "giving money, saving money and spending money." Each boy was allocated a small plot of land to raise and sell produce. Jobs for pay were available to the older children on campus for between 15 and 25 cents per hour. Through these opportunities the board hoped to impart the "moral effect" of honest labor and the "glow of satisfaction" of "doing of work for a useful purpose." [69]

To teach thrift Mooseheart followed the lead of the George Junior Republics by establishing a student bank. Half the money earned by students went automatically into their checking accounts. From this, students could "draw checks for candy, baseballs, baseball bats and the hundred and one things a boy or girl wants." Here again the authorities tempered freedom with control. They required a houseparent to countersign each check and set a limit of $3.00 at a time. The bank rested on the theory that children "are more apt to be spend-thrifts or misers than adults. Unless they actually save money and get into the habit of doing it as children they never will as adults." The authorities deposited the remainder of the student's earnings into a savings account in a bank in Aurora. It earned interest, but the students could not make withdrawals until graduation.[70]

As in so much else, Mooseheart strove to maintain a balanced approach in matters of money. Its urgings in favor of thrift rested alongside principles promoting good works. Each Sunday the staff encouraged children to donate a penny to their church. The board's annual report urged that students be taught "to give and to 'give till it hurts' in a worthy cause" and reminded them that "The Gift Without the Giver is Bare." If penury was a danger, so too was excessive altruism. The key was to steer clear of extremes.[71]

The *Mooseheart Weekly*, the newspaper published by the students, underlined this point. A story aptly titled "Self-Sacrifice" appeared in 1920. The main character was a hard-working man "who lived for his family." He spent little on himself and devoted his energy to making his family happy. After years of self-sacrifice he grew resentful; he "began to feel that the burden he had imposed on himself had been imposed by them." The next step was fear and paranoia. The man started to misinterpret innocent conversations as plots against him. Here was the moral: "If he hadn't tried so hard to do it all himself, they would all have been happier still. Self-Sacrifice is as bad as selfishness when it becomes a fixed idea."[72]

One of the best-known policies of Mooseheart was its prohibition of corporal punishment. Any employee who slapped a child was dismissed or transferred to another job away from children. Kelly, who was a student during the 1920s and 1930s, reflects the consensus of former staff and alumni when she insists that employees "knew they would be fired if they ever hit you." The authorities "wouldn't allow that for one minute."[73]

Instead, punishment involved a schedule of demerits that could be assigned by houseparents, teachers, or deans. The following infractions carried penalties of two demerits each: disobedience, lying, impertinence, disorder, fighting, and missing short assignments. A maximum of five demerits was levied for more serious offenses: possession of tobacco, truancy, bullying, destruction of property, or being "a little too demonstrative" with members of the opposite sex. The accumulation of demerits led to a gradual loss of privileges. Five or more demerits resulted in an assignment on the Student Work Line. Students who were SWL had to spend one hour per day for twenty days working in jobs such as weeding gardens and picking up rubbish.[74]

The authorities sent repeat offenders among the boys to one of several "punishment farms" on the outskirts of Mooseheart. The most onerous was Fez Hall. It was characterized by long hours of work, near-total isolation from the rest of the community, and a simple diet. Because the children said that the meals were mainly bean sandwiches, it became known as the beanery. A boy on the farm could gradually work his way back to a clean record.[75]

For the most part even troublesome boys committed relatively minor offenses. A list exists of nine boys in the vocational program who spent time on the farm between July 1, 1921, and July 1, 1922. Three had been sent to the farm for smoking; one, for stealing popcorn; two, for accumulating excessive demerits; two, for fighting (with a knife in one case); one, for general disobedience and impudence; and one, for possession of cigarettes and visiting North Aurora without a permit. The girls had a gentler system. They did not have a punishment farm but worked off demerits in their residence halls.[76]

A theme in the publicity for Mooseheart was its system of "self-government." Until the 1920s a junior and senior assembly met daily at 5:00 P.M. Each student over age eleven had voting rights. The assembly was compared to an "old town meeting." The names of students with five or more demerits were read as means to shame them into good behavior. "It was kind of humiliating," Cottingham recalls, "to stand up there and report that you were this sassy." The assembly heard appeals from children to reduce demerits and could make recommendations for leniency, although this did not happen often.[77]

While the children may have learned useful parliamentary skills, the assembly never exercised real power. Its decisions were subject to the veto of the superintendent. The board noted that the "Mooseheart Assembly is not a self-governing body in the same sense that the George Junior Republic is, but is instead what might be called a supervised self-government." For reasons that are somewhat obscure, the assembly fell into disuse and disappeared by the 1930s.[78]

The demerit system survived but with revisions. Reforms came after withering criticism by Albert Bushnell Hart, who noted that demerits (often for very minor offenses) tended to pile up quickly. Between 1922 and 1924 more than 200 students, or one-fourth of the children (not including preschoolers), were under some form of punishment at any given time. More than 40 were on the farms. For Hart these numbers indicated a flaw in the system. He expressed disbelief that "there is any state of things at Mooseheart that justifies such a number of continuing punishments."[79]

The board enacted reforms in punishment methods during the 1920s and 1930s. It increased the number of demerits necessary for a trip to the farm and placed much less reliance on the student work line. It took steps to ensure that more boys served their punishments in the residence halls rather than on the farms. Lastly, the board established incentives to counterbalance the punitive features. It instituted merits that could be earned for proficiency in twenty categories, including "Self Control in word and deed" and "Neatness and good taste in dress." Each merit resulted in extra privileges.[80]

The most serious discipline, of course, was expulsion (or "demission"). Between 1922 and 1924 (see table 4.4) the board approved demissions for 167 children. Most demissions were not related to a breach of discipline. More than 44 percent of the children were demitted at the request of a relative (usually the mother) because the family had become able to provide support. Only 13.7 of the demissions entailed a specific breach of discipline, most commonly running away. Serious infractions were rare. As a former student recalls, "You had to be a pretty bad actor in order to get it [demission for breach of discipline]. The average guy who was trying to obey the rules and stuff like that wouldn't be expelled."[81]

Conclusion

Mooseheart flourished during a period when orphanages began to fall into disfavor. Child care experiments increasingly gravitated toward solutions such as mothers' aid and foster homes. Many experts regarded orphanages as cruel, regimented, and harmful to the future success of the children. This view still holds sway among scholars who contend that orphanages "create children who tend to be behind other children in skills, achievement, and social adaptation."[82]

This characterization does not seem to apply to Mooseheart graduates. To be sure, the transition from a sheltered and well-regulated campus was not easy. Many graduates had to learn such mundane activities as paying bills and filling a car with gas. Others suffered homesickness for Mooseheart and lingered in nearby communities before venturing out. Some home lodges found jobs and housing for graduates, but others neglected this duty. More than a few graduates could not count on help because their home lodges had disbanded during the depression.[83]

TABLE 4.4. Decisions by the Board of Governors on Applications for Demission from Mooseheart, 1922–1924, Percentage of Children Approved for Demission

Demitted (no reason specified)	36.5
Demitted (for reasons other than breach of discipline)	49.7
Withdrawn by relative	32.7
Improved conditions at home	12.5
"Mentally deficient"	3.5
Not legally adopted by father	.5
Over 18 and failed coursework	.5
Under 18 and completed vocational degree	.5
Mother failed to give required services	1.1
Demitted (for breach of discipline)	13.7
Running away	6.5
Stealing and running away	1.7
Unspecified bad conduct	2.9
Incorrigible	.5
Improper letter written	.5

Source: Mooseheart Governors, minutes, and Mooseheart, superintendent's report [1922–24], folders 1–2: Moose and Mooseheart, Board of Governors, Correspondence and Reports, 1922–24, box 14, Albert Bushnell Hart Papers, Harvard University Archives, Pusey Library, Harvard University, Cambridge, Mass.

But the picture for new graduates was far from bleak. Alumni established an association to help them obtain "a start in life." By 1931 it had loaned $20,000 through a special revolving fund. More significantly, graduates entered the marketplace with vocational and academic skills and access to a network of alumni. The letters they wrote to Ralph Meister showed that although graduates underwent "a period of readjustment . . . they seemed to have managed it rather well on the whole." [84]

The most compelling evidence appeared in a study conducted by Martin Reymert of 402 graduates between 1919 and 1929. The response rate, 77.6 percent, was unusually high. The results point to a record of achievement. The male respondents (see table 4.5) earned weekly wages that exceeded the national average by 70.9 percent; the wages of the females were 62.5 percent higher than those of other American women. [85]

The gap was even wider when measured by standards of educational progress. Ironically, an institution founded to demonstrate the superiority of man-

TABLE 4.5. Average Weekly Wages, Mooseheart Graduates, 1919–1929, and
All Male and Female Wage Earners in the United States, 1930

	Mooseheart (1)	U.S. (2)	Percentage Difference $[(2)/(1)-1]$
Males	$36.00	$25.55	70.9
Females	$25.00	$15.64	62.5

Sources: Loyal Order of Moose, *Mooseheart Year-Book and Annual* (1931) (Mooseheart,
Ill.: Mooseheart Press, 1931), 142–45; "Average Earnings and Hours of Work: All Male
and Female Wage Earners," in National Industrial Conference Board, *Service Letter on
Industrial Relations*, n.s., 74 (February 28, 1931): 6.

ual education turned out a bumper crop of college students. Mooseheart alumni
were four times more likely than other Americans (ages 18–24) to have attended
institutions of higher learning. More than 34 percent of the graduates (female
and male) went to college, compared with a U.S. average in 1930 of 7.6 percent
for males and 4.8 percent for females.[86]

Interviews with alumni make clear the positive features of a Mooseheart
childhood. Its services enabled thousands of children to gain a superior academic education and learn marketable skills. These advantages equipped them
to make their ways in the world and excel. Moreover, despite certain missteps
by officials, Mooseheart taught the children less tangible but perhaps more important skills, such as a sense of right and wrong, tolerance for others, good
manners, and self-restraint. The financial cost of Mooseheart may have been
high, but it was money well spent.[87]

CHAPTER FIVE

From the Cradle to the Grave

The words were familiar to Americans, but the context was not: "Protection Now Furnished from the 'Cradle to the Grave.'" When the SBA made this promise, it embarked on a seemingly quixotic mission. In 1916 the leadership confidently vowed to build an old folks' home, an orphanage, and a hospital. A fraternal society had never before attempted so much. By 1925 doubts had been quelled, and one by one these goals were completed. The first and most modest was the SBA Children's Home.[1]

The SBA Children's Home and Mooseheart offer valuable opportunities to compare and understand fraternal orphanages as a whole. One lesson to be learned from them is that any quest to find a "typical" fraternal orphanage is probably fruitless. A wide variety of immigrant and native societies were sponsors. The number of children served by a given group varied from a handful to a thousand. At the same time a closer look at Mooseheart and the SBA home reveals features that appeared across the wide spectrum of fraternal orphanages. Neither Mooseheart nor the SBA home received governmental subsidies. Both appealed to the lodge model of the extended family. Each faced tensions between the stated ideals of the founders and practical realities. The differences serve to enrich the comparison. Mooseheart and the SBA home exhibited notable contrasts in discipline, degrees of social isolation, and postgraduate preparation.

The SBA (named the Knights and Ladies of Security prior to a merger with a smaller organization in 1920) started to lay the groundwork for an eleemosynary institution in 1916 when the National Council outlined plans to establish a hospital and home for "Old Folks, Invalids and Orphans." The first item on the agenda was a building site. After a spirited round of bidding among local lodges (or "councils"), Topeka, Kansas, the site of the national headquarters, won the prize. The deal was sealed when the Chamber of Commerce "and other citizens" donated 260 acres of farmland just outside the city.[2]

To circumvent a Kansas law prohibiting fraternal societies from owning homes and hospitals, the National Council created a separate Home and Hospital Association. It was little more than a technicality. Five of the seven trustees belonged to the executive committee of the Knights and Ladies of Security. Two others were Louis Emmerson, the secretary of state for Illinois and a future governor, and Arthur Capper, the governor of Kansas. Capper, who also belonged to the Board of Governors of Mooseheart, did not exercise perceptible influence and was selected for his prestige value.[3]

Voluntary contributions comprised most of the initial funds for the SBA Children's Home. The National Council asked each member to contribute 5 cents per month but left the local councils to enforce the quota. This appeal sparked great interest from the rank and file. Fifty thousand nickels poured in during the first ten days, and by 1920 the SBA had raised $131,000. Members also volunteered sundry in-kind contributions, from bedsheets to livestock. The voluntary approach, however, was inadequate as a permanent funding source. It worked best when supplemented by compulsory contributions or funds earmarked for specific projects.[4]

In 1920 the board shifted to a more secure funding arrangement. It began an annual money transfer from the society's general fund to the Homes and Hospital Association. The board calculated the amount of the transfer as the equivalent of 5 (later 10) cents of the monthly dues. This system remained in place throughout the history of the homes and hospital. Voluntary contributions nonetheless remained important. Well into the late 1930s, in-kind and cash donations were essential to the successful completion and operation of the homes and hospital.[5]

When the SBA Children's Home opened in 1919, it was a modest affair. Initially the children shared a building with the elderly residents. Living conditions were far from ideal. In 1920 about six elderly people and thirty children filled a lone dormitory of about twenty-six rooms. Harry Perry, a pioneer resident, was six when he arrived, and he recalls his travails on a "sleeping porch" that was "kind of cold in the winter and the snow came in." The crowding eased in 1921 when the elderly residents moved into the SBA Old Folks' Home.[6]

Probably the greatest change for the children was the opening of a school (grades K through 12) in 1925. It had three teachers, one of whom served as principal. The curriculum stayed well within the educational mainstream. The SBA never seriously experimented with a vocational approach. The school provided the children with a quality education, but it isolated them from the surrounding communities.[7]

The early 1930s represented the height of the SBA's effort to provide cradle-to-grave protection. SBA Hill was now the site of a substantial farm (complete with hogs, chickens, and fifty Holsteins), a separate water supply, and a power plant. In 1933 the population of the Old Folks' Home increased to eighty-six; sixty-five children lived in the Children's Home. The boys and girls had moved into separate halls, with about two children per room. Each building had a live-in matron or a married couple; a trained dietitian prepared all the meals. The annual per-child cost was $480.[8]

The application process began at each local council, which helped complete the paperwork. The chief concern of the board of trustees, which decided all cases, was to screen out children from families not in financial need. This policy reflected the SBA's aversion to "Charity, which shoots blindly into space, often reaching an unworthy mark and always bruising the target." Once admitted, the child obtained free room and board, medical and dental care, and a full high-school education. The board did not undertake a formal adoption and reserved the right to release the child to an official guardian. Nor did it admit mentally retarded children or those with severe physical deformities.[9]

Information on the children's backgrounds is not detailed. A list of occupations for the fathers of the teenagers admitted during the 1930s shows one each for the following: steelworker, merchant, railroad laborer, railroad engineer, carpenter, barber, railroad operator, automobile worker, city fireman, and bacteriologist. Five fathers were listed simply as laborers. Half-orphans were in the vast majority (see table 5.1), and fewer than 10 percent of those admitted lacked parents. Most of the time the remaining parent, who was almost as likely to be the father as the mother, lived at home as the official guardian. The board seems to have taken seriously the goal of holding families together. Although mothers could not be admitted, brothers and sisters could. Ninety percent of the children had siblings at the SBA home. The board's general policy was to return any children with one parent living if the parent remarried.[10]

The catalyst for a stay at the SBA home was invariably family tragedy: death, desertion, or institutionalization. The memories of former residents are often vivid after more than six decades. One person simply writes, "Parents unable to provide adequate support, Father a coal miner. Couldn't give us proper 'bringing up' after mother passed away." Another recalls that "Mother was dead and Dad was sick and the Dr. had told him he would not get well. . . . My dad thought it was the best place for all of us children to be raised so we could stay together." A third makes the blunt statement, "Step Grandmother didn't want me there." The trauma of the separation, though never forgotten, gradually

TABLE 5.1. Family Status of Children Admitted to the
SBA Children's Home, 1924–1935

Status of Parents	Number of Children
Both dead	9
One living	69
Mother widowed and at home	21
Father widowed and at home	23
Mother deserted child	7
Father deserted child	6
Mother in state asylum or other institution	5
Father in prison	2
Both living	16
Father deserted child, mother at home	5
Mother deserted child, father at home	2
Father in prison, mother at home	5
Father deserted child, mother in state asylum	2
Father in SBA Old Folks' Home, mother in asylum	2
Incomplete information available	16
Father in prison, no information on mother	4
Mother deceased, no information on father	4
Mother at home, no information on father	8
No information about either parent	6
Total number of children admitted	116

Source: Security Benefit Home and Hospital Association, minutes, 1924–35, Security Benefit Group of Companies, Records, Topeka, Kans.

wore off. On her trip to the SBA home, for example, Kathleen Colbert Sabo recalls that she "cried and cried and cried. I was just a kid, and I didn't want to go and leave grandma and grandpa; but after we were there, it was fine. We met lots of other kids, and they're still our friends to this day."[11]

After 1924 the superintendent of the Children's Home was Fredricka Sutherland, the national vice-president of the SBA. She had been appointed by J. M. Kirkpatrick, who soon became her husband. Sutherland-Kirkpatrick wrote a regular column for the *Security News*, which kept members abreast of the lives of the children. In a typical story, she wrote that "Zela Dalton has just finished another picture in art. She has spent several hours on this picture and is quite pleased with it."[12]

Shirttail Brothers and Sisters

When promoting the SBA home, Sutherland-Kirkpatrick and other officials regularly evoked the imagery of the extended fraternal family. They emphasized
the absence of uniforms and other signs of institutional life. They boasted that
the children did not appear to be orphans but were "becomingly clad, as much
as they would be—and probably often more so—if they were under parental
roofs. . . . They are a mighty fine looking family." Another writer advanced
more modest claims. "No one," he conceded, "can take the place of father and
mother," but in "our Home we come as near to it as is humanly possible."
The *Security News* assured members that the children "are a happy family of
splendid children, and upon us devolves the duty of preparing them for useful
citizenship." [13]

To re-create normal family life, the SBA home tried to observe the milestones
of childhood. The *Security News* published the birthdays of children and asked
members to send gifts. A standard procedure was to designate one day per
month for a modest celebration. Christmas was more memorable. The national
office gave gifts and allotted spending money to the children for a group shopping expedition. It also tried to drum up gifts from the grass roots. One appeal
netted the contribution of a small herd of Shetland ponies. [14]

The school's annual yearbook exuded normality. A soon-to-be graduate gave
this account: "We can easily bring to mind our struggles with algebra, geome-
try, history, and French . . . our delightful glee club trips, bridge parties, ban-
quets, picnics, and hikes." Sports represented the major contact with the outside world. The boys' basketball and baseball teams competed in the Topeka
Sunday School Association. The girls participated in intramural contests. Other
extracurricular activities included a school newspaper and an archery club. The
music program staged lavish operettas for fraternal members and the citizens of
Topeka. [15]

Religion, at least in a formal way, did not loom large in either the school or
the residence halls. Like other orphanages, fraternal or otherwise, the SBA home
required the children to attend weekly church services on the premises. At Sunday worship the residents of the Old Folks' Home and the Children's Home
came together. A retired Presbyterian minister performed the services and,
along with his wife, taught Sunday school. Although some of the children were
Catholic and one was Jewish, the Protestant cast of the services did not cause
conflict. Harry Perry, who had been raised as a Catholic, said that "it didn't mat-

Teachers, matrons, and children of the sba Children's Home at the National
Conference of the sba in Chicago, 1932. (Courtesy of Alex and Julia Kulscar)

ter whether you were Catholic or Protestant, you went to the services." Because
there were few children, the sba home could not afford to tailor religious instruction to the beliefs of the parents.[16]

All the basics were free at the Children's Home, including medical care, food,
and clothing. As Florence Paschke Ford notes, "We never had any need for
money because we never went anywhere where we could spend it." Teenagers
did, however, have opportunities to earn pay. The jobs for the boys were on the
farm or truck garden; the girls worked in the cannery or in the hospital. No options existed for outside work. The national office allowed the students to spend
half the money they earned and gave the rest to them upon graduation.[17]

The happiest memories of the alumni center on peer friendships. The children rather than the fraternal publicists proved most sincere about the model
of the surrogate family. Sabo still looks upon the other graduates as "shirttail
brothers and sisters." Other former residents remember that the "kids were all
family" and "kind of like brothers." In the yearbook for 1936 one girl wrote to
an older boy, "I only wish you were my brother along with some of the others."[18]

The "big brother and big sister" system reinforced familial solidarity. The
matrons paired an older and a younger child as roommates. Charles Ehrnfelt
experienced both roles during his stay. When he arrived, he shared a room with
an older boy who looked after him. Later Charles graduated to the status of big

brother. His job at that point was to ensure that his younger roommate completed tasks such as making his bed, brushing his teeth, and folding his clothes. Former residents credit this system with helping to smooth their transition to the SBA home and teaching responsibility. The home kept the big brother and sister approach to the end. One reason, perhaps, was that there were never more than two dorms, and thus the pairing of old and young did not pose logistical challenges. If anything, it lightened the burdens on the matrons.[19]

The Reign of the Matrons

Life at the SBA home had its advantages, but it was far from ideal. A chief complaint was social isolation. The few regular outings were annual visits to the state fair and trips to Topeka once a month to see a movie. A matron kept close watch. The children did have some opportunities to show off their theatrical and musical talents to local and national gatherings of councils, but there were no movies or dances on the premises. The children had time on their hands; "It got pretty tedious down there," an alumnus recalls.[20]

Furthermore, the authorities restricted contact with families. Visits had to be prearranged and were only allowed on Sundays. During the early years children could return home on holidays, but by the late 1920s this privilege had ended. The authorities were not receptive to communication between children and unrelated visitors. Evelyn Colbert Bezan, an SBA alumnus, sums it up: "We were not supposed to talk." The home was also intrusive in the regulation of mail. Although members of the staff urged children to write home, they carefully scrutinized and sometimes censored correspondence.[21]

The SBA home imposed strict boundaries on contact between the sexes. Dating was taboo. Almost no opportunities existed for boys and girls to socialize outside school. The matrons and teachers, Sabo remembers, "didn't like us to be together too much. We were pretty dumb. We wouldn't have known what to do anyhow." But within limits, the children found ways to circumvent the rules. Ehrnfelt confides that "like all youngsters that age, there were times and places. Nothing serious. Never a pregnant girl that I ever knew of. . . . But I had girlfriends; we held hands, and we snuck a kiss now and then."[22]

Most alumni agree that the authorities fell short in preparing the children for postgraduate life. The SBA home did not offer scholarships, and with a few exceptions, the local councils were of little help. As Wendell Taylor puts it, "They gave you a new suit of clothes and any money that you had from when you worked there, and they let you out the door and you were on your own. . . . You hit the ground running." Graduates had to learn anew, or for the first time, everyday skills. In part this neglect was a product of the depression, a time when local councils were weak and less able to give aid.[23]

sba home residents found it hard to bond with adults. There were no mothers on-site to provide emotional support, and the attitudes of the matrons compounded the problem. With some exceptions, the matrons were emotionally distant and mechanical in their work. For most of these women, according to Ehrnfelt, it was "just a job. We had no real relation with them. They never had conversations with us unless it was a lecture or something." Taylor echoes this assessment, estimating that "when I was there about half of [the matrons] were mediocre at best." Ford, who arrived when she was an infant, poignantly remarks, "We were well fed, clothed, and schooled. . . . The only thing we really lacked was love."[24]

The discipline enforced by the matrons could be severe. The usual punishments were revocation of privileges. Some matrons, however, were notorious for inflicting emotional and physical punishment. A female alumnus bitterly recalls that the matron "used to have what she called the paddle line for the older girls. . . . The one who had been bad had to crawl between [the older girls'] legs and was hit by another girl all the way through."[25]

One boy, a rare example of a runaway who never returned, used a poem to articulate his frustrations:

> If you steal in this world
> It's a sin
> If you love anothers' [sic] girl
> It's a sin
>
> If you give the "high ups" the "Yoohoo,"
> Or take what's not your due,
> With "authority" your're [sic] through
> For it's a sin. . . .
>
> If this sort of life seems dry,
> And you feel you would rather leave,
> awol you cannot try
> For it's a sin.[26]

If a single factor can account for the bleakness of life at the home, it was weak supervision. While Sutherland-Kirkpatrick meant well, she was naively trusting of those who worked under her. She took care that the children had the physical and educational amenities but failed to keep close tabs on the matrons.[27]

On the other hand, the life of a matron at the SBA home was not easy. She did not have the luxury of turning over the burdens of punishment to others and thus had to act as judge, jury, and executioner. It was a lonely, isolated existence with few recreational amenities. As importantly, a matron did not generally have her own children on the premises, in whom she could invest her hopes and find emotional satisfaction.

Nonetheless, the level of the punishment was out of proportion to disciplinary need. According to the board minutes and the recollections of alumni and teachers, the children were generally well behaved. No record exists of promiscuity. Running away, known as the "French leave," was the most visible breach of discipline. During the history of the home, the minutes of the board describe five runaways, all boys. One boy came back of his own accord and was readmitted, three were returned to their guardians, and one was never heard from again. One overnight absence, a lark rather than an attempt to escape, ended unceremoniously when a staff member happened upon the fugitives in Topeka. "It wasn't hard to spot us," Sabo recalls. "We were pretty dumb." According to Julia Peebles Kulscar, who took two French leaves, "We were very inquisitive; we weren't really bad. . . . We wanted to know things, but they didn't really want us to know anything except what they wanted us to know."[28]

A Superior School

Sutherland-Kirkpatrick's loose style of management was not entirely counterproductive. Her unwillingness to second-guess subordinates fostered a climate that enabled determined individuals with fresh ideas to have an impact. Because the SBA home was small, one person could make a positive difference. The downside, of course, was that there might be an abrupt return to the status quo if that individual left.

The school benefited the most from Sutherland-Kirkpatrick's laissez-faire attitude. She gave the first principal, Carl Westin, freedom to stress academic quality. Under Westin's tenure the state superintendent of education ranked the school as "Superior," spurring the Security News to exclaim proudly that it was "the only private school in Kansas to be given this high standing." Loose control from the top enabled the school staff to rely on far less punitive disciplinary methods than those exacted in the dormitories. A child with an average grade below C, for example, was allowed fewer supervised trips to the movies, a loss the entertainment-starved students genuinely feared. Half humorously, a writer for the high school annual asked readers to imagine the unlikely event of "Nobody having to stay home from the show."[29]

Several other individuals associated with the school loom large in the memories of alumni. They mention in particular Harley Garrett, the second principal, and his fellow teacher and wife, Orrisa Garrett. The couple breathed life into the original but often neglected character-building vision. The Garretts offered the counseling and emotional support that were woefully absent from the residence halls. For Harley the home presented an educational opportunity. While there, he conducted research for his M.A. at Stanford University. Completed in 1934, "Guidance in a Small School for Orphans" included a general description of Garrett's experiences and a psychological and academic profile of eighteen of the older children. This is probably the best source on the day-to-day activities and characteristics of the residents.[30]

Garrett's approach showed the influence of his mentor, William M. Proctor. Garrett took to heart Proctor's emphasis on character development. Proctor had stressed the duty of the teachers and counselors to foster "desirable character traits" such as "self-control, self-reliance, reliability, honesty or integrity, fair-play, cooperativeness, clean-mindedness, kindliness or goodwill, and loyalty to the best traditions of personal and national morality."[31]

Garrett cultivated a climate of trust, and the children opened up and confided in him. On one occasion some boys admitted that they had taken a French leave to date girls but assured Garrett that they had carefully policed one another. Garrett's account of another incident indicates his style of guidance and the rapport he enjoyed with the students. A girl who had participated in a French Leave "insisted that her conduct as well as that of the other girls and boys was above reproach. In the light of her record and character the writer is inclined to believe her." Through special assemblies and other devices, Garrett sought to instill traits of self-control, responsibility, "belief in God, being good to each other and the golden rule." Garrett, who had lost his parents at a young age, used this shared experience in his motivational talks. He urged each student to prepare for life "outside" and to "keep your mouth shut, your eyes open, and your ears perked up."[32]

From the beginning of his tenure Garrett detected deep-seated feelings of "discontent and dissatisfaction" among the children. This found expression in "disrespect for authority, laxity in their work, quarrelsomeness among themselves, and general rebelliousness." Gradually, as Garrett won their trust, the students voiced their frustrations. Finally they explained in a special assembly that "the trouble lay in not having enough activity in the summer time, excessive restrictions made on the whole group for the misdemeanors of a few, nagging on the part of those in charge and constant reminding that they could not be trusted." [33]

Garrett related these experiences in a letter to J. M. Kirkpatrick, the president of the SBA. He urged rejection of the older approach of enforcing rules "by reciting platitudes and doctrines of what is right and wrong. Morals and right conduct cannot be taught out of a text book." Instead, he touted the benefits of asking the children to articulate "their ideas of what proper conduct about the school and home should be [and] their desire for self-esteem." The result would be to "bring forth from them pretty much the rules of conduct which we older ones would have them obey, and they will obey them because they want to and not because they have to." [34]

Under his encouragement the students drafted a series of written resolutions. They began by admitting past misdeeds: "We have sneaked out of the buildings at night . . . plotted and executed fake scenes to aggravate the matrons and teachers . . . sneaked letters to our folks." The next section closed with a damning confession: "We have come to think of the home as a prison with conditions almost unbearable and have longed for the day when we would leave." The children pledged to mend their ways and promised to abstain from offenses such as running away, talking back, and sneaking notes. Interestingly, another pledge was "not to develop any case of love-sickness." Then the students threw themselves on the mercy of the officials. They expressed the hope that the "authorities will be more willing to give us the few privileges we desire, especially if we show our ability to appreciate them, and not to take advantage of them." [35]

Garrett's strategy bore fruit. Officials eased some of the more onerous restrictions. They gave the older children the right to earn pay on the SBA farm and have access to a pool and tennis court during the summer and, for the first time, permitted small groups of teenagers to visit Topeka. In addition, the authorities allowed the creation of an elected student council. It had no power over matters of substance, but it served as an outlet for students to express their views and vent their frustrations. The reforms had little impact on the part of the home that mattered the most: the residence dormitories. There the matrons continued to rule. Only Sutherland-Kirkpatrick had the power to change that. [36]

Nevertheless, some modest reforms affected life in the dorms. The Garretts made headway in creating forums for the older boys and girls to socialize. They had originally proposed heavily chaperoned dances, but the matrons and the straitlaced fraternal officials objected. Finally, Sutherland-Kirkpatrick assented to monthly "bridge parties" to be held in the residence halls. The Garretts served as chaperons and participants. The boys and girls took turns as hosts and followed the custom of starting each party with a formal receiving line. The bridge parties offered a welcome opportunity for students to interact with members of the opposite sex. Acting as a surrogate father, Harley Garrett advised the boys to "go from the first floor of your dormitory to the second floor and pick up your date and bring her over here and have some fun and take her back home and kiss her a few times if you wish but don't stand out there and neck all night." [37]

The Garretts left the SBA home in 1936 sensing that its days were numbered. Applications had fallen off dramatically. The population dwindled until it reached twenty-one in 1940. In 1942 the board of trustees closed the home for good. Kirkpatrick explained that the decision was the result of "a lack of demand or need for that form of benevolence attributable to public funds now available for the support of dependent children." [38]

The SBA Old Folks' Home was also marking time during this period. The board continued to consider applications after 1935, but far fewer were submitted. There were only five in 1939, down from a record thirty-nine in 1935. Meanwhile the percentage of applications rejected by the board increased. By 1936 the turn-down rate had risen to 50 percent. In 1946 the board closed the SBA Old Folks' Home. Kirkpatrick explained that "Social Security and other public assistance programs" had resulted in a situation where "the real need for our homes for aged members had practically ceased to exist." [39]

The Alumni of the SBA Children's Home

To better assess the quality of the SBA Children's Home, I sent a questionnaire to alumni who resided there during childhood. Twenty individuals responded, a substantial proportion considering the small population of the home. At its height it never had more than sixty-five residents. The questions asked about life before and during their stays at the facility. To provide a comparative framework, I used the same questionnaire that Richard B. McKenzie employed for his unprecedented survey of more than 1,600 orphanage alumni. McKenzie selected nine orphanages, including institutions sponsored by Baptists, Methodists, Presbyterians, Jews, Masons, Odd Fellows, and one state government.

TABLE 5.2. Pre-Orphanage Backgrounds of Alumni,
Percentage of Orphanage Respondents

	SBA	McKenzie
Reasons sent to orphanage		
One parent dead	75	60
Lack of support	40	34
Both parents dead	15	15
Other reasons	5	17
Broken homes	0	18
Abuse before orphanage stay		
Any form of abuse	20	21
Physical	20	10
Mental	10	9
Sexual	5	5

Sources: Richard B. McKenzie, "Orphanage Alumni: How They Have Done and How They Evaluate Their Experience," in *Rethinking Orphanages for the Twenty-first Century*, ed. Richard B. McKenzie (Thousand Oaks, Calif.: Sage Publications, 1999), 108, 116; SBA Survey Results (in author's possession).

Except for size of population, the environments were similar to that of the SBA home.[40]

The SBA home survey results show that the alumni shared numerous characteristics with those studied by McKenzie. They were elderly, with a median age of 78.5 years, compared to a mean age of 67 for McKenzie's respondents. The people in both surveys arrived at the orphanages at roughly the same age (about 8 years old) and stayed about the same length of time (9 to 10 years). When asked why they came to the orphanage, both sets of alumni most commonly answered that the loss of a parent or lack of support was the reason (table 5.2). Many respondents gave more than one explanation.[41]

One notable result, at least for the SBA home, was the low level of reported abuse (see tables 5.2 and 5.3) during the orphanage stay. The abuse rate was 15 percent, slightly higher than in McKenzie's survey. In addition, both sets of alumni indicated that they had been more likely to encounter abuse before they went to the orphanage. In the case of the SBA home, these figures do not seem to coincide with comments from individual interviews and the survey. It is tempting to explain the low level of reported abuse as the result of denial, but

TABLE 5.3. Overall Assessments of Orphanage Stay,
Percentage of Orphanage Respondents

	SBA	McKenzie
Forms of abuse at orphanage		
Any form of abuse	15	13
Physical	15	10
Mental	5	7
Sexual	0	2
Wanted to be adopted		
Never	95	81
Rarely	0	5
Sometimes	5	9
Frequently	0	2
Constantly	0	1
No answer	0	2
Wanted to return to family		
Never	35	31
Rarely	10	15
Sometimes	35	30
Frequently	10	10
Constantly	5	6
No answer	5	8

Sources: Richard B. McKenzie, "Orphanage Alumni: How They Have Done and How They Evaluate Their Experience," in *Rethinking Orphanages for the Twenty-first Century*, ed. Richard B. McKenzie (Thousand Oaks, Calif.: Sage Publications, 1999), 117; SBA Survey Results (in author's possession).

such an interpretation would fail to explain the willingness of former residents to volunteer information about the cruelty of the matrons. It might be a matter of historical context. Alumni of the SBA home grew to maturity during a time when the threshold for and definition of abuse was much higher than it is today. The behavior of the matrons, while generally viewed as harsh and capricious, may simply not have been considered abusive.[42]

Using the survey I tried to assess quality by asking alumni to compare the SBA home to the possible alternatives. Only a few individuals said that they had wanted to be adopted. This response was hardly surprising for the SBA home because adoption was never a possibility; it was far more realistic to expect a re-

TABLE 5.4. Personal Preference for Way of Growing Up,
Percentage of Orphanage Respondents

	SBA	McKenzie
Orphanage vs. own family		
Staying at orphanage	60	72
Staying with own family	15	16
Uncertain	20	9
No answer	5	0
Orphanage vs. foster care		
Staying at orphanage	85	89
Going in foster care	5	2
Uncertain	0	8
No answer	10	0
Overall evaluation of orphanage experience		
Very favorable	50	76
Somewhat favorable	0	8
Mixed	30	13
Somewhat unfavorable	5	.7
Very unfavorable	0	1
No answer	10	0

Sources: SBA Survey Results (in author's possession); Richard B. McKenzie, "Orphan-age Alumni: How They Have Done and How They Evaluate Their Experience," in *Rethinking Orphanages for the Twenty-first Century*, ed. Richard B. McKenzie (Thousand Oaks, Calif.: Sage Publications, 1999), 118–19.

turn to the family. The minutes of the board of trustees attest to thirty-one examples of children going back to their guardians before they reached the age of graduation. In all, 60 percent of SBA home alumni reported that they wanted, at one time or another, to return to their families. But most also said that they did not seriously consider this option. Only 15 percent said that they thought "frequently" or "constantly" about wanting to return to their families. Respondents (see table 5.4) shared an aversion to foster care. More than 80 percent would rather have stayed in the orphanage than a foster home. If given the choice, a lower but still substantial majority would have selected the orphanage over their families.[43]

The two groups of alumni showed the greatest difference when asked to give an overall rating to the orphanage experience (table 5.4). For the SBA home,

TABLE 5.5. Positive Attributes Cited, Percentage of Orphanage Respondents

	SBA	McKenzie
Education, skills development, and guidance	75	49
Basic amenities	55	50
Personal values and direction	45	60
Friendships and close sibling ties	40	38
Sense of self-worth	25	59
Religious and spiritual values	5	29
Sense of stability and permanence	5	13
All positives (specific claims that everything was positive)	0	1

Sources: SBA Survey Results (in author's possession); Richard B. McKenzie, "Orphan-age Alumni: How They Have Done and How They Evaluate Their Experience," in Re-thinking Orphanages for the Twenty-first Century, ed. Richard B. McKenzie (Thousand Oaks, Calif.: Sage Publications, 1999), 119.

50 percent of respondents checked the "very favorable" category, while 76 percent in McKenzie's study did so. The "very unfavorable" category did not get one SBA home alumni vote, and only 5 percent chose "somewhat unfavorable." Instead, "mixed" was the second most frequent choice.[44]

The significant difference in attitudes between each set of respondents is explained perhaps by the responses to the next question, which asked for the three most positive aspects of the orphanage (see table 5.5). From the list of positive aspects, 75 percent of the alumni from the SBA home cited advantages related to education and skills development, while the corresponding figure was 49 percent in McKenzie's survey. The Garretts and teachers like them account for much of the difference. A former resident of the SBA home called the Garretts "two of the nicest teachers a kid could have. They changed my life. We all still write to them." Another credits them as "the biggest and best influence for me—their talks and help. Positive attitude."[45]

Other strong emotional support came from sibling relationships both biological and fictive. For one male former student, two benefits of life at the SBA home were that "my brothers and sisters were together and dad [was] able to visit when he could," and that the "other boys and girls became like brothers and sisters."[46]

Second to education, the SBA home alumni expressed appreciation for basic amenities they received. When asked for specifics, more than 50 percent described, often at considerable length, the superior health care, good food, and

TABLE 5.6. Negative Attributes Cited, Percentage of Orphanage Respondents

	SBA	McKenzie
Lack of freedom	70	15
Excessive punishment	25	12
Lack of love and emotional support from institution and staff	20	31
Poorly trained, underpaid, and unmotivated staff	20	6
Separation from family and siblings	10	34
Lack of education, skill development, and guidance	1	27
Excessive work demands	5	6
Lack of amenities	5	6
No negatives (specific claims that there were no problems)	10	20

Sources: SBA Survey Results (in author's possession); Richard B. McKenzie, "Orphanage Alumni: How They Have Done and How They Evaluate Their Experience," in *Rethinking Orphanages for the Twenty-first Century*, ed. Richard B. McKenzie (Thousand Oaks, Calif.: Sage Publications, 1999), 120.

housing available at the home. Most of all, they appreciated the assurance of stability in a world of mass unemployment and economic deprivation. The SBA home excelled, according to one respondent, in providing "food, clothing and shelter during the depression years." Another said, "Excellent Food, Excellent Shelter, and Excellent Schooling."[47]

When asked to list negative aspects (see table 5.6), the SBA home alumni complained of the lack of freedom (including excessive isolation, too much routine, and unreasonable regimentation). Speaking for many, one man deplored the "lack of contact with the outside world, i.e., competition and association with other children." For others, the sheltered conditions meant that they "had no idea of how other kids were." But many tempered these criticisms. One respondent wrote, "Rules—They were necessary but we didn't always think so." Although 80 percent of SBA home alumni said that they never ran away, 15 percent rebelled against the constraints by taking French leave, mostly just "for fun."[48]

SBA home alumni were more likely than respondents from other orphanages to cite excessive punishment and the poor quality of the staff as negatives. In nearly every case they singled out the matrons. According to one, these women were "totally unfit for their positions"; another, when asked about negative aspects, bluntly declared, "Mean Matrons." A key concern was not the severity of discipline but the lack of fairness in carrying it out: "Our Matrons were not trained. . . . Group punishment instead of just guilty ones. . . . Being punished for things of little consequence." This was not a blanket critique of the entire staff, however. The teachers and principals were the objects of almost universal praise.[49]

Only a handful of SBA home alumni mentioned any serious problems adjusting to post-orphanage life. A woman who came to the home as an infant described "terrible experiences adjusting when I first went to public school." But such comments were rare; nearly all alumni deny that they had difficulty with adjustment. Problems existed, to be sure, such as finding work during the depression, but the possession of a valuable diploma provided a high level of self-confidence. Contrary to stereotypes, alumni did not generally feel stigmatized as "orphan kids." Ehrnfelt denies that he ever "felt like I was second grade or anything like that." Similarly, Bezan reflects that she "always told people I was there. I've never been ashamed of it." Sabo declares that "I never tried to hide it from anybody. I told them where I was raised."[50]

Acceptance of the past did not necessarily constitute an embrace of orphanages. The survey asked SBA alumni about recent proposals to bring back orphanages. The respondents were mostly favorable to the idea, although several included provisos. One former resident suggested that orphanages "would offer a more stable environment than foster homes. Too often children are moved from home to home at the whim of some social worker." Two alumni faulted foster homes for separating siblings; it "sure meant a lot to me to be able to be [with] my brother and sister." Another responded, "We had every thing we needed (nice clothing), clean rooms, clean bedding every week. Good food. If we were ill we were taken care of. We didn't have our Mother or Father but we had each other."[51]

Comments that were less favorable to bringing back orphanages were often ambiguous. The most negative response came from an alumnus who stated that the matrons were guilty of "'child abuse' in the first degree. If it hadn't been for the teachings of Dr. and Mrs. Garrett and Miss Childs not too many of us would have turned out as good as we have." Despite this complaint, the rest of this respondent's answer was a guarded endorsement of properly supervised orphanages over foster homes. Former residents less critical of the home nonetheless voiced similar concerns. They warned that any orphanage staff would have to be properly trained and supervised. A female alumnus articulated the views of many: "Kinder matrons, that would be the most important. School at the S.B.A. was great!"[52]

The recollections and opinions of orphanage alumni, although illuminating, need to be used with caution. One problem is the obvious risk of positive bias.

TABLE 5.7. Median Household Incomes of U.S. General White Population
(65 years and older) and Orphanage Respondents, 1994

| | | | Percentage Difference | |
| | | | SBA/U.S. | McKenzie/U.S. |
U.S. (1)	SBA (2)	McKenzie (3)	[(2)/(1)−1]	[(3)/(1)−1]
$18,670	$24,700	$30,000	24	61

Sources: SBA Survey Results (in author's possession); Richard B. McKenzie, "Orphan-age Alumni: How They Have Done and How They Evaluate Their Experience," in *Rethinking Orphanages for the Twenty-first Century*, ed. Richard B. McKenzie (Thousand Oaks, Calif.: Sage Publications, 1999), 113; conversation with Richard McKenzie, March 10, 1999.

The passage of sixty years may lead to glossing over bad memories and unduly accentuating fonder ones. Moreover, it is possible that the alumni who bothered to respond were more likely to be happier and successful in their lives. By the same token, biases toward the negative side should not be discounted. As countless Americans in psychotherapy can attest, adults do not necessarily regard childhood or early home life with nostalgia.

McKenzie's survey addressed a related issue, the long-term impact of the orphanage experience. The dominant view among anti-orphanage critics has been that institutional life impedes success and inflicts permanent psychological scars. To test whether these charges were true, McKenzie asked questions regarding household income, educational attainment, and attitudes about life: "It is expected that if the criticisms of long-term orphanages . . . are correct, both the respondents' family backgrounds and their orphanage experiences should be expected to have held the alumni back in life. Even with the potential upward biases in the survey methods, it might still be expected that the respondents, as a group, would have fared less well in life than their counterparts in the general population." His findings and mine cast doubt on the conventional assumption that orphanages held back children from success. Based on the responses, he concluded that alumni have "outpaced their counterparts of the same racial and age group in the general population by wide margins."[53]

The alumni of the SBA home excelled in nearly every category. Their median household income was 24.4 percent higher than that of other white Americans in their age cohort (table 5.7), and they were well above the norm in educational attainment (table 5.8). Ninety percent had high school diplomas, compared with 67 percent of the white population over age 65. Their record of achieve-

TABLE 5.8. Educational Background and Divorce Rates of
U.S. General White Population (65 years and older)
and Orphanage Respondents, 1994

	SBA	McKenzie	U.S.
Educational background			
High school diploma	90	86	67
College degree	10	22	12
Some college	35	27	11
Divorce rate	35	17	5

Sources: SBA Survey Results (in author's possession); Richard B. McKenzie, "Orphan-age Alumni: How They Have Done and How They Evaluate Their Experience," in *Re-thinking Orphanages for the Twenty-first Century*, ed. Richard B. McKenzie (Thousand Oaks, Calif.: Sage Publications, 1999), 111, 114; conversation with Richard McKenzie, March 10, 1999.

ment in higher education was generally good. Thirty-five percent had "some college, but no degree," while only 11.9 percent of the white population could make this claim. If there was a shortfall, it was in college graduation rates. Although 10 percent had earned college degrees, 12.5 percent of white Americans over age 65 had done so. This disparity, however, evaporates when the alumni (who had a median age of 78.5) are compared to all white Americans over age 75. Still, former residents of the SBA home, unlike those in McKenzie's survey, cannot claim a clear advantage in this respect.[54]

Both groups of orphanage alumni fared poorly in marital relationships (table 5.8). Thirty-five percent of former residents of the SBA home reported divorces, compared with only 5 percent of all white Americans over age 65. They had a greater likelihood of failed marriages than the alumni in McKenzie's survey. Their higher divorce rates offer the most compelling support for the prevailing theory that a long institutional stay lays the groundwork for insecure and un-loving adult relationships. It also lends credence to the view that orphanage alumni have suffered bad effects from inadequate parental role models.[55]

At the same time, the alternatives to the orphanage would not necessarily have been better. For most SBA home alumni, the choice was not between a loving and stable family and an orphanage but between an orphanage, a broken and disadvantaged family, and a foster home.

Other results of the survey called into question theories that orphanage alumni had a bleaker outlook on life. Several questions attempted to assess current attitudes. The survey asked the same question that has been used by the National Opinion Research Center at the University of Chicago for more than forty years: "All things considered, how would you say things are going these days?" Three categories could be selected: very happy, somewhat happy, and not too happy. If the standard critique of orphanages was right, the categories "not too happy" or "somewhat happy" would win hands down. The opposite was true: 29 percent of Americans said they were very happy, compared with 55 percent of the SBA home alumni and 61 percent in McKenzie's sample.[56]

The survey also attempted to use voting as an indicator of social "maladjustment." If orphanage alumni were, as one historian puts it, "behind other children in . . . social adaptation," they might be more likely to remain uninvolved and stay home on election day. Again, the answers revealed otherwise. The orphanage alumni in both surveys had a higher rate of turnout than the national average in the 1992 election. While 72 percent of Americans who were 45 years old and over voted in 1992, 100 percent of SBA home alumni and 88 percent of McKenzie's sample did so.[57]

The evidence of mental health and social adaptation is generally consistent with the observations recorded by Garrett. In his thesis he reported the results of the Bernreuter Personality Test developed by the Employment Stabilization Research Institute at Stanford University. The purpose of the test was to measure four traits: neurotic/stable tendencies, dependence/self-sufficiency, introversion/extroversion, and dominance/submission. The scores for the SBA home far exceeded Garrett's expectations and did not fit his preconceptions about "institutional children." He speculated that it was "possible that the strict discipline which is maintained both in the home and school together with the absence of outside contacts, has caused these children to become submissive, introverts and somewhat neurotic. However, this indication cannot be noticeably observed in working with the children. In fact, in many cases . . . the results of these tests seem to be contrary to the writer's opinion of the student."[58]

Conclusion

The history of the SBA home does not provide easy answers about orphanages. It was far from a perfect institution. Regimentation could be excessive, and the rules were often petty. Some of the personnel, especially the matrons, were ill suited for their duties. Fraternal leaders and the orphanage staff unduly sheltered the children from the realities of the outside world. Some permanent emotional scars may have resulted.

But there is more to the story. The SBA home excelled in other respects. Its record was especially good when compared with the probable alternatives: disadvantaged or abusive families and foster homes. The children were well fed and clothed, obtained superior health care, and received excellent educations. They could turn to caring and talented teachers; their possession of a high school diploma gave them a crucial edge. Partly as a result of their education they were more likely to attend college and earn higher incomes. Given their disadvantaged family backgrounds, they would probably not have fared so well without the SBA.

Far from supporting the stereotype of the emotionally deprived and maladjusted institutional child, the survey indicates that alumni have unusually upbeat attitudes about life. The typical respondent was far more likely than the average American to describe his or her state of mind as very happy. A key message is the need to compare orphanages to the possible alternatives rather than to ideals that did not or could not have existed. When judged by this standard, the SBA Children's Home generally brought improvements to the lives of its residents and gave them the wherewithal to succeed as adults.

CHAPTER SIX

The Lodge Practice Evil Reconsidered

S hortly after the turn of the century, articles about the "lodge practice evil" began to fill the pages of American medical journals. This term referred to a new method by which fraternal societies extended low-cost medical services to members. The usual approach was for a doctor to give basic health care in exchange for a salary based on the size of the membership. For obvious reasons, lodge practice was a popular innovation among members of fraternal societies. It inspired equally strong opposition, however, from key leaders in the medical profession. These critics charged that lodge practice posed a danger to prevailing fees and subjected doctors to the exploitative whims of the laity.

A long tradition of contract practice preceded the fraternal lodge experiments. In the colonial period, for example, planters had hired doctors on a per capita basis to care for slaves. After the Civil War, contract practice emerged in industries, such as railroads, lumbering, and mining, where workers did not have access to medical care. Unions made some forays into contract practice during the nineteenth century, especially among miners in the West. The best-known venture was the Coeur d'Alene Miners' Union Hospital in Idaho of the Western Miners' Federation.[1]

Lodge practice had its greatest impact before the turn of the century in immigrant and other ethnic societies. By the 1870s many of the predominantly black mutual benefit societies in New Orleans hired doctors on a per capita plan. Tampa, Florida, was another area of early activity. Beginning in 1887, La Igual, a Spanish-language fraternal organization, retained doctors on a contract basis. The society was probably influenced by the mutual aid tradition of the *centros* in Cuba.[2]

The slow development of lodge practice in the United States was in notable contrast to the growth of similar activities in Great Britain and Australia. More than half of wage earners in the latter countries may have had access to doctors from friendly societies before World War I. In part, American laggardness was the consequence of a different fraternal tradition. The British and Australian friendly societies always kept a near-exclusive focus on sick benefits. This may have offered a firmer foundation for the development of medical service plans. Demographic factors also were influential. Lodge practice may have been more feasible in Great Britain because of the higher population density, which made it easier for each doctor to serve large numbers of patients. In other words, the Americans could have been slower to adopt lodge practice for the same reasons that they took so much longer to embrace fraternal organizations.[3]

The Rise of Lodge Practice

Estimates greatly varied, but there was universal agreement that lodge practice was growing rapidly after the turn of the century. In 1909, for example, a doctor in Illinois calculated the magnitude of increase during the previous two decades at 500 percent. Seven years later an article in the *New York State Journal of Medicine* reckoned that the "number of people treated in this manner has, at a conservative estimate, been multiplied about fifty times during the last twenty years." In many communities, according to Dr. S. S. Goldwater, the health commissioner of New York City, lodge practice had become "the chosen or established method of dealing with sickness among the relatively poor."[4]

Lodge practice achieved an important foothold in urban areas, including Chicago and New York. In both cities it was especially popular among Italians, Greeks, and Jews. According to medical reformer Dr. Michael M. Davis Jr., the "idea that a 'society' exists to provide cash or medical benefits is so deeply ingrained in the immigrant's mind that he finds it hard to understand organization for any other purpose." Anna Kalet concluded that "practically the only voluntary health insurance agencies in New York City which furnish their members with medical care are the fraternal societies."[5]

Such estimates, often of the thumbnail variety, should be viewed with considerable caution. A few studies, however, were more rigorous. To uncover the extent of lodge practice in Pennsylvania, Dr. George E. Holtzapple mailed 231 questionnaires to physicians. Those responding reported that the system existed in some form in fifty-four urban areas. Drawing on Holtzapple's evidence, reasonably complete figures for twenty-seven communities can be studied.[6]

A comparison of this data with census statistics makes it possible to estimate the number of adult males in every community eligible for the services of a lodge doctor. The percentage ranged from a low of 2.3 in Harrisburg to a high

of 33 in Monaca. The overall median was 8.9. The average medical fee paid per
member was $2.00 a year. Four years later the author of a follow-up survey con-
cluded that the number of physicians under contract had more than doubled.[7]

The gaps in Holtzapple's survey, however, were noticeable. The membership figures were not always complete, particularly for the smaller lodges. Of
equal importance, because of inadequate replies, he could not include several
large cities, notably Philadelphia and Pittsburgh. It is possible to compare
Holtzapple's findings with another, more comprehensive survey. In 1906 the
King County Medical Society tabulated the membership figures and fees of
fraternal orders with lodge doctors in Seattle, Washington. The results suggested that 15,000 individuals (compared to "only a few hundred" in 1899) were
eligible. The average annual fee was $1.20. The participation rate was roughly
two of ten of Seattle's adult males over age twenty-one. While comparatively
small by British and Australian standards, this constituted substantial market
penetration.[8]

The urban environment in which lodge practice thrived had rich traditions
of innovation in health care delivery. Many philanthropic, religious, and business organizations had established dispensaries in cities. A majority of dispensaries were freestanding units centered at the neighborhood level. Generally,
some portion of their funding came from local governmental sources. As charitable institutions they could hold down costs because doctors donated all or
part of their services. The American Medical Association (AMA) estimated that
about one-fifth of the population of New York City in 1915 had applied at some
time for medical care in dispensaries. Both dispensaries and lodge practice
reflected a general readiness in urban neighborhoods to engage in health care
experimentation.[9]

Lodge Practice among Native Whites

Lodge practice was generally more prevalent among orders that concentrated
on sick and funeral benefits rather than life insurance. Two of the three largest societies among native whites that provided this service, the Loyal Order of
Moose and the FOE, primarily offered sick benefits. The major exception was
the third society, the IOF, a life insurance order. By 1910 these three groups
had several thousand doctors to look after the medical needs of a half-million
members.[10]

Of the three orders, the IOF had the oldest tradition of lodge practice. Although it was a life insurance order, it traced its origins to the AOF, a British

friendly society that provided sick and funeral benefits. As early as the 1830s the AOF had established lodges in the United States, but by the 1870s and 1880s many of these had split off to form the Foresters of America and the IOF. By 1907 the groups had 300,000 members in the United States, mostly in the Northeast and Midwest. Despite a tendency toward schism, the various Foresters organizations maintained similar rituals and operational structures. The ceremonies drew inspiration from Robin Hood and his men in Sherwood Forest. In keeping with the medieval motif, the lodges were "courts" and the supreme leader a "chief ranger." Women and men could join (in separate courts), and the only religious test was belief in a supreme being. The IOF was quintessentially internationalist.[11]

The IOF in the United States emulated the AOF's cosmopolitan outlook and emphasis on lodge practice. Each court, in the fashion common to a friendly society, hired a doctor whose salary was based on the number of members. An annual fee of about $2.00 purchased the doctor's services, including house calls, but usually did not pay the cost of medicine. Only members who had passed a physical examination and stayed on the rolls for one year were eligible.[12]

While the various organizations of Foresters eschewed nationalism, one of their leading rivals for lodge practice, the FOE, was almost a caricature of apple-pie Americanism. The first lodge opened in Seattle, Washington, in 1898. From a modest start, the FOE's ranks mushroomed to 300,000 by 1908, with heavy concentrations in the Mississippi Valley and the West. The members embraced a fun-loving and informal style. The "aeries," with their well-stocked bars, often served as local community centers. The freewheeling behavior led to an unsavory reputation. In 1910 *McClure's Magazine* dismissed the group as "a great national organization of sporting men, bartenders, politicians, thieves, and professional criminals." The FOE's leaders later refurbished their image by launching a highly visible and ultimately successful campaign for the proclamation of Mother's Day.[13]

From its beginning the FOE became noted (notorious in medical society circles) for engaging in lodge practice. Between 1906 and 1910 it dispensed a million dollars in salaries to physicians. Each aerie charged a standard $2.00 medical fee that not only guaranteed treatment to each member—including minor surgery—but, unlike the Foresters, extended to the member's family as well. Conditions not covered were venereal disease, pregnancy, and "any sickness or injury caused or brought about by the use of intoxicating liquors, or opiates, or by any immoral conduct."[14]

Until the 1910s the Loyal Order of Moose relied on lodge practice, not Moose-

heart, as the main inducement for new members. It adopted a system that did
not differ greatly from the plans offered by the Foresters and the Eagles. The national organization set minimum ground rules; the local lodges controlled the
selection and supervision of doctors. The pay scale for the lodge doctor was
usually less than $2.00 per member, although some lodges chose to pay higher
amounts. In many lodges this fee covered house calls and medicine. Lodges in
large urban centers employed several doctors at the same time. There were also
instances, such as in Helena, Montana, where doctors had contracts with more
than one society.[15]

Society Doctors in New Orleans

New Orleans had one of the oldest and most extensive traditions of lodge practice. While these arrangements existed among all ethnic groups, they were most
pervasive among blacks, especially Creoles. In 1937 Harry Walker identified 137
organizations that offered the services of a doctor. Among these were local affiliates of two prominent national organizations, the Eastern Star and the Household of Ruth. More common, however, were homegrown societies such as the
Ladies of Fidelity, the Young Men of Inseparable Friends, the Bon Secours, the
Holy Ghost, and the United Sons and Daughters. The names of black societies
indicate that no fewer than forty catered primarily to women.[16]

These societies had long been familiar features on the local landscape. More
than half dated their founding to the nineteenth century. A handful of societies
had been in continuous existence since the antebellum period. Before the Civil
War the focus had been on the payment of sick and funeral benefits, like fraternal organizations throughout the country. By the early 1880s, however, lodge
practice had become a standard feature of societies of New Orleans, anticipating developments elsewhere by twenty years.[17]

One explanation for the earlier development of lodge practice in New Orleans was the presence of a large Creole population. Members of this group provided the early leadership and seed money. The Catholic Church actively but
unofficially encouraged members to form societies. Another possible factor was
the influence of European antecedents such as the lay-controlled but religiously
based confraternities of France and early New Orleans.[18]

New Orleans's history of yellow fever epidemics and high death rates also
spurred the development of lodge practice. As late as 1929 the death rate in New
Orleans was 142.6 per 100,000, compared with 70.1 for rest of the United States.
Death rates for blacks were higher than in any other major southern city. The

relative lack of governmental social welfare spending encouraged people to form societies for mutual protection. New Orleans was always at or near the bottom in appropriations for indoor and outdoor relief. With a few exceptions it relied on the private sector to aid the poor. As late as 1930 the city spent considerably less per capita on all types of relief than did other large cities.[19]

The rank and file of these societies came from extremely modest backgrounds representing, according to one scholar, "a fair cross section of the Negro population." Most were unskilled in contrast to their counterparts in the Moose, Foresters, and Eagles, who tended to be skilled workers. A statistical sample in 1937 of 376 males and 443 females in thirty-four societies showed that most of the females worked outside the home, 55 percent in unskilled occupations (primarily domestic service) and 8.4 percent as professionals. Among the working males, 53.7 percent were unskilled, 30.8 were skilled and semiskilled, and only 4.7 percent were professionals or proprietors.[20]

An article in the *New Orleans Medical and Surgical Journal* in 1888 calculated that four-fifths of the population belonged to societies with lodge doctors. This estimate, however, was a better reflection of the exaggerated fears of organized medicine than of actual conditions. The Orleans Parish Medical Society published a more reliable estimate in 1897. The author sent questionnaires to 138 physicians in New Orleans. The results indicated that membership in a lodge entitled 55,000 individuals (or one-fifth of New Orleans's population) to medical care. Four of ten of the doctors who replied to the survey had contracts with societies.[21]

The social welfare activities of these societies extended beyond the provision of doctors. Funeral home owners, for example, vied in annual elections to become "society undertaker." The reward for victory was a steady and sometimes lucrative contract. The payment to the undertaker, much like the stipend to the doctor, was on a per capita basis. During the 1930s, lodges paid between $50.00 and $56.00 for funerals. Each lodge also relied on this system to elect a druggist to fill all prescriptions. Because these added responsibilities placed greater demands on management and accounting skills, a class of individuals known as "society mechanics" emerged. These were men and women with training and experience in parliamentary procedure, record keeping, and leadership. Society mechanics commonly held offices in several lodges, from which they received salaries. In many cases they founded their own lodges. For a well-educated black man and woman, experience as a society mechanic was a means to obtain economic benefits and community prestige.[22]

Primary data concerning lodge practice in New Orleans is in short supply.

Nevertheless, some records survive. Particularly helpful is a minute book covering the period from August 1914 through September 1916 from the Ladies Friends of Faith Benevolent Association, a black female society of about 170 members. In terms of organizational structure and benefits, the Ladies Friends of Faith fit the general local pattern. The rank and file voted annually to choose a "society" druggist, doctor, and undertaker, who provided services at a low, flat rate. Members taken sick collected $2.00 a week if they saw the lodge doctor and $3.00 if they did not. To guard against false claims, a visiting committee checked on the recipients. The rules stipulated that members who failed to visit claimants pay a $1.00 fine.[23]

During this two-year period the minute book records great activity. One hundred and thirteen individuals (slightly over half the membership) collected sick benefits. Of these, seventy used the lodge doctor at least once; several, a dozen times. Almost all applicants obtained cash payments and medical service (including free medicine) without eliciting objections. An exception was a member "discharged" because the "chairlady [of the sick committee] stated that she found the sister on the side of the bed sewing." This, of course, violated the requirement that recipients be unable to work.[24]

The deliberation process of the Ladies Friends of Faith was not a simple matter. At nearly every meeting the society heard at least one plea from a member unable to pay dues because of unemployment or poor health. One of the most desperate cases concerned a woman who was "out of Doors, and had no money." In such cases the society generally extended help. It allowed twenty-four members extra time to pay their debts, and it passed the hat for ten others. Not once did the Ladies Friends of Faith reject an appeal outright. Such liberality did not translate into open season on the lodge's treasury, however. The members readily voted to drop from the rolls delinquents who failed to explain their "unfinancial" status.[25]

The Response of the Medical Societies

Regardless of religious, ethnic, or political orientation, all fraternal societies, to the extent they provided medical services, faced similar obstacles. The most serious, without a doubt, was the organized opposition of physicians. The spread of the lodge practice evil elicited nearly universal condemnation from medical societies. Reflecting the intensity of feeling, the *Pennsylvania Medical Journal* bluntly demanded in 1904 "that the 'club doctor' must be shut out of the profession."[26]

At its core this antipathy represented fear for the survival of fee-for-service remuneration. Dr. W. F. Zierath of Sheboygan, Wisconsin, succinctly summed up the matter when he chided his colleagues for bowing to "the keen business instinct of the laity" who had "discovered in contract practice a scheme to obtain medical services for practically nothing." Once doctors allowed nonprofessionals to place them on fixed salaries, Zierath and others cautioned, loss of both income and independence would follow. The profession would then become tainted and demoralized by every physician's "undignified" scramble to "sell himself to the lowest bidder." Another opponent predicted that lodge practice, if not stopped, would depress fees to levels "comparable to those of the bootblack and peanut vendor."[27]

No opprobrium was off limits in depictions of the lodge doctor. He was a "scab" who broke ranks with professional solidarity, an incompetent "quack" spewed out by a low-grade diploma mill, and most unforgivably, a "huckster" bent on commercializing the noble art of medicine. Critics were quick to add, however, that lodge practice also harmed the patient who, in return for these low fees, received shabby service. It was a vain attempt, charged one opponent, to get "something for nothing." Another cited "the consensus of opinion that physicians generally give fraternal organizations their money's worth, no more."[28]

A constant refrain stressed the poor training of lodge doctors. Dr. A. B. Hirsh characterized most lodge physicians as the products of "short term, low-grade, proprietary institutions, men usually with little or no indoor hospital training ... who would probably prove failures in life without some such form of assured income." On a related note, Dr. Albert M. Eaton blamed inferior schools for "over-crowding our ranks," thus fueling the struggle that made lodge practice thrive.[29]

The critics warned that toiling under such conditions would demoralize and degrade even the best doctors. No one, they concluded, could long endure the strain of running at each patient's "beck and call." The physician shackled by a contract would inevitably neglect essential postgraduate study and lapse into "slip-shod methods of diagnosis and treatment," thus becoming "a real cheap doctor." Dr. H. A. Tomlinson claimed that lodge practice rendered promising young colleagues "slovenly [and] indifferent" and killed their "scientific spirit." Dr. Morris Clurman cited an extreme case of a lodge doctor obligated to make thirty house calls in a "routine day." He asked, How could any physician working under such conditions "conscientiously examine each patient and make the proper diagnosis?"[30]

A favorite target was the election process used to select doctors. Critics described these campaigns as carnivals of corruption in which victory depended on extravagant promises or outright bribery. Eaton recalled the case of a physician who garnered the necessary votes by paying the initiation fees of certain members. The detractors portrayed election contests as marred by unseemly "wire-pulling" and backslapping. Zierath argued that the successful candidate's campaign demanded "the handshaking, the button-holing, the treating to cigars and drinks in public houses . . . the hobnobbing with individuals far below him in the social scale and intellectuality." [31]

Lodge Practice Reconsidered

Any effort to reconsider the value of lodge practice is difficult. The bulk of the surviving sources point to a ringing verdict of guilty. But this research problem is not fatal. Ironically, when read from a modern perspective, the strident manifestos published in the medical journals paint a far less negative picture, and the professional critiques can be supplemented by justifications of lodge practice written by doctors and members of fraternal societies.

The leading beneficiary of lodge practice was, of course, the patient of modest means. He or she was able to obtain a physician's care for about $2.00 a year, roughly equivalent to a day's wage for a laborer. For comparable amounts, some lodges extended coverage to family members. The remuneration the lodge doctor received was a far cry from the higher fee schedules favored by the profession. The local medical society in Meadville, Pennsylvania, was typical in setting the following minimum fees for its members: $1.00 per physical examination, surgical dressing, and daytime house call and $2.00 per nighttime house call. Such charges, at least for ongoing service, were beyond the reach of many lower-income Americans. Hence it was not coincidental, an editorial in the *Medical Council* pointed out, that lodge practice thrived in communities populated by the working poor.[32]

Moreover, had it not been for the competition offered by fraternal societies, official fees probably would have been still higher. In this vein Dr. Charles S. Sheldon complained that lodge practice "demoralizes the scale of prices in a profession already too poorly paid. It causes dissatisfaction among those outside the lodges and makes them unwilling to pay regular prices." [33]

Lodges were able to maintain low fees partly because of organizational strengths peculiar to the fraternal structure. Lodges could entice doctors with a substantial and stable patient base, leaving them well positioned to purchase medical services at "wholesale" and sell at "retail." Elections also exerted downward pressure on fees. A lodge doctor in New Orleans lamented that every year a "fellow has to get out and bid his head off to get work."[34]

At the same time, allegations that elections encouraged shady tactics had some merit. In New Orleans, for example, shrewd politicking could be an essential part of a lodge doctor's repertoire. As a local physician who defended the practice remarked, "Yes, you've got to 'talk turkey' with them [the members]. If you serve them right they'll look out for you." The official historian of the WC (which had numerous lodge doctors) conceded that the early method of selecting physicians led to undue "favoritism." He blamed this on the doctor's dependence on "the good will of the leading members. . . . There was the temptation to show partiality to their friends both in the admittance of new members and in the issuance of sick certificates."[35]

The preponderance of evidence from both supporters and adversaries indicates that, on balance, the election process served members well. The main virtue was that it allowed patients to compare notes on the medical records of both challenger and incumbent. In 1909 John C. McManemin, the past worthy president of the FOE, maintained that as "the membership have the right of franchise in electing the lodge physician, so have they in deposing him, and it therefore results that unless the physician so selected, attends to the duties devolving upon him he is quickly brought to account."[36]

Inspection of the medical journals gives some cause for skepticism of blanket assertions that lodges heedlessly sacrificed quality to elect candidates with the lowest fee. The contrary, in fact, occurred in a campaign described by lodge practice adversary Dr. George S. Mathews of Providence, Rhode Island: "In one lodge two members in good standing in the State Medical Society openly in lodge meeting underbid the one the other [sic]. One volunteered his services at $2 a head. The other dropped his price to $1.75. The first bidder then acceded to this price with medicines furnished. This occasioned a drop in bidder No. 2 in his price to include medicine and minor surgery. To the vast credit of the lodge neither bid was accepted but a non-bidder was given the job at $2." In another case a Moose lodge asked the national organization to increase the salary of a doctor deemed particularly deserving.[37]

Even critics who disdained the quality of lodge practice acknowledged that it attracted some physicians of high ability and training. Although Hirsh gave a low overall rating to doctors who had arrangements with lodges, he noted that there were exceptions, including "graduates of schools of various standards, including even the universities." Goldwater stated that "many competent medical men" held these contracts, and "between the slip-shod service of the poorer kind of dispensary, and the painstaking care of the conscientious lodge doctor, the choice easily lies with the latter." Significantly, the greatest contempt was reserved for physicians with lucrative practices who took lodge contracts on the side. Holtzapple excoriated such individuals as "inordinately selfish and avaricious" men who "have no neighbors in the profession, for they are not Samaritans by practice."[38]

Citing low levels of medical education was also misleading. For many opponents it was sufficient merely to mention that lodge doctors came disproportionately from the proprietary medical schools. This charge was probably accurate but falls short of an indictment. Proprietary medical schools had two salient features: the owners were physicians in regular practice, and unlike endowed universities, they subsisted entirely on tuition. The physician/owners were paid from fees received in exchange for delivering lectures and from referrals tendered by grateful graduates. The students, because they often came from modest backgrounds, lacked both the connections and the financial resources enjoyed by many of their university-trained counterparts. Thus they had ample reason to embrace lodge practice. For a recent graduate, a lodge might be the sole route to the seed money and community contacts necessary to launch a practice. To call these doctors "quacks" was unjust. Like other aspiring physicians, they had to obtain state certification. Since the 1880s and 1890s, certification had tightened and failure rates had reached ever higher levels.[39]

The fraternal society, as the purchaser of services, had incentives to maintain the quality of care. An incompetent or arbitrary physician could prove fatal to actuarial soundness. Dr. A. Ravogli, an experienced lodge practitioner from Cincinnati, underlined this point. While agreeing that societies "desire to diminish their expenses," he noted that it was "in their interest to have their members well attended and speedily cured, in order that they may safeguard their own interests."[40]

Moreover, prospective members were wary of organizations with high mortality rates. The IOF repeatedly contrasted the death rate of members (6.66 per 1,000) with that of the same age group in the general population (9.30 per 1,000). It credited this low mortality to "Sherlock-Holmes-like acuteness in the detection of bad risks" exhibited by each court. Doctors in the courts of the IOF annually rejected between 10 and 20 percent of applicants.[41]

The fact that lodge doctors were the principal custodians of cash sick benefits put them under added pressure to look after the financial health of the organization. Although fraternal societies often dispensed generous quantities of money, they were equally eager to root out malingering. A member could collect only if the illness was both disabling and verified by a physician. The presence of the lodge doctor as an enforcer gave the requirement potency. In her study of voluntary health insurance in New York City, Anna Kalet, no friend of lodge practice, reported the general view "that private physicians, when asked for sickness certificates, are inclined to be lenient, whereas lodge doctors are more likely to be strict." [42]

In addition, doctors who neglected their duties faced stiff sanctions, mostly fines. Infractions included failure to report at meetings, fraudulent approval of sick claims, and refusal to respond to a house call. For the last-named violation, both the FOE and the IOF authorized a lodge to hire a substitute from the open market and then deduct the charges from the salary of the delinquent doctor. Unfortunately, a shortage of records makes it difficult to assess how rigorously societies enforced these rules. [43]

An important consequence of lodge practice for the patient was to facilitate habits of assertiveness, thus anticipating by several decades the "active patient." Many physicians, obviously humiliated by such treatment, denounced the quickness of patients to "quibble." Dr. J. W. Bolton of Warrensburg, Missouri, blamed excessive house calls for engendering fears in the physician "that he will lose his position if he fails to answer every call regardless of circumstances and his knowledge of the fact that he is being imposed on constantly by members who abuse their privileges." Lodge practice challenged the prevailing medical elitism that held, in its extreme version, that the "doctor should have absolute control of the patient." The fraternal society gave patients "the idea that they can go to the lodge doctor for anything and that he is duty bound to attend them." [44]

The medical journals betrayed more than a tinge of class bias as well. Clurman bristled that "laymen, especially those of the lower strata of working men, are not the best judges of the professional merits of a physician." He related the humiliation of a physician whom a tenement housewife had scolded for tardiness. Mathews bitterly cited the case of a colleague discharged for refusing "to meet a committee composed entirely of working men who were asked to pass judgment on his professional handling of a man who claimed that he was getting improper medical treatment for his disease." [45]

Professional journals also recounted complaints of patients who pestered doctors with "trivial" ailments. Zierath considered it inevitable that the lodge doctor would be called "to see cases repeatedly where a physician would not be called, were the regular fee to apply. One of the children in a family has abdominal pain, and the anxious mother promptly conjectures that it is appendicitis" when it was nothing more than "too much indulgence in mince pie." But, he continued, it "looks stylish to have the doctor's rig standing in front of the house and excites the curiosity and envy of the neighbors, therefore the 'free doctor' is summoned."[46]

As part of an effort to fight this perceived exploitation of doctors, the *Western Medical Times* prominently featured a poem titled "The Lodge Doctor":

> Here's to the foolish M.D.,
> Who would for a dollar agree
>   To doctor a lodge
>   For a livelong year,
> And never to dodge
>   Though the work be severe;
> May he ever scamper
> His patients to pamper
>   At all hours of the day and the night!
> For hives and phthisic
> May he ever give physic
>   To people who call him for spite![47]

For fraternal societies, by contrast, the ability to call on the doctor for any complaint was a major selling point. Lodge practice, declared an editorial in the official magazine of the FOE, "accords perfectly with the modern theory of the prevention of disease. . . . Many of the poorer members, under other circumstances, might delay in calling a doctor until the disease had made considerable headway." Tongue in cheek, Oronhyatekha of the IOF, himself a practicing physician, expanded on this theme. "I never could see the philosophy," he argued, "of curing a patient inside of a week or so, when he paid me two dollars a day. . . . But the Foresters' doctor gets one dollar a year for medical attendance. . . . What is the sense of allowing a man to remain ill under such conditions?"[48]

Lodge practice opened unusual opportunities for many working-class Americans to compare and experiment. It empowered them to break free from the confining view that health care was merely a generic good. For the first time, many individuals had the wherewithal to sample medical services as a menu of choices, each item adjustable to suit a particular need. Members expressed their discernment through selective patronization. They may have turned to the lodge doctor for prevention and initial screening, but many looked elsewhere for a cure. The *Maine Medical Society Journal* lamented that though members did not hesitate to use the doctor for "small matters," they would call on "some one else when seriously sick or compelled to pay for services." Drawing on more detailed evidence, the Beneficiary Committee of the FOE reported a participation rate of 83 percent. An extensive survey of lodge members in New Orleans revealed that 56 percent relied exclusively on their society doctors, while the rest also patronized other physicians.[49]

Probably the best sources of information on selective patronization in New Orleans were the interviews conducted by Walker. Especially revealing was a member's remark that "there is nothing better than a society[,] for when you're sick they give you the best possible attention, but if I were real sick, I'd prefer calling [another] doctor. . . . Society doctors are too busy to handle extreme illnesses." Walker found that respondents were "generally favorable to the institution," even the poorest members who relied exclusively on lodge doctors. One member asserted, "The society is a good thing to be in and the doctor is good. We are poor folks and if I needed a doctor to call regularly I'd use the society doctor."[50]

To professional critics, however, these examples of selective patronization indicated that better-off workers who could afford to pay prevailing fees were getting a free ride. For this reason, many physicians regarded lodge practice as a more serious threat to the profession than the free dispensary. Holtzapple wrote that because the poor were "better provided for to-day by dispensaries and free wards," there was "no legitimate need for fraternal organizations to furnish medical care practically free of cost to its members, especially those who are able to pay."[51]

Much to the frustration of the medical societies, many physicians benefited from contracts with fraternal societies. Several doctors in New Orleans defended lodge practice as a "stepping stone" to building a stable private practice. One predicted that "if you cut out benevolent organizations, you cut out contact of the colored physician with thousands of people. Few colored people have enough money to go to Negro physicians. Without benevolent organizations, most of the Negro patients would have gone to Charity hospital." A member of the Loyal Order of Moose argued that doctors sought lodge contracts because of "the advertising they get, and the work they do for our families. . . . I, myself, have paid $1,800 to a Moose doctor for treating my wife inside of two years. . . . It is not the 50 cents they are after. It is the work from our families, and the advertising they get from a big lodge of three or four thousand members."[52]

In one of the few editorials in a professional outlet favorable to lodge practice, the *New York State Journal of Medicine* underlined additional gains for the doctor, including opportunities to earn money by charging fees for medicine and for uncovered services, such as obstetrics. The author rejected allegations that excessive demands made lodge doctors deficient in "scientific skill." Such a contention, if true, would be applicable with equal force to independent practitioners who carried greater patient loads. Ravogli credited his lodge experience with providing a valuable introduction to the community: "Even at the present time, not infrequently do old members of the French society call at my office for consultation in my specialty."[53]

Most of the few medical professionals who were more favorable to lodge practice sought a vague middle ground between open tolerance and suppression. Hence, the label "regulationist," rather than defender, best fits their position. With scarcely an exception, they applauded united action by the profession to constrain, although not necessarily eliminate, the competition. Dr. Albert T. Lytle of Buffalo urged the medical societies to fix "minimum medical remuneration, or selling prices" for lodge contracts. Virtually absent among the regulationists was the zeal so evident in statements issued from the opposition. Ravogli's tepid suggestion that lodge practice not "be entirely stamped out" was fairly representative.[54]

A certain grudging tone marks the pronouncements of the regulationists. They tended to picture lodge practice not so much as a positive good but as an inevitable evil. An exemplar in this regard was the New York State Journal of Medicine. Only a few months after condemning attempts to expel lodge doctors from the state society, it effusively praised a successful boycott by the Port Jervis Medical Club of members with these contracts. It cautioned, however, that similar tactics were "scarcely applicable" to large cities where "owing [to] the lack of union and want of harmony among the thousands of individual members of the profession, . . . lodge practice has been of such insidious growth, fertilized by economical and revolutionary changes; its roots have penetrated so deeply that their dislodgment might do more harm than good."[55]

The apogee of regulationist influence came in 1913 when the Judicial Council of the AMA resolved that "lodge practice under certain circumstances is one of health insurance that must be accepted and controlled, not condemned and shunned." This lukewarm endorsement carried little force and was short on specifics. In the end even this minor regulationist triumph proved fleeting. Never again would the AMA give an imprimatur to a statement as favorable to lodge practice.[56]

The efforts by members of the medical profession to stem the lodge practice evil showed several parallels to campaigns launched at the time against "dispensary abuse." Dispensaries, like lodges, came under fire for serving patients who allegedly could pay regular fees. Other points of comparison were frequent claims by doctors that dispensaries subjected them to the exploitative whims of "the laity" (trustees), undercut prevailing fees in private practice, and encouraged patients' trivial complaints. On the other hand, many critics acknowledged that dispensaries, like lodges, afforded young doctors a means to build a patient base.[57]

From the standpoint of the patients, however, lodge practice had a significant advantage over the dispensary. The dispensary carried the unavoidable odor of charity and dependency. It had a reputation as a "medical soup kitchen." In this respect at least, lodge practice presented an appealing alternative to patients of modest means. In addition, prosperous members who did not use the medical services could receive satisfaction through helping other lodge members without inflicting the stigma of charity on either donor or recipient. The *Eagle Magazine* suggested that the chief beneficiaries were "those who need it most—the members in moderate circumstances, who have large families and much sickness. In furnishing a physician to such people, the Aerie is not only performing a brotherly act, but is doing service to the entire community." For much the same reason, a spokesman for the WC contrasted the mutual aid cheerily paid to the lodge member with the alms handed to "a charity patient, which is repugnant to the self-respecting man."[58]

The Decline of Lodge Practice

By the 1920s, lodge practice had entered a steep decline from which it never recovered. Large segments of the medical profession had launched an all-out war. Throughout the country, state societies imposed manifold sanctions against physicians who accepted lodge contracts. The medical societies of several states, including Pennsylvania, Michigan, California, Maine, and Vermont, recommended that offenders be barred from membership. "The evil is such a far-reaching one," warned the *Journal of the Michigan State Medical Society*, "that any measures to suppress it are justifiable." Other state professional organizations, such as those of West Virginia and Illinois, favored less draconian pressure on practitioners to sign pledges spurning lodge contracts.[59]

Some critics went even further and objected to any system of per capita payment. Zierath implored that contract practice "in every phase, as an institution, must be completely and absolutely abolished." The lodge doctor drew the heaviest fire. Even many of the fiercest critics, however, admitted some need for other forms of contract practice. The classic case was a company doctor in an isolated area, such as a lumber camp, where there were no fee-for-service alternatives. Contract practice could even be tolerated in an urban context when a doctor earned a high salary as an examiner for a commercial life insurance company.[60]

There was less willingness, however, to find extenuating circumstances for the lodge doctor. Dr. John B. Donaldson of Canonsburg, Pennsylvania, spoke for many: "As to lodge practice, to my mind it is simply contemptible and I see no excuse for its existence." The double standard did not escape the attention of lodges. An editorial in the *Eagle Magazine* claimed, with some exaggeration, that there were "few professional protests" against company doctors. "Does it make a difference," it asked, "whether the employer [of contract doctors] is a wealthy corporation, or a fraternity of humble citizens, most of them wage-earners?"[61]

County, rather than state, societies formed the vanguard of the movement to suppress lodge practice. The prototypical campaign began with the request that a doctor sign an agreement shunning lodge contracts or, at least, not provide services for fees under the "customary" rate. Sometimes this method worked, at least for a while. If the pariah failed to relent, he faced more serious retribution, such as forfeiture of membership or a boycott. In 1913, for example, members of the medical society in Port Jervis, New York, vowed that if any physician took a lodge contract, they would "refuse to consult with him or assist him in any way or in any emergency whatever." Sometimes the boycotts extended to patients. One method of enforcement was to pressure hospitals to close their doors to members of the guilty lodge. By 1914, in the *Journal of the American Medical Association* Dr. Robert Allen could write, with but slight exaggeration, "There is scarcely a city in the country in which medical societies have not issued edicts against members who accept contracts for lodge practice."[62]

Reports in the medical journals suggest that these restrictions were effective. One example occurred in Bristol, Pennsylvania, where local physicians boycotted the lone lodge doctor in the area. As word of the campaign spread, "patrons gradually withdrew from him, his calls for attendance were few, and this last summer he quietly left the town and vicinity." In a similar case a member of the Loyal Order of Moose in Fort Dodge, Iowa, charged that doctors in his community had run the local lodge "into the ground" by going on strike.[63]

In pursuing such tactics the medical societies consciously emulated the treatment of the "scab" by labor unions. Ironically, many of these same doctors roundly condemned the behavior of the working class in other contexts. Even so, the analogy they drew between the labor union and the medical society had merit. Both shared the pursuit of higher income for members and the desire to discipline nonconformists who refused to contribute to organizational solidarity. Holtzapple, for instance, sounded almost like Walter Reuther when he proclaimed that "we are 'our brother's keeper' and our liberty to accept a contract ceases when its effects are detrimental to the well-being of our profession." In like manner the *West Virginia Medical Journal* recommended that "working men themselves, the chief beneficiaries of this form of practice, should decline to enter into an arrangement that compels men of education to engage in the very thing that the labor unions so bitterly denounce, namely, the cutting in prices of labor, in effect, 'black sheeping.'" Zierath admired the labor union model and urged his coprofessionals to take heart from the "hard-earned" concessions that unions had extracted from "money-mad and oppressive corporations."[64]

As the medical profession tightened the noose around lodge practice, fraternal societies reacted with mounting frustration. In 1910 a national official of the FOE bemoaned that a "great many of our Subordinate Aeries have encountered no end of trouble during the last year trying to secure the services of a competent physician. Medical associations and societies every where have placed their mark of disapproval on the Aerie physician." Two years later the supreme leader of the Loyal Order of Moose complained of the "utter impossibility" for many lodges "to procure a competent physician under the terms provided by the laws of the Order."[65]

Fraternal societies tried to counterattack by coordinating efforts to import physicians from outside the community. This worked on occasion but, in general, was far too expensive and cumbersome. A few lodges contemplated payment of fees high enough to pass muster with the medical societies, but for the vast majority the expense was prohibitive. By the second decade of the twentieth century, stepped-up pressure from doctors motivated many orders to rethink and then reluctantly abandon lodge practice. Indicative of the transformation was the experience of the FOE. In 1905, after numerous queries from lodges, Conrad Mann, the grand worthy president, cautioned that it "would be unwise . . . to dispense with the services of the Aerie Physician entirely as this has undoubtedly proven one of the strongest factors in the upbuilding of our Order." By 1911 Mann had completely shifted his stance. He now advised that were he a member of an aerie facing a boycott of doctors, he would vote to pay higher cash sick benefits and dispense with the lodge doctor. A year later his counterpart in the Loyal Order of Moose suggested the same course of action.[66]

A court verdict in Montana significantly altered the situation. The details illustrate the difficulties faced by the proponents of lodge practice. The incident began when Clarence A. Case, an operator for the Associated Press, sought admission for an operation at the St. John's Hospital in Helena. Because the hospital did not employ physicians, it required patients to contract with and pay for their own doctors. Case selected Dr. John G. Thompson. The hospital managers denied admission to Case on the ground that the Lewis and Clark Medical Society had found his doctor guilty of unethical behavior. The sole charge against Thompson was that he had served as lodge doctor for both the FOE and the Loyal Order of Moose. Later that day, St. Peter's, another Catholic hospital in Helena, used the same justification to deny admission to Case. Case was one of Thompson's private patients. He was not a member of the FOE.[67]

Within a few days Thompson had filed suit in the district court to compel the hospital to admit Case. His attorney asserted that the action of the medical society was "simply a movement on the part of the doctors to so throttle and so coerce the hospitals in this city that they were compelled to assent to this agreement or else suffer a boycott." The suit also alleged that the hospital, as a tax-exempt charitable corporation, had an obligation to admit all licensed physicians in the state. Not surprisingly, Thompson obtained the enthusiastic support of the local lodges of the FOE and the Loyal Order of Moose. Four members of the Lewis and Clark Medical Society testified against him.[68]

Despite the determined efforts of the fraternal orders to rally public sympathy, Thompson lost. The district court ruled that the hospital had the power as a private corporation to deny access. The judge endorsed the contention of the Lewis and Clark Society that it was defending professional ethics. He concluded that the doctors had the "right to maintain the ethics of the association just the same as any labor union." The judge suggested that the fraternal societies always had the option of building and maintaining a hospital organized under "unethical rules."[69]

The officials of Helena Aerie of the FOE vowed to fight back. They boldly announced plans to build a hospital and sent a resolution to the national aerie asking its aid in appealing the case to the state supreme court. Helena Aerie warned that the ruling, unless reversed, would be a dangerous legal precedent in other states, "thus rendering inoperative one of the most important features of our Fraternity." After some consideration the national aerie recommended against an appeal, evasively suggesting that it was unnecessary because of the plans to establish a hospital. More importantly, it expressed concern that an adverse court decision "would be cited as authority by the Medical Associations all over the jurisdiction, and might operate to the great detriment of the Fraternal Order of Eagles generally." The Helena lodge's hospital, despite much talk, never materialized.[70]

Conclusion

The perception of the Grand Aerie that it would lose an appeal was realistic. The prevailing legal climate of the Progressive Era was not conducive to such a proposition. At few times in American history have elites, including judges, been so willing to defer to the acknowledged experts. The courts, when given a choice, took the side of medical associations as the recognized gatekeepers of the profession.

Some societies were able to withstand assault better than others. Lodge practice survived, and sometimes thrived, in the WC and many of the predominantly black lodges in New Orleans well into the 1930s and, in a few instances, still later. Until the 1950s, lodge practice was also an important feature of the International Worker's Order, a society affiliated with the Communist Party. Most of these organizations shared an important advantage over mainstream societies such as the FOE in that they could rely on ethnic or ideological solidarity to carry them through a crisis. Doctors remained loyal to the International Worker's Order for political as much as economic reasons. A slightly different dynamic applied to black organizations, which could draw upon a relatively closed ethnic market.[71]

Lodge practice was also a victim of an overall shrinkage in the supply of physicians due to a relentless campaign of professional "birth control" imposed by the medical societies. In 1910, for example, the United States had 164 doctors per 100,000 people, compared with only 125 in 1930. This shift occurred in great part because of increasingly tight state certification requirements. Fewer doctors not only translated into higher medical fees but also weaker bargaining power for lodges. Meanwhile, the number of medical schools plummeted from a high of 166 in 1904 to 81 in 1922. The hardest hit were the proprietary schools, a prime recruiting avenue for lodges.[72]

By the end of the 1920s, lodge practice had been pushed to the margins of health care. This rapid reversal of fortunes was startling. Until the 1910s both fraternalists and medical society leaders had regarded lodge practice as the wave of the future. A decade later the subject rarely rated even a mention in the medical journals. As lodge practice fell by the wayside, other forms of fraternal medical care actually enjoyed a period of expansion. The designers of these experiments often carefully crafted them to withstand or circumvent the objections of the medical profession. Some societies decided that it was time to take the boldest step of all: build their own hospitals.

CHAPTER SEVEN

It Almost Bled the System White

"Politics" was one of the dirty words of fraternalism. The writings and rituals of societies repeatedly celebrated the lodge's splendid isolation from the cares and controversies of the outside world, including those involving governmental policies. Reality increasingly dictated otherwise, however. By the late nineteenth century, fraternalists found that political questions could not be ignored. As early as the 1870s, legislatures in various states began to consider laws to regulate life insurance societies. Because "old liners" often supported these restrictions, fraternalists charged, with much accuracy, that the motivation was to quash bothersome competitors.[1]

In part, the formation of the NFC in 1885 was a defensive measure against this trend. Through cooperative effort, the organizers hoped to thwart inimical legislation. In 1890 the Committee on Legislation of the NFC recommended that no law "subjecting the fraternal orders to State control in any way should be permitted to be enacted." Even legislation that had the apparent purpose of shielding the established orders from "fraudulent" competitors met with suspicion. In 1891 an article in the *Fraternal Monitor* criticized a law recently passed for this purpose by New Hampshire's state legislature. The writer charged that such legislation invariably paved the way for unintended and highly destructive consequences: "If the people get in the dangerous habit of thinking that their law givers can protect them from frauds, they will lean upon a broken stick every time[,] for frauds can purchase or wheedle such laws out of our Solons with a small percentage of their plunder faster than solid, honest enterprise can procure their repeal."[2]

Even so, the NFC recommended a Uniform Law in 1892 for enactment by the states. The law defined the parameters of a fraternal society in broad terms: "Each Association shall have a lodge system, with ritualistic form of work and representative form of government, and shall make provision for the payment of benefits in case of sickness, disability or death of its members, subject to their compliance with its constitution and laws." It encouraged disclosure through required annual reports. Benefits such as child insurance, endowments, and tontines were not mentioned. This was no small matter, as it served to codify and reaffirm state legislation and court rulings that banned societies from providing these kinds of insurance.[3]

Keep Your Reserve in Your Pocket

The political debates about the Uniform Law are impossible to appreciate without a review of the financial methods of fraternal orders. During the late nineteenth century most societies relied on postmortem assessments. Usually members paid the same premium regardless of age. Under the simplest version, societies required an equal per capita assessment (usually $1.00) upon the death of a member. Some promised a death benefit of $1,000; others offered as much as $2,000. The earliest life insurance society to use this method, the AOUW, vested the power of assessment in a grand lodge. Later many organizations disbursed payments of death benefits through a national office. Gradually they adopted other reforms to make the process less ponderous and more predictable. Instead of charging a separate levy after each death, for example, societies tried to collect a fixed number of assessments to pay all claims.[4]

Despite some modifications, the postmortem approach continued to predominate until the 1890s. The appeal of this method rested on its simplicity and apparent equity. Fraternalists defended it as pay-as-you-go insurance that was sold at cost. Although some societies attempted to accumulate reserves, these never amounted to much. The consensus was that a reserve was a "fifth wheel for a wagon" and opened the door to corruption. When an official of the AOUW proposed creation of a reserve, the members overwhelmingly voted it down. Nathan S. Boynton, a former president of the NFC, declared in 1899 that a "nest egg is a good thing, but when one piles up the eggs, keeps on accumulating them, and does not dispose of them either in paying legitimate claims or putting them under the hen that hatches big, well developed chickens, they will soon spoil and become useless."[5]

On the surface the early experience with the assessment system was a stunning success. Societies attracted millions of Americans and posed stiff competition to the old-line companies. A direct comparison of fraternal and old-line rates shows why. In 1896 the median annual assessment paid by members of the twenty-nine leading fraternal orders was just over $10 per $1,000 of insurance. An annual premium for a leading old-line policy of the same value, by contrast, was about $20 for a man at age twenty-five and $48 at age fifty.[6]

From Financial Crisis to Readjustment

This happy state of affairs did not last as societies faced the demands of aging memberships. Between 1887 and 1895, for example, the average annual death rate for twenty-five large life insurance orders rose from 7.17 to 10.04. In several extreme cases it more than doubled. Increased death rates resulted in higher and more frequent assessment calls. The extra charges undermined an important attraction for joining: low-cost insurance. Unable to carry the added weight of mounting assessments, younger members dropped out by the thousands and turned to companies or newer, "cheaper rate" societies. As a result, the older organizations faced the bleak prospect of an elderly and dwindling membership base.[7]

Despite this problem, the assessment system was viable, at least in theory. Several special conditions were necessary for success, however. The prerequisite was an educated and dedicated membership fully aware of the long-term consequences of the arrangement. More specifically, the assessment system, at least for life insurance, stood and fell on the willingness of the old and the young to stay loyal even when that meant higher rates over time.[8]

The assessment method had its longest track record of success in the orders that offered primarily sick and funeral benefits. The local lodges in these organizations were responsible for raising the money for sick and funeral benefits. In an exhaustive study of the IOOF in British Columbia, John Charles Herbert Emery concluded that the system was sound and durable despite its reliance on the pure assessment principle. Lodges often paid substantial sick benefits for decades in open violation of the "eternal" rules laid down by the actuaries. The lodges accomplished this because of extra revenue generated from profits on assets, such as rentals from meeting halls. In addition, because of visiting committees, they were able to police malingering and maintain solidarity.[9]

For the life insurance orders these conditions did not generally apply, at least not to the degree necessary for long-term stability. During the early days their leaders, usually with complete sincerity, had held out the promise that a low assessment for all ages could always continue. When these promises proved unfounded, many members reacted with hostility and skepticism. Not surprisingly, their first inclinations were either to deny the problem or to blame it on incompetence or corruption.[10]

Even when they could no longer explain away the signs of crisis, some societies tried hard to sustain the assessment approach. They struggled to hold down increases in the average age by launching aggressive campaigns to infuse "new blood." If this strategy failed, as it generally did, societies appealed directly to the young to pay the higher assessments rather than drop out. By that time, however, it was usually too late. The leaders had the unenviable task of explaining to members why their earlier promises of cheap rates for both old and young had been wrong.[11]

A few societies tried to skirt the consequences by compromising or abandoning their reliance on whole life insurance and instituting term policies. Whole life extended throughout the entire life of the member; term policies either expired at a specific age or at the end of a set period. When a term policy expired, societies typically gave the member the option of renewing at a much higher assessment. Some fraternalists defended term policies, asserting that "old men" without dependents did not truly need life insurance. In the end, however, few societies were willing to abandon their reliance on whole life policies, at least for new members. The marketing appeal was too strong to resist.[12]

Efforts to retain members probably worked best when deeper loyalties, such as religious belief, ethnicity, or ideology, held together the rank and file. Such ties were strongest in small, neighborhood-oriented societies that depended on local knowledge and mutual trust. Officials in old-line companies noted the durability of fraternal ties with astonishment and more than a little envy. In 1904 Walter S. Nichols marveled that "associations which, measured by ordinary mercantile standards, would be pronounced hopelessly insolvent, have been carried along for years through the loyal support of their members."[13]

Even under the best conditions the assessment method included a bothersome element of instability. The number of assessment calls from year to year could vary wildly. They could reach almost unbearable levels during unanticipated crises such as the yellow fever outbreak of the late 1870s. More to the point, it was expecting a great deal of young members to remain loyal without firmer guarantees of future benefits.[14]

But fraternal societies were able to transform themselves to meet new conditions. They increasingly turned their backs on the old system, at least in its purest form. Most organizations founded during the late nineteenth century instituted graded rather than equal assessments. The size of premiums varied with entry but remained level throughout the life of the member. Two of the first societies to adopt graded assessments were the Royal Arcanum (1877) and the IOF (1881). Under the plan of the Foresters the lifetime annual dues for new members gradually increased from 40 cents per month at age eighteen to 60 cents at age forty and finally to $1.85 at age fifty-four. The trend was unmistakable even in the older societies. By the 1890s organizations such as the AOUW had adopted graded assessments, although many hedged by limiting the reform to new members.[15]

Graded assessments were a necessary but rarely sufficient condition for the achievement of actuarial solvency. Current fraternal rates, even under graded assessments, were still too low to accumulate an adequate reserve. By the middle of the 1890s, death rates and the numbers of assessment calls of the oldest societies continued to rise. An extreme example was that of the Knights of Honor established in 1873. By 1894 an aging membership had already resulted in a death rate of 16 per 1,000. Ten years later it was more than 34 per 1,000, while the membership had plummeted from 119,785 to 49,000. The steep decline of the Knights of Honor was unusual, but almost every society faced pressure. Fraternal leaders gradually became convinced that unless they took drastic action, there would be no revenue to pay future benefits as they came due.[16]

These continuing problems spurred the second phase of readjustment: increased premiums. The process began in earnest just after the turn of the century when several life insurance orders, including the Knights of the Maccabees, the LOTM, the AOUW, and the Knights of Columbus, made the plunge. Within the next decade scores of other societies had followed suit and substantially increased premiums. In 1895 the monthly premium for a new member of the IOF at age twenty-five was 67 cents, but by 1908 it was $1.05. During this same period premiums for those at age fifty-four rose from $3.00 to $4.31. The IOF followed the now standard practice of applying the increased rates to old as well as new members. The elderly, who had been the main beneficiaries of the old rates, therefore suffered the most from the rate hikes.[17]

The readjustment movement benefited greatly from the support of respected individuals and organizations in the fraternal world. The NFC became a major force for age-based premiums and the creation of reserve funds. Even the *Spectator*, an old-line journal, reported that the convention of the NFC in 1896 revealed that the "general trend of opinion seems to be toward a rearrangement of rates and the establishment of reserve funds by the leading orders."[18]

In 1898 the NFC took the bold step of authorizing a table of mortality for societies to use as the basis for their new rates. The campaign for readjustment won support from prominent fraternal publicists, officials, and actuaries such as Abb Landis, Myron Sackett, and Walter Basye. In 1905 George E. West wrote that most fraternal officials had realized "that the once popular doctrines of 'new blood,' 'average age,' 'reserve in the members' pockets,' etc., have little value [and are] as worthless and delusive as is a mirage to the wanderer in the desert."[19]

The critical challenge, of course, was to convince ordinary members. The best way to accomplish this was to discredit detractors as defenders of untenable cheap-rate and current-cost societies. The LOTM, one of the first societies to adopt new rates, made effective use of this method. In 1908 the theme of readjustment became a recruiting tool in "A Maccabee Playlet," which appeared in the *Ladies Review*. One of the characters delivered the following warning: "Now dear, don't you get led away with any of them cheap-rate societies. They can't give somethin' for nothin' any better than you or I could and keep it up. If they don't go to pieces altogether, they'll be collectin' so many assessments a month after a few years that you'll finally pay more than in ours where everything is planned out to be just at cost. Guess you wouldn't call your groceries cheap 'cause you were getting them on credit, would you?"[20]

The defenders of readjustment rejected claims that the adoption of old-line methods, such as reserves, would lead to the triumph of cold-blooded commercialism. To those who feared a diminution of fraternity, Abb Landis pointed to the experience of British friendly societies. Their ties of mutuality still remained powerful despite the fact that, unlike their American counterparts, they had embraced higher rates and reserves for several decades. Basye disputed the contention that readjustment was unfair to those who had "borne the heat and burden of the day." To the contrary, he declared, "appropriating the reserves belonging to new members to meet the deficiency of old members" would be "the grossest kind of inequity."[21]

Many societies were able to smooth the transition to readjustment by instituting level premiums. Under this arrangement, premiums did not increase throughout the life of the member but were still high enough to accumulate a sufficient reserve. A major advantage of this system was its appeal to the fraternal penchant for simplicity and equity. Conversion to a level-premium system, however, entailed enormous short-term costs. The greatest burdens fell on the elderly, who often paid the costs accumulated under the earlier reliance on cheap rates.[22]

Americans could have avoided much of the ordeal of readjustment had they heeded the experience of the friendly societies in Great Britain and Australia. As Basye put it, "History repeats itself. The conditions of the English societies described in 1850 were almost identical to the conditions of our societies of 1900." The first major organization to run into serious trouble was the Manchester Unity during the early 1840s. As the oldest friendly society, it faced creeping financial costs because of an aging membership. Internal debate racked the society, but in 1853 the central committee instituted graded rates for sick and funeral benefits as well as reserves. It completed the final phase of readjustment in 1870. One by one, other societies followed suit, including the AOF and the GUOOF. Though the leadership of both organizations faced bitter opposition, including secession, they were able to make the changes stick. The last wave of British readjustment came in the 1880s. In all, the process had taken nearly fifty years.[23]

At the time, events in England and Australia had made little to no impression on the American fraternal orders, which continued to embrace equal assessments and low reserves. In part, this attitude resulted from an understandable skepticism of the applicability of the British model. The friendly societies, after all, focused almost exclusively on sick and funeral benefits and medical services and thus seemed to be moving on an entirely different organizational track. But attitudes changed dramatically during the actuarial crisis of the 1890s and early 1900s. The American fraternal advocates of readjustment embraced the British model as their own. For Landis the actuarial crisis gave the lie to the view that American life insurance orders were unique. To the contrary, it illustrated that the "same underlying principles govern in the business operation of Friendly Societies and Fraternal Orders," including the eternal laws of mortality.[24]

Moreover, Landis asserted that closer scrutiny revealed that the other differences between British and American societies were not really large. He noted that the recent trend among the friendly societies was to offer life insurance as well as sick benefits. The leading example was the Manchester Unity. During the 1890s it began to guarantee death benefits of £200 (about $1,000), an amount comparable to the promises of many American life insurance orders. Unlike most fraternal orders, the Unity did not rely on the assessment method. From the beginning it backed its life insurance with sufficient reserves and rates. This insurance plan even inspired praise from the old-line *Life Insurance Independent*, a publication that rarely had kind words for American societies. Even so, attempts to draw parallels can be overdone. Despite the foray of the Manchester Unity into life insurance, sick and funeral benefits always remained the major focus of British societies.[25]

Fraternalism versus Paternalism

By the first decade of the twentieth century few fraternal leaders openly questioned the desirability of "adequate rates." Instead the topic of debate shifted to what role, if any, government would play in achieving this goal. On one side were advocates of a regulatory hands-off policy on rates and reserves. They drew support from the low-rate societies, as one might expect, and from some leading advocates of readjustment. On the other side were those who called for greater regulation through state law and insurance commissions. These individuals, once a small minority among fraternal officials, slowly gained influence. Others who addressed the issue shifted between camps, often with considerable ease and opportunism.

Both sides mobilized their forces in 1900 when the NFC recommended that states enact a new, uniform law. Critics called it the Force Bill. The name fit. The older societies had expressly tailored it to their needs. They inserted a provision denying approval to societies charging less than the rates given in the NFC table. The proposed law applied this standard selectively, however, through a grandfather clause that exempted societies that were already licensed. Few organizations, established or otherwise, had yet adopted these rates. Harsh though this provision was, the supporters of the Force Bill justified it as necessary to give breathing space for readjustment by preventing "unfair" competition from the cheap-rate societies. One proponent declared matter-of-factly that "competition is somewhat *too* rife" and described the formation of new societies as "an evil."[26]

The Force Bill met with determined fraternal opposition. The newer societies, of course, aligned against it. About forty of them organized the Associated Fraternities of America (AFA) as a rival to the NFC. In a characterization that came uncomfortably close to the truth, C. H. Robinson, the first president of the AFA, described the Force Bill as a paternalistic ploy by the fraternal old guard to quash rivals. Robinson and his allies wanted to leave the societies more or less alone to decide rates and reserves. He compared the leaders of the NFC to the "Pharisees and Hypocrites of the Scriptures" who while eager to "bind burdens grievous to be borne and place them upon the shoulders of others," do not "propose to touch the burdens with one of its fingers." As several advocates of stricter legislation later noted, the harsh double standard of the Force Bill was difficult to ignore.[27]

The AFA was not the only center of opposition to this legislation. Objectors included such longtime advocates of readjustment as Landis and the editors of the *Fraternal Monitor*, the chief publication among the life insurance orders. Nearly all the opponents had one thing in common: they linked their case to a general critique of expansive and meddling government. In 1900, for example, the *Fraternal Monitor* editorialized that the "government is best which governs least." Six years later it warned "that the State, as represented by State officials, should not undertake to think for the individual." It cited the recent wave of voluntary readjustment as evidence that the societies should "be left to work out their destinies according to the light and experience they have," and warned that "interests having nothing in common with the fraternal system should be required to keep hands off so long as it [the readjustment] is progressing so satisfactorily." [28]

In rhetoric reminiscent of Thomas Paine's *Common Sense*, Landis characterized the Force Bill as part of an effort by the bureaucratic forces of "the State" to stifle the creative forces of "Society." By Society he meant organizations for mutual assistance, such as fraternal orders. "Although the *Society* generally and the *State*," he declared, "are intimately connected with and dependent on each other, of the two, *Society* is greater." Landis exhorted Americans to be "more jealous of their sovereignty" and to "check the present tendency toward imperialism so plainly evidenced in the prevailing disposition of office holders to assume the attitude of *rulers* over subjects." Fraternalists who used this rhetoric often did not apply the theory to issues not involving rates and reserves. Many "laissez-faire" fraternalists had supported legislation and court rulings against societies that paid endowments or child insurance. [29]

The defenders of the hands-off approach, like the advocates of readjustment, favored the British model. They pointed out that the friendly societies had readjusted with a minimum of governmental interference. Legislation by Parliament, such as the Act of 1896, had rested primarily on the principle of publicity and featured a requirement that each society hire an actuary to undertake a valuation. This valuation, which included information on assets, liabilities, and contribution tables, took place every five years. The main purpose of the Act of 1896 was to keep members fully abreast of the condition of their societies and spur them to take the necessary measures to ensure solvency. The British made exception to regulatory laissez-faire by restricting death benefits to a maximum of £200 on adults and £10 on children. Most friendly societies did not find either provision a great hindrance. At the time, they paid average death benefits for adults of £10 (about $50). [30]

For critics of the Force Bill the British system represented a desirable model of bureaucratic restraint and simplicity. They singled out for praise the requirement for valuations of the Act of 1896. The process was relatively unobtrusive because it occurred in five-year intervals, and it was more likely to reflect long-term financial stability than a valuation conducted annually. More importantly to opponents of the Force Bill, the British act left the friendly societies otherwise free to exercise self-government and implement corrective measures on their own terms. "Abuses cannot thrive in the light of day," Landis asserted, "and the only needed legislation is that which will assure full and complete publicity." The critics of the Force Bill summed up their legislative agenda by taking every opportunity to reiterate the slogan "Freedom and Publicity."[31]

The campaign against the Force Bill was largely successful. Through extensive lobbying and publicity the AFA fought the NFC to a standstill. In the end the Force Bill became law in only seven states. Hopes for achieving the general goal of limiting legislation to the principles of freedom and publicity, however, gradually dissipated. By 1908 the leaders of the AFA increasingly accepted the view that restrictive legislation would come. The terms of debate no longer centered on the desirability of increased regulation on rates and reserves but on the details.[32]

The shift in attitudes did not primarily occur because fraternalists had lost faith in the progress and inevitability of readjustment. Indeed, the number of societies willing to take significant steps in this direction continued to increase. The best explanation for the change of heart was the growing influence of new power alignments. For fraternalists the course of events increasingly demonstrated that if they did not control the law-writing process, others who were antagonistic to their interests would. This defensive strategy coexisted with and reinforced the older goals of the established societies, such as curtailing bothersome competition and speeding readjustment.

The first decade of the twentieth century brought a handful of proposed schemes for the federal government to regulate fraternal societies. One was put forward in 1904 by Senator John Dryden, better known as the founder and president of the Prudential Insurance Company. The bill would have barred from the mails all printed matter of fraternal life insurance orders. In justifying the proposal Dryden equated the societies with lotteries and fraudulent enterprises. Although the bill was never taken seriously, fraternalists viewed it as an ominous portent.[33]

Proposals in state legislatures to regulate fraternal insurance made more headway. The most serious was the Vorys model law, which had been put forward by the National Convention of Insurance Commissioners in 1902. It proposed restrictions on rates, assets, business operation, and valuation for old and new societies that made the NFC's Force Bill look liberal by comparison. The pressure continued to build. Speaking to the convention of the commissioners in 1909, James R. Young, the insurance commissioner of North Carolina, summarized the views of his colleagues. He vowed that if fraternal societies did not take the legislative initiative, it would become "the imperative duty of the members of this body . . . to take hold of and do their best to perform the task." [34]

The Mobile Law

Within a year of Young's not so subtle threat (and others like it), the NFC and the AFA forged a working alliance with the National Association of State Insurance Commissioners. Representatives from the three groups met, framed, and proposed a new uniform law. Known as the Mobile Law, it formalized the existing case and statutory law. It defined a fraternal society as a nonprofit organization with a lodge system, representative government, ritual, and tax exemption. Other provisions recognized powers that the societies could exercise and their commercial competitors could not. For example, it recognized a "reserve right to assess" under which societies were able to raise rates on existing policies by permission of the membership. In addition, the law made it illegal to garnish any fraternal policy for debt. [35]

The Mobile Law was a big step away from the old ideals of freedom and publicity. Its restrictions hindered organizational operation and served to limit fraternal behavior to a narrower realm. The most controversial requirement was that each society must show a gradual improvement in reserves. In the event a lodge failed to achieve this goal, the state insurance commission could revoke its license. With minor exceptions the Mobile Law barred rates that were any lower than those in the NFC table. Additionally, the Mobile Law required a doctor's examination for all policies, stipulated payment of death benefits, and most importantly, proscribed "speculative" enterprises such as the payment of endowments or extension of credit to members. One proponent of this type of regulation argued that it was unfraternal to "supply credit for business deals, to provide money for the payment of a member's debts, or to do a banking business." [36]

Opponents of the Mobile Law, emulating the tactics of the AFA, marshaled their forces into a separate organization, the Federated Fraternities, and embraced the old rallying cry of "freedom and publicity." One of the critics, Z. H. Austin, a consulting actuary, classified the Mobile Law as a scheme to confer "arbitrary powers upon insurance commissioners" and undermine the freedom of action and competitive edge of societies through debilitating constraints.[37]

Another opponent, Carl W. Kimpton, feared that the Mobile Law would bring the death of societies by eliminating a defining feature of fraternalism: self-government. He argued that such power was meaningless unless it embodied the right of the members to establish operating plans on an assessment basis. According to Kimpton, advocates of regulation had become so obsessed with the flaws of cheap rates that they had been blinded to the virtues. Assessment insurance, he noted, had successfully provided years of low-cost insurance protection for millions of lower-income Americans. Kimpton quoted a well-known fraternal leader who was convinced that if "these societies should fail to-day, no one would have lost a penny because the money collected has been properly expended and gone to the widows and orphans."[38]

Despite these efforts the critics were on the losing side. The power alignments had changed greatly since the ill-fated Force Bill. Most importantly, the economic constituency for a hands-off policy on rates and reserves, which had once been formidable, had dwindled. Ironically, the new attitudes resulted in part from the success of readjustment. The recent willingness of societies to abandon the postmortem approach and raise rates also weakened the motivation to fight legal rate restrictions.[39]

By 1910 more restrictive legislation seemed inevitable. A factor in the shift was the increased political power and legitimacy of state insurance commissions, but there were also ideological reasons. Like other Americans, fraternalists had lost much of their suspicion of interventionist legislation during the Progressive Era. In a speech at the National Convention of Insurance Commissioners, D. P. Markey of the Knights of the Maccabees noted that some still thought "that there should be no standard whatever; but that valuation and publicity should govern wholly here as in England . . . that each should have whatever rates it pleases, use whatever standard it pleases." Markey rejected this position, stating that this "is not the feeling in America generally. We have become educated along the line of legislation." None other than Abb Landis joined the campaign for restriction by becoming an active player in the effort to draft and implement uniform legislation.[40]

The backers of the Mobile Law soon routed their opponents. Victory came in 1912 when the Federated Fraternities capitulated by endorsing the proposal, now rechristened the New York Conference Law, after securing several minor amendments. As a result, the Federated Fraternities no longer had a rationale for existence and dwindled into oblivion. There were other signs of an emerging legislative consensus among societies. In 1913 the NFC and the AFA merged to form the National Fraternal Congress of America (NFCA). This new organization soon had no rivals, and by 1919 its campaign for the ideals of the New York Conference Law, widely dubbed the "fraternal law of the land," had achieved victory in forty states.[41]

Conclusion

By the early 1920s the process of readjustment was substantially complete, at least for the societies in the NFCA. It had truly been a baptism by fire. During the transition period, societies had to contend not only with the normal costs of raising premiums but also the disruptions of World War I and the deadly influenza epidemic in 1918 and 1919. According to Edward J. Dunn, the process of readjustment had "literally played hell with the fraternal beneficiary system and with our individual societies. Second and third readjustments, forced upon our already mangled societies, made matters all the worse and almost bled the system white."[42]

Dunn overstated the problem somewhat. As a whole, the membership in life insurance orders continued to increase. The number of fraternal certificates nearly doubled from 4.7 million in 1904 to 8.5 million in 1920. In relative terms, however, the societies were losing ground. Fraternal policies represented 49.3 percent of the value of all life insurance in force in 1908, but by 1928 the percentage had fallen to only 9.1. For both the members and the leaders of societies, the 1920s proved to be a time of questioning. Would there be a future for fraternal orders, many asked, and if so, what form would it take?[43]

CHAPTER EIGHT

It Substitutes Paternalism for Fraternalism

T he endorsement of the New York Conference Law by the NFCA did not signal a complete change of heart about the role of government. The leading fraternal publications, such as the *Fraternal Monitor* and the *Western Review*, provide ample evidence of a continuing aversion to intrusive bureaucracy and paternalism. This hostility greatly intensified when the NFCA and other fraternal organizations launched a vigorous and ultimately successful campaign against proposals for compulsory health insurance.

It would have been easy to dismiss opponents as foolishly swimming against an inexorable tide. Many academicians and politicians predicted that compulsory insurance, which had spread throughout much of Europe, was only a matter of time. The American Association for Labor Legislation (AALL) began to lay the groundwork in 1912. At first it moved slowly because it was still in the midst of a successful push for workmen's compensation. The membership of the AALL included such progressive luminaries as John R. Commons, Irving Fisher, and Richard T. Ely. Its campaign slogan touting compulsory health insurance as the "next great step in social legislation" did not seem out of line.[1]

In 1915 the AALL put forward a model law for enactment by the states. The provisions combined elements of the German and British systems. The proposed law would have covered nearly all manual workers earning less than $1,200 per year. It would have offered extensive services including burial benefits, maternity insurance, cash disability, hospitalization, and nursing home care. Employers and workers would each pay 40 percent of the total costs; the rest would come from taxpayers. The law also provided for the creation of hundreds of district mutual funds to serve as "carrier organizations." Employers and workers would each select half the officials in charge of the funds. An insurance commission appointed by the governor would have ultimate authority.[2]

Initially, organized medicine seemed to be favorable to compulsory insurance. Dr. Frederick Green, the secretary of the Council on Health and Public Instruction of the AMA, praised the model law as "so entirely in line with our own that I want to be of every possible assistance." In the next few months the AALL made further revisions to please organized medicine, including free choice of doctors through a panel system and pro rata compensation based on the number of visits. These changes represented a departure from foreign models, which relied on capitation or straight salaries.[3]

Many doctors were receptive because they hoped that compulsory insurance would free them from lodge practice. At an early stage in the campaign the AMA's Committee on Social Insurance predicted that it would finally end the "commercial haggling" of lodges and their practice of "bidding down the struggling doctors to a minimum." It depicted compulsory insurance as a lifeline to rescue "the unfortunate physician who, facing starvation, must accept this lodge practice." At the meeting of the Committee on Medical Economics of the New York Academy of Medicine, a defender of the AALL's plan pointed out that the average income of physicians in Britain had increased since the introduction of compulsory insurance. In addition, the medical societies of Pennsylvania and Wisconsin gave compulsory health insurance their official support. The resolution in Wisconsin carried without a dissenting vote. Its author was W. F. Zierath of Sheboygan, one of the most spirited opponents of lodge practice.[4]

The Opposition to Compulsory Health Insurance

Before 1916 the main opponents to compulsory insurance were the commercial casualty and life companies, labor unions, and fraternal societies. The commercial companies drew the hardest line, especially after the AALL proudly (and as events proved, foolishly) announced that they would not have any role in the system. Organized labor was more divided. Although several state labor federations endorsed compulsory insurance, the American Federation of Labor was emphatically opposed. Like fraternalists, labor opponents condemned the AALL's plan as paternalistic and destructive to self-help. They also voiced fears that such a plan would be used as precedent to undermine the independence of unions.[5]

Fraternal opposition predated the AALL proposal. In 1907, for example, the *Fraternal Monitor* condemned state-provided health, accident, and life insurance and predicted that it would sap "that spirit of self-reliance so essential for continued progress and prosperity. We become a people of leaners instead of workers." Two years later the *Ladies Review* featured an editorial about a pension law recently enacted in Great Britain. According to the writer, most Americans regarded such plans "as savoring too strongly of the paternal in govern-ment and putting a premium on improvidence." Any government scheme would fail, she warned, if it ignored the moral of the old story about the race be-tween the "ant and the sluggard."[6]

Fraternal hostility hardened and intensified after Great Britain took steps to enact compulsory old-age insurance. "No thoughtful person who has studied history," the Fraternal Monitor commented, "and who realizes that govern-ments are consumers not creators of wealth, can watch the drift of things with-out a growing feeling of apprehension." Smith W. Bennett expanded on this theme at the joint conference of the NFC and the AFA. He criticized assorted movements for social welfare legislation and warned that state insurance could sound the "death knell of fraternal insurance in this country."[7]

Despite the mounting evidence of fraternal opposition, the officials of the AALL hoped to win over "farseeing labor and fraternal leaders." The basis for their optimism was the favorable precedent of Great Britain, where the friendly societies had initially fought compulsory insurance but had later given their assent. One reason for this about-face was a provision in the Act of 1911 that gave the societies official status as carrier organizations. The leaders of the AALL sensed that the same shift in opinion was beginning in the United States. They took heart from the few American fraternalists who had made positive refer-ences to compulsory insurance.[8]

The FOE was particularly receptive to the idea. In 1914 an article in the Eagle Magazine praised that part of the British plan that designated friendly societies as carrier organizations. The article pointed out that certain American societies, the "foremost" of which was the FOE, were in an excellent position to perform this role. Despite these statements, however, the FOE never went on record in favor of compulsory health insurance.[9]

A more vocal fraternal supporter of compulsory insurance was former con-gressman John J. Lentz, the founder and president of the American Insurance Union and a member of the Board of Governors of Mooseheart. In 1916 he spoke in favor of compulsory insurance at a conference sponsored by the AALL. Lentz contended that it was impossible "to meet the awful problems of misery and poverty except by universal insurance." He charged that those who cried the loudest against "paternalism or some other 'ism' [had] always served the purpose of mud on the wheels of progress." As an alternative he appealed to Giuseppe Mazzini's dictum, "Democracy is the progress of all, through all, un-der the leadership of the wisest."[10]

As part of the AALL's effort to woo fraternal orders, its model law offered them certain advantages. One provision gave workers the right to opt out of the state fund entirely and have that portion of the premiums paid to a fraternal order or a labor union. Should they do this, the employer's portion would be paid into a central guarantee fund for times of emergency. There was a catch. Had the model law been enacted, the societies and the unions would have paid a heavy price for the privileges. They would have forfeited these special exemptions if their benefits were lower than those received by workers in the compulsory plan. Under the AALL's proposal they had to pay cash sick benefits for a maximum of twenty-six weeks equivalent to two-thirds of wages (about $16 for a person earning $100 per month). By comparison, societies in California and Illinois typically paid between $5 and $10 per week for no more than thirteen weeks. Additional requirements of the model law would have mandated free medical, surgical, and nursing care.[11]

The Fraternal Response to the Model Law

Most fraternalists rejected the AALL's overtures. They generally predicted that the model law would lead to the same results for them as had befallen the friendly societies. The *Western Review* emphasized that the national insurance law in Great Britain had corrupted and weakened the societies by overwhelming them with red tape and malingerers. It also charged that the high cost of compulsory insurance had driven many members of friendly societies to drop the voluntary portion of their dues.[12]

John B. Andrews, the secretary of the AALL, did his best to put a good face on the situation in a letter to the *Western Review*. He warmly praised the "excellent service" of the societies as providers of insurance, asserting that the AALL's proposal "should have your hearty support." He promised that the AALL's plan would avoid British mistakes; it did not set up fraternal societies as the central carriers, thereby avoiding the danger of "swamping" them "in a compulsory scheme." He noted that the model law exempted members from premiums to the state fund and gave them access to a guarantee fund in times of crisis. Andrews reassuringly concluded that as long as societies met the "specified conditions" of the law "and if the benefits equal those provided in the act, fraternal society members are exempt from further insurance. This arrangement will avoid double insurance and its attending evils in England."[13]

Andrews's statement did not address the critical objection that it was impossible for most societies to meet the minimum standards. Then again, it is doubtful whether Andrews truly desired an important role for fraternal societies. The day after he wrote to the *Western Review*, he penned a much different letter to a supporter of compulsory insurance. Andrews characterized the position of the fraternal societies as "a difficult one," adding that "the requirement that they offer the same benefits as those given under the act will do much to raise the standard and will probably prevent many from qualifying." [14]

Andrews was not the only proponent of compulsory insurance to have ambiguous views about the fraternal role. On one hand, he and other supporters generally acknowledged that the societies had been trailblazers in sick and other medical benefits. For example, Isaac Rubinow, a statistician, leading writer on compulsory insurance, and adviser to the AALL, characterized fraternal insurance as "a valuable form of social insurance." John R. Commons predicted that the societies would inevitably play "a most important part in a universal health program." He particularly credited them with discovering how to lower costs by letting out contracts to the lowest bidder. The societies had learned, Commons added, that "if expenses go up, their assessments go up. For this reason they are careful to watch their members and to prevent them from feigning sickness and getting the benefits fraudulently." [15]

The other side to this praise was fear that the fraternal societies would upset the harmony and uniformity of a centralized plan. A committee of the Progressive Party rejected fraternal involvement and suggested that the British reliance on friendly societies as carrier organizations had set the stage for wasteful duplication and inefficiency. Instead the committee recommended the German method of entrusting administration to geographically based mutual funds composed of employers and employees. Other comments in the Progressive Party's report revealed a deep distrust of voluntarism. "These lodges," it proclaimed, "have a further defect, from a patriotic standpoint, in that they form centers of association for the different foreign nationalities instead of creating through a strong local sick fund, a nucleus for loyalty to the state." [16]

The Battle Begins in the States

The supporters of compulsory insurance faced their first major test in California. A crucial player was Governor Hiram Johnson, the vice-presidential candidate of the Progressive Party in 1912, who was clearly receptive to the AALL's plan. In 1915 Johnson appointed a Social Insurance Commission to study the issue. The commission's membership almost guaranteed a favorable recommendation. All the appointees were men and women with long track records in the fight for progressive social welfare legislation. The commission first tipped its hand by selecting Isaac Rubinow as chief consultant. Rubinow had helped to draft the social insurance plank of the Progressive Party and had written an encyclopedic advocacy work, *Social Insurance, with Special Reference to American Conditions* (1913).[17]

The witness list at the commission's public hearings revealed the emerging battle lines. An executive from the Aetna Life and Aetna Accident and Liability Companies testified in opposition. Physicians lined up on both sides, indicating that organized medicine did not speak with a single or even predominant voice. The same was true for the labor unions. The former vice-president of the San Francisco Labor Council praised compulsory insurance as beneficial to workers; the editor of the *Labor Clarion*, the journal of the council, condemned it for creating class distinctions.[18]

The chief fraternal witness was John A. Falconer, the California general secretary of the AOF, which had more than 10,000 members in the state. The AOF, unlike its distant cousin the IOF, provided primarily sick and funeral benefits, not life insurance. Like the IOF, however, its lodges offered the services of doctors. Falconer testified that for about $1.00 per month in dues a thrifty worker could obtain sick benefits "and he will get them if he is employed at the time he gets sick or not." He pointed out that the sick benefits of the AOF averaged $7.00 per week. In response to Falconer, Rubinow asserted that the AALL's plan would pay higher cash benefits than the AOF's and cover major operations. The early signs of opposition did not bode well for the AALL's proposal. As Rubinow pointed out, "Fraternal orders are perhaps stronger in California than in many other states."[19]

Even as Falconer spoke, other fraternal opponents were beginning to act. George W. Miller, the new president of the NFCA, pledged that "the fraternal beneficiary system will stand in opposition to an attempt to establish State insurance." Officials from a wide array of organizations, including the MWA, the IOF, the Protected Home Circle, the Royal League, and the WBA, took visible roles in the fight against compulsory insurance.[20]

Opposition came from other sources as well. Many doctors began to mobilize against compulsory insurance. The AALL found it increasingly difficult to exploit professional fears about lodge practice. By 1917 organized medicine had become more confident about its prospects as its long campaign to limit the supply of new doctors was finally bearing fruit. According to some estimates, the income of physicians had risen as much as 41 percent from 1916 to 1919.[21]

For the first time, opponents of compulsory insurance were able to use the specter of lodge practice to go on the offensive. They began to suggest that compulsory insurance, rather than ending lodge practice as the AALL had asserted, would enshrine its worst features, such as low pay scales, loss of autonomy, and overwork. Reports in the medical journals began to criticize the condition of doctors under compulsory insurance in Britain. As Rubinow later recalled, opponents of compulsory insurance were able to harness the "traditional antagonism to all forms of contract practice, the contempt towards the 'lodge doctor.'"[22]

The Impact of World War I

As might be expected, World War I heightened the intensity of fraternal opposition. For some fraternalists the war and the postwar Red Scare were invitations to indulge in xenophobia. In testimony before the New York Senate, Alice B. Locke, a member of the Supreme Board of Trustees of the WBA, depicted compulsory health insurance as the brainchild of "well-known radical Socialists, chief among whom was Eugene Debs, now serving a well-merited sentence of imprisonment for sedition." By contrast, she described people who fought against compulsory insurance as "100 percent Americans." Ronald Numbers has quoted similar examples of superpatriotic rhetoric from the leaders of medical associations, entitling one of his chapters, "Death by Hysteria."[23]

In the case of fraternal societies, however, terms such as "hysteria" are misplaced. Their attitudes were far too deep seated to be dismissed as excessive home-front zeal. The war was an important motivating factor, to be sure, but primarily because it reinforced much older suspicions. Fraternalists took it as an object lesson in the eternal dangers of excessive governmental control. Most obviously, they drew a direct link between compulsory insurance and Prussian autocracy. In 1918, for example, John Sullivan of the MWA characterized the enactment of compulsory insurance under Chancellor Otto von Bismarck as the first installment in a plan to wrest autonomy from citizens by "tying them in their family affairs directly to the Imperial Government." As a result the masses had become "dependent and subservient," and the liberty of the individual had been dethroned. In 1919 the *Fraternal Monitor* singled out the Iron Chancellor in a caustic special editorial, "Menace of Social Insurance." It described how the "wily Bismarck took the situation in hand and, while appeasing the socialists, foisted upon the people . . . a system that made them mentally, morally and industrially subservient to the Junkers."[24]

Fraternal leaders warned that American domestic wartime mobilization also created dangers. Minnie W. Aydelotte, deputy supreme commander of the WBA for the West Coast, described proposals for compulsory health insurance as part of a broader trend to force citizens to rely on government during wartime. She conceded that governmental regulations were necessary on a temporary basis but feared that Americans were now "trusting blindly" to official edicts. Such behavior opened the door for political power to increase to levels "which it was never intended any government should assume or undertake, even in time of war." R. H. Gerard, the president of the NFCA in 1918, also sounded the alarm. He warned his listeners that "democracy may become as despotic as King or Czar and there is danger that our people may fall into the heresies" that led to tyranny after the French Revolution.[25]

To fraternal opponents, wartime events brought out in sharp relief the contrast between European practices of dependence and American principles of self-reliance. Aydelotte declared that "our men and women can and do stand on their own feet." Europeans, on the other hand, had become accustomed to letting their leaders "do most of their thinking." Thus she regarded compulsory health insurance as the product of a "socialistic, paternalistic, and undemocratic movement."[26]

Compulsory insurance, according to the critics, would corrupt America by introducing a new form of graft. When several leaders of Tammany Hall endorsed the AALL's proposal, the *Fraternal Monitor* had a field day. The editor reasoned that Tammany politicians had not acted out of principle but because they knew that "the compulsory health insurance bill would provide over fifty thousand jobs to the faithful." Mary MacEachern Baird agreed, predicting that the floodgates would be open to graft and "political office seekers of which the world is full."[27]

Social Workers Must Make a Noise

Fraternalists were eager to make the AALL into a whipping boy. They repeatedly reminded their audiences that despite its name, the American Association for Labor Legislation was not a labor union. To the contrary, the *Fraternal Monitor* warned, the AALL was primarily an organization of "social reformers and college professors." Support of compulsory insurance by "professional social workers" was not only paternalistic but demonstrated their need to "make a noise in order to earn their salaries." The *Monitor* clearly did not share the fascination with professional expertise that was so prevalent during the Progressive Era: "Theorists in the class room have produced few measures of practical progress. The application of their doctrines usually has led to oppression and bloodshed." The editorial concluded that the academics and reformers in the AALL subscribed to the elitist notion that people of "superior intelligence 'should do something for the lower class.'"[28]

Fraternal critics feared that compulsory insurance was but a beginning. The Social Insurance Committee of the NFCA portrayed compulsory insurance as the "opening wedge" in the AALL's program, which provided "insurance by the State against old age life, against unemployment and that eventually all forms of insurance—life, casualty, fire and every other form—shall be carried solely by the Government." This claim, although exaggerated, was not unreasonable. Key officials of the AALL, such as Rubinow, often depicted compulsory insurance as only one phase in a broader campaign.[29]

One persistent claim of the opposition was that compulsory insurance would strike a blow against individual independence and self-respect. It would, according to John Sullivan, turn each recipient into "a ward of the Government." He asserted that compulsory insurance snatched away an essential learning experience for successful human development. Each person "discovers his powers generally; through the necessity of being held to resolve his course himself." The approach was much like that of Abb Landis, who cited the work of Herbert Spencer as justification for rejecting compulsory insurance. In Landis's view, Spencer had proved the impossibility of making people good through legislation. Instead, according to Landis, the best way to reach this goal was "entirely by self-development."[30]

Gender occasionally appeared as a subtext in the arguments. John Sullivan echoed the concerns of Samuel Gompers and others when he blamed compulsory insurance for causing the "devitalization of manhood." Such appeals, however, were highly malleable. Groups such as the WBA had never found it difficult to appropriate the "manly" values of independence, self-reliance, and competition. Hence, Bina West almost instinctively perceived compulsory insurance as a threat to the progress of women. She feared that it would weaken those habits of female autonomy and thrift so carefully nurtured by participation in fraternal life. She advised female lodge members that they had a special obligation to uphold "for Americans the privilege we have always enjoyed of taking care of ourselves and helping one another." Agreeing, Locke detected in compulsory health insurance a "program that looks to . . . the nationalization of women."[31]

Fraternal leaders agreed that compulsory insurance threatened to weaken the vibrancy of mutual aid in general and lodges in particular. Baird perceived an attack on the "mutual idea" that encourages "the individual to do that which he can do best, and inspires him to be an independent, provident, and self reliant being." In a more direct sense, of course, a leading concern was that compulsory insurance would crowd out fraternal services. The *Fraternal Monitor* predicted that it would mean that "the protection of several million people in voluntary societies will become unnecessary and cease to exist."[32]

Fraternalists also charged that compulsory insurance was unnecessary. Why adopt a new, risky initiative, Sullivan asked, when societies already gave Americans access to low-cost "social insurance"? In these organizations, any member secured "the Social element of the lodge room, fraternal assistance obtaining through distress of whatever nature, including unemployment and sickness, carrying its educating influence as to the beneficence of protection." Sullivan cited the trend among societies, including the MWA, to erect sanitariums for members with communicable diseases such as tuberculosis. In like vein, Bina West characterized compulsory insurance as a potential competitor to the WBA's services of hospitalization and maternity insurance.[33]

While fraternal critics conceded that many societies did not offer medical services, they rejected the AALL's conclusion that such groups were therefore "inadequate." To the contrary, they took it as evidence that those societies had not yet reached their potential. As a means to speed this process, Sullivan endorsed the Raker Bill, which had been proposed in Congress to allow societies to establish sanitariums on federal public land. William Gale Curtis, a leading publicist against compulsory insurance, called for a systematic fraternal campaign for more preventive care. He threw down a question and a challenge: "Why not a Health Warden for every lodge, and a Deputy for every Ward?" As president of the NFCA, Gerard urged each lodge to create a health conservation committee charged with the task of eliminating "the economic waste, due to disease."[34]

Like other critics, fraternalists questioned the record of compulsory insurance. Both Sullivan and the *Fraternal Monitor* cited statistics that the per capita frequency of sickness, as well as its duration, had increased markedly in Great Britain and Germany. They noted that both countries had higher death rates than the United States. The reiteration of these statistics kept proponents of compulsory insurance on the defensive. They found it especially difficult to explain the divergence in death rates. With little effect, advocates of compulsory insurance ascribed the increase in German and British sickness rates to the greater willingness of workers to ask for treatment.[35]

Despite their celebration of mutual aid and declamations against paternalism, few fraternalists were willing to launch a full-scale attack on two other cornerstones of the emerging American welfare state, mothers' pensions and workmen's compensation. One important society even campaigned for mothers' pensions. In 1911 the FOE helped to secure passage of the first pension laws in Missouri. But the FOE's position was exceptional. The general approach of fraternalists was to stay on the legislative sidelines during the debates over mothers' pensions and workmen's compensation.[36]

Timing provides part of the explanation for why societies did not oppose these initiatives. Both reforms had first been proposed when fraternal societies were preoccupied with readjustment and regulatory legislation. The movement for compulsory health insurance, by contrast, largely dated from the middle and late 1910s. At this time the financial situation had improved considerably, and the campaign for uniform legislation was nearly complete. Thus societies were in a better position to expend the necessary political resources. But this explanation only goes so far. Although the finances of societies had generally improved after 1915, they were still shaky. Moreover, by 1918 many societies had suffered setbacks because of devastating costs from the influenza epidemic. Another, more plausible explanation was that the stakes were much higher. Had compulsory health insurance become law, it would have covered a substantial portion of the working class, a key fraternal constituency. Workmen's compensation, by contrast, applied to the limited realm of workplace accidents, and mothers' pensions involved very few recipients.

Moreover, in any fight against mothers' pensions or workmen's compensation, the societies would have been on the losing side. These laws enjoyed broad and overwhelming support. As Molly Ladd-Taylor observes, mothers' pensions "spread like 'wildfire' in the 1910s, achieving more rapid legislative success than any other social justice reform of the Progressive Era." From 1911 to 1913 twenty states had enacted pension laws. By 1920 twenty more had jumped on the bandwagon. Supporters relied heavily on "maternalist" arguments that government had a duty to support motherhood. Most objections to mothers' pensions came from charity society leaders such as Edward Devine. Their case, which emphasized the dangers of paternalism and the threat to self-help, had much in common with the arguments leveled by fraternal orders against compulsory health insurance.[37]

Workmen's compensation enjoyed a breadth and depth of support nearly as formidable as mothers' pensions. The movement grew out of intense dissatisfaction with the high costs and unpredictability of the old common-law system of dealing with accidents on the job. Workmen's compensation became law in twenty states between 1911 and 1913. By 1920 the total had increased to forty-two.[38]

A speech by S. H. Wolfe, a member of the Committee on Social Insurance of the NFCA, illustrated the fraternal attitude toward workmen's compensation. Like a nineteenth-century classical liberal, Wolfe opened by lauding the prescience of William Graham Sumner, the quintessential exponent of laissez-faire. He advised emulation of Sumner's dictum on "The Great Advisability of Minding One's Own Business" and argued that any diminution of "self-reliance tends to make us less fit to take the place in the world for which we were intended, and therefore tends to destroy." [39]

Wolfe's conception of self-reliance, however, did not rule out workmen's compensation, which he denied was "social relief," much less "social insurance." According to Wolfe's conception, compulsory insurance qualified as social insurance because the benefits were based on class distinction, while workmen's compensation did not qualify because all employees, regardless of income, were eligible. "The universal applicability of these benefits," Wolfe explained, "and their disregard of the social status of the beneficiaries remove them . . . from the sphere of social insurance activities." Much like Wolfe, Gerard denied that recipients of workmen's compensation lost "self-respect or standing," because payments depended on "the extent of the injury suffered and not upon the assumption, as in Germany, that the sufferer is a pauper." [40]

Wolfe depicted workmen's compensation as essentially a conservative modification of the previous but far more cumbersome method of settling liability claims through the courts. Following this line of analysis, the Committee on Social Insurance of the NFCA held that "there is a difference between compensation and the matter of charitable relief. Compensation has some idea of a *quid pro quo*." The committee ascribed much of this difference to the comparative ease in assigning responsibility, and thus liability, for injuries in the workplace. The causes of sickness were more difficult to trace. [41]

Umbrella Organizations

By the end of 1917 fraternal opposition to compulsory insurance had come into its own. The societies had joined forces with their old enemies, the commercial insurers, to form umbrella organizations. Despite past differences the coalition was a natural one. Both fraternal and commercial insurers had long stressed the dangers of excessive governmental paternalism and the virtues of self-reliance. Some of the earliest and most effective umbrella organizations were insurance federations at the state levels. First appearing in Ohio but then spreading to other states, the federations vowed to battle "State insurance." Both executives and policyholders could join. Although members came primarily from the commercial sector, fraternal societies also participated. The vice-president of the Insurance Federation of New York, for example, was George A. Scott, president of the New York State Fraternal Congress. In addition, I. I. Boak, head council of the Woodmen of the World, Pacific Jurisdiction, was a former president of the Insurance Federation of Colorado. In 1915 representatives of the state federations met to form the Insurance Federation of America (IFA).[42]

The IFA worked in tandem with the smaller, well-financed Insurance Economics Society of America (IESA), organized by William Gale Curtis, the president of the National Casualty Company of Detroit. In contrast to the IFA, which opposed all forms of state insurance, the IESA kept the focus centered on compulsory health insurance. It funneled seed money to organizations such as the New York League for Americanism and the California Research Society of Social Economics. The IESA also published a series of bulletins between 1916 and 1919. Curtis, who was often the author, took special pains to stress the dangers of compulsory insurance to fraternal orders. The bulletins received wide circulation in the fraternal world.[43]

The most prestigious group that served as an umbrella organization was the National Civic Federation (NCF). Founded by Ralph M. Easley, it had been around since 1900 as a vehicle to forge cooperation between labor, business, and the public sector. The NCF had played a pivotal role in state and federal legislation during the Progressive Era in fields such as banking regulation, workmen's compensation, and labor mediation. By the middle of the 1910s its enthusiasm for wide-ranging interventionist legislation had waned considerably. Easley gradually nudged the NCF in a more conservative direction.[44]

The NCF's reaction to compulsory insurance was one of the first clear signs of its shift. In 1914 it commissioned a survey of compulsory insurance in Europe. The final report was highly critical. In reference to the British system, the authors, who included J. W. Sullivan of the Typographical Union and P. Tecumseh Sherman, an attorney in New York, faulted "the utter inadequacy and comparative inefficiency of the medical treatment provided." Fraternalists often quoted the finding that compulsory insurance had led to a diminution of organized mutual aid in Britain. The NCF's report estimated that the number of friendly societies had declined by more than 200 because of the Act of 1911.[45]

The NCF's reform credentials proved a stumbling block for advocates of compulsory insurance. It was one thing to dismiss the IESA as a narrow and selfish front group, but such a charge carried much less weight against the NCF, especially after Frederick L. Hoffman volunteered his services. Since the 1890s Hoffman, the chief statistician of the Prudential and a former president of the American Statistical Association, had accumulated a long and often controversial record as a researcher on subjects ranging from the pauper burial rate to tuberculosis in the dusty trades. He was perhaps best known as an exponent of white racial superiority. Nevertheless, officials in the AALL thought enough of his progressive credentials, including a record of advocacy of industrial regulation and workmen's compensation, to select him in 1912 as a member of its Committee on Social Insurance. It was a decision they would regret.[46]

During his three years on the committee, Hoffman stood out as a dissenting voice. Significantly, his initial objections were not against compulsory insurance per se but against the AALL's plan to exclude commercial companies as carriers. By 1915 Hoffman was publicly attacking the committee's work and favorably citing the NCF's critical survey. Tired of his lone-wolf status, he resigned from the committee in 1916.[47]

Even before the break, Hoffman had considerably broadened his objections to compulsory insurance. He increasingly depicted it as unduly paternalistic and destructive of self-help. In his letter of resignation Hoffman rejected the contention that "fraternal insurance cannot meet these [American health] needs" and praised it as "a commendable form of voluntary thrift." [48]

By this time Hoffman was closely working with the Department of Social Insurance of the NCF. The relationship became official in 1919 when he was named consultant to the NCF's new Committee on Constructive Plan of Health Insurance. The committee had a diverse membership. The chairman was Warren S. Stone, the grand chief of the International Brotherhood of Locomotive Engineers and a close ally of Samuel Gompers. Other members included A. C. MacLean, the president of the NFCA; Magnus W. Alexander, the managing director of the Industrial Board; and Mark Daly, the general secretary of the Associated Manufacturers and Merchants of New York.[49]

Hoffman traveled to Great Britain to conduct a follow-up study to the NCF's original report. Despite his old-line background, he was careful to stress issues that would appeal to his fraternal allies. In his report he described at length the weakened state of the friendly societies. Like William Gale Curtis, Hoffman adeptly steered clear of raising acrimony between fraternal societies and medical professionals. His report charged that compulsory insurance had destroyed the independence of doctors through panels but, at the same time, avoided condemning lodge doctors. This approach paid off. Fraternal critics often cited Hoffman's report.[50]

They also found it easy to embrace the critique put forward by Samuel Gompers. With relish the *Fraternal Monitor* quoted Gompers's attack on the AALL: "Here comes along a movement of men and women led by sophistry as to the cause of the ills and as to the hoped-for better life, and willing to rivet the masses of labor to the juggernaut of government." Gompers, a lifelong Mason, had always been an exponent of voluntary methods to solve problems. At a convention of the National Casualty and Surety Agents, he stated that he did not carry insurance in any private company but was "insured in the union of my trade. I wish that there would be more of that insurance of a fraternal and mutual character."[51]

California: Defeating the Inevitable

By 1917 there were signs that the tide was turning against compulsory insurance. The insurance federations, medical associations, and fraternal societies had stepped up the pressure. The AALL's model law had gone down to defeat in the fifteen states where it had been proposed. Nonetheless, officials of the AALL continued to exude optimism. They yearned for the chance to present the issue to the voters.

California offered that chance. At the governor's urging, the state legislature scheduled a public vote in November 1918. Rubinow optimistically characterized California as "a state in which there probably exists a stronger popular health insurance movement than in any other part of the country." Supporters had lined up a popular progressive governor who appointed a favorable state commission of respected reformers. Even the state medical society, under its president J. Henry Barbat, was still generally supportive. The campaign's literature had effectively featured endorsements from state and national figures such as Governor, later Senator, Hiram Johnson; Governor William D. Stephens; Ray Lyman Wilbur, the president of Stanford University; Daniel C. Murphy, the president of the California State Federation of Labor; Theodore Roosevelt; and William G. McAdoo, the U.S. secretary of the Treasury.[52]

Yet despite such outward signs of pending success, the AALL had cause for concern. Fraternalists, dissident elements of organized medicine, and insurance companies were on the offensive. The societies mounted an attack on several fronts and forged close ties with the Insurance Federation of California. Like the insurance federations in other states, it was open to all elements of the insurance industry. In January 1917 opponents placed a full-page advertisement in the *San Francisco Chronicle* charging that a compulsory plan "would destroy the usefulness of many splendid fraternal benefit societies" and vitiate fraternalism by replacing "brotherly love" with "cold-blooded compulsion."[53]

Fraternalists also rallied with other opponents in a somewhat broader organization, the California Research Society of Social Economics. The group had been organized and funded by the IESA. Curtis, the president of the IESA, recruited Carlton Babcock to head the organization. By all accounts Babcock, a former newspaper publisher and secretary of the Insurance Federation of Idaho, had formidable public relations talents. The NFCA also threw itself into the fight. Carlos Hardy, a member of the NFCA's Social Insurance Committee, visited the state to coordinate opposition. Female fraternalists, such as Minnie W. Aydelotte, lent their names to a special women's committee organized by the California Research Society.[54]

The leaders of the AALL looked on this mounting fraternal opposition with dismay. Some had seen it coming. As early as April 1917 John B. Andrews had lamented the evidence of cooperation between commercial companies and fraternal societies. He warned that "in California, the insurance companies apparently have been egging on the fraternals to urge that under health insurance there should be free competition between all classes of carriers. And the fraternals fell for it!"[55]

Even so, events in the week before the election seemed to bode well for supporters of compulsory insurance. Californians, like other Americans, were in the middle of the influenza epidemic. Reminders were everywhere. Newspapers in the state repeatedly carried front-page photographs of ordinary citizens wearing protective masks. Pro-amendment forces were confident that the epidemic would win voters to their cause. They were wrong. Despite the efforts of Rubinow and the AALL, the final results were a stunning repudiation of compulsory insurance. The amendment crashed to defeat by a vote of 358,324 to 133,858.[56]

New York: The Last Battle

Although greatly discouraged, advocates of compulsory insurance were not quite ready to give up. They mounted a determined campaign to pass a modified version of the AALL's model law in the New York legislature. The cosponsors were Senator Frederick Davenport, a leading progressive Republican, and Assemblyman Charles D. Donohue, the Democratic minority leader. Despite the AALL's earlier failures in the state, the prospects looked good this time. It had amassed an impressive list of supporters, including Al Smith, the New York State Federation of Labor, the City Club of New York, and the Consumers League. The AALL was even able to defuse opposition from the Christian Scientists by inserting a religious "conscientious objector" clause.[57]

Flushed with victory, however, the opponents of compulsory health insurance were not prepared to let New York slip away. As in California, the societies cooperated closely with the commercial companies through umbrella organizations. The New York State Fraternal Congress, under the leadership of George A. Scott, joined forces with the Insurance Federation of New York. Fraternalists also worked through the New York League for Americanism, the state version of the California Research Society. The IESA threw itself into the fight by "donating" the services of Carlton Babcock to act as secretary. Babcock published a steady stream of pamphlets. He carefully pitched the appeal, predicting that compulsory insurance would bring "the complete ruin of fraternalism."[58]

The involvement of the New York League for Americanism became a lightning rod. Pointing to its financial support from upstate manufacturers, critics depicted the entire movement against compulsory health insurance as a small cabal of selfish interests. They were equally confident that the AALL's proposal represented the popular will. Isaac Rubinow claimed that the "general public, or at least that part of it which is interested in matters of social progress, is already almost unanimously in favor of the health insurance principle."[59]

Such an approach may have scored debating points, but it was a poor reflection of reality. The movement against compulsory insurance clearly had struck a popular chord. A poll of factory workers in Utica indicated that 12,875 respondents opposed the idea, while 112 were for it. As Ronald Numbers observes, the result was "an obvious embarrassment to an association that claimed to represent the working class." It was equally difficult for supporters of compulsory insurance to dismiss the large following of fraternal societies. Membership in the New York State Fraternal Congress was about 700,000.[60]

The struggle culminated in 1919. Witnesses representing the full gamut of interests turned out at public hearings before the state senate in March. In April a coalition of progressive Republicans and Democrats in the state senate approved the Davenport-Donohue bill. It looked like compulsory insurance might become law, but then conservative Republicans successfully prevented a vote, thus killing compulsory insurance for the third year in a row.[61]

In 1920 the AALL and its allies tried once again to resurrect a bill. As they had before, fraternalists made their voices heard. A witness at the public hearing was Alice B. Locke of the WBA, which had 30,000 members in the state. Locke depicted compulsory insurance as "class legislation of the most vicious type. It would compel the thrifty, moral, independent citizen to accept a thinly disguised form of poor relief, which he neither needs nor desires." She mentioned as a positive sign that the National American Woman Suffrage Association and the League of Women Voters had never endorsed compulsory health insurance. Locke spoke from personal experience. It was on her motion that a combined national conference of the two organizations had referred a proposed endorsement back to committee. Commenting on this victory, Locke exclaimed with joy, "And there it still slumbers!" This time the bill never made it to a vote. The movement for compulsory insurance was dead. The defeat had dealt a major setback to the emerging welfare state in the United States.[62]

The End of Compulsory Insurance

In 1934 a now chastened Isaac Rubinow reflected self-critically that it "seems as if literally everyone" had opposed compulsory insurance. He continued, "And who was for it? An energetic, largely self-appointed group . . . which carried with it the profession of social work, to some extent the university teaching groups, the economic and social sciences, and even the political progressive organizations, but very little support beyond these narrow confines."[63]

Fraternal societies had made much of the difference in the margin between victory and defeat. At the beginning of the campaign the AALL had reason to expect that the societies would be more sympathetic. Despite longtime fraternal criticisms of state insurance, it was questionable whether societies had either the ability or the inclination to back up action with words. The AALL had miscalculated. The debate over compulsory health insurance had proven that fraternal opposition to governmental paternalism was alive and well.

CHAPTER NINE

Our Dreams Have All Come True

Orphanages and homes for the elderly were not the only social welfare institutions established by fraternal societies during the first three decades of the twentieth century. Many lodges embarked on endeavors ranging from state-of-the-art hospitals and sanitariums to preventive health centers staffed by nurses and volunteers.[1]

The life insurance orders were responsible for many of the grand projects, especially in health care. Much of this fraternal activism was a legacy of readjustment. The end of cheap rates made it harder for the life insurance orders to compete with the commercial companies, who now had the edge. In 1923 the average annual premium for ten representative life insurance orders for a man who joined at age thirty was $20.81 per $1,000, while the same policy in a commercial company cost $18.29. Under such circumstances, societies responded by returning to their roots as *fraternal* rather than merely cheap-rate societies.[2]

They made the fight against tuberculosis a priority. Causing 140.1 deaths per 100,000 in 1915, the "white plague" was truly a pandemic. But there was reason to believe that individuals could make a positive difference. Evidence was mounting that tuberculosis was curable if detected early. Experts regarded a stay in a sanitarium as a promising form of treatment. In a healthful environment, they suggested, the afflicted could partake of the benefits of improved ventilation, sunshine, a balanced diet, and rest.[3]

The fraternal war against tuberculosis began with a proposal by H. A. Warner, the president of NFC from 1901 to 1902. He appealed to member organizations for cooperation in establishing a national fraternal sanitarium in Las Vegas, New Mexico. Warner recommended that construction costs be met by a per capita fee of a penny per month on each of the 3.5 million members. Under this scheme members of the cooperating societies would get free treatment, while nonmembers would pay reduced rates.[4]

Despite an endorsement by the NFC and the AFA, the project never came to fruition. Part of the problem was that Warner had acted just when the societies had perhaps the weakest incentives to cooperate. They were embroiled in a battle for economic survival and had to fight off inimical legislation. Although Warner's proposal failed, it spurred a debate that had important long-term consequences. It revealed a potential demand not just for sanitariums but for other eleemosynary institutions. For the first time, practical questions of building, financing, and patient eligibility were on the table. As a result, several societies launched their own sanitarium projects. Leading examples included the WC, the Royal Circle, the Woodmen of the World, and the IOF.[5]

One of the first groups to take the plunge was the MWA, which opened a sanitarium in Colorado Springs in 1908. With a million members the MWA was the largest fraternal life insurance order. The choice of Colorado Springs reflected the popular belief that the climatic conditions were ideal for treatment. The Denver Chamber of Commerce had described Colorado as the "mecca of consumptives, and rightfully; for dry air, equitable temperature are as of yet the most reliable factors in the care of that disease." Several religious and ethnic groups also established sanitariums in Colorado.[6]

The head camp of the MWA financed the construction and operating costs through an annual per capita fee of 3 cents. The amount was woefully inadequate. The MWA gradually increased the fee to 5 cents per month in 1921. One of the head camp's strategies for raising money was to appeal to lodges ("camps") and members ("neighbors") to contribute for buildings and other improvements. This method helped pay for dozens of tent-cottages (each costing $250) for patients. As a means of recognition, the Head Camp inscribed the names of the contributors over each entrance.[7]

The MWA rapidly expanded the facilities. By 1923 the sanitarium, which covered 1,368 acres, had 205 tent-cottages, a two-story central building, greenhouses, a recreation hall, a herd of Holsteins, an elaborate conduit of sewer and steam heat pipes, a barn, a power plant, a library, and a post office. There were 175 employees. Most impressive was a four-story hospital of seventy beds with state-of-the-art technology "to aid in diagnosis and treatment, not only of tuberculosis, but of incidental troubles as well." The hospital employed four doctors, two consultants, and two dentists. The nursing staff, which included several former patients, received training in classes conducted by the doctors.[8]

The sanitarium admitted all insured members (men only) in good standing. Everything was free except travel expenses and personal incidentals. The sanitarium was deluged with requests for admission. It had to turn away 70 percent

The tuberculosis sanitarium of the MWA, near Colorado Springs, Colorado, ca. 1910s. Each tent-cottage included an inscription identifying the camp (lodge) that had paid for it. (Courtesy of the Modern Woodmen of America, Archives, Rock Island, Ill.)

of the applicants during the first year and 50 percent in the second. As of January 1, 1926, the sanitarium had treated 7,071 patients at a cost of $4 million. By this time there were usually 245 patients on any given day.[9]

As the physical plant grew more imposing, so did the patient capacity. A critical factor that helped to guarantee space for patients was the declining incidence of tuberculosis in the United States. The death rate per 100,000 had fallen to 39.9 in 1945. Between 1909 (the first full year of operation) and 1925, the sanitarium's median annual rejection rate of applicants as a percentage of annual discharges was 8.3. It fell to 3.6 in 1925. Most rejections were of "cases which offered no possible chance for improvement." The management gave priority to patients in the early stages of the disease. Even so, about 40 percent of those admitted were advanced cases. During this period the sanitarium gradually increased the maximum length of stay from six months to fourteen. Even with the higher limit, the average stay for patients in 1926 was six months.[10]

The sanitarium complemented the older fraternal conception of benefits as reciprocal obligations; the services were "not given in charity, but in fulfillment of the Society's contract with all its Beneficial members." At the same time, each patient was subject to a "certain degree of discipline." If he failed "to subscribe to reasonable rules for his own good there is another Neighbor on the waiting list ready to take his place." The management enforced a regimen of diet, regular exercise, and rest, and it strongly discouraged outside contacts. Patients could receive special permission to leave the premises, but they had to return by evening. The underlying goal was to "free patients from all possible domestic cares and responsibilities." In pursuing this goal the management discouraged the "too solicitous attentions of relatives" by reserving the right to prohibit family members from staying in the county.[11]

The MWA did not hesitate to use the sanitarium to drum up new members. It featured the project in movies, illustrated booklets, and other promotional literature. Field agents made it the theme of speeches to assemblies of "Neighbors." Although the MWA was leery of allowing too many visits to patients by relatives, it encouraged "thousands" of tourists to make the trip.[12]

Judging the effectiveness of the treatment at the MWA sanitarium, or any of its competitors, is problematic. There is controversy among medical historians about why the tuberculosis epidemic waned. The promoters of American sanitariums trumpeted their success rates, but firm conclusions are elusive in part because most institutions did not maintain contact with patients after release. Fortunately, the MWA, as an insurance organization, did keep such data, including details such as the date and cause of death. These records show that 7,071 men were patients from 1909 to 1925. By the end of 1925, 4.5 percent had died while at the sanitarium and 50.5 percent still survived. This record compared favorably to other tuberculosis sanitariums. Throughout the history of the sanitarium movement, 25 percent of patients in the United States died in an institution, and about 50 percent more died within five years of release. Because the MWA sanitarium admitted advanced cases, about 30 to 50 percent of the total, its performance was impressive. A possible reason for success was that it permitted longer stays than other institutions. An episode of tuberculosis, and thus the period of treatment, could last for several years.[13]

Specialists and Hospital Care

Fraternal organizations experimented with health care in other ways as well. Some societies began to consider comprehensive programs of hospitalization.

Two of them, the WC and the IOF, built on existing systems of lodge practice. Both began the transition to more comprehensive programs during the 1910s and 1920s.

At the turn of the century the medical program of the WC was like that of countless other societies. The individual branches employed doctors on a capitation basis. Each branch had a high degree of autonomy to determine compensation, working conditions, and quality. During the 1910s a group of reformers within the organization began to raise objections, pointing to two problems. One was purely demographic. As the membership began to disperse from crowded neighborhoods, it was increasingly difficult to guarantee ready access to a branch doctor. The other objection, as mentioned earlier, was that the status quo led to excessive favoritism.[14]

The reformers united around a fairly modest proposal that branches appoint rather than elect doctors. They made little headway. Then the reform elements persuaded several branches in New York City to create a citywide medical department, with optional participation by branches. The medical department appointed and supervised each "district" doctor who served several branches. The plan was so popular that the number of participating branches quickly jumped from 80 to 100. In 1920 the medical department took the next step of establishing a specialist service, with doctors in fields such as surgery, obstetrics, dentistry, optometry, and orthopedics. A member could consult a specialist upon obtaining a referral from a district doctor.[15]

By the end of the 1930s, the specialists, then operating out of WC-owned clinics in New York City, saw 8,000 patients annually. At the same time, forty district general practitioners averaged about 100,000 house calls each year. The annual fee was $3.00 per individual and $5.00 per family. The services included house calls and, in contrast to many other fraternal societies, "extras" such as medicine, x-rays, bandages, and treatment for venereal disease. A member paid a higher fee for major surgery. Branches in other cities, such as Chicago, responded by creating medical departments of their own.[16]

The evolution of the medical program of the IOF showed parallels with the WC's. Reformers at the grass roots took initiatives to create a new system. The high courts, most notably Northern California, Southern California, and Central Ontario, established programs of free surgical benefits to supplement the lodge doctors of individual courts. The high court contracted with private hospitals for rooms and hired salaried surgeons to perform operations. With some variation, the fees were about $1.25 per month. The service paid for all expenses.

Family members could obtain care either for free or at reduced rates based on ability to pay. In addition to the fees, high courts raised revenue through voluntary contributions by staging special events such as bazaars. Thousands of members used these surgical services. Between 1910 and 1932 the high court of Northern California provided 4,064 major and minor operations. Some indication of the extent of the coverage was that although the high court had 8,727 members in 1932, there were 212 operations that year.[17]

As the IOF's medical programs expanded, the old-style lodge doctor increasingly took a back seat. While many courts still hired general practitioners, others phased them out and relied exclusively on the high court physicians. In 1934 C. D. Parker, the secretary of the IOF's medical board, explained that "times have changed, methods that were valuable twenty years ago are now obsolete." Parker stated that the old method of attaching medical services to individual courts was no longer tenable because of dispersed population.[18]

The WBA: From Hospitalization to Health Centers

The evolution of the health care program of the WBA was almost the reverse of the process followed by the WC and the IOF. The WBA had no previous experience with lodge practice, and its hives did not hire doctors or offer sick benefits. The main benefit was life insurance paid through the national organization. By the first decade of the twentieth century there was a rising chorus from the grass roots to establish broader services. The experience of other societies probably informed this discussion. Because the WBA was an active participant in the NFC, members would have been aware of the health care experiments of the MWA and the IOF.

Several local and state hives decided on their own to establish medical services. In locations as diverse as Chicago, Illinois; Birmingham, Alabama; and Yankton, South Dakota they endowed rooms and beds for members in hospitals and sanitariums. The practice spread rapidly after 1905. Eventually the Supreme Hive Review (national office) took measures to bring the service to the entire membership. In 1915 it established a special fund financed by a monthly fee of 2 cents from each member. The supreme hive disbursed all receipts to state and local hospital committees of volunteers who, in turn, contracted with private hospitals to reserve or endow beds and rooms.[19]

Members who were otherwise unable to pay and in need of surgery were eligible for hospitalization. They generally obtained free service, including room,

"DON'T BOTHER MOTHER, DEARIES, TRY TO BE GOOD CHILDREN".

"THERE NOW, YOU ARE MORE COMFORTABLE, ARE YOU NOT?"

Advertisement for the hospital program of the LOTM (later Woman's Benefit Association), from the *Ladies Review*, July 1914. (Courtesy of the Woman's Life Insurance Society, Port Huron, Mich.)

food, and nursing care. A requirement with each application was a diagnosis by the physician recommending surgery. The local hospital committee and the national medical director gave final approval. The WBA recruited many of its surgeons from the ranks of its medical examiners who examined new members for life insurance purposes. The success of the plan hinged on the willingness of these surgeons to donate their services to indigent patients.[20]

Medical examiners for the WBA had more reason than most doctors to feel loyal to the organization and thus donate services. Many were women, often homeopaths, who did not have the usual professional connections. Probably the most famous was Marcena S. Ricker of Rochester, New York, who had been Susan B. Anthony's personal physician. The position of medical examiner served as a springboard to build a private practice and opened doors for female doctors who otherwise suffered from discrimination. As the *Ladies Review* pointed out, there were "certain compensations for the medical examiner aside from the money consideration." Younger doctors could study methods of diagnosis and extend "acquaintance in the community."[21]

The WBA's existing medical infrastructure of examiners made expansion of the hospital service possible. By early 1919 the organization had signed contracts with eighty-seven hospitals in thirty states, the District of Columbia, and British Columbia. From 1919 to 1922, 5,720 women obtained care through the hospital service, 3,825 in surgical and 1,895 in medical cases. The influenza epidemic offered a severe test, accounting for 410 patients and making the disease the largest single diagnosis among the medical cases.[22]

Within a few years the WBA had phased out the hospital service. Several factors prompted this decision. The fee of 2 and, later, 5 cents per month was far too small to meet the surgical needs of the members. Questions of who was eligible had become increasingly nettlesome. The restriction of care to indigents only was difficult to enforce. Many better-off members were resentful that they had paid the fee yet were not eligible. Both hospital administrators and doctors complained that patients were taking advantage of the system. For instance, a letter from the superintendent of the hospital bluntly warned Bina West that if "some arrangement cannot be made so that the cases that are not charity will come into the hospital with the understanding that they are to arrange the surgeon's fee with the surgeon, I do not wish to continue this work." After quoting the letter, West issued a public warning: "There is no stigma attached to financial inability to pay for hospital care, but there *is* a stigma attached to those who request this service and who are *able to pay for it*, and who keep some deserving sister from receiving the fraternal care planned for her by the splendid members of our great Association."[23]

By the 1920s the WBA faced hard choices. One possibility was to extend the hospital service to all members, essentially the approach of the WC and the IOF. The WBA rejected this alternative because it would mean a sizable boost in fees. Instead of 5 cents, each member would pay a monthly medical bill of close to $1.00. Another daunting obstacle was finding personnel. The adoption of a program like those of the WC or the IOF would entail hiring salaried physicians, thereby alienating organized medicine. The precedents were not encouraging. Hospitals had already revoked contracts with the WBA for less important reasons.[24]

Instead the WBA moved in a completely different direction. It began to focus on "prevention of disease" through the establishment of local health centers. The WBA had opened thirty-six centers by 1931. At no cost, members could obtain a "general physical survey . . . such as the taking of temperature, weight and measurements, pulse and blood pressure, examination of eyes, ears, nose, throat, and teeth, and urinalysis." Staffing was by volunteers from the members who were primarily nurses or doctors. Financing came from the same fraternal fund that had supported the hospital service.[25]

The centers sponsored lectures, special events, and classes in home nursing and first aid. A supervisor of the health center in Kansas City described the flavor of the work. "We had a lovely afternoon," she wrote, "with music, recitations, and a health talk. Thirty-two juniors and nine mothers were present. I examined 25 children—tonsils, teeth, and weighed and measured, and gave leaflets to all." A supervisor in Chicago reported the results of twenty-five examinations of babies, including twins who "were in very poor health due to improper care and feeding, and have been put on feeding formulas, and they are now averaging a gain of seven to eight ounces a week." Through a system of card files, the centers kept track of expectant mothers and sought them out to arrange consultations.[26]

To supplement the health centers, the national WBA inaugurated a free visiting nurse service. Members in areas without a health center were not charged. Those near health centers paid a reduced per-visit fee. For the most part the WBA hired through existing visiting nurse associations. Each member was entitled to a maximum of eight visits for any "acute medical or surgical" case, including maternity. The duties of a nurse included bathing the patient, changing her clothes, and helping to prepare her food. Contagious cases, such as tuberculosis, were not eligible for full coverage, although "an occasional visit may be made for investigation and instruction."[27]

The transformation of the WBA's health program came with a price: the demise of the hospital service. The national organization still paid for some surgical cases but in far fewer numbers. While the WBA sacrificed hospitalization, the membership gained corresponding benefits. The new plan was a "universal service," much like the hospital and sanitarium plans of other societies. In 1923 the *Ladies Review* stressed that the health centers and visiting nurses were "for *all* members who are within their reach. Do not wait to be urged to find out your physical condition, rather try to avoid illness and suffering." The WBA, in fact, advertised that it could not maintain the centers "in any place unless the members receive the benefits."[28]

The health centers also enabled the WBA to serve a much higher proportion of the membership. From 1923 to 1934 members had the benefit of 902,097 health center consultations and 28,000 examinations by doctors. There were thirty-eight health centers by 1934 in seventeen states and one Canadian province. The visiting nurses, who numbered 800 that year, were busy. They logged 47,960 visits from 1923 to 1934. The classes on home nursing and first aid continued to be filled throughout the depression. Between 1931 and 1935, 873 "diploma awards" in first aid and 306 in home nursing were awarded.[29]

Another flaw with the old hospital service was that the WBA could not use it for recruiting. Indeed, the *Ladies Review* bluntly warned against any who "hold out our hospital service as an inducement to the prospective new member." The health centers and visiting nurses did not suffer from this weakness. In 1935 Dr. Annie E. Reynolds, the supreme health supervisor of the WBA, proudly declared that during the year, "our health supervisors personally secured 302 new members and 631 new juniors." The health program continued until the 1950s, when it suffered a precipitous decline. In 1949 there were thirty-six health centers; sixteen remained in 1957.[30]

Latin Hospitals in Tampa

The first fraternal hospitals were usually built on an ethnic base. Probably the oldest and longest lived were those of the French and German mutual benefit societies in San Francisco and Los Angeles. El Centro Asturiano and El Centro Español supported two early twentieth-century hospitals. Contenders in a spirited rivalry for the loyalties of Cuban and Spanish cigar workers who lived in Tampa, they were extensions of cooperative clubs, or *centros*, which had arisen in Cuba during the late nineteenth century. These organizations provided financial mutual aid and operated clubhouses.[31]

The first of Tampa's fraternal hospitals opened in 1905 under the auspices of El Centro Asturiano. For an average of $1.50 per month, members obtained coverage for themselves and their families. Ultimately the hospital boasted sixty beds, a pharmacy, an up-to-date operating room, and an x-ray laboratory. Historians Gary R. Mormino and George E. Pozzetta reckon that it "ranked among the most modern and best equipped in Florida." The staff treated nearly 8,000 patients and performed 1,623 surgical operations by the 1930s. Jealous of this success, El Centro Español opened a facility. The second hospital maintained a fee structure and standard of quality analogous to its rival's.[32]

Centro Asturiano in Tampa was originally an affiliate of Centro Asturiano in Havana. Like the Cubans the Tampans proved to be pragmatic. Almost immediately the societies added members who were from different ethnic and cultural groups. The only restrictions of the Tampa El Centro Asturiano were that the initiate be white and "of good character and in good health." Southern Italians were among the outsiders to join. Within a few years native white Florid-

The hospital of El Centro Asturiano, Tampa, Florida, ca. 1930. (Courtesy of Special Collections, University of South Florida Library, Tampa, Fla.)

ians who wanted low-cost hospital care began to apply. By 1942 so many persons had joined that perhaps 20 percent of the members were "of Anglo-Saxon stock."[33]

The SBA Hospital

During the 1920s the SBA established what became probably the largest of the fraternal hospitals. It was an indirect legacy of the agitation for a national tuberculosis sanitarium, led by H. A. Warner, the medical director of the SBA. His sanitarium proposal had failed, but the campaign had encouraged the members to ponder the idea of a grand project.[34]

In 1916 the National Council of the SBA inaugurated plans to raise money for an old folks' home, an orphanage, a cooperative farm, and a "general hospital for the treatment of all diseases, specializing in surgery." William A. Biby, the chief backer of building the hospital and homes, noted that the old-line companies had long ago established a "system of inspections and instructions in healthful living and the preservation of health." A fraternal hospital would make it possible to "go a step further than they do and materially assist our risks to live longer." No life insurance order had ever established a general hospital. The closest facsimiles were the hospitals of groups such as the MWA, which were ancillaries to sanitariums.[35]

The SBA collected the seed money from its members. It set a per capita quota of a nickel per month and then allocated the proceeds to the Home and Hospital Association. Additional help came from voluntary cash and in-kind donations of members. The adoption of a compulsory funding method after 1920 complemented the SBA's emphasis on universality. J. M. Kirkpatrick, the national president, underlined this point. In 1924 he declared that because every member was eligible for the benefits, "all should contribute equally and thus obviate the necessity of conducting campaigns for the raising of money through subscriptions." The commitment to universality contrasted with the mission of the WBA, which had always tried to restrict benefits to indigents. From the beginning the SBA serviced members without regard to financial need.[36]

The hospital rapidly surpassed the orphanage and the old folks' home as the crown jewel of the SBA. This was almost inevitable. The hospital was an imposing edifice with three stories, forty beds, an x-ray machine, and two operating rooms. Within three years the staff increased to two surgeons; an eye, ear, nose, and throat specialist; ten nurses; a lab technician; and a dietitian. The compensation of the doctors was by salary rather than fee for service, and the salaries were high by contemporary standards. The SBA proudly announced that it would employ only registered rather than student or practical nurses.[37]

The cost to members was free as long as they kept up their life insurance payments. The amount of these varied with age. In 1925 a man or woman at age thirty paid $1.50 per month for a whole life policy of $1,000, while the premium for a person who joined at fifty-five years was $4.35 per month. These premiums remained level throughout life. The right to receive care extended to children who held juvenile certificates. Girls and boys between six months and sixteen years paid monthly premiums of 20 cents for small whole life policies. According to Kirkpatrick, the "hospital benefits are not costing members one cent" in higher premiums. Officials claimed that this had been accomplished through savings in the cost of management.[38]

The SBA's medical plan specialized in dealing with major medical expenses or, in modern parlance, catastrophic coverage. Admission to the hospital was open to all surgical cases and those involving "acute non-contagious diseases," but it excluded members who were bedridden or maternity cases. This approach differed from the more comprehensive plans of the WC and the IOF. While a comprehensive plan greatly facilitated regular examinations and preventive services, it added to the cost. Under a catastrophic system, such as that offered by the SBA Hospital, the patient received fewer general services but paid much lower fees. The only preventive service was the provision of a free urinalysis through the mail twice a year.[39]

The use of the hospital far exceeded expectations as 5,246 patients came from twenty states from 1925 to 1928. Doctors performed 1,750 major and 2,158 minor operations, with a death rate of under 2 percent. Requests for free urinalysis also kept the hospital busy. In the first two years the laboratory analyzed 16,387 samples. Despite the exclusion of maternity cases, more than 60 percent of the patients were women. Just over 10 percent were "juvenile members." By 1928 the commodious wards had become crowded as the daily average number of patients rose from 28 to 61. To find additional space, more beds were installed in a building that had formerly been a residence for nurses.[40]

Crowding, while an inconvenience, did not detract from the success of the hospital, and that, in turn, gave a boost to the SBA. Between 1925 and 1928 membership increased from 211,979 to 224,807. President Kirkpatrick framed the matter succinctly when he proclaimed that each patient who returned home became "a living, walking advertisement." He estimated that the hospital alone accounted for "fully 50% of the insurance protection being written by our Association today."[41]

The SBA used the *Security News* to advertise the benefits of the hospital. A column regularly featured letters from satisfied patients. "Since I have come home from that wonderful S.B.A Hospital," wrote one member in March 1926, "I often found myself wondering if it isn't all a dream that there is really such a fine place for the service of those who really need it." Many patients commented on the homelike atmosphere. Gus Lading of Topeka wrote that the patients were "like one family" who "visit one another and see how everybody is getting along. So you cannot get lonesome there." Mrs. E. R. Gunnerson, commenting on her son's tonsillectomy, wrote that the experience had made her family "ardent boosters for the Home and Hospital of the Security Benefit Association."[42]

The testimonials, along with mounting demand for the hospital's services, fueled the enthusiasm of the SBA's leadership. In 1928 Kirkpatrick announced an ambitious plan to increase the size of the hospital. His goal was to end the crowding and build a solid foundation for future membership growth. A bigger hospital would make it possible to raise money through fees charged to nonmember paying patients. Kirkpatrick looked forward to the day when the hospital would surpass "in magnitude the great Mayo Brothers Clinic." [43]

Transfers from the SBA fund paid part of the costs of the expansion, but voluntary contributions were critical. In many ways the expansion effort represented a repeat performance of the earlier building campaign. As before, the Home and Hospital Association encouraged contributions by tying gifts to specific improvements. The price for furnishing a two-bed room, for example, was $250. The name of the contributing individual or council would be inscribed "in enduring stone at the door." Contributors during the drive were geographically diverse, but not surprisingly, Kansans stood out, with donors such as the Mystic Sewing Club of Council 1362 in Leavenworth. [44]

The expanded hospital, which opened in 1930, was nothing like the Mayo Clinic, but it was still something to brag about. The building, modeled after Independence Hall in Philadelphia, had 250 beds, two extensive wings, and a 160-foot clock tower in the middle. Costing about $800,000, it was probably the largest general hospital ever built by a fraternal society and one of the best in Kansas. To commemorate the occasion the SBA held a "great homecoming" that brought 10,000 participants to Topeka. [45]

All of this was expensive. As the depression began, the SBA had more need than ever to uncover new sources of revenue. The transfers from the general fund and voluntary contributions no longer met the increase in operating costs. The National Council met in January 1930 to consider the possibilities. One, which it immediately ruled out, was to boost monthly insurance rates. Such a move was unpalatable "because of the dissatisfaction and consequent lapsation which it was believed would result." As seasoned fraternalists, members of the board were well aware of the connection between economic hard times and lapsation. Raising rates could also alienate members in outlying areas who did not use the hospital. [46]

In the end the board implemented a middle course. It announced a sliding scale of out-of-pocket charges for patients. A member who lived in zone one—Kansas, Missouri, Nebraska, and Oklahoma—paid an entrance fee of $10.00 and $1.00 for every day in the hospital. Zone two, which encompassed the next closest thirteen states, including Arkansas, Colorado, and Wisconsin, had an entrance fee of $5.00 plus 50 cents per day. Members in zone three—the rest of the country—continued to receive the service free. Another motivation for the

The SBA Hospital, ca. 1930. (Courtesy of the Security Benefit Group
of Companies, Topeka, Kans.)

zone system was to increase support from members who lived in outlying areas. The plan was not successful. In 1933 the board of trustees replaced the zone
system with a flat $10.00 entrance fee and a per-day charge of $1.00.[47]

Even with these increases, the room rate for zone one was about one-fourth
that of other hospitals. Patients in the SBA Hospital enjoyed other comparative
savings as well. They did not have to pay extra charges for the operating room,
nursing care, anesthetic, x-rays, and lab tests. A study of 10,000 full-pay patients
in 100 private hospitals found that the average patient paid $72.00 for a stay of
eleven days. The equivalent stay at the SBA Hospital cost $21.00.[48]

Coping with Depression and War

The SBA weathered the economic storms of depression rather well. Throughout
the crisis it continued to pay all claims and kept debt to a minimum. Much of
the credit lay with the conservative financial management during the 1920s. The

SBA had generally avoided the temptation to finance expansion through borrowing. The combined construction costs of the original and expanded hospital, as well as the homes, had come primarily from voluntary contributions. This abhorrence of debt, which was a characteristic of other societies as well, was a natural reaction to years of bad experience with overexpansion and cheap rates. Even so, the leaders of the SBA faced a crisis. Membership plummeted throughout most of the 1930s. In 1928, 224,807 men, women, and children belonged to the SBA, but by 1936 their ranks had thinned to 93,458.[49]

The SBA may have lost ground nationwide, but it became more popular than ever in Kansas. In 1925 the state membership was 42,127, or 19.8 percent of the nationwide total. By 1949 the number of Kansans who belonged to the SBA reached an all-time high of 70,818, or 53.6 percent of the entire membership. Not surprisingly, nearby Missouri was second with 11.1 percent of the national total. These figures corresponded with hospital use. Between 1925 and 1928, 62.4 percent of the patients were Kansans, while 14.6 percent were Missourians. From July 1948 to June 1949 a whopping 71.3 percent of the 3,478 members who used the hospital were from Kansas; Missouri was second at 14.1 percent.[50]

The domination of Kansas and Missouri was a double-edged sword. On one hand, it gave convincing evidence that the founders were right in their perception that there was a demand for the hospital. Clearly, Americans wanted far more from a fraternal society than life insurance. On the other hand, the existence of the SBA Hospital impeded the work of organizers in distant states. It dramatically weakened the incentive for individuals who had neither the time nor the money to travel to Topeka. Unfortunately for the SBA, it was impossible to stake all hopes on Kansas and Missouri. The membership in these states was much higher than ever but was still not enough to support a 250-bed hospital.

The larger hospital had not translated into a busier one. If anything, the annual number of patients began to decline. From 1932 to 1940 the patient load stabilized at 1,200 to 1,500 per year. After 1930, however, it was unusual if patients filled more than one-third of the available 250 beds. The figure would have been even lower had not the SBA also made efforts, albeit with limited success, to attract full-pay private patients.[51]

The hopes for generating revenue from membership fees also fell short. At no time were they sufficient to cover operating costs. The amount of costs covered by fees gradually increased to 29 percent in 1937. After that it never dipped below 25 percent. Transfers from the general fund continued to pay the bulk of the costs throughout the 1940s. Only in 1945 did fees from patients cover more than one-third of total expenses.[52]

To a considerable extent the SBA Hospital was a white elephant. The operating costs were higher than ever, but because of the slippage of membership, the revenue base had never been lower. From this standpoint the expansion of 1930 had been a mistake. The old sixty-five-bed hospital probably had the capacity to accommodate the member-patient loads of the 1930s. At the time, however, the decision to expand the hospital seemed sensible. The leadership had fairly good reason to expect that the rapid increase in the annual number of patients from 524 in 1925 to 2,045 in 1928 would continue.[53]

In retrospect, perhaps the board of trustees should have listened to members who called for building an additional hospital rather than expanding the existing one. This strategy, of course, would have carried its own risks. In 1928 the SBA National Council rejected a resolution to establish a second hospital in the Northwest on the grounds that the "present hospital with proposed enlargement in our opinion will better meet the needs of our membership by providing a more skilled professional service than is possible should we attempt to locate and maintain a large number of inferior institutions."[54]

The SBA faced another obstacle during the 1930s and 1940s: opposition from organized medicine. Doctors and hospital administrators looked suspiciously on the SBA hospital as an expanded version of the old lodge practice evil. At various times the three doctors on the SBA staff had difficulty gaining admission to professional organizations such as the American College of Surgeons. In a letter to Kirkpatrick, S. R. Boykin, the chief of staff, lamented that many doctors in Topeka "would welcome the opportunity to black ball one of the men from the Security Benefit Association Hospital."[55]

The SBA Hospital had trouble winning a place on the approved lists of medical, surgical, and hospital associations. The American College of Surgeons persistently refused to include the hospital despite an assurance from the inspector that he would issue a favorable report. The inspector later confided to Boykin that the real basis for the rejection was that "there was not a doctor on the Board of Trustees." Boykin suggested that the AMA wanted to punish the SBA for practicing contract medicine. Not surprisingly, the resultant bad blood discouraged cooperation between the hospital and members of local medical societies on matters such as referrals and consultations.[56]

For the SBA as a whole the AMA's rules against advertising were probably more troublesome. In 1938 William Cutter, secretary of the Council on Medical Education and Hospitals of the AMA, denied the SBA Hospital inclusion on the AMA's approved list, contending that it violated the canons against advertising and the corporate practice of medicine. Cutter accused the SBA of extending "medical and hospital service . . . into communities outside of the local area" and thus competing "with hospitals and physicians in those communities." Somewhat perplexed, Kirkpatrick asked Cutter to provide a specific example of how the SBA Hospital had violated the rules. "Perhaps we could change our literature," he plaintively suggested, "to meet your requirements." Despite Kirkpatrick's plea, the AMA continued to keep the SBA Hospital off the list.[57]

Kirkpatrick tried again in 1943 with greater success. After an all-out lobbying campaign by the SBA's attorney in Chicago, the hospital returned to the AMA's roster. The victory was short lived, however, as the AMA withheld approval in 1946. The ostensible reason once again was the SBA's advertising policy. F. H. Arestad, the assistant secretary of the Council on Medical Education and Hospitals, cited as evidence the SBA's recent circular, "Are Your Postwar Plans Protected?" The most serious offense for the AMA was that the advertisement featured testimonials from former patients. It was hard to deny the obvious, but Kirkpatrick presented the SBA's policy as consistent with the AMA's rules. He explained that "we advertise not to secure patients but to solicit members for our life insurance organization. We feel that our advertising policy . . . must be followed in order to serve the best interests of this organization." The SBA Hospital stayed off the AMA's list.[58]

Meanwhile, another threat arose from the rapid spread of employer-based, third-party payment systems of health care. Blue Cross and Blue Shield were examples. The purpose of Blue Cross was to pay hospital expenses. It had been formed in the 1930s by hospitals to achieve a larger and more stable source of income from patients. The goal of Blue Shield, an offshoot of Blue Cross, was to provide cash compensation to physicians.[59]

Most subscribers to Blue Cross and Blue Shield did not join as individuals, as was the case with the SBA, but were enrolled in groups by their employers. Changes to the federal tax code greatly spurred the growth of these plans. The Revenue Act of 1942 was especially important because it exempted fringe benefits, such as health insurance, from the income tax. The act opened the door for employers to compete for workers during a period of wage controls. It better enabled unions to secure lucrative tax-free fringe benefits for their members.[60]

Members of groups such as the SBA were the losers because they had purchased policies on an individual rather than a group basis. They could not deduct their dues from their taxable income. The spread of "free" health insurance coverage meant an ever shrinking market for the SBA product. By 1946 the number of subscribers to Blue Cross had risen to approximately 20 million. Seven million people alone had signed up in the preceding. Blue Shield had about

2 million subscribers by the beginning of 1946. These totals do not include commercial insurance plans.[61]

Blue Cross and Blue Shield reinforced, at least for the time being, the traditional prerogatives of the medical profession. Neither plan posed a serious challenge to the autonomy of doctors and hospitals or to fee-for-service compensation. Their main purpose was simply to reimburse the bills of providers. Blue
Cross and Blue Shield never aspired to assume control of the medical means of
production. If anything, the means of production controlled them. Members of
medical associations and hospital boards generally dominated the state boards
of directors of Blue Cross and Blue Shield.[62]

The upward spiral in health care costs during the 1940s also contributed to
the demise of the SBA Hospital. Inflation forced hospitals to pay more for med-
ication, building supplies, and technology. Wartime conditions, including a
shortage of doctors, exerted tremendous upward pressure on salaries and led to
rapid staff turnover. Between 1935 and 1945 the average cost per patient-day at
the SBA Hospital rose from $5.00 to $6.64. By 1949 the average cost to the SBA
Hospital per patient-day was $10.84. This was substantially lower than the na-
tional average. For 1949 all short-term general hospitals showed an average cost
of $14.33 per patient-day.[63]

A direct cost comparison between the SBA Hospital and other hospitals, however, would miss a key issue. Blue Cross and other third-party payers were less
vulnerable to medical inflation. Because third-party payers reimbursed health
care providers on the basis of their costs, hospitals and doctors lacked incentives
to economize. The same was true of patients. Both providers and recipients
could shift costs to the third-party payers. With the real medical costs obscured,
incentives to be cost-conscious or shop around for less expensive alternatives
were significantly undercut. The SBA Hospital was less able to hide or shift the
financial burden. Because of its reliance on individual subscribers, higher costs
added greater pressure to economize. The SBA tried to relieve the drain by closing the orphanage in 1942 and the home for the elderly in 1946. In addition, it
raised the per diem rate for new members to $2.00. Members who had joined
before August 1944 continued to pay the old rate of $1.00 per day.[64]

These measures failed to address and may have even worsened the underlying financial dilemmas. Because of the fee increases, people had fewer reasons
to join the SBA. The budget deficit improved somewhat, but the gains were
marginal and temporary. Even after the fee boost, patients still directly paid for
about one-third of costs. The rest of the hospital's budget continued to come
from transfers through the general fund. In 1930 the combined transfer from the

general fund for the expenses of the orphanage, the home for the elderly, and the hospital amounted to $246 million; by 1949 it was $232 million for the hospital alone.[65]

The SBA suffered from another telling weakness. The old fraternal ties seem to have waned considerably since the 1920s. One indicator was the content of the news coverage of the *Security News*. By the 1940s it carried far fewer stories about councils and members who were trying to improve the homes and hospital through fund-raising drives. Vibrant voluntarism had nearly disappeared. Perhaps the successful completion of the hospital encouraged complacency among the leaders and inspired them to regard the local council as an organizational fifth wheel. Not surprisingly, several top officials in the SBA began to ponder conversion of the SBA into a commercial company.[66]

The necessary critical mass for making this change came in 1948 after a bleak report by the Nebraska Insurance Commission. The commission threatened to deny the SBA a license to operate on the ground that it no longer fulfilled the necessary legal requirements of a fraternal society. As a result, the board of directors concluded that the fraternal method of operation was not viable and started conversion to a mutual company. The process was complete by 1950. The Security Benefit Association formally became the Security Benefit Life Company. The hospital continued to serve fraternal members at the old rates, but because of legal restrictions the same service was not available to policyholders in the commercial company. After a brief but failed drive to sell hospital services as private insurance, the hospital closed for good in 1954. Security Benefit Life (now the Security Benefit Group of Companies) still exists as a commercial company.[67]

Conclusion

The 1940s and 1950s witnessed the end of the second wave of fraternal health care expansion. During this period the rise of third-party insurance began to invade markets traditionally served by fraternal alternatives such as the IOF, the WC, and the WBA. There were exceptions. The *centros* of Tampa and the French Hospital of the French Mutual Benefit Society of San Francisco remained open until the 1980s, although there was a growing tendency to cater to third-party payers rather than members. Despite this general record of decline, there were also examples of fraternal expansion in hospital care during the postwar period. Two of the most impressive were in the little town of Mound Bayou, Mississippi.[68]

CHAPTER TEN

Our Temple of Health

I n 1942 more than 7,000 black people gathered in the small town of Mound Bayou, Mississippi, to celebrate the opening of the Taborian Hospital. The project had been undertaken by the Mississippi Jurisdiction of the International Order of Twelve Knights and Daughters of Tabor. To many celebrants it seemed a miracle. Through their combined efforts they had raised enough money to build a hospital in one of the poorest counties in the nation. For the first time, men and women could visit a doctor by walking through the front door rather than the side entrance for the "colored section." [1]

The hospital of the Knights and Daughters of Tabor was neither the first nor the last such institution among blacks. Black fraternal organizations had established various hospitals during the first three decades of the twentieth century. In Indianapolis, for example, the Sisters of Charity, an independent women's lodge, founded a small hospital during the 1910s. The movement to build hospitals thrived especially in the South. By 1931 black fraternal societies had founded nine fraternal hospitals in the South. Of the six or so that remained in 1950, three had opened since 1940. [2]

The organizations sponsoring black fraternal hospitals included the Mosaic Templars (Arkansas), the United Friends of America (Arkansas), the Working Benevolent Society (South Carolina), and a group with a remarkable name for a black fraternal order, the Lily White Security Benefit Association (Florida). By the end of the 1920s Arkansas was home to four such hospitals; the largest was the 100-bed facility of the Woodmen of Union in Hot Springs. About 70,000 members belonged to the organization, each of whom paid annual dues of $15.00. The supreme custodian was John L. Webb, a graduate of Tuskegee Institute and an enthusiastic booster of the self-help ideas of Booker T. Washington. [3]

In 1928 Thomas J. Huddleston, a former member of the Woodmen of Union and a wealthy black landowner, established the Afro-American Hospital in Yazoo City, Mississippi, which straddled the southeastern border of the Delta.

Plans to build the hospital had been formulated in 1924 when Huddleston founded the Afro-American Sons and Daughters. He had promised to begin construction if a thousand people joined the organization. Each new member paid an annual fee of $1.50, which flowed into a building fund. For three years Huddleston carefully tallied and published the receipts to update contributors. After he had sufficient money in hand, he secured a loan from a white-owned bank in Yazoo City to finance the rest of the construction costs.[4]

The Taborian Hospital

Huddleston's success was the inspiration for the builders of the second fraternal hospital in the state, the Mississippi Jurisdiction of the International Order of Twelve Knights and Daughters of Tabor. Unlike the Afro-American Sons and Daughters, the society had a long history not only in Mississippi but elsewhere in the South. It had been founded in 1872 by Moses Dickson, a free black man from Ohio who had fought in the Civil War. He derived the name of the organization from the mountain of Tabor in Galilee as mentioned in Psalm 89:12: "Tabor and Hermon shall rejoice in thy name." Like countless other fraternal societies, the Knights and Daughters of Tabor featured a ritual, secret passwords, and well-practiced drill teams. The major benefits were a small burial policy and weekly cash payments for the sick. Along with this program of mutual aid, the society dedicated itself to "Christianity, education, morality and temperance and the art of governing, self reliance and true manhood and womanhood."[5]

The Knights and Daughters of Tabor allowed men and women to join on equal terms although in separate lodges. In fact, female members in the Mississippi Jurisdiction outnumbered males by nearly two to one in 1942. While most of the top officials were men, women obtained leadership positions at the lower and middle levels. A drawing card for women was that the Knights and Daughters of Tabor had close ties with the church, the bastion of black female social life.[6]

The genesis of the hospital can be traced to the election of Perry M. Smith as chief grand mentor. Smith was a schoolteacher from Mound Bayou and had belonged to both the Woodmen of Union and the Afro-American Sons and Daughters. His father had been chief grand mentor at the turn of the century, and Smith benefited from careful grooming by his father to take on a leadership role. He had considerable talents of his own; he projected the image of a dignified, quiet aristocrat who was above the fray. But behind the scenes, he could be

forceful. Widely known as "Sir P. M." because he was the chief knight, he headed
the Mississippi Jurisdiction until his death in 1970 at age ninety-four.[7]

Smith began his tenure by trying to breathe life into an organization that had
recently been in receivership. To accomplish this he called for the establishment
of a hospital. The state grand session of 1929 rejected this proposal and voted instead to raise money for a new temple. Smith did not give up easily and continued pushing his idea. He finally succeeded in 1938 when the membership
voted ten to one in favor of the hospital plan. After much debate about where
to build it, the grand session selected Mound Bayou, an all-black community
of 800 people in the heart of the Delta. Not coincidentally, it was also Smith's
hometown.[8]

Few people doubted the need for a hospital in that part of the Delta. The
health care options for blacks were limited; only people in the small middle
class were able to afford the continuous services of general practitioners. The
poor had to depend on whatever was provided by planters. Some planters paid
the full cost of medical care, but others deducted the expense from the wages
or crop shares of their workers. The most ubiquitous health care practitioners
for poorer blacks were midwives. There were more than 100 in Bolivar County
alone in 1929.[9]

As for hospitals, the Afro-American Hospital of Yazoo City was the closest
black-owned facility, and it was ninety miles south of Mound Bayou. Many
white hospitals did not admit blacks under any circumstances, and those that
did offered substandard service. A common practice was to relegate black patients to the basement. Even when there was access to hospital care, only a few
black residents had the money to purchase it. Six state hospitals provided limited charity care in 1929, but all were in southern Mississippi rather than the
Delta. In Bolivar County twenty beds were designated for blacks in private and
public hospitals. These beds served a black population of approximately 52,000
and had to be shared by paying and charity patients.[10]

Even full-pay hospital patients had to endure humiliating second-class treatment. Many hospitals required black patients to bring eating utensils, sheets,
and toothbrushes and to pay for a black nurse if none was on staff. Smith had
confronted the system firsthand in a personally defining moment. He had taken
one of his children to a white hospital, entering through the back door. He
waited in vain for a doctor and eventually left. According to Smith's sister-in-
law he then "carried the patient to the Afro-American Sons and Daughters Hospital in Yazoo City, Mississippi. There they entered the front door" and were

"treated with courtesy and respect. That day, he decided to organize Tabor in Mound Bayou."[11]

There were pragmatic reasons for locating in Mound Bayou. It was one of a handful of towns in the South where blacks could vote and hold office. The community had been established in 1887 by two cousins, Benjamin T. Green and Isaiah T. Montgomery. Montgomery had been the personal slave of Joseph E. Davis, the brother of Jefferson Davis. By the turn of the century, Mound Bayou had earned a reputation as a haven for black entrepreneurship and self-help. In 1911 it inspired praise from Booker T. Washington, who called the community "a place where a Negro may get inspiration by seeing what other members of his race have accomplished." Mound Bayou later fell on hard times because of the depressed market for cotton, but it remained a powerful symbol of racial pride. As importantly, the town's black-controlled political environment offered protection for a hospital. As Mayor Benjamin A. Green (the son of Benjamin T. Green) pointed out, Mound Bayou, unlike other municipalities in Mississippi, did not impose a curfew. Curfews greatly hindered blacks who sought emergency treatment after dark.[12]

Once the location had been selected, Smith organized a conservative and incremental building campaign. Beginning in 1938 each member of the Knights and Daughters of Tabor paid an annual assessment into a hospital fund. The money gradually accumulated. To drum up support Smith visited plantations throughout Mississippi to speak to sharecroppers and tenants. One effective fund-raising method was to ask individuals to contribute the cost of a single brick. The hospital plan attracted 5,000 new members in four years.[13]

Although the membership financed the lion's share of construction costs, Smith won some financial and moral backing from white planters and doctors in the Delta. Many no doubt looked on the Taborian Hospital as a means to relieve themselves from paying medical costs for poor blacks. In addition, Smith carefully cultivated the goodwill of his future competitor, the Afro-American Hospital. He took the precaution of asking Huddleston to speak at the dedication ceremony in 1942. According to the *Taborian Star*, Huddleston "spellbounded the audience with real facts and figures of the successful operation of an all-Negro owned and operated hospital."[14]

In the months before the opening, Smith sought staff for the hospital. To take charge of the outpatients, he hired Dr. Phillip Moise George of Mound Bayou as the medical director. The most prominent black general practitioner in that part of the Delta, George was the logical choice. He was a community leader and had participated in an unsuccessful campaign to win a grant from the Julius

Rosenwald Fund to convert the former home of Isaiah T. Montgomery into a hospital.[15]

To find a chief surgeon, Smith visited Meharry Medical College in Nashville. Smith asked Dr. Matthew Walker, then an assistant professor, to become the chief surgeon. Although Walker did not accept the offer, he later played a pivotal role in the development of the Taborian Hospital. On Walker's recommendation Smith hired Dr. Theodore Roosevelt Mason Howard to fill the post.[16]

Howard's influence proved crucial. He left a deep imprint on fraternal hospitalization in the Delta and became a pioneer in Mississippi's early civil rights movement. A native of Kentucky, Howard had attended Oakwood College, a Seventh-Day Adventist school in Alabama for blacks. He finished his undergraduate education at Union College in Lincoln, Nebraska, which was also affiliated with the church. While in Lincoln, Howard developed a lifelong aversion to the color line. His letters to a former professor described his personal experiences with racial bigotry in Lincoln and revealed his growing outrage about discrimination. During this period Howard first showed his legendary gift for gab as a paid lecturer for the National Saloon League. He earned his medical degree in 1935 as the only black person in the graduating class of the College of Medical Evangelists in Loma Linda, California. Opinions about Howard's character diverge sharply. Some describe him as a zealous community builder, courageous crusader for civil rights, and kind-hearted doctor. Others remember him as egotistical and self-aggrandizing. He was a man not easily pigeonholed.[17]

When the Taborian Hospital opened in 1942, the final cost of construction had been over $100,000. The facilities included two major operating rooms, an x-ray room, a sterilizer, incubators, an electrocardiograph, a blood bank, and a laboratory. The hospital usually had two or three doctors on the staff; all were black. In 1944 annual dues of $8.40 entitled an adult to thirty-one days of hospitalization, including major or minor surgery; the dues also covered a $200 burial policy. The fee for a child was $1.20 per year for the same services and a $50 burial policy. Nonmember patients could obtain care but at higher rates.[18]

The hospital met with an enormous response from blacks in the Delta. Membership in the Knights and Daughters of Tabor in Mississippi mushroomed from 25,000 in 1942 to more than 47,000 in 1945. Lists of 338 patients from a total of four months in 1942 and 1945 reveal that 86.6 percent came from the four-county area of Bolivar, Coahoma, Sunflower, and Washington. A few had traveled from as far away as Chicago, Illinois. Given that Bolivar County residents made up nearly half the patients and the membership nearly doubled to 47,000

The Taborian Hospital, Mound Bayou, Mississippi, 1940s. (Florence Warfield Sillers, comp., *History of Bolivar County, Mississippi* [Jackson, Miss.: Hederman Brothers, 1948].)

between 1942 and 1945, one might surmise that somewhere near a majority of the county's blacks in 1945 were members and thus eligible for care at the hospital. The eligibility percentage for the whole Delta, which was home to about 380,000 blacks, was much smaller.[19]

Virtually all the patients were black. The vast majority worked as sharecroppers or farm laborers. They came to the hospital with varied maladies such as hernias, peptic ulcers, fibroid tumors, hypertension, bone and joint disease, fevers, and occasionally, gunshot and stab wounds. High blood pressure was probably the most common problem.[20]

Many members exercised their rights and came to the hospital for seemingly minor complaints. In so doing they obtained a limited form of preventive medicine, and the practice was encouraged to some degree. In 1944 a report issued by the Taborian Hospital Board of Management had concluded, "DON'T stay at home until you are DOWN and OUT, then come to the Hospital. Remember: 'A stitch in time saves nine.' Our Medical Staff is efficient but God alone can do the impossible." According to a former doctor, "There was quite a deal of that [patients asking to be seen for minor complaints]. That was not a great deal to our liking. That was preventive care, however. . . . That is exactly what the HMOs are doing now."[21]

The danger, of course, was that this open-door attitude might lead to malingering and abuse. To prevent this Smith urged that great discernment be exercised in recruiting efforts, warning that the "timber to build Tabor must

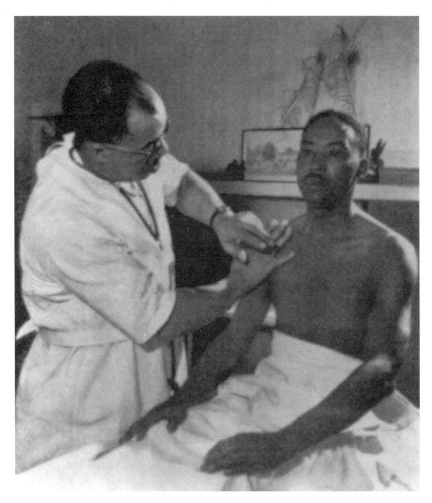

Dr. T. R. M. Howard of the Taborian Hospital examining a patient, 1946. (Hodding Carter, "He's Doing Something about the Race Problem," *Saturday Evening Post*, February 23, 1946, 30; photograph by Wilbert H. Blanche)

be chosen with greatest care. Don't enlist them when they are too old, or when they are in bad health and when they are of bad morals." Despite such strictures, it was rare for anyone to be disqualified for preexisting health conditions. Louella Thurmond, later the head nurse, remembers that the membership form included "a few health questions but it didn't seem to hinder anyone from joining." [22]

During the first decade prominent visitors gave the hospital generally glowing reviews and praised it as an exemplar of black self-help. Articles about it appeared in national magazines such as *Coronet* and the *Saturday Evening Post*. In 1946, for example, Hodding Carter, a prominent journalist in the Delta, reported that "Taborian is crowded but the clean, light wards, the cream-and-brown hallway and the operating rooms are spick and span."[23]

A New Rival: The Friendship Clinic

Even as Carter wrote, however, a dispute between factions of the Knights and Daughters of Tabor was coming to a head. By the end of 1946 Howard had been dismissed as chief surgeon. A major bone of contention involved Howard's private clinic, just across the street. During the early 1940s the hospital's board of management required all applicants for care to be examined by the chief surgeon in this clinic. Each patient who did not need hospitalization paid Howard $1.00. Objections to this practice mounted. Many critics charged that it unfairly benefited Howard and contradicted the guarantee of free hospitalization. Smith and his allies also feared that the order's ambitious chief surgeon would soon run for chief grand mentor.[24]

After Howard's dismissal, his supporters launched a counterattack by running their own candidate against Smith at the state grand session in late 1947. The bitterness was heated on both sides. Howard's followers accused Smith of dictatorial methods, nepotism, and favoring Mound Bayou's elites at the expense of the "little people." Smith's supporters fired back by alleging that Howard was power hungry and had lined his pockets as chief surgeon. The political infighting rose to such intensity that the white county sheriff was asked to keep order and tally the vote. Smith prevailed, but the contest was fairly close.[25]

The dissidents would not be appeased. Shortly after the grand session, they formed a rival fraternal society, the United Order of Friendship of America, and launched a campaign for a second hospital. The new organization had 149 lodges and 5,000 members, almost all former Taborians. R. L. Drew, a longtime leader in the Knights and Daughters of Tabors, became grand worthy master and, predictably, Howard took over as chief surgeon. As a fraternal society the United Order of Friendship of America differed little from the old Knights and Daughters of Tabor. There was a ritual, including passwords and higher degrees, and the men and women belonged to separate "palaces" and "chapters."[26]

The Friendship Clinic, which opened in 1948, was not as large as the Taborian Hospital but offered essentially the same services, including obstetrics, internal medicine, and major surgery. The small staff immediately faced the prob-

lem of keeping pace with the needs of the patients. With only one doctor to assist him, Howard had to perform as many as twelve operations a day.[27]

For Howard both fraternal hospitals were springboards to the creation of an
array of business enterprises in Mound Bayou. He established the first swimming pool for blacks in Mississippi, a 1,600-acre cotton and cattle plantation,
a restaurant with a beer garden, a home construction firm, and even a small
zoo. He purchased the Magnolia Mutual Life Insurance Company, a purely
commercial venture. It sold both burial and hospitalization insurance to blacks.
Later he became chairman of the board of the National Negro Business League
and the president of the National Medical Association (NMA), the medical society for black doctors.[28]

Meanwhile the Knights and Daughters of Tabor scrambled to find a re-
placement for Howard. With some desperation Smith again turned to Matthew
Walker, who had since become head of the surgery department at Meharry
Medical College. Walker helped to secure several short-term replacements, but
the heavy patient load continued to put high demands on the surgical staff.
Smith and Walker worked out an official arrangement which provided that surgical residents from Meharry, under the supervision of Walker, be sent to the
hospital on a rotating basis. For two decades both a junior and a senior surgical
resident came to Mound Bayou for stays of four to six months. In addition, first-
and second-year students visited for three weeks. Many alumni from Meharry
recall working at the Taborian Hospital initially as students and later as residents. For the more serious operations, a surgical team, often composed of
a specialist, a surgeon, and an anesthetist, drove down from Nashville. Walker
himself made the trip about 200 times.[29]

Jim Crow and Civil Rights

Both hospitals had to adapt to the highly segregated racial environment that
characterized the Mississippi Delta. To some extent they benefited from this
state of affairs. Racial discrimination was an important, although certainly not
the sole, factor that accounted for their clientele. The leaders of both societies
were well aware that great dangers awaited any person who challenged the status quo. Politicians and state officials had the ability to hinder or destroy the
hospitals through regulations and other restrictions. Planters, for their part, always had the power to deny fraternal collectors and recruiters access to their
properties.[30]

Despite these impediments both societies not only supported but were often in the forefront of the emerging opposition to Jim Crow and disfranchisement. Obviously their influence reflected the rise of a growing, better-educated, and self-aware black middle class. Many civil rights activists learned their leadership skills through fraternal orders. In Mound Bayou they had two thriving hospitals that stood as visible reminders of the wider potential for black organizational talent and assertiveness.[31]

Officials of the United Order of Friendship were more assertive in challenging the racial status quo. In 1951 Howard played a pioneering role when he organized the Regional Council of Negro Leadership (RCNL). Other participants included R. L. Drew and Howard's assistant at the Friendship Clinic, Dr. E. P. Burton, who cared for most of the outpatients. The RCNL quickly sparked controversy when it distributed bumper stickers calling for boycotts of service stations that did not provide rest rooms for black patrons. This demand, though consistent with the doctrine of separate but equal, was a risky one to make in Mississippi. By 1954 Howard took a more radical stand. At a meeting with the governor, he drew intense criticism from whites when he called for strict enforcement of the Supreme Court's ruling in *Brown v. Board of Education*. A year later he organized a rally of 10,000 blacks in Mound Bayou for voter registration.[32]

Howard's example had a crucial impact on the political education of future civil rights leader Medgar Evers. Fresh from college, Evers had arrived in Mound Bayou in 1952 after accepting a job offer from Howard to sell insurance for the Magnolia Mutual Life Insurance Company. He later won a promotion to acting agency director. Evers's wife, Myrlie, worked for the company as a typist and gave birth to her first child at the Friendship Clinic. Howard made quite an impression on the young mother. "One look told you," she later wrote, "that he was a leader: kind, affluent, and intelligent, that rare Negro in Mississippi who had somehow beaten the system." She described how her husband, while making his insurance rounds, encountered the "absolute squalor" of sharecroppers in "shacks on the nearby cotton plantations. Here, on the edges of the cotton fields, life was being lived on a level that Medgar, for all his acquaintance with the poor of both Mississippi and of Chicago's teeming black ghetto, found hard to believe." Medgar Evers not only sold insurance; he also promoted membership in the NAACP. He left Mound Bayou in 1954 to become the first field secretary for the NAACP in Mississippi.[33]

During the 1940s Howard's relations with local whites generally had been cordial. They grudgingly gave him some respect because of his business and organizational acumen. This goodwill rapidly evaporated with Howard's growing political involvement. The breaking point came after a highly publicized effort by Howard to find and protect witnesses to the murder of Emmett Till. He became the target of financial harassment; his family received death threats. Unable to weather the storm of hatred, in 1956 Howard sold his properties at a loss of $100,000 and moved to Chicago, where he established a practice. He transferred control of the hospital of the United Order of Friendship to Burton and Drew and gradually phased out the operations of the Magnolia Mutual Life Insurance Company. Despite Howard's departure, his compatriots at the Friendship Clinic did not abandon political activity. Burton and Drew continued to be leaders in the RCNL, and Drew helped to organize boycotts of segregated bus stations as president of the NAACP of Coahoma County during the early 1960s.[34]

Like their counterparts in the United Order of Friendship, the leaders of the Knights and Daughters of Tabor generally promoted civil rights. Smith persistently but discreetly supported voter registration and membership in the NAACP. Edward Verner, a surgical resident at the Taborian Hospital, described Smith's approach as one of "suggestion rather than an overt clarion call. It was pretty much low key." The hospital's most visible involvement came in the 1960s. During the freedom rides and other protests, the Taborian Hospital extended refuge and medical aid to Fannie Lou Hamer and Amzie Moore. In 1975 Andrew Young recalled that as "we marched in those glory days, flanked by police cordons shielding us from angry crowds, we knew that there was the little hospital at Mound Bayou that would care for us."[35]

At the same time Smith tried to remain on friendly terms with the white community. In 1953, as a publicity coup, he persuaded the governor, the lieutenant governor, and the speaker of the state house to deliver addresses in Mound Bayou on the anniversary of the hospital's opening. Smith's strategy of quiet but firm protest was generally effective. Staff and surgical residents describe the hospital's relationship with planters and politicians as cordial. But for the most part there was little direct contact with whites.[36]

Patient Care, Fund Raising, and Staffing

Both fraternal hospitals enjoyed a brisk business during the 1950s and 1960s. At the Taborian Hospital there were 135,208 visits by outpatients between 1942 and 1963 and a yearly average of 1,400 stays by inpatients. The number of births was

Patients waiting to see doctors at the Taborian Hospital, 1946. (Hodding Carter,
"He's Doing Something about the Race Problem," *Saturday Evening Post*,
February 23, 1946, 31; photograph by Wilbert H. Blanche)

2,871. The Friendship Clinic also turned in a busy record. Between 1961 and 1965
the numbers of patients and newborns averaged a little over half of those recorded by the Taborian Hospital.[37]

It was a challenge to cope with the stream of patients. Seventy-six beds sometimes filled the space at Taborian Hospital, which had been designed for forty-
two. The staffs of both hospitals vehemently deny that anybody was turned
away or forced to leave prematurely because of crowding, although in a few cases
they referred patients who required special equipment to other facilities.[38]

One indelible memory of the caregivers was the unusually cooperative attitude of the patients. By all accounts, patients were grateful and ready to follow
medical advice. Dr. Robert J. Smith, a former student and resident at the Taborian Hospital, remarked that "I have never enjoyed the practice of medicine any
place as much as I did in the town of Mound Bayou. Everybody you helped was
very appreciative." On the face of it, this patient behavior stands in contrast to
lodge practice, a precursor to fraternal hospitalization. Lodge practice had a
reputation for encouraging patients to be assertive and demanding. The spe-

cial conditions of the Delta had much to do with the difference. Dr. Charlotte Walker, who worked at the Taborian Hospital as a medical student in the early 1960s, notes that "many of these people came from plantation-type situations . . . where they were not treated with kindness or respect, and we always treated the patients kindly and courteously. They were Mr. Smith and Mrs. Jones not Jerry and Jane." [39]

During this time the two societies, in their struggle to keep the hospitals afloat, benefited from high levels of organization. The United Order of Friendship had more than 140 lodges throughout the state in the late 1940s. The Knights and Daughters of Tabor had an even more extended network. As late as 1963 it had 688 affiliates in the state, including temples for the Knights, tabernacles for the Daughters, and tents for the Maids and Pages of Honor (girls and boys). Much like the Shriners of the Masons, the Taborians had an elite unit for members with higher degrees, the Royal House of Media. The tabernacles, temples, and tents were under the jurisdiction of twenty-two districts throughout the state, each led by a high presider. The high presiders were responsible for collecting the quarterly dues of members. They were familiar sights on plantations as they walked from door-to-door with their receipt books. As an inducement, each high presider could keep 10 percent of the funds collected. They also vied for awards at the state grand session. The report for 1962 praised "Dtr. Beulah Stokes, Bobo, who raised $105.00 and was crowned Queen and received a beautiful trophy and one dozen red roses." [40]

Local and state auxiliaries in each society raised additional funds to equip the hospital and make up deficits. They often focused campaigns on the kinds of specific capital improvements that members could readily appreciate, such as the purchase of new bassinets for the baby ward. Many people gave contributions in kind. In February 1953, for instance, the state hospital auxiliary reported that members had donated fifty-eight pillow cases, seventy-four washcloths, thirty-two bars of soap, two boxes of grits, and other items. Hospital stays could spur fund-raising efforts. In 1943 the officials of a tabernacle in Metcalf wrote that their members had used the hospital for "four successful operations in the past year. It is a God Send. We mean to do our bit and more for the hospital." [41]

The grand session of the Mississippi Jurisdiction of the Knights and Daughters of Tabor was a major opportunity for the high presiders and members of the auxiliary to raise money and attract recruits. It featured activities ranging from spelling bees to beauty contests. In addition, the Maids and Pages vied for college scholarships in oratorical contests. In 1952 the star attraction was a parade of forty floats. The United Order of Friendship followed a similar strategy.

The organizers of the five-day annual conclave in Greenwood tailored the events to specific groups through Men's Day, Women's Day, and Children's Day. The festivities concluded with a street parade and a Hospital rally.[42]

To pay for the relief of members in need, both societies relied on Annual Sermon Day. This event combined altruism and financial self-interest. For the Knights and Daughters of Tabor, annual Sermon Day took place on the third Sunday in June at 3:00 P.M. It was the duty of each high presider to reserve a church and recruit a minister to deliver "a good, gospel sermon." The sermon culminated in an appeal for donations. Jessie Dobbins, a high presider in the 1940s, induced people to start giving by offering a personal contribution. Half the proceeds could be kept by the minister. The Taborian Relief Fund and the participating church divided the rest.[43]

Both societies used their auxiliaries to recruit volunteer labor. In one case the leaders of the auxiliary of the Friendship Clinic made a deal with fifteen local farmers to donate a total of 100 pounds of cotton and arranged for another farmer to gin it for free. The only condition was that the auxiliary arrange for someone to do the picking. It completed the job, sold the final product, and used the proceeds to purchase tiles for the floor of the hospital. Several nurses at the Friendship Clinic picked the cotton and installed the tiles.[44]

The relative lack of state regulation contributed to the success of the hospitals. This environment had been fostered by Mississippi's history of segregation and low welfare spending. Many white leaders feared that if the hospitals disappeared, white taxpayers, doctors, and planters would have to foot the medical bills of poor blacks. Therefore, regulation was virtually nonexistent. Officials of the Mississippi Commission on Hospital Care rarely, if ever, inspected the facilities. Only at the end of the 1950s did regulators begin to assert their authority.[45]

Even then, both the Friendship Clinic and the Taborian Hospital could rely on support from members of the local white political and medical establishment. For example, in 1961, when the Mississippi hospital commission threatened to shut the Friendship Clinic for regulatory infractions, the administrators persuaded seven prominent white doctors from Bolivar County to write letters of support. One doctor warned that closure would "cause many of the patients that go there to become charity or state aid patients and overload and overtax our present facilities in the state," while another opined "that it would have been impossible for these patients to have secured hospital service at all except for the existence of the Friendship Clinic."[46]

The light hand of regulation also helped the hospitals to save on expenses. Salaries were extremely low. The medical director of the Taborian Hospital earned $500 per month in 1958; the pay for the head nurse was half that amount. The ability to minimize payroll costs enabled the hospitals to hire entry-level personnel (often teenagers) and train them incrementally in a kind of apprenticeship. Over time, talented employees could look forward to gradual increases in pay and responsibilities. For example, Annyce Campbell began as a nurse's aide at $18 per month with the Taborian Hospital. Later she worked for nearly two decades as the head nurse of the obstetrics unit at the Friendship Clinic.[47]

With the exception of the doctors, most of the staff at the two hospitals did not have formal training. They either learned on the job or in special in-house courses supervised by the chief surgeon. In 1958 the nursing staff of the Taborian Hospital consisted of one registered nurse, five licensed practical nurses, and six nurse's aides. The doctors showed pride in their capacity to manage this system. "We took a girl out of the cotton field," Walker often declared, "and taught her to give anesthesia with drop ether." Although on-the-job training was the norm, both hospitals strongly encouraged and sometimes paid for staff to take courses and upgrade their skills.[48]

Despite the reliance on salaried doctors, neither hospital encountered significant trouble from medical associations. Observers do not recall any hostility from either the state affiliate of the AMA or the all-black NMA. A probable reason was that the hospitals catered to a rural, low-income, and racially marginalized market. Black doctors were not likely to object to fraternal hospitals, at least in rural areas, because they were sources of extra work. Even so, it is surprising that medical associations, given their aversion to contract practice, did not raise some objections.[49]

The Decline of the Fraternal Hospitals

By 1960 both hospitals were feeling financial pressures. Former employees cite the impact of new regulation as the culprit. The files of the Mississippi Commission on Hospital Care bear them out. The commission gradually shifted from its previous policy of regulatory laissez-faire and started to issue citations, finding the hospitals guilty of infractions such as inadequate storage and bed space, failure to install doors that could swing in either direction, and excessive reliance on uncertified personnel. In response to one mandate, the Taborian Hospital expended hefty sums to replace cane fiber walls with fire-resistant material that could be more easily scrubbed. The two hospitals never seemed able to satisfy the demands of the commission, however. In 1965 a consultant from the commission roundly chastised the Taborians for their slowness in responding to regulatory edicts. He complained that "when we have asked your facility to take the necessary steps to upgrade same, we are constantly told that you do not have funds with which to do these things, yet if you are to operate a hospital, something has to be done to meet the Minimum Standards of Operation for Mississippi Hospitals."[50]

Heavy-handed regulation was also a factor in the decline of at least two other fraternal hospitals in the Deep South, the Afro-American Hospital in Yazoo City and the United Friends Hospital in Little Rock. The Afro-American Hospital closed down (as a fraternal entity) in 1966; the United Friends Hospital, which had opened in 1922, lingered until 1975. Marginal enterprises were unable to keep pace with increasingly voluminous regulatory standards. In addition, desegregation meant that white and, for that matter, black doctors had fewer reasons to shield fraternal hospitals from the regulators.[51]

Another factor that impinged on the stability of black fraternal hospitals in Mound Bayou and elsewhere was growth of technology in health care. The rise of third-party payment systems speeded this trend. When the government or private insurers paid the bill, as they did to an increasing extent for blacks in the Delta, patients had incentives to patronize facilities that featured the latest and most expensive technology. Black fraternal hospitals, which were relatively low-tech enterprises, could ill afford to shift additional costs onto their impoverished memberships.[52]

The shift toward third-party payers had already become apparent in the Delta by the 1950s. With increased automobile ownership, it was easier for patients to travel to Memphis or Jackson to obtain free care. An even more important catalyst for change was the Hill-Burton Hospital Construction Act of 1946. The act offered states federal grants to build and modernize hospitals, outpatient clinics, and public health centers. Two provisions cut deeply into the patient base of black fraternal hospitals. The act required that hospitals use a portion of the funds for indigent care, and it stipulated that all services be offered "without discrimination on account of race, creed, or color." Of course there were gaping loopholes, and enforcement was poor. For example, the act allowed southern states to maintain hospital segregation as long as they gave blacks care "of like quality." On the whole, however, these grants slowly helped to make both free and paid hospital care available to blacks, albeit under conditions of segregation.[53]

Even more directly, the Hill-Burton Act hindered the ability of the two fraternal hospitals to make necessary capital improvements to compete successfully. Neither the Friendship Clinic nor the Taborian Hospital received any federal funds, while other hospitals in the area reaped a windfall. Overall, health facilities in the counties of Bolivar, Coahoma, Sunflower, and Washington obtained $4.6 million from the federal government between 1948 and 1965. The state also allocated funds. This money enabled nonfraternal hospitals to upgrade their equipment and add more than 450 beds. A small number were for blacks in segregated hospitals. By the early 1960s more beds for blacks had been added or were being added in both Bolivar and Sunflower Counties. Yet change came slowly. Only in 1961 did blacks have hospital beds in Cleveland, the seat of Bolivar County.[54]

During the 1960s, Medicare and Medicaid vastly accelerated the trend toward reliance on third-party payers. The lure of reimbursement dollars led white doctors and hospitals to seek the low-income black patients they had once shunned. Another development was the appearance of a small but growing segment of the local black population with private coverage through organizations such as Blue Cross and Blue Shield. A result of both trends was, according to John Hatch, the first director of community health action at the Delta Health Center, that "people who had real choices, like good solid health insurance, elected to go elsewhere."[55]

A final factor that led to the decline of the hospitals was massive migration to the North. Motivated by the mechanization of southern agriculture, the black population of the Delta dropped precipitously. Because so many workers who moved were younger and better educated, the fraternal hospitals had to carry the burdens of an impoverished, aging, and declining membership. In 1945 the Knights and Daughters of Tabor had 47,450 members in Mississippi. By 1960 the combined membership of the United Order of Friendship of America and the Knights and Daughters of Tabor had dwindled to 22,237.[56]

These developments put unavoidable upward pressure on the dues. By 1964 the Knights and Daughters of Tabor had raised dues to $30 per year for adults and $4 for children. It also added extra fees of $4 for an EKG, $2 for an x-ray, and $15 for a normal delivery. Although these rates were considerably higher than they had been in the 1940s, the coverage still included thirty-one days of hospitalization, major and minor surgery, basic examinations, and routine tests and drugs. The Friendship Clinic followed the same trend by raising dues to $32 for adults and $5 for children and by refusing to take any financial obligation for contagious diseases that required "strict isolation" and procedures involving "the services of highly trained and skilled technicians; such as brain surgery." Despite the increased fees, the budgets of both hospitals began to fall periodically into the red.[57]

In 1966 the federal Office of Economic Opportunity (OEO), the major front-line agency in the War on Poverty, entered the scene with subsidized health care. The Department of Community Medicine at Tufts University established the Delta Health Center in Mound Bayou with a planning grant from the OEO. The center sponsored an extensive program of community health education, preventive medicine, and free outpatient services to people below the poverty line. The next year witnessed the end of fraternal hospitalization in the Delta. In 1967 the inducement of a second planning grant from the OEO persuaded the two societies to merge their hospitals and sell the property to the federal government. The new federally owned Mound Bayou Community Hospital used the building of the old Taborian Hospital and was the first inpatient facility of the OEO. As in most OEO projects, the board of directors included representatives from the community. As part of the deal with the federal government, the leadership of both societies, including Smith and Drew, was given control of one-third of the board.[58]

Despite this power-sharing arrangement, fraternal membership fell off dramatically. The loss of fraternal ownership and financing left members with little motivation to keep paying dues. The hospital was just another OEO project. The dilemma created by this change was illustrated in a letter from P. M. Smith and other leaders of the Knights and Daughters of Tabor to the Mississippi state insurance department. The letter requested legal authorization to upgrade the level of fraternal life insurance coverage: "Since 90% of our membership is composed of people who are classified in the poverty category—they are eligible for free care at the Mound Bayou Community Hospital. Therefore, we are losing their membership in the order. This puts the Order in a declining position in membership and financial income. We aren't sure of our proper direction, but we feel that with the enactment of an additional line of policies to sell we will be able to survive."[59]

The rapid inflow of federal money dampened the community's old habits of medical mutual aid and self-help. According to Dr. Louis Bernard of Meharry Medical College, "The dollars available from the so-called antipoverty program ruined the International Order of the Knights and Daughters of Tabor." Many former staff members of both hospitals share Bernard's opinion. According to Annyce Campbell, who worked at the Delta Health Center after the merger, "Everybody was reaching for money." She reports warning at the time "that it's not helping because this ain't gonna last and then when this is gone, we'll still be standing around not wanting to do those things for ourselves that we can do."[60]

The Quality of Patient Care

One obvious question is How well did the Taborian Hospital and the Friendship Clinic serve their patients? Critical assessments have been put forward by the founders of the Delta Health Center. Hatch characterizes patient care at the Taborian Hospital as "awful" and remembers that the equipment was antiquated. He declares bluntly, "I know if I were really very sick, I would not have wanted to be there. . . . I think that they made a mighty effort to be kind and decent to people, but they were always at the edge of resources." He emphasizes that the hospitals did not encourage preventive medical care strategies such as immunizations and better nutrition. Dr. H. Jack Geiger, also a veteran of the Delta Health Center, asserts that the surgical residents at the Taborian Hospital were "cutting everything that moved without real teaching or supervision" by a fully trained and certified board surgeon. Geiger and Hatch agree, however, that most deficiencies resulted from a need to stretch scarce resources rather than from a lack of good intentions.[61]

Others express favorable opinions about the care provided by the hospitals. Today in Mound Bayou any mention of the Taborian Hospital and the Friendship Clinic to people over age forty is likely to evoke fond memories. The former patients and staff who were interviewed exclaim "wonderful" and "beautiful" when asked about the quality of care. A qualified secondhand source is L. C. Dorsey, a social worker who started at the Delta Health Center in 1966 and served as executive director for more than two decades. Based on numerous conversations with former patients, Dorsey summarizes the attitudes as "almost always positive for the 1950s and 1960s" but more of "a mixed bag" for the 1970s and 1980s.[62]

To some extent, sunny memories can be attributed to nostalgia for a simpler past. On the other hand, praise for the hospital is equally enthusiastic from staff who have also worked in more modern and generously financed facilities. Louella Thurmond, now employed at the Delta Health Center, remembers the Taborian Hospital as a "family type setting [where] everybody seemed to be concerned about each other." She agrees with her coworker Earlee Thompson, who emphasizes that "we gave good quality care." Campbell voices the same sentiment. "I truly say," she declares, "that the service was tops. . . . I've learned this since I've been in nursing. You can't deal with one part of the man. You have to deal with the whole man."[63]

Former doctors, surgical residents, and medical students from Meharry who worked at the hospitals temporarily express similar views. They had ample opportunities to compare the Taborian Hospital and the Friendship Clinic with more up-to-date medical facilities elsewhere. Dr. Asa G. Yancey, who succeeded Howard for one year as chief surgeon at the Taborian Hospital, characterizes the physical plant during the late 1940s as "pretty much state of the art," although he suspects that it later lagged behind. Bernard describes the level of care as "superb," while Smith remembers that the hospital in the early 1960s was "clean as a pin and the food was excellent. . . . It was a better run hospital than some of the hospitals that I go to in Memphis today." Smith did not detect any decay in patient care or technical quality between his visits in the 1950s and 1964. His impression was that "it was not on a shoe-string budget. They kept things up." Smith and Bernard underscore the dedication and competency of the support staff.[64]

Bernard agrees that it would have been preferable to have had a fully board certified surgeon present during operations but contends that this was "not feasible at Mound Bayou" because of the cost. Smith emphasizes that the senior residents had accumulated considerable surgical experience before their arrival. Most were in the fifth or sixth year of their residencies. "Dr. Walker," he declares, "loved those patients. . . . He would never send a chief resident down there unless he was sure that chief resident was ready to go." For the more serious cases, the doctors either transferred the patients to other hospitals or requested help from specialists at Meharry, who could make the trip "in a matter of hours."[65]

Smith speculates that the founders of the Delta Health Center and other officials from the OEO were victims of "culture shock." They might have been unrealistically preoccupied with the stark contrast between rural hospitalization in Mississippi and the more familiar, technologically advanced institutions of the Northeast: "If they came from Harvard to Memphis today, there would be some difference in technology. For basic and nuts and bolts, the things that 90 percent of the patients that go in a community hospital need, we could do. When there was something we couldn't do, we had places where we could send people."[66]

The medical students and surgical residents also have much to say about the role of on-the-job training. They remember that this system worked well, although not all would recommend it for current public policy. Smith characterizes his subordinates as "better than some of the nurses and anesthetists I have now." Verner fondly recalls that "you could take a person with a certain amount of natural ability and just train them. Some of those girls were actually brilliant kids." Bernard and Smith contend that the hospital anticipated the recent

TABLE 10.1. Death Rates and Average Length of Stay:
Taborian Hospital and Friendship Clinic, 1961–1966

	Taborian Hospital	Friendship Clinic
Patient deaths (excluding newborns)	5.0 percent	3.9 percent
Newborn deaths	0.9 percent	2.0 percent
Average stay (excluding newborns)	9.8 days	7.9 days

Sources: Friendship Clinic, Application for Hospital Renewal, Mississippi Commission on Hospital Care, 1958–66, and Taborian Hospital, Application for Hospital Renewal, Mississippi Commission on Hospital Care, 1961–66, Mississippi Department of Health, Jackson; Duke Endowment, Hospital and Orphan Section, *Annual Report* [1958–62].

trend to entrust more responsibility to nurse's aides, health care technicians, and nurse practitioners. Both men credit the Taborian Hospital with making efficient use of limited financial resources. Bernard favorably compares the fraternal hospitals to the current health care system, where "every new piece of technology that comes out is twice as expensive as the first piece." By contrast, he contends that the administrators of the Taborian Hospital realized that "you cannot give everybody a Rolls-Royce."[67]

These subjective evaluations are not the only sources on the quality of patient care. Between 1961 and 1966 both hospitals filed annual reports with the Mississippi Commission on Hospital Care. The reports included data on basic measures of quality such as the numbers of inpatient deaths and average stays (table 10.1). Although comparable figures are not available for hospitals in Mississippi as a whole, they do exist for South Carolina. During the late 1950s and early 1960s the Hospital Section of the Duke Endowment tabulated annual statistics (table 10.2) on fifty-three general hospitals in the state. They offer a reasonably objective standard of comparison.[68]

Patient outcomes at the Taborian Hospital and the Friendship Clinic were not significantly different from those for blacks in South Carolina. The record of the Taborian Hospital in obstetrics appears to have been excellent. Fewer than 1 percent of newborns died during this period. This percentage was lower than that for both blacks and whites in South Carolina. One surprise was the fairly strong performance of the Friendship Clinic, which was generally regarded as the less technically advanced and more financially strained of the two institutions.[69]

TABLE 10.2. Death Rates and Average Length of Stay: Black and White Patients in
Fifty-three General Hospitals in South Carolina, 1958–1962

	Blacks	Whites
Patient deaths (excluding newborns)	4.8 percent	2.2 percent
Newborn deaths	2.8 percent	1.7 percent
Average stay (excluding newborns)	7.3 days	7.3 days

Sources: Friendship Clinic, Application for Hospital Renewal, Mississippi Commission on Hospital Care, 1958–66, and Taborian Hospital, Application for Hospital Renewal, Mississippi Commission on Hospital Care, 1961–66, Mississippi Department of Health, Jackson; Duke Endowment, Hospital and Orphan Section, *Annual Report* [1958–62].

The most notable contrast with South Carolina was the longer than average patient stay in Mississippi. It was 9.8 days at the Taborian Hospital and 7.9 days at the Friendship Clinic. In South Carolina, blacks and whites both had average stays of 7.3 days. These statistics are consistent with the perception, widely echoed by observers, that the patient base of the Friendship Clinic and the Taborian Hospital had aged considerably by the 1960s, since the elderly tend to have longer hospital stays. In South Carolina, for example, blacks who were over age sixty-five had an average stay of 12.5 days. Probably the most convincing evidence of aging was the relatively low number of newborns at the Taborian Hospital and the Friendship Clinic. The percentage of newborns among the patients was roughly half that for blacks in South Carolina.[70]

Another reason for the longer stays may have been malingering. Geiger speculates that many patients who were not really sick checked into the hospitals to "take it easy" after the harvest. While such cases did exist, former doctors at the hospitals deny that they imposed a significant burden. "I might have had three of those," Smith reports. "You would take the guy in. . . . He felt he might have had something. [The doctors] took the guy, maybe kept him a day; if there wasn't anything wrong, they talked to him nice and he'd leave. That was never a problem. Ninety-eight percent of the people I saw in that clinic every day needed to be seen."[71]

Conclusion

The years after the demise of the hospitals as fraternal entities were highly troubled. Soon after the creation of the new Mound Bayou Community Hospital in 1967, it became a battleground between federal officials and the fraternal members who had been appointed to the board of directors. By the early 1970s some former officials at the Delta Health Center called for shutting the hospital down because of regulatory infractions. In 1974 Bernard ordered the end of the rotation program because the "increasing requirements of the Mississippi State Hospital Commission made it an impossible situation." It was not an easy decision. Bernard still had fond memories of the hospital because of his experiences there as a student, a resident, and for a brief time, chief surgeon.[72]

In 1983 the Mound Bayou Community Hospital finally closed due to mounting pressure from regulators, allegations of decaying standards of care, and federal funding cutbacks. Only the empty shell of the original building remains on Highway 61. Today the Delta Health Center, controlled by the federal Department of Health and Human Services, still provides outpatient care and preventive medical services.[73]

For twenty-five years before 1967, thousands of low-income blacks in the Mississippi Delta obtained affordable hospital care through fraternal societies. Although there were clear deficiencies, the quality was reasonably good, especially given the limited resources. Most importantly, the Taborian Hospital and the Friendship Clinic excelled in providing benefits to patients that were not easily quantifiable, including personal attention, comfortable surroundings, and community pride. Both societies accomplished these feats with little outside help. The Knights and Daughters of Tabor and the United Order of Friendship of America forged extensive networks of mutual aid and self-help for thousands of low-income blacks.

CHAPTER ELEVEN

The End of the Golden Age

E ven after the readjustment of the 1910s, fraternalism was a powerful force. As had been true for well over a century, more Americans
belonged to lodges than any other kind of organization aside from
churches. The President's Research Committee on Social Trends
counted 20 million members in 1930. It estimated that the actual total, however,
was as high as 35 million. But despite these high numbers, the age of rapid expansion had ended.[1]

A slowing trend in membership growth appeared across a wide spectrum
of societies. The ranks of the life insurance orders rose from 9.9 million to
10.8 million between 1920 and 1929; the number of lodges remained stable at
roughly 124,000. This performance, while respectable in absolute terms, compared poorly with that of the commercial companies. Between 1920 and 1929
the number of commercial ordinary policies increased from 16.7 million to
31.3 million. Growth for orders and secret societies providing funeral and sick-
funeral benefits, such as the Moose, the Eagles, and the Masons, slowed too. Between 1920 and 1929 the membership of the eleven leading societies climbed
from 9.2 million to 10.8 million. The Masons, who added a million initiates,
were responsible for most of the gain and by 1930 represented a record-breaking
12 percent of white adults.[2]

For the black societies as well, the growth rate tapered off. The *Negro Year
Book*, published periodically by the Tuskegee Institute, lists 21 national insurance and noninsurance fraternal societies in 1916, 30 in 1925, and 32 in 1931. The
membership statistics in the *Year Book*, while limited to just a few societies, suggest a leveling off: 888,557 (1916), 1.4 million (1925), and 1.4 million (1931).[3]

The limited growth resulted from various factors. Lingering doubts about
stability and reliability hampered recruiting efforts. Societies, particularly
among blacks and immigrants, had to contend with accusations of mismanagement and corruption. Another stumbling block was the emergence of rival en-

tertainment sources such as the movies and radio. A third factor was specific to the immigrant organizations: the drying up of "new blood" from Europe. Fourth, the core values of fraternalism, including character building, thrift, and mutual aid, came under increasing assault. Finally, societies suffered from laws that hindered their operation and subsidized competitors.

Questions about fraternal stability still arose during the 1920s. Though societies had generally completed the transition to higher rates, bitterness lingered among the rank and file and the public. A related issue, especially plaguing black organizations, was bad publicity from corruption and mismanagement. Memories were fresh of the fate of the once prestigious UOTR. During the 1910s it had fallen prey to a cycle of bad management, nepotism, and embezzlement that culminated in the collapse of its bank and other enterprises.[4]

At the same time, too much emphasis can be placed on negative practices. Financial scandals, such as those which befell the UOTR, were the exceptions. Only rarely did societies disappear because of insolvency or corruption. Moreover, commercial companies were not immune to such problems. Well-publicized financial scandals had rocked the old-line companies in the 1870s and, in fact, had helped usher in the rise of fraternal insurance. After societies confronted similar difficulties in the early twentieth century, they too showed an ability to learn and recoup. For example, black organizations such as the American Woodmen, the Knights and Daughters of Tabor, and the IOSL showed financial stability and continued growth after the 1920s.[5]

A more general threat to fraternalism during the 1920s was competition from new varieties of entertainment and recreation. Thomas M. Howell, the supervisor of degrees for the Moose, lamented that "the radio, the automobile, the jazz band, the outdoor entertainment, the fast means of travel" had placed "the old style lodge meeting, in which the same ceremonies, week after week, and month after month, are carried on, somewhat in discard." People in search of spectacle and drama could find them in the latest film of Cecil B. DeMille. Yet the importance of the recreational and ritualistic components of fraternalism can be overemphasized. While attractive to many members, they were never the primary inducements to join. If this had been the case, societies would not have invested so much time and emotional capital in social welfare and mutual aid. The Grand Aerie Commission of the FOE (an organization well known for conviviality) had warned that "no fraternity can depend entirely on its recreational features to attract members."[6]

Some sources of fraternal decline were specific to particular categories of societies. Immigrant organizations lost recruits as a consequence of World War I and restrictive federal quotas limiting immigrants from Europe. J. Weinberg, the chairman of the National Executive Committee of the wc, lamented that his society "once had a ready made source from which to take new members. The members looked for us. Conditions in Russia and Galicia and conditions here gave us the ready material. But now, it is different. Now we must look for the material and we must adopt other methods."[7]

Immigrant-based societies also fell victim to economic successes. As the first and second generations scaled the economic ladder, they had less need for fraternal financial and cultural benefits. In his study of Italians in Chicago, for example, Humbert S. Nelli states that "numerous prewar members and subscribers turned away from institutions that reminded them of the colony from which they had recently departed and which seemed alien to the middle-class life to which they aspired."[8]

Assimilation as an explanation for the decline of mutual aid can only carry us so far, however. Millions of immigrants in the nineteenth century experienced the same process. They, too, had dropped their ethnic societies after assimilation but had lined up to join organizations such as the IOOF and the AOUW. Studies by historians have failed to explain why later immigrants were not nearly as likely as their earlier counterparts to remain joiners. Another flaw in positing immigration as a necessary precondition for mutual aid is the inability to explain the vibrancy of voluntarism in countries lacking large foreign populations. The native-born of Great Britain, for example, established a ubiquitous network of mutual aid through thousands of friendly societies.

Endowments

Adverse legislation also contributed to fraternal decline. Laws regulating societies became increasingly restrictive. Nearly every state had adopted versions of either the Mobile Law of 1910 or the New York Conference Law of 1912. Not all these laws were inimical to societies. Some codified certain special advantages previously recognized by the courts, such as the nonprofit and tax-exempt status. Others protected fraternal certificates from attachment or garnishment for debt and authorized the open contract. The open contract enabled societies to raise premiums on existing policies by a simple vote, a power not enjoyed by commercial companies. During critical periods it was a useful tool to address unanticipated financial exigencies and to speed readjustment.[9]

But legislation cut both ways. For every benefit incurred, there was a price. Black societies in the South especially suffered. Early in the twentieth century the legislatures of Georgia, Kentucky, Mississippi, Virginia, and other states required societies to pay deposits ranging from $5,000 to $10,000. Smaller organizations found it almost impossible to meet this demand. In 1905 the imposition of a $5,000 deposit in Georgia devastated the black societies and forced many to disband. Mississippi followed suit with higher financial requirements. In 1915 the insurance commissioner of the state proudly recounted that he had personally denied or revoked licenses to 50 percent of the applicants during the previous two years. While some of these laws stemmed from a sincere desire to shield blacks from fly-by-night organizations, others arose from decidedly less altruistic considerations. Although the attempt failed, Georgia tried to raise its deposit requirements as high as $20,000 in 1909. The proposed law carefully exempted "those individual lodges which have among their members any legal descendants of Revolutionary, Mexican or Civil War sires." [10]

Other laws hampered societies both large and small by limiting the varieties of insurance that they could offer. The initial restrictive legislation during the 1890s centered on endowment insurance. An endowment could take a multitude of forms, but typically it entailed a contract that ran for a specified number of years and promised the insured, if he or she were still alive at the end of the time period, a stipulated sum. A leading motivation to purchase endowments was to save for old age. This goal contradicted the "die to win" philosophy of traditional life insurance. The tontine was probably the most controversial species of endowment. The basic concept was simple although the methods of application varied greatly. Under a pure tontine, a group of individuals paid annual sums into a common fund, and after a term of years, the survivors divided the proceeds. [11]

Several societies specialized in endowments during the 1880s and 1890s. These organizations never constituted a majority of fraternal orders, but they were influential for a time. A few endowment societies relied on the tontine principle. These fell into two categories: short term (paying out in five years or less) and long term (paying out in five to twenty years). One of the largest and better run of the long-term endowment societies was the Order of the Iron Hall. In addition, some mainstream life insurance societies experimented with endowments on the side. The best known among these were the MWA, the IOF, and the endowment division of the Knights of Pythias. [12]

Most life insurance orders, however, stoutly rejected endowments as contrary to fraternalism. The NFC went on public record against them and barred from its ranks all societies offering these policies. The critics charged that endowments were improper because they advanced the "selfish" interests of living members. In a speech to the NFC in 1891, James E. Shepherd expressed the new consensus when he asserted that endowments were "irreconcilable" with fraternalism because they were speculative and "purely banking and not insurance of any kind." Similarly, fraternal actuary William Francis Barnard defined endowments as the "exact converse of insurance. Its function is investment and its benefits are always for self."[13]

Scholars have attributed the demise of endowment societies to their reliance on assessment methods and low rates, but this is not a convincing explanation. Low assessments and cheap rates, after all, had not destroyed the life insurance societies. They survived by readjustment, not by eliminating the basic form of the benefit. As Edward J. Dunn pointed out, as "a matter of principle no one can successfully deny that a fraternal society can make adequate provision for endowment benefits as well as for death and disability benefits. The matter of adequacy is merely a question of rates."[14]

But any process of readjustment and higher rates took time, and the endowment societies did not have time. Restrictive laws, often enacted at the behest of life insurance societies, precluded this option. A major goal of state legislation was to deprive endowment societies of the legal protections extended to the life insurance societies, such as exemption from taxes and debt garnishment and the right to make assessments to cover deficiencies. Some laws banned outright any sale of fraternal endowment policies. Furthermore, the courts generally ruled that endowments to living, healthy members were inconsistent with an organization's nonprofit status.[15]

Sale of endowments by commercial companies, however, continued to be permissible under state law. The life insurance companies first monopolized the field by relying on the semi-tontine policy. It combined features of the pure tontine with conventional life insurance. The purchaser paid a portion of the premium for a standard life insurance policy, but unlike regular life insurance, the dividends (or surplus over the reserve) flowed into a common fund, which usually expired after twenty years. If the insured died before the end of the term, the beneficiaries collected the face of the policy. If the insured survived, he or she, along with other members of the fund, divided the accumulated proceeds, plus interest. The beneficiaries of the insured had no claim on the fund.[16]

Semi-tontines earned higher rates of return than savings accounts in banks. "In addition to securing conventional life insurance," wrote Roger L. Ransom and Richard Sutch, "the purchaser . . . was creating a retirement fund for old age. Moreover, the rate of return earned by survivors on the investment of the deferred dividends could be expected to be unusually generous since they would share in the accumulated dividends contributed by deceased policyholders and all forfeitures of those who allowed policies to lapse." Nine million semi-tontine policies were in force just after the turn of the century.[17]

In 1905 semi-tontine insurance came under heavy fire from the Armstrong Committee of the New York state legislature. In its final report the committee recommended prohibition of further sales, contending that these policies appealed to the "gambling instinct," produced disappointing returns, and invited corruption. As a result of the investigation the State of New York halted further sales of semi-tontine policies by requiring that dividends be returned annually rather than deferred into a common fund. Other states quickly followed suit. By the 1910s semi-tontine insurance was largely forgotten.[18]

Many fraternalists cheered the Armstrong Committee. To the *Fraternal Monitor* the results of the investigation proved the superiority of the fraternal philosophy of "the granting of benefits for dependents and avoiding investment and speculative insurance." Bina West regarded the attack on semi-tontine insurance as a welcome sign that the masses were beginning to understand that "insurance and investment can not properly be combined. The principles involved are fundamentally antagonistic." More than a decade later, Basye praised the New York Conference Law for prohibiting societies from engaging in business that violated their "mutual and non-profit taking character." For Basye, it was beyond dispute that the "investment business should be left to savings banks and bond brokers, and the issuing of tontines or other features of chance should be done, when permitted by law, by the various semi-lottery companies in the business for profit." In a more direct sense the New York Conference Law and the Mobile Law precluded societies from operating banks and other profit-making businesses on the side.[19]

Despite the assertions of West and Basye, a few examples indicate that fraternal societies could offer endowment insurance on a sound financial basis. During the 1920s the SBA successfully sold endowment (although not tontine) policies. It evaded legislative restrictions by incorporating and indirectly controlling a trust company to sell the policies. For monthly premiums of $3.50, a twenty-year plan gave the insured a monthly endowment of $50 for four years and nine months. The length of the endowment payout period could be extended for as long as thirty-one years for higher monthly premiums. This plan was actuarially sound and popular with members.[20]

The record of the friendly societies in Great Britain shows that fraternal endowments could flourish under the right legal regime. Prior to the twentieth century, British law did not enforce a rigid dichotomy between nonprofit and profit organizations. As a result the friendly societies were freer to specialize in endowments, tontines, investments, and savings plans. The chief examples of these specialist organizations were the dividing, Holloway, and deposit societies. These specialist organizations shared features with the mainstream friendly societies, including sick benefits, but put greater emphasis on savings. In the dividing societies the members divided the surplus each year. Members of the deposit and Holloway societies paid annually into a sick benefit fund, and any surpluses were deposited into interest-earning personal accounts that could be used for old age and other purposes, such as home loans.[21]

Although these arrangements were usually illegal in the United States, state laws often permitted societies to offer limited benefits to the aged. The New York Conference Law authorized benefits "for disability on account of old age" but required that the recipient be seventy years old and disabled. A considerable number of societies took advantage of this option although not all followed the rule that the member be physically disabled at seventy. In 1929 the U.S. Department of Labor sent an inquiry to seventy-one fraternal orders and found that twenty-one granted cash benefits for elderly members. Some distributed the cash value of death benefit certificates in regular installments, while others extended "paid up" coverage under which premiums ceased at seventy but the policy stayed in force.[22]

Child Insurance

Child insurance was another potential opportunity for societies that was precluded by state laws. As early as the 1890s, legislation and court rulings restricted fraternal coverage to adult members. Fraternalists did not necessarily object to the restrictions and, indeed, often supported them, charging that insurance on children encouraged "selfish" behavior and thus detracted from the goal of protecting dependents.[23]

Fraternalists were not alone in holding these views. Many Americans condemned child insurance as exploitative and, more ominously, as an inducement for parents to murder their children. The New York Times described it as a "temptation to inhuman crimes" and regarded agents who sold these policies as "pests of society." For fraternal orders, however, opposition to child insurance proved a costly mistake. It paved the way for commercial companies selling small industrial policies to dominate the field. Industrial insurance of this type became a standard feature of the budgets of wage earners. From 1900 to

1920 the number of industrial policies rose from 1.4 to 7.1 million and by 1925 surpassed the number of fraternal policies.[24]

A few societies tried to offer child insurance despite legal obstacles. The IOSL launched a pioneering foray in 1909 by announcing a plan to insure the children of members at low rates. The experiment did not last long. Almost immediately the commissioner of insurance for Virginia denied permission, citing the law restricting fraternal insurance to adults. In 1915 several large societies launched a public campaign to repeal legislative prohibitions on fraternal insurance of children. Without immediate action, they warned, the flow of "new blood" to the industrial companies would reach critical proportions. George A. Scott of the New York State Fraternal Congress chastised societies for "allowing the old-line, industrial insurance companies to teach our youths the need of protection. Unwittingly, the fraternalists of this country have been raising children as prey for their opponents."[25]

This belated effort to change laws proved to be an uphill struggle. In 1917 nine states permitted fraternal societies to admit children under sixteen as beneficial members. Predictably, the old-line companies stoutly opposed repeal of the restrictions. Joining them were many insurance commissioners who pointed to the actuarial troubles of societies as evidence that they were not ready for new responsibilities. Despite these obstacles the fraternal supporters of child insurance gradually made headway in repealing restrictions and in extending coverage. By 1930 societies had 912,700 juvenile members, and forty states allowed fraternal child insurance. Legal liberalization, while certainly helpful, came too late. The societies never recovered more than a small fraction of the business that they had lost to the industrial insurance companies.[26]

Group Insurance

The response of fraternal societies to group insurance progressed through a similar cycle of rejection, competition, and belated accommodation. The Equitable Life Assurance Society sold the first large group policy in 1912, the same year the New York Conference Law was passed. The company contracted with Montgomery Ward to insure 2,912 of its employees. Group insurance represented a major departure from commercial and fraternal precedents because employers paid the premiums and the insured individuals did not have to take a medical examination.[27]

The explosive growth of group insurance caught fraternal societies com-

pletely off guard. Restrictive legislation left them helpless to respond. By requiring medical examinations, the law effectively ruled out fraternal group insurance. Instead of seeking permission to enter the field, however, the societies
demanded legislative prohibition. The joint meeting of the NFC and the AFA
condemned group insurance as "imprudent" and "unsafe" because it dispensed
with the medical examination.[28]

More importantly, fraternal critics argued that group insurance would subject employees to "American Serfdom." The report of the Committee on Statutory Legislation of the NFC and AFA in 1913 asked, "Is it not true to human nature that the employe [sic] [in a group plan] will drop whatever other family
protection he may have? Losing his employment a few years afterward . . . he
thus loses the only form of family protection he has and the family is left a
charge upon the state." Fears ran wild when the Metropolitan Life Insurance
Company offered group coverage to the entire membership of a fraternal order
in Michigan.[29]

The well-orchestrated legislative campaign by fraternalists to stem the group
insurance tide ended in failure. By the end of the 1910s, commercial policies of
this type were legal in nearly every state. The only fraternal "victories" were of
a highly dubious character. In certain states, societies secured laws prohibiting
companies from insuring lodges as groups. In the meantime, the sale of group
insurance, almost all through commercial insurers, spread like wildfire. The
number of persons covered rose from 99,000 in 1915 to 1.6 million in 1920. A
decade earlier many of these workers would have been prime prospects for fraternal deputies. Now societies had to write them off to the competition.[30]

As group insurance made steady inroads, a rising chorus of fraternal leaders
proposed fighting fire with fire. As early as 1915 Abb Landis urged societies to
experiment with insuring in groups by using the lodge, rather than the individual, as the insurance unit. According to Landis the largest of the British friendly
societies had "successfully carried on an insurance business with the individual
lodge as an insurance unit." But Landis's recommendation was not the only
possible avenue to pursue. Another was for the societies to use the workplace as
the insurance unit by, perhaps, insuring all the workers of an employer and offering them fraternal memberships. But either method entailed potential pit-
falls, not the least of which was adverse selection. In a speech before the Casualty Actuarial Society, James D. Craig underlined the dangers of using the lodge
as the insurance unit. He stressed that without a medical examination, fraternal
group plans would become prey to poor risks.[31]

A handful of fraternal experiments in group insurance occurred during the

1920s. Probably the largest was a plan sponsored by the Arkansas Grand Lodge of the AOUW. It entered into contracts with several employers, including the Green Chevrolet Group and the First National Bank in North Little Rock. To get around a state law requiring members to pass a medical examination, the grand lodge gave the insured the option of enrolling as fraternal members at higher rates.[32]

The Arkansas Grand Lodge underscored the portability of fraternal coverage as a selling point. As one observer noted, the new fraternal members in Arkansas "possess legal reserve certificates which are their own property, and if they leave the employ of the company they may carry on payments and keep the insurance in force." Under a commercial group policy, by contrast, a lost job meant loss of benefits. Based on this experience, John Frazer, the grand master workman in the state, recommended fraternal group insurance as best suited for workers in small businesses. The costs of monitoring were low, and the less impersonal atmosphere made it easier to convince the insured of the benefits of lodge membership. To accommodate heterogeneity, Frazer suggested that societies engage in cooperative efforts to establish a framework for workers in the same plant to choose from several fraternal affiliations. Unfortunately there is a lack of sufficient information on either the effectiveness of the plan or its subsequent history.[33]

Fringe Benefits

The rise of group insurance had more long-term consequences. As one of the first fringe benefits, it marked the increasing centralization of benefits, such as life insurance, in the workplace. Because of the third-party payment method, thousands of workers for the first time no longer obtained insurance on an individual basis. This change had vast consequences for the future of fraternal orders.

The 1910s and 1920s also brought the full flowering of another fringe benefit, the company pension. As late as 1900 only about 8 companies (mostly railroads) offered pensions; by 1925, 248 did so. These plans covered 2.8 million workers and continued to flourish until the depression. Despite the existence of models such as group life insurance, however, few employers chose to insure their pensions through commercial companies. Instead most paid the entire cost and did not require contributions from workers.[34]

Another factor that fostered the centralization of benefits under the control of employers was workmen's compensation. State laws enabled employers to contract with commercial insurers to underwrite accident coverage. These arrangements sowed the seeds that later flowered into the modern third-party payment system in health care. After Massachusetts required employers to contract with commercial accident insurers during the 1910s, Morris J. Vogel points out, "many patients who had hitherto received free treatment now payed for their hospital care, indirectly at least, through third-party payment." Workmen's compensation spurred centralization of benefits in a subtler way by motivating firms to create an infrastructure for the disbursement of financial benefits. Once established, this infrastructure was available for other purposes, including health insurance. Simply put, workmen's compensation lowered the transaction costs for centralized employer-based benefits and third-party payment systems.[35]

The federal government was instrumental in speeding this centralization through amendments to the tax code. The Department of the Treasury exempted from the income tax all "reasonable" contributions made by employers to pension funds but did not extend this exemption to employees. It did not take long for group insurance to receive favorable tax treatment as a fringe benefit. In 1920 the Treasury ruled that the premiums of group policies paid by employers and employees were tax exempt. Again this exemption did not apply to premiums on individually purchased policies.[36]

Are We Burdened with Too Many Laws?

Rising discontent with legislation provoked a general debate among fraternalists about the desirability of governmental regulation. Essentially, three schools of thought emerged: defenders of existing fraternal regulation, advocates of a laissez-faire policy, and those who favored a middle ground. These debates played out at the annual conventions of the NFCA and in the pages of the *Fraternal Monitor*.[37]

A zealous defender of the laissez-faire approach was George A. Scott. In a speech to the NFCA in 1920, he chastised fraternalists for their eagerness to stake their hopes on government. According to Scott, the effect of legislation, "which we ourselves have secured after years of hard struggle," was to ossify the fraternal system and undermine its former appeal:

> No Fraternal Society can today go into this field [health insurance for the entire family] and supply what the Commercial Companies are supplying. *The law which we made will not permit it.* No Fraternal Society can today

write group insurance, not even on so small a group as a member's family. *The law which we made will not permit it.* No Fraternal Society can to-day write insurance contracts in combination with savings bank deposits which are being written by Commercial Companies in every town and city that has savings banks. *The law which we made will not permit it.*[38]

Scott and other critics disputed the contention that legislation insulated so-cieties from the corrosive effects of "commercialism." Instead they argued that it confined fraternity to an ever shrinking domain and fostered a form of com-mercialism that was narrow, bureaucratic, and unimaginative. Scott concluded that the "Fraternal Beneficiary System came into being without the aid of statutes and ran until 1892 without statutory guide. During that time . . . the sys-tem made greater growth than it has since. We may now well exclaim, give us less law and more fraternity." In 1915 William Lloyd Harding, the chairman of the Mystic Toilers, expressed this attitude in a speech, "Are We Burdened with Too Many Laws?" According to Harding the life insurance societies had become "almost wholly commercial. The fraternal has been legislated out of the plan. In other words, we have too many laws that go into the minutest details."[39]

From Mutual Aid to Service

These debates on the proper role of governmental regulation coincided with the emergence of an equally important cultural challenge to the underlying prem-ises of fraternalism. The result was an acute identity crisis. The traditional fra-ternal worldview was under attack. Age-old virtues such as mutual aid, charac-ter building, self-restraint, thrift, and self-help, once taken for granted, came under fire either as outmoded or as drastically in need of modification. The transformation was not universal, of course. None other than Calvin Coolidge repeatedly emphasized the benefits of saving. At the local level, some public schools and a few settlement houses established savings clubs. Trends in the op-posite direction were equally pronounced, however.[40]

Challenges, both explicit and subtle, to the old ideas came from a wide range of opinion leaders. Some reformers, such as Isaac Rubinow, increasingly questioned the efficacy of mutual aid, family networks, and neighborhood cooperation as solutions to poverty and dependence. Similar concerns had ap-peared in the comments of the proponents of mothers' pensions who worried that stressing self-help, character building, and mutual aid detracted from the united action needed to address the broader problems of the community and the nation. In the *Survey*, for example, M. L. Hale asked whether in "the present vast and intricate plan of society is not the real responsibility with the state rather than with the neighborhood?" Rubinow left little doubt about his belief in the inadequacy of voluntarism. He warned that any movement for compulsory insurance "must meet its strongest opponent in the fetishism of self-help." He regarded thrift as a "positive vice" when it reduced "the standard of life, not only below the desirable social standard, but even below the physiological standard." Similarly, John A. Lapp, who later served as the president of the National Conference of Social Work, warned that if "a worker saps his physical power for the sake of a money savings, he will soon exhaust his physical bank account." These attitudes represented a culmination of environmentalist ideas as reflected in Abraham Epstein's contention that poverty was "beyond the control of the individual." The old emphasis on character and distinctions between the worthy and the unworthy were deemed moralistic and unfair.[41]

This orientation found champions among some, although not all, social reformers and appeared in the writings of bankers and home economists, long regarded as guardians of thrift and self-restraint. In 1918 Clarence W. Taber used his textbook, *Business of the Household*, to warn that if savings "means stunted lives, that is, physical derelicts or mental incompetents . . . through enforced self-denial and the absence of bodily comforts, or the starving of mental cravings and the sacrifice of spiritual development—then the price of increased bank deposits is too high." An earlier generation would have dismissed these statements; now they were in the mainstream. Bruce Barton, the public relations pioneer and author of the best-selling life of Christ, *The Man Nobody Knows*, espoused the ideal of self-realization rather than self-reliance, declaring that "life is meant to live and enjoy as you go along. . . . If self-denial is necessary I'll practice some of it when I'm old and not try to do all of it now. For who knows? I may never be old."[42]

For Barton the best substitute for the old folk wisdom was "service." He was only one of many to join this crusade. Throughout the 1920s, paeans to service laced the speeches of businessmen and professionals. In 1924 Edward W. Bok described service as the "greatest word in the English Language." All this talk of service was not new, of course. At the turn of the century a key belief of the Social Gospelites was the necessity that service be enlisted in a crusade to advance the Kingdom of God on Earth. As promoted in the 1920s, however, the concept had become secularized and was not tied to a specific political agenda.[43]

The agenda of service clashed with the most valued traditions of fraternalism. Societies stressed reciprocity and mutual self-interest; the byword of service was stewardship. The duty of the good steward was to promote altruism for the betterment of society as a whole, not the members of a single organization. To Bok there was nothing worthwhile in "the service that serves self, for, like lip service, that accomplishes naught." While mutual aid was accessible to all classes through the lodge, stewardship was for the well-off. As businessmen or professionals, stewards were under special moral obligation to share their bounty with others.[44]

A good indicator that change was afoot was the rise of service clubs, such as Rotary International (1905), Lions International (1917), and Kiwanis International (1915). Unlike fraternal societies, they catered exclusively to professionals and businessmen. In the name of service the members pledged themselves to community and national betterment. They paid homage to a generalized altruism rather than reciprocity toward peers. The policy of the Lions was "No club shall hold as one of its objects financial benefits to its members." Shunning of mutual self-interest struck a chord with individuals who had lost faith in the old ways of mutual aid.[45]

While fraternal societies struggled to hold their ground during the 1920s, the membership of the Lions, Rotary, and Kiwanis doubled to 287,086. In their seminal study, *Middletown*, Robert S. and Helen Merrell Lynd elaborated on the success of service organizations in undermining the fraternal loyalties of many professionals and businessmen. They noted that "business men are 'too busy' to find the time for lodge meetings that they did formerly; the man who goes weekly to Rotary will confess that he gets around to the Masons 'only two or three times a year.'"[46]

In response many fraternal officials tried to remake their societies, in subtle ways, into the more fashionable image of service. For example, John Chapman Hilder noted that "in almost every case the big fraternities are finding the appeal to self-interest—with which they started—less attractive to the average prospective member than the idea of doing something for others." The rhetoric of the Loyal Order of Moose reflected this trend and found expression in a new definition of charity. In 1928 Edward J. Henning, a member of the executive committee, praised charity as a word to be embraced, not shunned. Charity, according to Henning, represented a higher form of altruism and thus best encapsulated the mission of the Loyal Order of Moose. "When you succor the needy," he exclaimed, "when you furnish food and shelter to those who need it—not because of a contract that is written to be fulfilled according to its

TABLE 11.1. Death, Permanent Disability, Sickness and Accident, Old-Age, and Other Benefits for 174 Fraternal Societies: Annual Amount Paid (in millions of dollars), 1910, 1920, and 1930

	1910	1920	1930
Death	76.3	129.3	122.3
Permanent disability	2.2	2.4	3.6
Sickness and accident	1.6	3.0	7.2
Old age	.5	3.6	3.6
Other	3.6	5.4	16.6
Total benefits	84.3	143.9	153.6

Source: Fraternal Monitor, *The Consolidated Chart of Insurance Organizations*, 1910, 1920, 1930.

terms—but as a pure impulse to serve—then you are engaged in charity." By 1931 the Supreme Council offered a symbolic endorsement of the new lexicon by renaming the Extension Service (to aid members in need) the Charity Fund.[47]

A driving force behind these changes was James J. Davis. Davis, who had once subscribed to the philosophy of mutual aid, now portrayed his organization as an exemplar of the twin virtues of charity and service. He described both ideals as resting on the same premise of an "open hand and the open heart." In 1935 Davis carried the emphasis on service to its logical extreme. In his annual address he urged that official publications "hereafter refer to our Fraternity as a *service* organization, rather than a fraternal organization."[48]

Davis even pondered the unthinkable: elimination of cash sick and funeral benefits. He asked whether this insurance unduly pandered to self-interest at the expense of fostering "that heart-warming glow which comes from the knowledge of good deeds well done without thought of personal reward." Pointing to a stagnant membership, he speculated that the benefits were no longer attracting new blood. They had become increasingly redundant in an age when "workmen's compensation, group insurance, and other similar features are rapidly coming into vogue." In particular such benefits had little meaning to businessmen and professionals who joined because of their desire to serve humanity. Davis's hopes were somewhat premature, and his revolution did not succeed. Either because he pulled back himself or because the members resisted, the Loyal Order of Moose retained sick and funeral benefits and even increased

TABLE 11.2. Death, Permanent Disability, Sickness and Accident, Old-Age,
and Other Benefits for 174 Fraternal Societies: Spending per Member
(in dollars), 1910, 1920, and 1930

	1910	1920	1930
Death	11.00	14.03	12.84
Permanent disability	.31	.26	.38
Sickness and accident	.23	.32	.75
Old age	.07	.39	.38
Other benefits	.52	.59	1.74

Source: Fraternal Monitor, *The Consolidated Chart of Insurance Organizations*, 1910,
1920, 1930.

them during the depression. At the end of the 1930s it was still a fraternal organization in its methods of operation.[49]

Despite the inroads of service clubs, mutual aid for social welfare remained a powerful force in the 1920s. Ethnic communities in Chicago, according to Lizabeth Cohen, "provided more assistance than other institutions, public or private, which were only viewed as a last resort." In fact, statistics show that a broad spectrum of societies *increased* their social welfare commitments to members. Projects such as the sanitarium of the MWA, the hospital of the SBA, and the health program of the WBA would have withered on the vine without the fraternal enthusiasm of lodges and auxiliaries. The *Consolidated Chart of Insurance Organizations*, an annual survey of 174 life insurance orders, shows substantial expansion in benefits for disability, sickness, accidents, and disability because of old age.[50]

The *Consolidated Chart* also indicates that the concentration on life insurance continued in the 1920s but became somewhat less important. If allocations are measured in both dollar amounts and percentage of budgets, societies designated more money for benefits for disability, sickness, accident, and old age (tables 11.1, 11.2, and 11.3). The percentage of the 174 societies carrying each type of benefit also increased throughout the period (table 11.4).

On the other hand, the *Consolidated Chart* is an imperfect guide to the state of fraternalism. Its chief flaw is its failure to include information about orders offering sickness and funeral benefits, such as the Loyal Order of Moose, the IOOF, and the AOF. These are not small matters. In 1910, for example, the life in-

TABLE 11.3. Death, Permanent Disability, Sickness and Accident, Old-Age,
and Other Benefits for 174 Fraternal Societies as Percentage
of All Losses Paid, 1910, 1920, and 1930

	1910	1920	1930
Death	90.5	89.8	79.6
Permanent disability	2.6	1.7	2.4
Sickness and accident	1.8	2.0	4.7
Old age	.6	2.5	2.4
Other benefits	4.3	3.7	10.8

Source: Fraternal Monitor, *The Consolidated Chart of Insurance Organizations*, 1910,
1920, 1930.

TABLE 11.4. Payment of Benefits for Permanent Disability, Sickness,
Accident, and Old Age in 174 Fraternal Societies: Percentage
of Societies Offering, 1910, 1920, and 1930

	1910	1920	1930
Permanent disability	30.4	46.5	57.4
Sickness	21.8	28.7	33.9
Sickness (lodges free to decide)	0	11.4	15.5
Accident	28.7	34.4	50.0
Accident (lodges free to decide)	0	4.0	4.0
Old age	28.7	34.4	45.9

Source: Fraternal Monitor, *The Consolidated Chart of Insurance Organizations*, 1910,
1920, 1930.

surance orders paid more than $76 million for death benefits, compared with
$5.1 million for sickness, disability, and old age. By contrast, the spending of the
fourteen leading orders providing sick and funeral benefits was far greater than
the outlays of all the life insurance societies combined. During seven months in
1910 and 1911, according to the *Fraternal Monitor*, the fraternal societies devoted
$25 million to sick and funeral benefits. Unfortunately, statistics of this exacti-
tude do not exist for subsequent years. Moreover, too much should not be made
of the distinction between kinds of fraternal insurance. Several of the life insurance societies listed in the *Consolidated Chart*, including the wc, the Polish National Alliance, and the Ancient Order of Hibernians, also disbursed substantial sick benefits.[51]

Conclusion

Most revolutions do not achieve complete success, and the service revolution, if it qualifies as such, was not an exception. Despite the mournful statements of Scott and Harding about the death of fraternity and the calls by Davis to substitute a mission of service, the old ideas of mutual aid retained power.

Still, change was in the air. The public statements of fraternal leaders during the 1920s showed waning zeal for traditional conceptions of mutual aid and a willingness to consider alternative approaches. As a strategy to attract members, this was probably a mistake. By deemphasizing their commitment to thrift, mutual aid, and self-help, societies abandoned the qualities that had made them distinctive. A rededication to service, no matter how zealous and heartfelt, was unlikely to result in the creation of organizations that were anything more than imitations of genuine service clubs. Yet even if the new strategy was futile, it was an entirely understandable response to a perplexing state of affairs.[52]

CHAPTER TWELVE

Vanishing Fraternalism?

O
n the whole, fraternal societies were in good shape on the eve of
the Great Depression. Membership, although dropping relative
to population, remained at high levels, and lodges continued to
wield enormous influence. Even the data in *Middletown*, a study
that often presents a bleak portrait, testifies to this fact. The authors found that
48 percent of working-class adult males in 1924 were lodge members. Fraternalism was still formidable.[1]

This was not nearly as true by the end of the 1930s, a decade characterized by
a dramatic and demoralizing fall in memberships and prestige. The ranks of six
leading orders and secret societies stressing sick and funeral benefits—the Masons, the IOOF, the Knights of Pythias, the Improved Order of Red Men, the Junior Order of American Mechanics, and the Loyal Order of Moose—fell from
7.2 million in 1930 to 5.9 million in 1935. By 1940 membership had receded to
4.7 million. The life insurance orders suffered a similar decline. In 1930 10.1 million Americans belonged to these organizations, but by 1935 this number had
fallen to 7.6 million. Although the bloodletting of the depression years had
abated by 1940, membership recovered to only 7.8 million. By comparison the
number of commercial ordinary insurance policies was more than 5.6 million
higher that year than it had been in 1930.[2]

While information on black fraternal societies is far less precise, the leading
indicators pointed downward. In 1940 J. G. St. Clair Drake summarized the results of extensive interviews with black lodge members and officials in Chicago.
The consensus was that "there are fewer lodges and societies than before 1910,
and their influence has been drastically weakened since the depression." In 1934
a survey of 500 black families in Chester, Pennsylvania, recorded that 404 individuals had lapsed in their fraternal memberships. Studies for Richmond; New
Orleans; New Haven; Evansville, Indiana; and the State of West Virginia showed
a similar trend.[3]

Both white and black organizations suffered from the consequences of high unemployment that crested at 25 percent in 1933. As economic conditions worsened, thousands of men and women gave up their struggles to pay dues and dropped out. "Every study of unemployed families in Chicago during the early years of the depression," writes Lizabeth Cohen, "recorded that large percentages, usually around 75 percent, had been forced to let some or all insurance policies lapse." By early 1933 the *Moose Docket* noted that about 30 percent of the membership was in arrears because of joblessness. A lapsed member of a black society in Mississippi summarized a recurrent fraternal complaint: "People ain't got no work. How dey gonna pay dues when they cain't eat?"[4]

This gloomy picture contrasted with those of previous depressions. During hard times in the past, workers had kept their dues current through strategies such as drawing from savings, borrowing money, or turning to kin networks. In some cases they had persuaded their lodges to carry them on the rolls. Previously, overall membership during depressions and recessions tended to grow or remain level. During the 1890s, for example, the membership of the life insurance orders rose every single year save two. It climbed from 3.6 million to 4.9 million between 1893 and 1897, probably the worst time of economic decline. The same tendency was apparent after the panic of 1907. In Homestead, Margaret Byington found it "significant that with the exception of three Slavs, all the families continued their insurance payments during the period of depression."[5]

To be sure, workers in the 1930s also dipped into savings, borrowed money, and petitioned lodges for help, but the odds were increasingly against them. The chief obstacle was the unprecedented duration of the Great Depression. High unemployment persisted for a decade. Hence the traditional fall-back mechanisms were more likely to buckle. Credit and savings dried up, and family networks frayed.

Even with these constraints, fraternal finances held up rather well during the depression. In 1935 Edgar Bennett, the president of the congress of the AOUW, proudly stated that not one fraternal order had "succumbed to the old law of the survival of the fittest." This claim, which was widely advanced by fraternal leaders, was not far from the truth. A study of sixty-five life insurance orders found that only five had ceased operation as fraternal societies in the 1930s. Three of these converted into commercial companies, and one merged with another society. The only failure, the American Benefit Society, had entered the depression with just a few hundred members. This sample left out the sick and funeral benefit orders, many of which did not extend beyond a local or statewide base, but it is striking how few national societies failed.[6]

The individual lodges did not fare nearly as well as the national organizations. In 1935 there were 98,836 lodges, a drop of over 20 percent from 1930. Contrary to the standard view, however, it is not evident that their demise can be explained by bankruptcy or inability to pay benefits. A study of the IOOF in British Columbia from 1891 to 1950 does not find a single example of a lodge that ceased operations because of financial insolvency or failure to pay benefits. Far more common explanations were mergers with nearby lodges or memberships reduced to levels insufficient to maintain official standing. Although the membership of the IOOF in British Columbia fell off during the depression, the benefit system did not collapse or lead to bankruptcy.[7]

Fraternal Social Services in the 1930s

If most fraternal societies in the United States remained financially viable during the depression, and there is good reason to believe that they did, such a view is at odds with the historical literature. Lizabeth Cohen, for example, contends that to the extent that societies in the United States survived, they did so only by shedding expensive benefits other than life insurance. Essentially she suggests that they abandoned their roles as social welfare organizations. For example, the Slovene National Benefit Society responded to economic exigencies by slashing sick benefits and loans to members. Accordingly, fraternal orders "like the Slovene National Benefit Society that made it through the depression did not offer members the same kinds of benefits afterward as they had before." Her general conclusion is that fraternals "failed" ethnic workers.[8]

The statistics in the *Consolidated Chart of Insurance Organizations* generally support Cohen's findings for the Slovene National Benefit Society, but they do not bear out her overall conclusion. In 1935 societies allocated more in per capita dollars in combined spending for sickness, accident, disability, and old-age benefits (tables 12.1 and 12.2) than they had in 1930, although total spending declined. Dispersals on these items inched up as a percentage of fraternal benefits (table 12.3).[9]

In short, the data for the life insurance orders do not show that societies failed their members during the depression. On the contrary, they responded with resourcefulness and redoubled commitment to social welfare. The proposition that societies tried to save money by discontinuing benefits other than life insurance also does not find support (table 12.4). While a lower percentage of organizations offered accident benefits in 1935, a *higher* percentage promised sickness, disability, and old-age benefits. Finally, the statistics do not suggest that the

TABLE 12.1. Death, Permanent Disability, Sickness and Accident, Old-Age, and Other Benefits for 174 Fraternal Societies: Annual Amount Paid (in millions of dollars), 1930, 1935, and 1940

	1930	1935	1940
Death	122.3	93.0	87.9
Permanent disability	3.6	3.3	1.9
Sickness and accident	7.2	5.1	5.8
Old age	3.6	3.2	3.1
Other benefits	16.6	14.5	21.5
Total benefits	153.6	119.3	120.4

Source: Fraternal Monitor, *The Consolidated Chart of Insurance Organizations*, 1930, 1935, 1940.

TABLE 12.2. Death, Permanent Disability, Sickness and Accident, Old-Age, and Other Benefits for 174 Fraternal Societies: Spending per Member (in dollars), 1930, 1935, and 1940

	1930	1935	1940
Death	12.84	12.82	11.72
Permanent disability	.38	.46	.26
Sickness and accident	.75	.70	.77
Old age	.38	.45	.41
Other benefits	1.74	2.00	2.87

Source: Fraternal Monitor, *The Consolidated Chart of Insurance Organizations*, 1930, 1935, 1940.

life insurance orders were pushing the limits of financial exhaustion because of this commitment. Taken as a whole, the 174 societies boasted a ratio of assets to liabilities of nearly two to one in 1935.

But a cautionary note is in order. The *Consolidated Chart* may give an inadequate picture of the general state of fraternalism because it does not include information on the leading orders supplying sick and funeral benefits. For example, the Loyal Order of Moose (not listed on the *Consolidated Chart*) spent $1.1 million in benefits (nearly $4.00 per member) in 1935. By comparison, the combined amount spent by the 174 life insurance orders that year was $5.1 million in sick and accident benefits, or less than $1.00 per member.[10]

TABLE 12.3. Death, Permanent Disability, Sickness and Accident, Old-Age,
and Other Benefits for 174 Fraternal Societies as Percentage
of All Benefits, 1930, 1935, and 1940

	1930	1935	1940
Death	79.6	77.9	73.0
Permanent disability	2.4	2.8	1.6
Sickness and accident	4.7	4.2	4.8
Old age	2.4	2.7	2.5
Other benefits	10.8	12.1	17.8

Source: Fraternal Monitor, *The Consolidated Chart of Insurance Organizations*, 1930,
1935, 1940.

TABLE 12.4. Payment of Benefits for Permanent Disability, Sickness, Accident,
and Old Age in 174 Fraternal Societies: Percentage of Societies
Offering, 1930, 1935, and 1940

	1930	1935	1940
Permanent disability	57.4	66.0	46.5
Sickness	33.9	35.0	33.3
Sickness (lodges free to decide)	15.5	13.7	11.4
Accident	50.0	45.9	39.6
Accident (lodges free to decide)	4.0	3.4	2.8
Old age	45.9	50.5	35.6

Source: Fraternal Monitor, *The Consolidated Chart of Insurance Organizations*, 1930,
1935, 1940.

Information gathered from several detailed studies of fraternal orphanages,
sanitariums, and homes for the aged shows that these institutions came through
the depression providing services to an increased number of residents. The first
major study, completed by the U.S. Bureau of the Census, reported that there
were 5,701 children and adults in seventy-four institutions in 1910. The next two
decades brought rapid growth. By 1929 (see table 12.5) the population of fraternal homes for the elderly was more than 7,000 adults. Rather than phasing out
spending on these institutions during the depression, societies increased capacity by 18.5 percent. For both 1929 and 1939 the bureau provided details on the
six societies with the most members in homes for the elderly: the Improved

TABLE 12.5. Fraternal Homes for the Elderly: Numbers of Homes,
Numbers of Residents, and Residential Capacity, 1929 and 1939

	1929	1939	Percentage Increase
Homes	112	129	13.1
Residents	7,678	9,550	19.6
Residential capacity	10,895	13,371	18.5

Sources: U.S. Department of Labor, Bureau of Labor Statistics, "Care of Aged Persons in the United States," *Bulletin* 489 (Washington, D.C.: Government Printing Office, 1929), 162, and "Homes for the Aged in the United States," *Bulletin* 677 (Washington, D.C.: Government Printing Office, 1941), 7, 13.

Order of Redmen, Patriotic Order of Sons of America, the Knights of the Maccabees, the Knights of Pythias, the Masons, and the IOOF. Not one had reduced residential capacity between 1929 and 1939.[11]

The population and numbers of fraternal orphanages also grew, albeit at a slower rate (see table 12.6). In 1933 these institutions housed 2.4 percent more children than in 1923. Although statistics are fragmentary thereafter, a slow decline probably had set in by the eve of World War II. Writing in 1943, Noel P. Gist guessed that "for several years there has been a decrease in the juvenile population of fraternal homes, and first-hand observations by the writer in visits to a number of fraternal institutions confirm these reports." Gist ascribed the source of much of the decline to the aging of adult society members.[12]

Several studies confirm a general graying of fraternalism during this period. According to a survey of insurance ownership in greater Boston in 1939, more than three of ten fraternal policyholders were over age fifty, compared to less than two of ten of those enrolled in commercial group plans. Two years later another study of black voluntary associations in Johnstown, Pennsylvania, indicated that more than three of ten fraternal members were over fifty, twice the proportion for the membership of other voluntary associations. Clearly, young adults of the late 1930s had much less direct experience with societies than did their parents or grandparents. An obvious consequence was that fewer children were eligible for care.[13]

Fraternal orphanages also fell prey to the popular social welfare trend of substituting foster homes for institutional care. Federal policy enshrined this approach through cash benefits under the Aid to Dependent Children provision of the Social Security Act. After 1935 the number of children living in institu-

TABLE 12.6. Fraternal Orphanages: Numbers of Orphanages
and Children in Residence, 1923 and 1933

	1923	1933	Percentage Increase
Orphanages	90	100	11.1
Children	9,178	9,409	2.4

Sources: U.S. Department of Commerce, Bureau of the Census, *Children under Institutional Care, 1923* (Washington, D.C.: Government Printing Office, 1927), 25, 48–254, and *Children under Institutional Care and in Foster Homes, 1933* (Washington, D.C.: Government Printing Office, 1935), 63–125; C. W. Areson and H. W. Hopkirk, "Child Welfare Programs of Churches and Fraternal Orders," *Annals of the American Academy of Political and Social Science* 121 (September 1925): 87.

tions of all kinds declined substantially. By 1951 it was one-third lower than in 1933, and more children were in foster homes than orphanages.[14]

Few if any fraternal tuberculosis sanitariums closed their doors during the depression. The NFCA conducted several often fragmentary and incomplete surveys between the 1930s and the 1950s. In 1930 six life insurance societies had sanitariums: the IOF (which had two facilities), the Knights of Columbus, the MWA, the Royal League, the Woodmen of the World, and the WC. Other organizations, such as the AOUW, cared for tubercular patients through special arrangements with private or state hospitals. Nearly all these institutions survived the depression intact. Only in the 1940s did they start to disappear, and not primarily for financial reasons but because new drugs provided better and less expensive treatment. By 1949 three sanitariums remained.[15]

The fraternal commitment to institutional and cash benefits remained impressive throughout the depression. Societies, as a whole, did not use hard times as a pretext to abandon or reduce resources devoted to social welfare. After the middle of the decade, the first discernible signs of retrenchment in fraternal allocations for social welfare became apparent, but not until the 1940s did societies promise significantly less in social welfare aid for their members.

The New Deal and Social Security

There is reason to believe that a relationship existed between the emerging welfare state and the decline of fraternal services. Most notably, the first signs of benefit retrenchment appeared after 1935, the year the Social Security Act became law. Officials of the homes for the elderly and orphans of the SBA cited Social Security and other welfare programs as justification not only for rejecting applicants but for closing down entirely. In 1939 Malcolm R. Giles, the supreme secretary and comptroller of the Loyal Order of Moose, urged the Supreme Council to consider restricting sick benefits to members under age sixty-five. As justification he stressed that these individuals were eligible for aid under the Social Security Act. The same year Norman G. Heyd, the chairman of the Moosehaven Board of Governors, reported that Moosehaven had the smallest population since 1931. He asserted that the major reason "for this decrease is undoubtedly the operation of the old-age pensions in most of the states."[16]

By the middle of the decade more fraternal leaders than ever defended the expanded welfare state as both consistent with and a logical extension of fraternalism. In 1935, for example, James J. Davis asserted with pride that "practically every provision embodied in the Social Security Act has been carried successfully by the fraternal societies of America for years, and all of it without cost to the taxpayer." No fraternal organization was more supportive of Social Security than the FOE, which was not a newcomer to the issue. It had pushed hard for government old-age pensions at both the state and the national levels. For good reason Franklin D. Roosevelt, while governor of New York, credited the FOE as the most important force for "showing the need for Old-Age Pension legislation." Conrad Mann, Frank Hering, and other officials justified increased governmental provision as a means to banish the poorhouse, which they depicted as the growing refuge of the elderly.[17]

There were also financial reasons for some fraternalists to welcome the prospect of an expanding welfare state. The establishment of Social Security and other programs provided excuses to shed costly services. Though societies had maintained social welfare spending at high levels during the depression, it was becoming an expensive proposition. The burdens were especially great because the membership base was older and smaller. If government assumed responsibility, societies would be freed to function in less-challenging roles as life insurance or convivial organizations.

Despite this shift in outlook, many fraternalists still voiced opposition to the expanding welfare state, although they were far less influential than in the past. Walter Basye agreed with Davis that fraternal societies "have provided a great deal of social security in this country, and their efforts continue." Unlike Davis, however, he concluded that this experience proved that an old-age pension system was not a proper function of the federal government: "'Security' that creates paupers is not security at all. . . . Charity and pauperism create a condition which is the same, no matter what it is called. . . . The only reason social security is politically popular is because some people have an idea that they will receive something for nothing at the expense of their neighbors. They are bound to be disappointed."[18]

Another fraternal opponent of New Deal welfare programs was De Emmett Bradshaw, the president of the Woodmen of the World. In 1943 Bradshaw predicted that higher taxes for Social Security would worsen unemployment and thus undermine self-help. For Bradshaw full employment was "the only guarantee to us that we can expand our membership and continue to collect from present members payments on existing insurance." He imagined the following scenario under an expanded welfare state: "Rugged individualism is crowded out, and the people lose their ambition and become listless as they drop toward the valley of delusions called socialism."[19]

Bina West of the WBA also condemned New Deal programs. As an alternative, however, she supported a Republican plan to pay small fixed pensions to the poor. West ridiculed suggestions that Social Security was just an expanded form of cooperative insurance or represented a culmination of fraternal principles. She charged that the trust fund was not a true reserve but instead a mere "bookkeeping entry." The premiums to finance the program, she asserted, could be used by the government for "any purpose, good or bad." As with compulsory health insurance, West worried that Social Security would pose a threat to American practices of mutual aid. She asked, "Is there any beautiful ritualism or human tenderness in a governmental bureau?"[20]

West was not alone in suggesting the clash between the values of fraternity and those associated with governmental welfare. Even fraternal supporters of Social Security, such as Giles, shared these concerns. While Giles praised Social Security as proof that "imitation is the sincerest flattery," he cautioned that government was incapable of approximating the warm handclasp from a fellow member or "the friendly visitation of fraternalists to a stricken brother." A top official of the SBA went further by declaring that fraternal societies, not federal bureaucrats, were best able to teach individuals how to be "self-sustaining and to provide for their own future."[21]

Fraternalism since the Depression

During previous eras fraternal societies had bounced back from hard times. This was not the case following the Great Depression. Membership recovered somewhat, but it never approximated the 1929 level relative to population. By

the beginning of the 1940s the societies were in full retreat as social welfare institutions. Conviviality or life insurance, instead of mutual aid, became the order of the day. But these inducements were rarely enough to attract and hold
members. By assuming fraternal welfare burdens, governments had undermined much of the reason for the existence of societies and thus for people
to join.[22]

This loss might not have been devastating had other niches been left for fraternal orders to fill. Though medical care had once seemed a promising area for
growth, experiments in this area had floundered in great part because of opposition from the medical associations. Other cooperative plans based on the principle of individual subscription suffered from the same obstacles. Probably the
most famous example was the medical cooperative plan of Dr. Michael Shadid,
the head of the Community Hospital of Elk City, Oklahoma. For more than
twenty years after 1929 Shadid fought a running battle with medical associations and state regulators. In its fight against cooperative and fraternal plans, organized medicine effectively used political weapons such as revocation of li-
censes, adverse insurance regulations, and restrictions on the corporate practice
of medicine. Later, health plans encountered the formidable stumbling block
posed by the rise of third-party payment systems. A wide gamut of tax, economic, and legal incentives discriminated against health service based on individual—rather than group—subscription.[23]

There were still some fraternal success stories in the postwar period. Societies
catering to groups or geographical areas characterized by weak third-party payment systems continued to flourish in the provision of medical care. Certain organizations, such as the Mississippi Jurisdiction of the Knights and Daughters
of Tabor and the Lily White Security Benefit Association of Florida, increased
social welfare services during the 1940s and 1950s. The hospitals of organizations
such as El Centro Español and the French Mutual Benefit Society remained
in operation until the 1980s. Although they eventually closed, their survival
indicates that societies could be important service providers under the right
conditions.

Even among the middle class there were instances of fraternal philanthropy
on a substantial scale. The experience of the Moose International (formerly the
Loyal Order of Moose) stands out. Its continuing commitment to social welfare
runs contrary to the scenario of fraternal failure. The Loyal Order of Moose
came under severe stress during the depression, and membership, which was
541,463 in 1930, plunged to 265,664 in 1936. Massive unemployment put a tremendous strain on retention and recruitment efforts. The response, however,

was not to eliminate or prune services to members. While the membership base fell, the population of Mooseheart (over 1,000 children) was maintained at pre-depression levels.[24]

The leaders weathered this storm by finding creative ways to adapt. For example, they persuaded the Women of the Moose, the ladies' auxiliary of the society, to assume the funding for the Mooseheart Laboratory for Child Research as well as Moosehaven. On a more fundamental level, the Supreme Council addressed the problem of reduced membership. Working through thousands of subcommittees at the local level, it launched a vigorous campaign to help members pay arrears and remain in good standing. These measures bore fruit. Membership began to recover and, by the middle of the 1940s, actually surpassed the levels of the 1920s.[25]

Although some fraternalists in the Loyal Order of Moose had expressed doubt during the 1920s about the need for sick and funeral benefits, the society did not use the depression as a pretext to abolish them. Indeed, spending for this purpose rose. In 1929 the Loyal Order of Moose spent $4.44 per member on sick and funeral benefits; by 1935 the expenditure had nearly doubled to a record-breaking $8.34 per member. That year the Supreme Council limited each member to a maximum of $100 in sick benefits. This rule arose not only from a desire to save money but to comply with insurance regulations. Even with the limit, per capita spending on sick and funeral benefits was still $4.06 in 1940, an increase in real terms from 1929 and higher in constant dollars than most of the 1920s. An influx of initiates helped keep the funds of lodges in good shape by holding down the average age. As a result the report on the state of the benefit funds was upbeat in 1942: "The Order has been well within the safety zone in maintaining its benefit plan," and "the member lodges have accumulated over one million dollars in beneficiary fund reserve. . . . While some have made the suggestion that the Moose Fraternity might eliminate sick benefits and funeral expenses, I am firmly convinced this feature of Moose Service . . . will continue to remain an important factor in our success."[26]

The decline of sick and funeral benefits did not become a reality until the 1940s. Much of the decrease occurred because lodges increasingly allowed the amount of per capita benefits to fall rather than raise the dues to keep pace with inflation. By 1953, when per capita spending was less than $3.00, the annual convention approved a resolution to make it optional for lodges to pay these benefits. As justification it noted the "continued development and extension of social security and unemployment compensation by both the national and state government . . . thereby making the payment of the contractual benefits by member lodges less appealing to the average man than it was when the program was instituted many years ago." Simply put, the Supreme Council did not phase out the program because of the financial stresses of the depression but because, in an era of wartime prosperity, it no longer deemed it necessary.[27]

By contrast the Loyal Order of Moose jealously preserved and in many ways expanded Mooseheart. In 1941 the Supreme Council voted to lower the admission requirements by opening the doors to more children with fathers who were alive and to "children and their mothers who did not show complete dependency." This took place in tandem with efforts to improve the quality of the service by expanding the physical plant and increasing the amount and variety of scholarships. The Loyal Order of Moose raised much of the money by strengthening the fraternal tie through the establishment of state Moose associations. In 1998 the children received a full college scholarship as long as they maintained a B− average for four years at Mooseheart.[28]

Despite the liberalization of admission requirements and increased spending on services, the population of Mooseheart continued to fall for most of the postwar period. By 1950 it had declined to 766 children, and despite a comfortable endowment of $150 million, fewer than 300 residents were left in 1998. The decline was caused by the rise of alternatives such as foster homes and Aid to Families with Dependent Children. Despite the continued opportunity for mothers to work and live at Mooseheart, fewer than ever exercised this option. According to Kurt Wehrmeister, the head of media relations for Mooseheart, "We'd like to encourage a bit more of that. We think we have too many mothers who are too likely to say, 'No, thanks. You look after them for awhile.'"[29]

Moosehaven also faced reduced demand, although to a lesser degree. After the advent of Social Security, the number of residents declined. During the 1940s and 1950s the Supreme Council refurbished the physical plant and began to advertise Moosehaven as a "retirement community" rather than an "old folks' home." By the early 1990s it housed 450 residents although it had a capacity for 600. The admission requirements, however, had not changed greatly since the 1930s. All residents (spouses excepted) had to be members in good standing for fifteen years.[30]

Conclusion

In 1953 Richard de Raismes Kip ended the last paragraph of *Fraternal Life Insurance in America* with the topic heading "Vanishing Fraternalism." Thirty-six years later Mary Ann Clawson echoed that theme by writing that while fraternal societies continued to exist after the depression, "their greatly diminished size, aging memberships, and public marginality mark them as anachronisms. Their inflated rhetoric and unselfconscious depiction of hierarchy has made them the stuff of comedy for at least a generation. So much is this the case that we take them seriously only through an effort of imagination and scholarship." Yet despite such pronouncements, Moose International and other societies stubbornly refused to assume their assigned fates as anachronisms by vanishing.[31]

During the 1980s and 1990s there were modest signs of resurgence, although these were not entirely unambiguous. In 1987 there were 9.1 million fraternal insurance certificates in force; by 1996 this had increased to 10.7 million, while the number of lodges rose from 42,669 to 43,282. Meanwhile, the official annual disbursements on "charity," though a far cry from the extensive social welfare of earlier periods, more than tripled from $10 million to $30 million. Information on the secret societies also does not neatly fit the scenario of looming extinction. Many once great organizations, such as the Knights of Pythias, the AOUW, and the Knights of the Maccabees, either do not exist or are mere shadows of their past glories; but others thrive. The Benevolent and Protective Order of Elks and the FOE each had a million members in 1996. The membership of Moose International was 1.7 million, more than at any time during the 1920s and 1930s.[32]

By the same token there has been a fundamental transformation in the nature of fraternalism. For the most part, fraternal membership, although still heavily working class, no longer includes the very poor. The rise of alternative forms of social welfare has dramatically reduced the demand for social welfare services among members. Mutual aid was a creature of necessity. Once this necessity ended, so, too, did the primary reason for the existence of fraternalism. Without a return to this necessity, any revival of mutual aid will remain limited.

The shift from mutual aid and self-help to the welfare state has involved more than a simple bookkeeping transfer of service provision from one set of institutions to another. As many of the leaders of fraternal societies had feared, much was lost in an exchange that transcended monetary calculations. The old relationships of voluntary reciprocity and autonomy have slowly given way to paternalistic dependency. Instead of mutual aid, the dominant social welfare arrangements of Americans have increasingly become characterized by impersonal bureaucracies controlled by outsiders.

NOTES

Abbreviations

In addition to the abbreviations used in the text, the following abbreviations appear in the notes.

SBAP   Security Benefit Association Papers, Kenneth Spencer Research Library, University of Kansas, Lawrence, Kans.
SBLP   Security Benefit Life Papers, Kenneth Spencer Research Library, University of Kansas, Lawrence, Kans.
SBG   Security Benefit Group of Companies, Records, Topeka, Kans.

Introduction

1. *Security News* 40 (September 1934): 27.

2. This book is not a general history of fraternal societies. My goal is to offer a broad overview of fraternal mutual aid among the working class since the late nineteenth century. Hence, the focus is not on elite organizations such as Freemasonry. For more information on these aspects of fraternalism, see Lynn Dumenil, *Freemasonry and American Culture, 1880–1930* (Princeton: Princeton University Press, 1984); Steven C. Bullock, *Revolutionary Brotherhood: Freemasonry and the Transformation of the American Social Order, 1730–1840* (Chapel Hill: University of North Carolina Press, 1996).

3. Este Erwood Buffum, *Modern Woodmen of America: A History* (Rock Island, Ill.: Modern Woodmen of America, 1935), 2:5.

4. Richard de Raismes Kip, *Fraternal Life Insurance in America* (Philadelphia: College Offset Press, 1953), 12.

5. Lizabeth Cohen, *Making a New Deal: Industrial Workers in Chicago, 1919–1939* (New York: Cambridge University Press, 1990), 64; August Meier, *Negro Thought in America, 1880–1915: Racial Ideologies in the Age of Booker T. Washington* (Ann Arbor: University of Michigan Press, 1963), 130.

The estimates for fraternal society membership are from U.S. President's Research Committee on Social Trends, *Recent Social Trends in the United States: Report of the President's Research Committee on Social Trends* (New York: McGraw-Hill, 1933), 2:935. The population statistics for Americans age twenty and over are in U.S. Department of Commerce, *Historical Statistics of the United States: Colonial Times to 1970*, pt. 1 (Washington, D.C.: Government Printing Office, 1975), 21.

6. Mark C. Carnes, *Secret Ritual and Manhood in Victorian America* (New Haven: Yale University Press, 1989); Mary Ann Clawson, *Constructing Brotherhood: Class, Gender, and Fraternalism* (Princeton: Princeton University Press, 1989), 246.

7. U.S. Department of Labor, Children's Bureau, *Mothers' Aid, 1931* (Washington, D.C.: Government Printing Office, 1933), 8.

Chapter One

1. Alexis de Tocqueville, *Democracy in America* (New York: Random House, 1981), 403–4.

2. John Hamill, *The Craft: A History of English Freemasonry* (Leighton Buzzard, Bedfordshire: Crucible, 1986), 15–16, 21, 27–40; David Stevenson, *The Origins of Freemasonry: Scotland's Century, 1590–1710* (Cambridge: Cambridge University Press, 1988), 7, 22, 123–24, 197–98, 216–33. For another recent study, see Margaret C. Jacob, *Living the Enlightenment: Freemasonry and Politics in Eighteenth-Century Europe* (New York: Oxford University Press, 1991).

Originally, "freemason" was a contraction of "freestone mason." The term referred to a specialist "who worked in freestone—usually limestone—capable of being immediately carved for decorative purposes" (Hamill, *Craft*, 27).

3. Dorothy Ann Lipson, *Freemasonry in Federalist Connecticut* (Princeton: Princeton University Press, 1977), 23, 48–49.

4. Ibid., 50–62; Conrad Edick Wright, *The Transformation of Charity in Postrevolutionary New England* (Boston: Northeastern University Press, 1992), 213–19; Steven C. Bullock, *Revolutionary Brotherhood: Freemasonry and the Transformation of the American Social Order, 1730–1840* (Chapel Hill: University of North Carolina Press, 1996), 92–93, 207–11.

5. Wayne A. Huss, *The Master Builders: A History of the Grand Lodge of Free and Accepted Masons of Pennsylvania*, vol. 1, *1731–1873* (Philadelphia: Grand Lodge, 1986), 61–62; Lipson, *Freemasonry*, 210.

6. Huss, *Master Builders*, 62–63.

7. Bullock, *Revolutionary Brotherhood*, 187–91; Lipson, *Freemasonry*, 207.

8. Leonard P. Curry, *The Free Black in Urban America, 1800–1850: The Shadow of the Dream* (Chicago: University of Chicago Press, 1981), 208–9; William A. Muraskin, *Middle-Class Blacks in a White Society: Prince Hall Freemasonry in America* (Berkeley: University of California Press, 1975), 31–35.

9. E. P. Thompson, *The Making of the English Working Class* (New York: Vintage, 1966), 418–19; P. H. J. H. Gosden, *Self-Help: Voluntary Associations in the Nineteenth Century* (London: Batsford, 1973), 6, and *The Friendly Societies in England, 1815–1875* (New York: A. M. Kelley, 1967), 71–93; Lipson, *Freemasonry*, 201.

10. Gosden, *Friendly Societies*, 26–30, 129–31.

11. J. M. Baernreither, *English Associations of Working Men* (1889; reprint, Detroit: Gale Research, 1966), 162; Thompson, *Making*, 419.

12. Wright, *Transformation*, 63, 66; Gosden, *Friendly Societies*, 5.

13. Richard D. Brown, "The Emergence of Voluntary Associations in Massachusetts, 1760–1830," *Journal of Voluntary Action* 2 (April 1973): 69–70; Wright, *Transformation*, 55–56.

14. Don Harrison Doyle, *The Social Order of a Frontier Community: Jacksonville, Illinois, 1825–1870* (Urbana: University of Illinois Press, 1978), 189–90; Mary Ann Clawson, *Constructing Brotherhood: Class, Gender, and Fraternalism* (Princeton: Princeton University Press, 1989), 24–25.

The six societies were the Scots' Charitable Society of Boston, the Massachusetts Charitable Mechanic Association, the Charitable Irish Society of Boston, the Boston Marine Society, the Episcopal Charitable Society of Boston, and the Massachusetts Charitable Society. Copies of the original bylaws from the eighteenth century can be found in

The Constitution and By-Laws of the Scots' Charitable Society of Boston (Boston: Farrington Printing, 1896), 36–40; Joseph T. Buckingham, *Annals of the Massachusetts Charitable Mechanic Association* (Boston: Crocker and Brewster, 1853), 6–9; *The Constitution and By-Laws of the Irish Charitable Society of Boston* (Boston: Cotter, 1876), 22–26; William A. Baker, *A History of the Boston Marine Society, 1742–1981* (Boston: Boston Marine Society, 1982), 302–3, 308–9; "The Articles and Rules of the Episcopal Charitable Society of Boston" (1724), in *Early American Imprints, 1639–1800*, ed. Clifford K. Shipton (Worcester, Mass.,: American Antiquarian Society, 1967–74); Massachusetts Charitable Society, "Rules and Articles" (1762), in Shipton, *Early American Imprints*.

15. *Constitution and By-Laws of the Scots' Charitable Society*, 22, 24–25, 29.

16. Baker, *History of the Boston Marine Society*, 302–3.

17. Clawson, *Constructing Brotherhood*, 107; Wright, *Transformation*, 209, 213–19.

18. Gosden, *Friendly Societies*, 88–93, 224–28.

19. Brian Greenberg, *Worker and Community: Response to Industrialization in a Nineteenth-Century American City, Albany, New York, 1850–1884* (Albany: State University of New York Press, 1985), 90–93; James L. Ridgely, *History of American Odd Fellowship: The First Decade* (Baltimore: James L. Ridgely, 1878), 234; Alvin J. Schmidt, *Fraternal Organizations* (Westport, Conn.: Greenwood, 1980), 243–45; Albert C. Stevens, *The Cyclopedia of Fraternities* (New York: E. B. Treat, 1907), 113, 235.

American Freemasonry was too decentralized to meet the necessary criteria for an affiliated order. State lodges were the highest level of authority, and proposals to establish a national grand lodge never were implemented. Freemasonry in the United States is better characterized as a confederacy of state grand lodges.

20. John S. Gilkeson Jr., *Middle-Class Providence, 1820–1940* (Princeton: Princeton University Press, 1986), 156; Greenberg, *Worker and Community*, 93; Stuart M. Blumin, *The Emergence of the Middle Class: Social Experience in the American City, 1760–1900* (Cambridge: Cambridge University Press, 1989), 223–25. Blumin asserts that "within the repeated assertion of a class-free brotherhood and hierarchy of merit a hint of the old working-class radicalism, if not of the Ricardian then at least of the 'Jack's as good as his master' variety," existed (225).

21. Albert Case, "The Principles of Odd Fellowship," *Gavel* 1 (January 1845): 128.

22. Ridgely, *History of American Odd Fellowship*, 16, 233; Editor's Table, *Gavel* 2 (September 1845): 64; "Educating the Orphan," *Emblem: An Odd Fellows Magazine* 1 (May 1856): 444; "I.O.O.F. Orphan Asylum—Ossinsing Lodge," *Gavel* 2 (May 1846): 284–86.

23. "The Order of Odd Fellows and the Pittsburgh Sufferers," *Gavel* 2 (May 1846): 287–88; Editorial, *Emblem* 1 (November 1855): 201.

24. "Board of Relief of Boston Lodges," *Emblem* 1 (August 1855): 53–54.

25. G. W. Clinton, "Objections to Our Order Answered," *Gavel* 2 (September 1845): 29; Mark C. Carnes, *Secret Ritual and Manhood in Victorian America* (New Haven: Yale University Press, 1989), 140. As Carnes points out, the widespread appeal of ritualism was multifaceted and defies simple explanations.

26. Joel Walker, "The Social Welfare Policies, Strategies, and Programs of Black Fraternal Organizations in the Northeast United States, 1896–1920" (Ph.D. diss., Columbia University, 1985), 33; Curry, *Free Black*, 210–11; Charles H. Brooks, *The Official History and Manual of the Grand United Order of Odd Fellows in America* (1902; reprint, Freeport, N.Y.: Books for Libraries Press, 1971), 91, 101.

For a discussion of the social and political context of the Odd Fellows, see Nick Salvatore, *We All Got History: The Memory Books of Amos Webber* (New York: Times Books,

1996), 163–67, 256–61. Another study that includes a valuable discussion of black fraternal societies is Peter J. Rachleff, *Black Labor in Richmond, 1865–1890* (Urbana: University of Illinois Press, 1984).

27. Myron W. Sackett, *Early History of Fraternal Beneficiary Societies in America: Origin and Growth, 1868–1880* (Meadville, Pa.: Tribune Publishing, 1914), 25–26.

The Knights of Labor was founded in 1869, a year after the AOUW. For a comparison of the two organizations, see Clawson, *Constructing Brotherhood*, 138–43.

28. Sackett, *Early History*, 27, 130–33, 197; Walter Basye, *History and Operation of Fraternal Insurance* (Rochester, N.Y.: Fraternal Monitor, 1919), 10–14, 47.

29. Abb Landis, *Life Insurance* (Nashville, Tenn.: Abb Landis, 1914), 105, 107.

30. *Fraternal Monitor* 18 (February 1, 1908): 23; Basye, *History and Operation*, 72; J. Owen Stalson, *Marketing Life Insurance: Its History in America* (1942; reprint, Bryn Mawr, Pa.: McCahan Foundation, 1969), 553; Harris Dickson and Isidore P. Mantz, "Will the Widow Get Her Money? The Weakness in Fraternal Life Insurance and How It May Be Cured," *Everybody's Magazine*, June 1910, 776.

31. Frederick L. Hoffman, "Fifty Years of American Life Insurance Progress," *American Statistical Association* 95 (September 1911): 88; U.S. President's Research Committee on Social Trends, *Recent Social Trends in the United States: Report of the President's Research Committee on Social Trends* (New York: McGraw-Hill, 1933), 2:935; U.S. Department of Commerce, *Historical Statistics of the United States: Colonial Times to 1970*, pt. 1 (Washington, D.C.: Government Printing Office, 1975), 21.

32. Richard de Raismes Kip, *Fraternal Life Insurance in America* (Philadelphia: College Offset Press, 1953), 30–31; Stalson, *Marketing Life Insurance*, 451–52, 553; Basye, *History and Operation*, 29; "The Cheapest Insurance," *World's Work* 11 (April 1906): 7398; Landis, *Life Insurance*, 88; Viviana A. Rotman Zelizer, *Morals and Markets: The Development of Life Insurance in the United States* (New York: Columbia University Press, 1979), 93; Carnes, *Secret Ritual*, 1.

33. Connecticut Bureau of Labor Statistics, *Annual Report* (1892), 1:70–71, 106–7, 114, 129–31, 643–770.

34. Ibid., 106–7.

35. Stevens, *Cyclopedia*, vi–vii, 70–72, 388–94; Carnes, *Secret Ritual*, 6–9; Noel P. Gist, "Secret Societies: A Cultural Study of Fraternalism in the United States," *University of Missouri Studies* 15 (October 1, 1940): 32–33, 48; Schmidt, *Fraternal Organizations*, 38, 197; Clawson, *Constructing Brotherhood*, 136–38; Robert C. McMath Jr., *American Populism: A Social History, 1877–1898* (New York: Hill and Wang, 1993), 58–59, 63, 70.

Michael W. Fitzgerald writes that the ritual of the Union League, an organization dedicated to protecting the civil rights of southern blacks during Reconstruction, "resembled that of the Masons, from which it clearly derived; like those of many fraternal organizations, it extolled civic virtue, universal brotherhood, and other worthy causes" (Fitzgerald, *The Union League Movement in the Deep South: Politics and Agricultural Change during Reconstruction* [Baton Rouge: Louisiana State University Press, 1989], 114).

36. Charles Moreau Harger, "The Lodge," *Atlantic Monthly*, April 1906, 494.

Chapter Two

1. Thomas J. Archdeacon, *Becoming American: An Ethnic History* (New York: Free Press, 1983), 112–13, 127, 141–42; Dernoral Davis, "Toward a Socio-Historical and Demographic Portrait of Twentieth-Century African Americans," in *Black Exodus: The Great*

Migration from the American South, ed. Alferdteen Harrison (Jackson: University Press of Mississippi, 1991), 10–11.

2. Samuel P. Hays, *The Response to Industrialism, 1885–1914* (Chicago: University of Chicago Press, 1957), 95; John R. Commons, *Races and Immigrants in America* (New York: Macmillan, 1907), 165; Robert Hunter, *Poverty: Social Conscience in the Progressive Era* (New York: Harper and Row, 1965), 313.

3. Carolyn L. Weaver, *The Crisis in Social Security: Economic and Political Origins* (Durham: Duke University Press Policy Studies, 1982), 20; "Special Census Reports: The Institutional Population of the United States," reviewed by Lilian Brandt, *Charities and the Commons* 16 (May 26, 1906): 488–91; Lee K. Frankel, "The Relation of Insurance to Poverty," in National Conference of Charities and Correction, *Proceedings* (1916), 444–45; Amos G. Warner, *American Charities* (New York: Crowell, 1908), 196.

4. Raymond A. Mohl, "The Abolition of Public Outdoor Relief, 1870–1900: A Critique of the Piven and Cloward Thesis," in *Social Welfare or Social Control? Some Historical Reflections on Regulating the Poor*, ed. Walter I. Trattner (Knoxville: University of Tennessee Press, 1983), 42; Warner, *American Charities*, 228–29.

5. Frank A. Fetter, "The Subsidizing of Private Charities," *American Journal of Sociology* 7 (September 1901): 361–64; U.S. Department of Commerce, *Historical Statistics of the United States: Colonial Times to 1970*, pt. 2 (Washington, D.C.: Government Printing Office, 1975), 1120, 1128; National Industrial Conference Board, *Cost of Government in the United States* (New York: National Industrial Conference Board, 1926), 89, 99, 103.

6. U.S. Department of Labor, Children's Bureau, *Mothers' Aid, 1931* (Washington, D.C.: Government Printing Office, 1933), 8.

Per capita social welfare spending for cities with populations over 30,000 nearly quadrupled in real terms between 1903 and 1928. The greatest increases were in outdoor relief. See U.S. President's Research Committee on Social Trends, *Recent Social Trends in the United States: Report of the President's Research Committee on Social Trends* (New York: McGraw-Hill, 1933), 2:1251.

7. U.S. Department of Labor, *Mothers' Aid*, 17; Gwendolyn Mink, *The Wages of Motherhood: Inequality in the Welfare State, 1917–1942* (Ithaca: Cornell University Press, 1995), 50.

8. Louise Bolard More, *Wage-Earners' Budgets: A Study of Standards and Cost of Living in New York City* (New York: Henry Holt, 1907), 117–18.

9. Edward T. Devine, "Pensions for Mothers," *Survey* 30 (July 5, 1913): 458–59; Frederic Almy, "The Relation between Private and Public Outdoor Relief," *Charities Review* 7 (March 1899): 22.

10. Christopher Lasch, ed., *The Social Thought of Jane Addams* (Indianapolis: Bobbs-Merrill, 1965), 91; Peter Roberts, *The New Immigration: A Study of the Industrial and Social Life of Southeastern Europeans in America* (New York: Macmillan, 1912), 188, 190; John Daniels, *America via the Neighborhood* (New York: Harper and Brothers, 1920), 53; Marion Booth and Ordway Tead, "Roxbury and Dorchester," in *The Zone of Emergence: Observations of the Lower Middle and Upper Working Class Communities of Boston, 1905–1914*, ed. Robert A. Woods and Albert J. Kennedy (Cambridge: MIT Press, 1969), 159.

11. Paul S. Taylor, *Mexican Labor in the United States* (1928–34; reprint, New York: Arno Press, 1970), 1:185; Konrad Bercovici, *On New Shores* (New York: Century, 1925), 268; Alan M. Kraut, *The Huddled Masses: The Immigrant in American Society, 1880–1921* (Arlington Heights, Ill.: Harlan Davidson, 1982), 92, 99–101; Robert E. Park and Herbert A. Miller, *Old World Traits Transplanted* (New York: Harper and Brothers, 1921), 159–67.

12. John Daniels, *In Freedom's Birthplace: A Study of the Boston Negroes* (Boston: Houghton Mifflin, 1914), 199; Howard W. Odum, "Social and Mental Traits of the Negro: Research into the Conditions of the Negro Race in Southern Towns," *Studies in History, Economics, and Public Law* 37 (1910): 99, 102–3; Fannie Barrier Williams, "Social Bonds in the 'Black Belt' of Chicago," *Charities and the Commons* 15 (October 7, 1905): 42.

13. Jerome Dowd, *The Negro in American Life* (New York: Century, 1926), 100; Hace Sorel Tishler, *Self Reliance and Social Security, 1870–1917* (Port Washington, N.Y.: Kennikat Press, 1971), 96; Commons, *Races and Immigrants*, 50.

14. Robert Coit Chapin, *The Standard of Living among Workingmen's Families in New York City* (New York: Charities Publication Committee, 1909), 208–9, 245; More, *Wage-Earners' Budgets*, 269.

15. Chapin, *Standard*, 288.

16. Illinois Health Insurance Commission, *Report* (Springfield, 1919), 228; Chapin, *Standard*, 193.

17. Illinois Health Insurance Commission, *Report*, 189, 228.

18. Margaret F. Byington, *Homestead: The Households of a Mill Town* (New York: Charities Publication Committee, 1910), 90–91, 163.

19. Ibid., 113, 115, 161.

20. Illinois Health Insurance Commission, *Report*, 223.

21. Byington, *Homestead*, 91; Sadie Tanner Mossell, "The Standard of Living among One Hundred Negro Migrant Families in Philadelphia," *Annals of the American Academy of Political and Social Science* 98 (November 1921): 200; Asa E. Martin, *Our Negro Population: A Sociological Study of the Negroes of Kansas City, Missouri* (1913; reprint, New York: Negro Universities Press, 1969), 150; Chapin, *Standard*, 196.

22. William H. A. Carr, *From Three Cents a Week: The Story of the Prudential Insurance Company of America* (Englewood Cliffs, N.J.: Prentice-Hall, 1975), 14–18; Marquis James, *The Metropolitan Life: A Study in Business Growth* (New York: Viking, 1947), 43–45.

23. Illinois Health Insurance Commission, *Report*, 218.

24. Mossell, "Standard," 200; Martin, *Our Negro Population*, 150.

25. More, *Wage-Earners' Budgets*, 43.

26. Sophonisba P. Breckinridge, *New Homes for Old* (1921; reprint, Montclair, N.J.: Patterson Smith, 1971), 194; William I. Thomas and Florian Znaniecki, *The Polish Peasant in Europe and America* (1921; reprint, New York: Dover Publications, 1958), 2:1519; Phyllis H. Williams, *South Italian Folkways in Europe and America: A Handbook for Social Workers, Visiting Nurses, School Teachers, and Physicians* (1938; reprint, New York: Russell and Russell, 1969), 193; *The Jewish Communal Register of New York City, 1917–1918* (New York: Kehillah [Jewish Community] of New York City, 1918), 991–92.

27. James Borchert, *Alley Life in Washington: Family, Community, Religion, and Folklife in the City, 1850–1970* (Urbana: University of Illinois Press, 1982), 98, 217.

28. Warner, *American Charities*, 59–60; Daniels, *In Freedom's Birthplace*, 214; William L. Pollard, *A Study of Black Self-Help* (San Francisco: R and E Research, 1978), 52; Odum, "Social and Mental Traits," 282–83.

For other comments on the ability of blacks to avoid dependence, see Woods and Kennedy, *Zone*, 81; Bureau of Negro Welfare and Statistics, *The Negro in West Virginia* (1923–1924), 89.

29. Mary Willcox Brown, *The Development of Thrift* (New York: Macmillan, 1900), 156; Martin, *Our Negro Population*, 153.

30. Martin, *Our Negro Population*, 45–46.

31. Quincy L. Dowd, *Funeral Management and Costs: A World Survey of Burial and Cremation* (Chicago: University of Chicago Press, 1921), 75; John F. Dryden, *Addresses and Papers on Life Insurance and Other Subjects* (Newark: Prudential Insurance Company of America, 1909), 50–51.

32. L. M. Thomas, "The Bulwark of Our Republic," *Knights and Ladies of Security* 21 (May 10, 1915): 1.

33. William P. Burrell and D. E. Johnson, *Twenty-five Years History of the Grand Fountain of the United Order of True Reformers, 1881–1905* (1909; reprint, Westport, Conn.: Negro Universities Press, 1970), 27; Ladies of the Maccabees of the World, *Ritual* (Port Huron, 1910), 19; Independent Order of Saint Luke, *Degree Ritual* (Richmond, 1904), 24; Security Benefit Association, *Ritual* (Topeka, n.d.), 32; Loyal Order of Moose, *Historical Souvenir of the Loyal Order of Moose* (Chicago, 1912), 51, 61.

34. Security Benefit Association, *Ritual*, 36. The version of the song in Ladies of the Maccabees, *Ritual*, 40, includes this stanza:

Pledged sisters now are we
In blest fraternity,
Our hopes, our aims, our plans are one
Till passing years are done.

35. Ladies of the Maccabees, *Ritual*, 66; Loyal Order of Moose, *Historical Souvenir*, 67.

36. Independent Order of Saint Luke, *Historical Report of the R.W.G. Council, I.O., Saint Luke, 1867–1917* (Richmond, 1917), 41; Loyal Order of Moose, *Historical Souvenir*, 67.

For the pervasive use of the family analogy, see David Thelen, *Paths of Resistance: Tradition and Dignity in Industrializing Missouri* (New York: Oxford University Press, 1986), 166; Mark C. Carnes, *Secret Ritual and Manhood in Victorian America* (New Haven: Yale University Press, 1989), 119–20; Mary Ann Clawson, *Constructing Brotherhood: Class, Gender, and Fraternalism* (Princeton: Princeton University Press, 1989), 24–25.

37. "No Poor House for Members of the S.B.A. or Their Families," *Security News* 30 (March 1924): 1; Ladies of the Maccabees, *Ritual*, 58.

38. Independent Order of Saint Luke, *Degree Ritual*, 8; Ladies of the Maccabees, *Ritual*, 42–43.

For African antecedents, see Betty M. Kuyk, "The African Derivation of Black Fraternal Orders in the United States," *Comparative Studies in Society and History* 25 (October 1983): 559–92.

39. Independent Order of Saint Luke, *Degree Ritual*, 19.

40. Editorial Comment, *Ladies Review* 22 (January 1916): 1 and 20 (September 1914): 1.

41. Burrell and Johnson, *Twenty-five Years*, 138.

42. Loyal Order of Moose, *Historical Souvenir*, 35, 51.

43. Mary MacEachern Baird, Editorial Comment, *Ladies Review* 22 (Dec. 1916); Independent Order of Saint Luke, *Degree Ritual*, 20; Woman's Benefit Association of the Maccabees, *Ritual and Laws: The Order of the Rose* (Port Huron, Mich., 1917), 25–26.

44. Fanny L. Armstrong, "Woman as a Factor in Fraternal Organizations," *Review, Ladies of the Maccabees* 5 (May 1, 1899); "Address Delivered by Honorable William Jennings Bryan," *Mooseheart Magazine* 1 (October 1915): 18; Loyal Order of Moose, *Historical Souvenir*, 33.

45. Burrell and Johnson, *Twenty-five Years*, 216; Ladies of the Maccabees, *Ritual*, 37; Loyal Order of Moose, *Historical Souvenir*, 33.

46. Harvey F. Songer, "The Lodge System," *Security News* 30 (July 1924): 4; Ladies of the Maccabees, *Ritual*, 41–42; Burrell and Johnson, *Twenty-five Years*, 386.

47. Louis Hartz, *The Liberal Tradition in America: An Interpretation of American Political Thought since the Revolution* (New York: Harcourt Brace, 1955), 20.

48. Keith L. Yates, *An Enduring Heritage: The First One Hundred Years of North American Benefit Association (Formerly Woman's Benefit Association)* (Port Huron, Mich.: North American Benefit Association, 1992), 15–16, 29–54, 160, xxiv.

49. Alice E. Boyd, "Our Order," *Review, Ladies of the Maccabees* 4 (January 20, 1898): 2; Yates, *Enduring Heritage*, 101–4; 135–36; "History of Order and Biographical Sketches of Officers and Representatives of the Third Biennial Review," *Review, Ladies of the Maccabees*, supplement (July 1, 1899): 19–24; "The National Council of Women," *Ladies Review* 15 (September 1909): 188; Alice B. Locke, "Compulsory Insurance Opposed by Women's Benefit Societies," *National Civic Federation Review* 5 (July 10, 1920): 14, 16.

50. Elizabeth E. Brown, "The Work of Women," *Ladies Review* 7 (April 1, 1901): 2.

51. "The Seneca Falls Declaration of Sentiments and Resolutions, July 19, 1848," in *Documents of American History to 1865*, ed. Henry Steele Commager (New York: Appleton-Century Crofts, 1949), 1:315; Aileen S. Kraditor, *The Ideas of the Woman Suffrage Movement, 1890–1920* (Garden City: Anchor Books, 1971), 40.

Angelina Grimké, one of the founders of the suffrage movement, had expressed this view long before the Civil War: "I recognize no rights but *human* rights—I know nothing of men's rights and women's rights; for in Christ Jesus, there is neither male nor female" (Grimké, "Human Rights Not Founded on Sex," in *Freedom, Feminism, and the State: An Overview of Individualist Feminism*, ed. Wendy McElroy [New York: Holmes and Meier, 1982, 1991], 31).

52. Emma E. Bower, "Women in the World's Work," *Western Review* 15 (January 1909): 11.

53. Bina M. West, First Address, Vanderbilt, Michigan, October 21, 1891, Woman's Life Insurance Society Papers, Port Huron, Mich.

54. Elizabeth B. McGowan, "The Scope of Woman's Influence and Its Greatest Avenue for Good in Fraternal Organizations," *Ladies Review* 7 (January 1, 1901): 1; Emma Olds, "The Twentieth Century Woman as Fraternalist," *Fraternal Monitor* 11 (October 1, 1900): 35.

55. Elsie Ada Faust, "The Advantages of Fraternalism for Women," *Ladies Review* 22 (January 1916): 4.

56. Emma E. Bower, "Benefit of Fraternalism to the Home," *Review, Ladies of the Maccabees* 5 (March 1, 1899): 1; Bina M. West, First Address, Woman's Life Insurance Society Papers; Mary MacEachern Baird, Editorial Comment, *Ladies Review* 23 (Oct. 1917).

57. Bower, "Women in the World's Work," 11; Fraternal Actuarial Association, *Proceedings* (1918), 66.

Hollister asserted that "the walls that have naturally been built up between women, because of their social position, are thrown down in the lodge room" ("Greetings to the National Federation of Clubs," *Review, Ladies of the Maccabees* 2 [June 1896]).

58. "Protect the Home," *Ladies Review* 14 (May 1908) and 15 (August 1909); Ladies of the Maccabees, *Ritual*, 55–56.

59. "A Chat with Our Members," *Ladies Review* 19 (April 1913): 58.

60. Ella J. Fifield, "The Twentieth Century Woman as Fraternalist," *Ladies Review* 7 (December 1, 1901): 1; Lillian Hollister, "The Supreme Commander's Department,"

Ladies Review 15 (August 1909): 166; Louis I. Dublin, *After Eighty Years: The Impact of Life Insurance on the Public Health* (Gainesville: University of Florida Press, 1966), 47–49.

"If a woman dies, she will leave just as large a doctor's bill, just as much funeral expense and just as gloomy a husband as a man would leave if the reverse were true" ("Women Protected," *Security News* 28 [December 1922]: 2).

61. Fifield, "Twentieth Century Woman," 1; Editorial Comment, *Ladies Review* 21 (April 1915); Editorial and Personal, *Ladies Review* 25 (June 1909): 1; Clara P. Roberts, "The Collection of Money by Our Order," *Study Course: Port Huron, Hive No. 1, Mich.*, 18, Woman's Life Insurance Society Papers.

62. Lillian Hollister, "The Czar's Peace Conference," *Review, Ladies of the Maccabees* 5 (May 1, 1899); Herbert Spencer, *The Principles of Sociology*, vol. 1 (New York: D. Appleton, 1897), 729–30.

Hollister, in making a positive reference to Spencer, a strong opponent of woman suffrage, may have been aware, as were many other feminists, that it had not always been so. In 1850, two years after the declaration at Seneca Falls, Spencer had called for extending full political equality to women. See Herbert Spencer, *Social Statics: The Conditions Essential to Human Happiness Specified, and the First of Them Developed* (1850; reprint, New York: Robert Schalkenbach Foundation, 1954), 138–53.

63. David M. Fahey, *The Black Lodge in White America: "True Reformer" Browne and His Economic Strategy* (Dayton, Ohio: Wright State University Press, 1994), 13–19. Fahey gives the most thorough historical account and analysis of the UOTR.

64. Ibid., 4, 19–21, 30–31, 40.

65. Burrell and Johnson, *Twenty-five Years*, 15; Elsa Barkley Brown, "Uncle Ned's Children: Negotiating Community and Freedom in Postemancipation Richmond, Virginia" (Ph.D. diss., Kent State University, 1994), 141–42; Fahey, *Black Lodge*, 30–33.

66. Burrell and Johnson, *Twenty-five Years*, 75, 87.

67. Fahey, *Black Lodge*, 19, 52, 150, 256–57; United Order of True Reformers, Grand Fountain, *Minutes* (1907), 12.

68. Burrell and Johnson, *Twenty-five Years*, 90, 170–71; Fahey, *Black Lodge*, 30.

69. Burrell and Johnson, *Twenty-five Years*, 80, 117.

70. Ibid., 135, 171, 322; Fahey, *Black Lodge*, 27.

71. Burrell and Johnson, *Twenty-five Years*, 119, 173–74.

72. Alexa Benson Henderson, *Atlanta Life Insurance Company: Guardian of Black Economic Dignity* (Tuscaloosa: University of Alabama Press, 1990), 9; John Sibley Butler, *Entrepreneurship and Self-Help among Black Americans: A Reconsideration of Race and Economics* (Albany: State University of New York Press, 1991), 184, 188; Fahey, *Black Lodge*, 22.

73. Independent Order of Saint Luke, *Fiftieth Anniversary—Golden Jubilee, Historical Report* (Richmond, 1917), 5–6; Margaret Reid, "Mary Ann Prout," in *Black Women in America: An Historical Encyclopedia*, ed. Darlene Clark Hine, Elsa Barkley Brown, and Rosalyn Terborg-Penn (Brooklyn, N.Y.: Carlson Publishing, 1993), 948–49.

For more on the relationship between mutual aid and black churches, see Alexa Benson Henderson, *Atlanta Life Insurance Company*, 7–17.

74. Elsa Barkley Brown, "Uncle Ned's Children," 207, 500–503; Elsa Barkley Brown, "Womanist Consciousness: Maggie Lena Walker and the Independent Order of Saint Luke," *Signs* 14 (Spring 1989): 615–17, 624–30; Gertrude W. Marlowe, "Maggie Lena Walker," in Hine, Brown, and Terborg-Penn, *Black Women in America*, 1216; Fahey, *Black*

Lodge, 22; Wendell P. Dabney, *Maggie L. Walker and the I.O. of Saint Luke: The Woman and Her Work* (Cincinnati: Dabney Publishing, 1927), 38.

75. Elsa Barkley Brown, "Womanist Consciousness," 617, 630.

76. Dabney, *Maggie L. Walker*, 12–13; Marlowe, "Maggie Lena Walker," 1218–19; Elsa Barkley Brown, "Womanist Consciousness," 618–19; Maggie L. Walker, "Traps for Women," 16–18, 24, Addresses, n.d., Maggie L. Walker Papers, Maggie L. Walker National Historical Site, Richmond, Va.

In 1921 Walker ran unsuccessfully for state superintendent of instruction in Virginia on the "Lily-Black" Republican ticket. See Elsa Barkley Brown, "Womanist Consciousness," 618.

77. Dabney, *Maggie L. Walker*, 13; Maggie L. Walker, "Nothing but Leaves," 11–12, unpublished speech, Addresses, 1909, Maggie L. Walker Papers.

78. Maggie L. Walker, "Nothing but Leaves," 16; Maggie L. Walker, "Stumbling Blocks," 15, Addresses, February 17, 1907, Maggie L. Walker Papers; Elsa Barkley Brown, "Womanist Consciousness," 623.

79. Elsa Barkley Brown, "Womanist Consciousness," 624.

80. Ibid., 620, 622.

81. Dabney, *Maggie L. Walker*, 12; Marlowe, "Maggie Lena Walker," 1218–19; Elsa Barkley Brown, "Womanist Consciousness," 618–19.

82. Walker framed the issue in personal terms: "Well, when next you send your banking committee down to the white man's bank, to take your club money, your society money, your church money . . . don't forget, that with your own hands, you are placing a stumbling-block in the pathway of that boy and that girl you are sending to school, which will, probably, take them all their lives to overcome" (Walker, "Stumbling Blocks," 38).

83. Maggie L. Walker "Benaiah's Valour," Addresses, March 1906, 8, 15, Maggie L. Walker Papers.

84. Dabney, *Maggie L. Walker*, 121–22; "B.E. Banks," *Black Enterprise*, June 1998, 181.

Chapter Three

1. Walter Basye, *History and Operation of Fraternal Insurance* (Rochester, N.Y.: Fraternal Monitor, 1919), 49; Ancient Order of United Workmen, Nevada Jurisdiction, *Journal of Proceedings* (1903), 1351; Independent Order of Foresters, Supreme Court, *Minutes* (1905), 134; Knights and Ladies of Security, National Council, *Constitution and Laws* (1908), 50–51.

2. *The Ritual of the Independent Order of Foresters for Companion Courts* (Chicago, 1898), 65.

3. Knights and Ladies of Security, *Constitution*, 38; Selena Mountford, "Medical Examinations in Our Order," in *Study Course: Port Huron, Hive No. 1, Mich.* (n.d.), 9, Woman's Life Insurance Society Papers, Port Huron, Mich.; Connecticut Bureau of Labor Statistics, *Annual Report* (1892), 1:633; Illinois Health Insurance Commission, *Report* (Springfield, 1919), 123.

4. Ancient Order of United Workmen, *Proceedings*, 1350–51; Knights and Ladies of Security, *Constitution*, 38, 51; Independent Order of Foresters, *Minutes*, 134; Christopher J. Kauffman, *Faith and Fraternalism: The History of the Knights of Columbus, 1882–1982* (New York: Harper and Row, 1982), 123.

5. "Revision and Amendments," *Ladies Review* 10 (June 1, 1904): 11.

6. Knights and Ladies of Security, *Constitution*, 40; Knights and Ladies of Security, *Proceedings* (1912), 65; "Revision and Amendments," 11.

7. Connecticut Bureau of Labor Statistics, *Annual Report*, 119; Noel P. Gist, "Secret Societies: A Cultural Study of Fraternalism in the United States," *University of Missouri Studies* 15 (October 1, 1940): 129; Ladies of the Maccabees, *Approved Decisions and Rulings* (1912), 57. For other examples, see Ancient Order of United Workmen, *Proceedings*, 1350; Loyal Order of Moose, *Historical Souvenir of the Loyal Order of Moose* (Chicago, 1912), 15.

8. Gist, "Secret Societies," 129; Ladies of the Maccabees, *Approved Decisions*, 57. While the Connecticut Bureau of Labor Statistics listed the number of societies that excluded blacks, it did not describe the rules for Indians.

9. "Oronhyatekha," *Forester* 22 (January 1901): 48–50; A. Macgillivray, "Oronhyatekha," *Forester* 28 (March 1907): 40–41.

10. "Oronhyatekha," *Forester* 22 (January 1901): 48–50; A. Macgillivray, "Oronhyatekha," *Forester* 28 (March 1907): 40–41; David M. Fahey, *Temperance and Racism: John Bull, Johnny Reb, and the Good Templars* (Lexington: University Press of Kentucky, 1996), 182.

11. "Oronhyatekha," *Forester* 22 (January 1901): 48.

12. "Capital Contributes," *Forester* 24 (December 1903): 209; Fahey, *Temperance and Racism*, 84; "Official Circular No. 14," *Independent Forester* 21 (April 16, 1900): 292.

13. Mary Ann Clawson, *Constructing Brotherhood: Class, Gender, and Fraternalism* (Princeton: Princeton University Press, 1989), 110.

14. Joel Walker, "The Social Welfare Policies, Strategies, and Programs of Black Fraternal Organizations in the Northeast United States, 1896–1920" (Ph.D. diss., Columbia University, 1985), 71–72; Ladies of the Maccabees, *Approved Decisions*, 52–53.

15. Alvin J. Schmidt, *Oligarchy in Fraternal Organizations: A Study in Organizational Leadership* (Detroit: Gale Research, 1973), 27; Don Harrison Doyle, *The Social Order of a Frontier Community: Jacksonville, Illinois, 1825–70* (Urbana: University of Illinois Press, 1978), 182; Gist, "Secret Societies," 105–6; David P. Thelen, *Paths of Resistance: Tradition and Dignity in Industrializing Missouri* (New York: Oxford University Press, 1986), 166–67; *The Ritual of the Independent Order of Foresters for Companion Courts*, 4.

16. For the role of visiting committees in the prevention of malingering, see Connecticut Bureau of Labor Statistics, *Annual Report*, 143–45, 633–34; Anna Kalet, "Voluntary Health Insurance in New York City," *American Labor Legislation Review* 6 (June 1916): 148.

17. Paul Boyer, *Urban Masses and Moral Order in America, 1820–1920* (Cambridge: Harvard University Press, 1978), 150–52.

18. Michael B. Katz, "The History of an Impudent Poor Woman in New York City from 1918 to 1923," in *The Uses of Charity: The Poor on Relief in the Nineteenth-Century Metropolis*, ed. Peter Mandler (Philadelphia: University of Pennsylvania Press, 1990), 240; Katz, *In the Shadow of the Poorhouse: A Social History of Welfare in America* (New York: Basic Books, 1986), 291; Katz, *The Undeserving Poor: From the War on Poverty to the War on Welfare* (New York: Pantheon, 1989), 179–80, 184, 239.

19. James T. Patterson, *America's Struggle against Poverty: 1900–1980* (Cambridge: Harvard University Press, 1981), 20–25; Linda Gordon, "The New Feminist Scholarship on the Welfare State," in *Women, the State, and Welfare*, ed. Linda Gordon (Madison: University of Wisconsin Press, 1990), 25–26; Glenn C. Altschuler, *Race, Ethnicity, and*

Class in American Social Thought, 1865–1919 (Arlington Heights, Ill.: Harlan Davidson, 1982), 80–82.

20. Charles B. Wilson, *The Official Manual and History of the Grand United Order of Odd Fellows in America* (Philadelphia: Grand United Order of Odd Fellows, 1894), 11–17; Monroe N. Work, *Negro Year Book: Annual Encyclopedia of the Negro* (Tuskegee: Tuskegee Institute, Alabama, Negro Year Book Pub. Co., 1916–17), 397.

21. Wilson, *Official Manual*, 20, 153–56, 158; Work, *Negro Year Book*, 397.

22. William A. Muraskin, *Middle-Class Blacks in a White Society: Prince Hall Freemasonry in America* (Berkeley: University of California Press, 1975), 89–97; Dennis N. Mihelich, "A Socioeconomic Portrait of Prince Hall Masonry in Nebraska, 1900–1920," *Great Plains Quarterly* 17 (Winter 1997): 43.

The black version of the Knights of Pythias, with 250,000 members in 1916, was the second largest fraternal organization among blacks. See Work, *Negro Year Book*, 397.

Of fifty-one lodge members who could be identified in Ansonia, Connecticut, in 1922, twenty were laborers and seventeen were (probably unskilled) brass and foundry workers. See Knights of Pythias of North America, South America, Europe, Asia, Africa, and Australia, *Eighth Biennial Report of S. W. Green, Supreme Chancellor* (Nashville, Tenn., 1923), 95–97; *Ansonia, Derby, Shelton, and Seymour Directory* (1922, 1923).

For a description of black workers in the Ansonia area, see Jeremy Brecher, *Brass Valley: The Story of Working People's Lives and Struggles in an American Industrial Region* (Philadelphia: Temple University Press, 1982), 79, 93–101.

23. Application forms, St. Paul Lodge, Household of Ruth, box 21, Knights of Pythias Records, Schomburg Center for Research in Black Culture, New York Public Library, New York, N.Y.; Joseph A. Hill, *Women in Gainful Occupations, 1870–1920* (Washington, D.C.: Government Printing Office, 1929), 78, 76; Joanne L. Goodwin, "An American Experiment in Paid Motherhood: The Implementation of Mothers' Pensions in Early Twentieth-Century Chicago," *Gender and History* 4 (Autumn 1992): 330.

24. The canvas defined economic clubs as "insurance societies, labor unions, building associations, or some form of organization for economic advantage." See Federation of Churches and Christian Workers in New York City, *Second Sociological Canvas* (1897), 95; Robert Coit Chapin, *The Standard of Living among Workingmen's Families in New York City* (New York: Charities Publication Committee, 1909), 208.

25. Sojourna Household of Ruth, *Constitution, By-Laws, and Members' Financial Book* (ca. 1910), 7–13, box 21, Knights of Pythias Records.

26. Ibid., 14–15, 23–24.

27. Minute Book of Sojourna Lodge, Household of Ruth, April 17, 1914 to July 21, 1916, box 10, Knights of Pythias Records.

Lodges no doubt engaged in many unauthorized acts of "charity." Zora Neale Hurston recalled that a friend, a treasurer of the local Daughter Elks, advanced her funds during the depression to mail a manuscript. The money had been "borrowed" from the lodge treasury. See Hurston, *Dust Tracks on a Road: An Autobiography* (Urbana: University of Illinois Press, 1984), 210.

28. Minute Book of Sojourna Lodge, May 21, 1915, March 17, April 21, 1916, Knights of Pythias Records.

29. Ibid., April 17, 1914, April 21, 1916, and Sojourna Household of Ruth, *Constitution, By-Laws, and Members' Financial Book*, 11, Knights of Pythias Records.

The GUOOF allowed members to collect benefits as long as they had six months or less of arrears. See Grand United Order of Odd Fellows of the City of New York, *Consti-*

tution, By Laws, and Rules of Order of Excelsior Lodge (ca. 1907), box 21, Knights of Pythias Records.

30. Muraskin, *Middle-Class Blacks*, 46, 67, 84. For a critique, which I essentially share, of Muraskin's interpretation, see Loretta J. Williams, *Black Freemasonry and Middle-Class Realities* (Columbia: University of Missouri Press, 1980), 117–19.

31. David M. Fahey, *The Black Lodge in White America: "True Reformer" Browne and His Economic Strategy* (Dayton, Ohio: Wright State University Press, 1994), 255; Independent Order of Saint Luke, *Revised Constitution of the Right Worthy Grand Council* (Richmond, 1921), 39–40, 85; Mosaic Templars of America, Europe, Asia, and Africa, *Ritual* (Dallas: World Print, 1901), 16.

32. International Order of Twelve Knights and Daughters of Tabor, Georgia Jurisdiction, *Minutes* (1913), 21. For other examples, see Asa E. Martin, *Our Negro Population: A Sociological Study of the Negroes of Kansas City, Missouri* (1913; reprint, New York: Negro Universities Press, 1969), 144–45; Howard W. Odum, "Social and Mental Traits of the Negro: Research into the Conditions of the Negro Race in Southern Towns," *Studies in History, Economics, and Public Law* 37 (1910): 143–44; Wilson, *Official Manual*, 234–35.

33. Knights of Pythias of North America, South America, Europe, Asia, Africa, and Australia, Supreme Lodge, *Proceedings* (1915), 224. Echoing this point, David Thelen concludes that fraternal orders in Missouri at the turn of the century "were interested mainly in the social and personal, not the economic, characteristics of their prospective brothers" (Thelen, *Paths of Resistance*, 163).

34. Linda Gordon, "Black and White Visions of Welfare: Women's Welfare Activism, 1890–1945," *Journal of American History* 78 (September 1991): 565, 586–87. For a highly nuanced discussion of the moral values of the very poor, see Gordon's *Heroes of Their Own Lives: The Politics and History of Family Violence, Boston, 1880–1960* (New York: Viking, 1988).

The question of whether black societies strictly enforced their moral restrictions, while important, should not detract from the significant fact that so many bothered to adopt them. The mere existence of a "paper rule" tells much about the attitudes of those who approved it.

35. Workmen's Circle, *Report* (1907), 20–23.

36. Arthur A. Goren, *New York Jews and the Quest for Community: The Kehillah Experiment, 1908–1922* (New York: Columbia University Press, 1970), 190–91; Frederick Shulman, "Fraternal Orders," *Call of Youth* 3 (July 1935): 7; Judah J. Shapiro, *The Friendly Society: A History of the Workmen's Circle* (New York: Media Judaica, 1970), 100–101; Workmen's Circle, National Executive Committee, minutes, February 1928, Workmen's Circle Papers, YIVO Institute for Jewish Research, New York, N.Y.; "The Medical Department of the Workmen's Circle," *Call of Youth* 2 (June 1934).

37. Workmen's Circle, minutes, May 1926, December 1927, Workmen's Circle Papers.

38. Ibid., August 1928, June, December 1932; "The Medical Department of the Workmen's Circle," *Call of Youth* 1 (May 1933); Shapiro, *Friendly Society*, 165.

39. Workmen's Circle, minutes, June, September, October, December 1926, and February, November 1928, Workmen's Circle Papers.

40. Thomas J. E. Walker, *Pluralistic Fraternity: The History of the International Worker's Order* (New York: Garland, 1991), 142; Arthur J. Sabin, *Red Scare in Court: New York versus the International Workers Order* (Philadelphia: University of Pennsylvania Press, 1993), 13, 222; M. Mark Stolarik, "A Place for Everyone: Slovak Fraternal-Benefit Societies," in *Self-Help in Urban America: Patterns of Minority Business Enterprise*, ed. Scott

Cummings (Port Washington, N.Y.: Kennikat Press, 1980), 138; Joseph Stipanovich, "Collective Economic Activity among Serb, Croat, and Slovene Immigrants in the United States," in Cummings, *Selp-Help*, 168–69; Margaret E. Galey, "Ethnicity, Fraternalism, Social and Mental Health," *Ethnicity* 4 (March 1977): 42–43; Hannah Kliger, ed., *Jewish Hometown Associations and Family Circles in New York: The WPA Yiddish Writers' Group Study* (Bloomington: Indiana University Press, 1992), 61, 63; William E. Mitchell, *Mishpokhe: A Study of New York City Jewish Family Clubs* (The Hague: Mouton, 1978), 78.

41. Basye, *History and Operation*, 20.

42. *History and Manual of the Colored Knights of Pythias* (Nashville, Tenn.: National Baptist Publishing Board, 1917), 448–49; Maximilian Hurwitz, *The Workmen's Circle: Its History, Ideals, Organization, and Institutions* (New York: Workmen's Circle, 1936), 178.

"In most ethnic cultures," Lizabeth Cohen notes, "there was a deep distrust of public assistance. . . . Often the people of European countries that had state assistance, such as Italy, regarded dependence upon public charity rather than poverty itself as the disgrace. . . . To spare themselves the shame of watching their compatriots appeal to American institutions, ethnic groups found their own solutions" (Cohen, *Making a New Deal: Industrial Workers in Chicago, 1919–1939* [New York: Cambridge University Press, 1990], 57).

43. National Fraternal Congress, *Proceedings* (1901), 299; Editorial Comment, *Knights and Ladies of Security* 23 (February 1917): 4. For other fraternal statements stressing the distinction between charity and mutual aid, see E. J. Dunn, *Personal Efficiency in Fraternal Salesmanship* (Rochester, N.Y.: Fraternal Monitor, 1926), 261; Editorial Comment, *Knights and Ladies of Security* 22 (December 10, 1916): 4.

44. *The Jewish Communal Register of New York City, 1917–1918* (New York: Kehillah of New York City, 1918), 732.

45. Fraternal Order of Eagles, *Journal of Proceedings* (1909), 124; Independent Order of Saint Luke, *Degree Ritual* (Richmond, 1904), 14, 20, 30.

Many parallels appear between the restrictions on benefits imposed by fraternal societies and by labor unions. The socialist and self-consciously working-class Western Miners' Federation (a predecessor of the Industrial Workers of the World) was typical in denying benefits "when sickness and accident was caused by intemperance, imprudence, or immoral conduct" (Alan Derickson, *Workers' Health, Workers' Democracy: The Western Miners' Struggle, 1891–1925* [Ithaca: Cornell University Press, 1988], 66).

46. Max Weber, *From Max Weber: Essays in Sociology* (New York: Oxford University Press, 1958), 308.

"Membership in these societies," Doyle writes, "served as certification of good moral character and personal discipline, and this was, in effect, an endorsement as a good credit risk" (Doyle, *Social Order*, 186).

47. "The Meaning of Fraternity," *Ladies Review* 14 (March 1908): 61; Lynn Dumenil, *Freemasonry and American Culture, 1880–1930* (Princeton: Princeton University Press, 1984), 21; Muraskin, *Middle-Class Blacks*, 154–55.

48. Michael R. Weisser, *A Brotherhood of Memory: Jewish Landsmanshaftn in the New World* (New York: Basic Books, 1985), 17; James R. Orr and Scott G. McNall, "Fraternal Orders and Working-Class Formation in Nineteenth-Century Kansas," in *Bringing Class Back In: Contemporary and Historical Perspectives*, ed. Scott G. McNall, Rhonda F. Levine and Rick Fantasia (Boulder: Westview Press, 1991), 109; David M. Emmons, *The Butte Irish: Class and Ethnicity in an American Mining Town, 1875–1925* (Urbana: University of Illinois Press, 1989), 107–10, 139–41.

49. Peter Roberts, *Anthracite Coal Communities: A Study of the Demography the Social, Educational and Moral Life of the Anthracite Regions* (New York: Macmillan, 1904), 309; Donald E. Pienkos, *PNA: A Centennial History of the Polish National Alliance of the United States of North America* (New York: Columbia University Press, 1984), 253.

50. Loyal Order of Moose, *Minutes* (1921), 72; Terence O'Donnell, *History of Life Insurance in Its Formative Years* (Chicago: American Conservation Company, 1936), 631.

51. Elizabeth Jameson, *All That Glitters: Class, Conflict, and Community in Cripple Creek* (Urbana: University of Illinois Press, 1998), 106–7.

National organizations seem to have been more restrictive than local lodges. In both April and May 1905, for example, the Medical Board of the IOF reviewed and rejected 15 percent of the membership applications; see *Forester* 16 (July 1905): 63, 65. Between January and July 1904, the medical examiners of the LOTM had a rejection rate of 12.8 percent; see Ladies of the Maccabees, Supreme Hive, *Regular Review* (1903), 207.

52. Kauffman, *Faith and Fraternalism*, 133; Fraternal Order of Eagles *Journal of Proceedings* (1907).

53. Charles Edward Dickerson II, "The Benevolent and Protective Order of Elks and the Improved Benevolent and Protective Order of Elks of the World: A Comparative Study, Euro-American and Afro-American Secret Societies" (Ph.D. diss., University of Rochester, 1981), 293; "The Maccabee California Relief Fund," *Ladies Review* 12 (September 1906): 188; "The I.O.F. San Francisco Relief Fund," *Forester* 27 (July 1906): 34–35.

54. National Council of the Knights and Ladies of Security to the Various Councils of the Knights and Ladies of Security, 1906, and Hugh Gowan to ——, May 14, 1906, SBLP.

55. Mary J. Crum to —— Wallace, June 24, 1902, SBLP.

56. Clawson, *Constructing Brotherhood*, 11.

Chapter Four

1. Vivienne Cottingham, interview, June 27, 1996. Unless otherwise noted, all interviews were conducted by the author.

2. Ibid.

3. Ibid.

4. U.S. Department of Commerce, Bureau of the Census, *Benevolent Institutions, 1910* (Washington, D.C.: Government Printing Office, 1913), 44; Eve P. Smith, "Bring Back the Orphanages? What Policymakers of Today Can Learn from the Past," *Child Welfare* 74 (January–February 1995): 118; C. W. Areson and H. W. Hopkirk, "Child Welfare Programs of Churches and Fraternal Orders," *Annals of the American Academy of Political and Social Science* 71 (September 1925): 87; U.S. Department of Commerce, Bureau of the Census, *Children under Institutional Care and in Foster Homes, 1933* (Washington, D.C.: Government Printing Office, 1935), 63–125.

In 1910 governmental subsidies paid for 28.8 percent of the income of all orphanages; see U.S. Department of Commerce, *Benevolent Institutions*, 79.

Fraternal homes were far less common among blacks. The costs of building, equipping, and maintaining a facility could be enormous, and blacks were more likely to rely on informal adoption and extended family networks; see Peter C. Holloran, *Boston's Wayward Children: Social Services for Homeless Children, 1830–1930* (Rutherford, N.J.: Fairleigh Dickinson University Press, 1989), 144.

5. Loyal Order of Moose, *Historical Souvenir of the Loyal Order of Moose* (Chicago,

1912), 27, 57, 59; Warner Olivier, *Back of the Dream: The Story of the Loyal Order of Moose* (New York: Dutton, 1952), 118–19.

6. Guy H. Fuller, ed., *Loyal Order of Moose and Mooseheart* (Mooseheart, Ill.: Mooseheart Press, 1918), 15–17; James J. Davis, *The Iron Puddler: My Life in the Rolling Mills and What Came of It* (New York: Grosset and Dunlap, 1922), 246–47; Olivier, *Back of the Dream*, 78; Loyal Order of Moose, *Proceedings* (1927), 43–45.

7. Olivier, *Back of the Dream*, 124–25.

8. Ibid., 122.

9. Fuller, *Loyal Order of Moose*, 31–33; Olivier, *Back of the Dream*, 137.

10. Olivier, *Back of the Dream*, 135–36; *Mooseheart Magazine* 5 (September 1919): 1; "New Arrivals," *Mooseheart Weekly* 2 (March 21, 1919): 2; Albert Bushnell Hart to John W. Ford, May 7, 1923, folder: Moose and Mooseheart Vocational Training, 1921–25, box 14, Albert Bushnell Hart Papers, Harvard University Archives, Pusey Library, Harvard University, Cambridge, Mass.; Warner Olivier, "City of Children," *Saturday Evening Post*, September 14, 1948, 32.

Before 1915 the board of governors had admitted a few elderly members to Mooseheart, but the experiment did not work. In 1922 the Supreme Lodge opened a separate old folks' home in Orange Park, Florida. Dubbed Moosehaven, it had 203 residents by 1930 (29 women and 174 men). See Olivier, *Back of the Dream*, 175–79; Loyal Order of Moose, *Proceedings* (1930), 292.

11. "Mooseheart," *Mooseheart Magazine* 9 (June 1923): 1; Rudolph M. Binder, "Mooseheart's Aim Is Education for Life," *Literary Digest*, July 14, 1934, 30; Loyal Order of Moose, *Mooseheart Year Book* (1919–20) (Mooseheart, Ill.: Mooseheart Press, 1920), 47, 150; Martin L. Reymert and Ralph T. Hinton Jr., "The Effect of a Change to a Relatively Superior Environment upon the IQ's of One Hundred Children," in National Society for the Study of Education, *Thirty-ninth Yearbook* (Bloomington, Ill.: Public School Publishing, 1940), 258; "What We Find at Mooseheart: The School That Trains for Life," *Mooseheart Weekly* 2 (May 9, 1919): 1.

12. James J. Davis, *Iron Puddler*, 249–50; Martin L. Reymert, "The Mooseheart System of Child Guidance," *Nervous Child* 1 (October 1941): 88; Rudolph M. Binder, "Education at Mooseheart," *Education* 55 (November 1934): 153; Loyal Order of Moose, *Mooseheart Year Book* (1918–19) (Mooseheart, Ill.: Mooseheart Press, 1919), 134; Mooseheart, superintendent's report, January 12, 1923, folder 2: Special Topics, box 14, Hart Papers.

13. Olivier, *Back of the Dream*, 78; Mooseheart High School, *Seniors' Book*, vol. 7 (Mooseheart, Ill.: Mooseheart, 1925), 112; "From the Philadelphia Record, July 14, 1919," *Mooseheart Magazine* 6 (October 1920): 15.

14. Martin L. Reymert to Charles Spearman, November 4 1930, folder: Charles Spearman Correspondence, Martin L. Reymert Papers and Collection, Archives of the History of American Psychology, University of Akron, Akron, Ohio; Reymert, "Mooseheart System," 80–81, 92–95; Leonora Stumpf, interview, April 5, 1996.

15. Loyal Order of Moose, *Mooseheart Year Book* (1918–19), 38–40.

16. "An Achievement of the Common Man," *Moose Docket* 1 (November 1932): 47. In descending order of frequency the leading occupations were miners, railroad employees, laborers, farmers, and carpenters. See "Classification of Mooseheart Students According to Fathers' Occupation," *Mooseheart Weekly* 7 (June 21, 1924): 5.

17. Neva R. Deardorff, "The New Pied Pipers," *Survey Graphic* 52 (April 1, 1924): 47; Ralph Meister, interview, April 24, 1996.

18. Loyal Order of Moose, *Mooseheart Year Book* (1918–19), 22; Holloran, *Boston's Way-*

ward Children, 171; Reena Sigman Friedman, *These Are Our Children: Jewish Orphanages in the United States, 1880–1925* (Hanover, N.H.: University Press of New England for Brandeis University Press, 1994), 162–63; Nurith Zmora, *Orphanages Reconsidered: Child Care Institutions in Progressive Era Baltimore* (Philadelphia: Temple University Press, 1994), 69.

19. Loyal Order of Moose, *Proceedings* (1930), 13.

20. Loyal Order of Moose, *Mooseheart Year Book* (1918–19), 21; folders 1–2: Moose and Mooseheart, Board of Governors, Correspondence and Reports, 1922–24, box 14, Hart Papers.

21. Mooseheart Governors, minutes, and Mooseheart, superintendent's report [1922–24], folders 1–2: Moose and Mooseheart, Board of Governors, Correspondence and Reports, 1922–24, box 14, Hart Papers; Loyal Order of Moose, *Mooseheart Year Book* (1918–19), 21; Helen Koepp, interview, June 28, 1996.

22. Loyal Order of Moose, *Mooseheart Year Book* (1918–19), 21; Mooseheart, superintendent's report, March 29, 1924, Hart Papers; Loyal Order of Moose, *Proceedings* (1929), 21, and (1947), 247; Cottingham interview; Meister interview; Suzanne Kelly, interview, June 26, 1996; Koepp interview.

23. Binder, "Education at Mooseheart," 151; Deardorff, "New Pied Pipers," 47; Reymert, "Mooseheart System," 83; Meister interview; Stumpf interview.

24. Deardorff, "New Pied Pipers," 47; Hart to James J. Davis, September 19, 1924, folder 1: Moose and Mooseheart, Board of Governors, Correspondence and Reports, 1922–24, box 14, Hart Papers; Loyal Order of Moose, *Minutes* (1925), 15.

25. Loyal Order of Moose, *Minutes* (1925), 15, 93–95; Olivier, *Back of the Dream*, 79–80.

26. "Impressive Figures with Which Every Lodge Officer Should Be Familiar," *Moose Docket* 1 (October 1932): 85; Loyal Order of Moose, *Proceedings* (1929), 21, 240; Edward J. Henning, "First, Learn *All* the Facts, Then If You Must—Criticize," *Moose Docket* 1 (March 1933): 65–66.

Complete information is not available for mothers' pensions in California and New Jersey. See U.S. Department of Labor, Children's Bureau, *Mothers' Aid, 1931* (Washington, D.C.: Government Printing Office, 1933), 8–9, 28–29.

27. Olivier, *Back of the Dream*, 79–80.

28. "Strengthen the Degree Staff," *Moose Docket* 1 (October 1932): 32; Loyal Order of Moose, *Proceedings* (1930), 13.

29. Olivier, *Back of the Dream*, 233–36; Loyal Order of Moose, *Proceedings* (1929), 285–89.

30. Zmora, *Orphanages Reconsidered*, 16; Loyal Order of Moose, *Minutes* (1925), 209A; *Mooseheart Year Book* (1919–20), 29; and *Proceedings* (1931), 289.

31. Louis W. Harvison, "Mooseheart Service," *Mooseheart Magazine* 6 (July–August 1920): 11.

32. Loyal Order of Moose, *Mooseheart Year Book* (1919–20), 31, 42–43, and *Minutes* (1925), 212A; Kelly interview; Reymert, "Mooseheart System," 76–77, 83.

33. Reymert, "Mooseheart System," 76; Binder, "Mooseheart's Aim," 30; memo from A. S. Baylor, Visit to Mooseheart Vocational School, October 22, 1923, folder 1: Moose and Mooseheart, Board of Governors, Correspondence and Reports, 1922–24, box 14, Hart Papers; Koepp interview.

34. Loyal Order of Moose, *Mooseheart Year Book* (1919–20), 42, 46, and *Minutes* (1925), 212A.

35. Cottingham interview; Kelly interview.

36. Reymert, "Mooseheart System," 76; Cottingham interview; Stumpf interview; Marie Smejkal, interview, February 14, 1996.

37. Mooseheart, superintendent's report, December 15, 1922, Hart Papers; Cottingham interview.

38. Mooseheart, superintendent's report, December 15, 1922, Hart Papers; Kari Morlock, interview, April 8, 1996; Cottingham interview.

39. Matthew P. Adams, "The Home Atmosphere at Mooseheart" pt. 2, *Mooseheart Weekly* 4 (December 17, 1921): 2; Cottingham interview; Kelly interview; Smejkal interview; Meister interview.

40. Reymert and Hinton, "Effect of a Change," 257.

41. Leonard Burch, interview, April 29, 1996; Morlock interview.

42. Morlock interview; Meister interview; Burch interview.

43. Loyal Order of Moose, *Proceedings* (1932), 88−92; Mildred E. Whitcomb, "First Grade, the School's Last Chance: An Interview with Martin L. Reymert," *Nation's Schools* 43 (March 1949): 23−24; Martin L. Reymert, "The Mooseheart Graphic Rating Scale for Housemothers and Housefathers," *Journal of Applied Psychology* 22 (June 1938): 288−94; Olivier, *Back of the Dream*, 139−50; Meister interview; Burch interview; Kelly interview.

44. Cottingham interview; Smejkal interview.

45. Cottingham interview; L. W. Merryweather, "The Argot of an Orphans' Home," *American Speech* 7 (August 1932): 398, 400−404; Edmund Kasser, "The Growth and Decline of a Children's Slang at Mooseheart, a Self-Contained Community," *Journal of Genetic Psychology* 66 (1945): 131−36.

46. Burch interview; Meister interview; Kelly interview.

47. Binder, "Education at Mooseheart," 151; Mooseheart, Board of Governors, minutes, December 15, 1923, folder 2: Moose and Mooseheart, Board of Governors, Correspondence and Reports, 1922−24, box 14, Hart Papers; Burch interview; Meister interview; Kelly interview; Koepp interview.

48. Mooseheart, superintendent's report, March 29, 1924, Hart Papers.

49. Ibid.; Meister interview; Koepp interview.

50. Mooseheart, superintendent's report, March 29, 1924, Hart Papers; Meister interview; Koepp interview; Kelly interview.

51. Koepp interview; Burch interview.

52. Adams, "Home Atmosphere," 2; Loyal Order of Moose, *Minutes* (1925), 209A; Binder, "Mooseheart's Aim," 30; Joe Mitchell Chapple, *"Our Jim": A Biography* (Boston: Chapple Publishing, 1928), 237.

53. Fuller, *Loyal Order of Moose*, 55; Binder, "Education at Mooseheart," 152; Adams, "Home Atmosphere," 2.

54. Mooseheart, superintendent's progress report, January 23, 1934, Hart Papers; Rudolph M. Binder, "Mooseheart; A Socio-Pedagogical Experiment," *School and Society* 35 (June 25, 1932): 856−57; Mooseheart High School, *Seniors' Book*, 68, 76, 84, 88; Burch interview; Meister interview; Loyal Order of Moose, *Mooseheart Year Book* (1919−20), 86, and *Proceedings* (1934), 191; (1940), 90−91; (1941), 258.

55. Loyal Order of Moose, *Proceedings* (1932), 57; Lyle R. Rolfe and Kurt Wehrmeister, "The Amazing Story of Mooseheart Football," *Moose* 78 (October/November 1992): 16−17; Mooseheart High School, *Seniors' Book*, 134, 172, 178, 195.

56. Mooseheart, Board of Governors, minutes, March 29−30, 1924, folder 2: Special

Topics, box 14; Mooseheart, superintendent's report, July 20, 1924; Mooseheart, Board of Governors, minutes, July 27, 1924, folder 1: Moose and Mooseheart, Board of Governors, General Correspondence, box 13, all in Hart Papers.

57. Kelly interview; Morlock interview; Fuller, *Loyal Order of Moose*, 53; Reymert, "Mooseheart System," 91.

58. Mooseheart, superintendent's report, July 20, 1924, Hart Papers; Kelly interview; Cottingham interview; Morlock interview; Smejkal interview; Meister interview; Stumpf interview; Burch interview; Rudolph M. Binder, "Mooseheart: A Model Community," *Sociology and Social Research* 19 (March–April 1935): 322; Reymert, "Mooseheart System," 91.

59. Burch interview; Smejkal interview; Cottingham interview; Meister interview; Reymert, "Mooseheart System," 78–79.

60. Olivier, "City of Children," 42; Cottingham interview; Binder, "Mooseheart: A Socio-Pedagogical Experiment," 855; Burch interview; Smejkal interview.

61. Mooseheart, superintendent's report, May 19, 1923, Hart Papers; Burch interview.

62. Loyal Order of Moose, *Minutes* (1925), 219A.

63. Ibid. (1915), 65.

64. Olivier, *Back of the Dream*, 152–58; Mooseheart High School, *Seniors' Book*, 92; "Protestant Church Services Started at Mooseheart," *Mooseheart Weekly* 2 (May 2, 1919): 9.

65. Olivier, *Back of the Dream*, 160–61; *Mooseheart Annual* 15 (1930), 80.

66. Loyal Order of Moose, *Minutes* (1925), 218A; Mooseheart, superintendent's report, March 15, May 19, 1923, Hart Papers.

67. Mooseheart, Board of Governors, Action Taken on the Superintendent's Docket by Executive Committee, February 14, 15, 1923, folder 2: Special Topics, box 14, Hart Papers.

68. For more on the George Junior Republics and related experiments, see Jack M. Holl, *Juvenile Reform in the Progressive Era: William R. George and the Junior Republic Movement* (Ithaca: Cornell University Press, 1971); LeRoy Ashby, *Saving the Waifs: Reformers and Dependent Children, 1890–1917* (Philadelphia: Temple University Press, 1984), 133–69.

69. Loyal Order of Moose, *Minutes* (1925), 214A–216A, 220A, and *Mooseheart Year Book* (1918–19), 134; Binder, "Mooseheart: A Socio-Pedagogical Experiment," 856.

70. Mooseheart, superintendent's report, March 15, 1923, Hart Papers; "Rules and Regulations for Use of Savings Fund," *Mooseheart Weekly* 2 (April 25, 1919): 3; Loyal Order of Moose, *Mooseheart Year Book* (1919–20), 66–67.

71. Cottingham interview; Loyal Order of Moose, *Mooseheart Year Book* (1919–20), 67.

72. "Self-Sacrifice," *Mooseheart Weekly* 3 (September 4, 1920): 4.

73. "About Mooseheart and the Loyal Order of Moose," *Mooseheart Magazine* 2 (June 1916): 8; Kelly interview.

74. Loyal Order of Moose, *Mooseheart Year Book* (1919–20), 55–59; Matthew P. Adams to Hart, November 16, 1923, folder 2: Moose and Mooseheart, Board of Governors, Correspondence and Reports, 1922–24, box 14, Hart Papers.

75. Loyal Order of Moose, *Mooseheart Year Book* (1919–20), 59–60; Merryweather, "Argot," 400; Meister interview; Burch interview; Hart to Adams, October 1, 1924, folder: Moose and Mooseheart, Discipline, 1922–24, box 13, Hart Papers.

76. Robert F. Havlik to Adams, August 7, 1922, folder: Moose and Mooseheart, Discipline, 1922–24, box 13, Hart Papers; Smejkal interview.

77. Loyal Order of Moose, *Mooseheart Year Book* (1918–19), 122–23; Mooseheart, superintendent's report, March 15, 1923, Hart Papers; Cottingham interview.

78. Mooseheart, superintendent's report, March 15, 1923, Hart Papers; Loyal Order of Moose, *Mooseheart Year Book* (1918–19), 122–23; Smejkal interview; Meister interview; Stumpf interview.

79. Hart to John W. Ford, December 8, 1923; Adams to Hart, September 17, 1924; Hart to Adams, October 1, 1924, all in folder: Moose and Mooseheart, Discipline, 1921–24, box 13, Hart Papers.

80. Hart to Adams, October 1, 1924, ibid.; "New Conduct Rating Plan for All Halls Now in Effect," *Mooseheart Weekly* 17 (July 31, 1931): 1; Loyal Order of Moose, *Proceedings* (1930), 284.

81. Mooseheart Governors, minutes, and Mooseheart, superintendent's report [1922–24], Hart Papers; Burch interview; Kelly interview. According to Meister, the children who were most likely to be demitted for reasons of discipline were those closest to graduation. "I postulated that there was a separation anxiety where the kid was afraid of leaving on the one hand and couldn't wait to leave on the other" (Meister interview).

82. Eve P. Smith, "Bring Back the Orphanages?," 138.

83. Cottingham interview; Kelly interview; Burch interview; Morlock interview; Smejkal interview; Stumpf interview; Meister interview.

The publications of the Loyal Order of Moose also carried ads listing the job skills of individual graduates; see "When a Feller Needs a Friend," *Moose Docket* 2 (June 1933): 10–11.

For the check-out procedure for graduates, see Mooseheart, superintendent's report, March 15, 1923, Hart Papers.

Alumni with whom I spoke insist that they did not feel a stigma. "We were told what a great place it was for so long," states one, "that I don't think we felt any stigma. I didn't perceive any and I never felt any" (Burch interview).

84. Loyal Order of Moose, *Mooseheart Year-Book and Annual* (1931) (Mooseheart, Ill.: Mooseheart Press, 1931), 145, and *Proceedings* (1931), 37–38; Meister interview.

85. Loyal Order of Moose, *Mooseheart Year-Book and Annual* (1931), 142–45, and "Average Earnings and Hours of Work: All Male and Female Wage Earners," in National Industrial Conference Board, *Service Letter on Industrial Relations*, n.s., 74 (February 28, 1931): 6. Because the median age of respondents was only twenty-two, these figures tended to understate the earnings potential of Mooseheart graduates.

86. My source for the raw data on male and female college attendance (1929–30 school year) is U.S. Department of the Interior, Office of Education, *Statistics of Higher Education, 1931–32* (Washington, D.C.: Government Printing Office, 1935), 25. The source for the numbers on Americans ages 18–24 is U.S. Department of Commerce, Bureau of the Census, *Abstract of the Fifteenth Census of the United States* (Washington, D.C.: Government Printing Office, 1933), 185.

87. Burch interview; Meister interview; Kelly interview; Smejkal interview; Stumpf interview; Koepp interview; Morlock interview.

Chapter Five

1. "Protection Now Furnished from the 'Cradle to the Grave,'" *Knights and Ladies of Security* 23 (April 1917): 7; Dean L. Smith, *A Nickel a Month* (St. Louis: MidAmerica Publishing, 1979), 13–14.

2. "Old Folks, Invalids, and Orphans Commission Appointed," *Knights and Ladies of Security* 22 (December 10, 1917): 1; Dean L. Smith, *Nickel a Month*, 22.

3. Dean L. Smith, *Nickel a Month*, 15–18.

4. Ibid., 20, 27; Security Benefit Association, National Council, *Proceedings* (1920), 166; "Sidelights on the H & H," *Knights and Ladies of Security* 25 (February 1919): 10.

5. Security Benefit Association, National Council, *Proceedings* (1924), 36–38.

6. Harley Garrett, "Guidance in a Small School for Orphans" (M.A. thesis, Stanford University, 1934), 9; Harry Perry, interview, March 3, 1996.

7. Security Benefit Association, National Council, *Proceedings* (1924), 38–39; Garrett, "Guidance," 9–10, 12.

8. Dean L. Smith, *Nickel a Month*, 28, 33, 48–49, 152–53; Garrett, "Guidance," 9–10; Security Benefit Home and Hospital Association, Board of Trustees, minutes, February 15, December 12, 1933, SBG; "The Security Benefit Home and Hospital Association, 1933," Security Benefit Life Insurance Company, Record Department, General Correspondence, reel B-11, SBG.

9. "Cooperative Relief of Distress," *Knights and Ladies of Security* 22 (December 10, 1916): 4; Dean L. Smith, *Nickel a Month*, 43–44, 52.

10. Garrett, "Guidance," 82–159; Security Benefit Home and Hospital Association, minutes, 1924–35, SBG.

11. SBA Survey Results, in author's possession; Kathleen Colbert Sabo, interview, March 9, 1996.

12. Dean L. Smith, *Nickel a Month*, 50; "Interest Centers in Home and Hospital," *Security News* 36 (June 1930): 24.

13. "None Can Equal Its Benefits," *Security News* 32 (August 1926): 4; "A Dream Becomes Vivid Reality," *Security News* 31, supplement (September 1925): 3; "Our Children and Our School," *Security News* 32 (February 1926): 1.

14. "Interesting Incidents of the H. & H.," *Security News* 27 (May 1921): 10; Dean L. Smith, *Nickel a Month*, 58; Florence Paschke Ford, interview, February 26, 1996; Evelyn Colbert Bezan, interview, March 2, 1996; LeRoy Paschke, interview, February 25, 1996.

15. Dean L. Smith, *Nickel a Month*, 106; Garrett, "Guidance," 77; *Fraternalist* 1 (1933). The *Fraternalist* is a student annual that was published for four years during the early 1930s. Copies are in possession of Charles Ehrnfelt, Bridgeport, Conn.

16. Garrett, "Guidance," 138; Perry interview; Paschke interview; Bezan interview; Ford interview.

17. Dean L. Smith, *Nickel a Month*, 45; Garrett, "Guidance," 46; Ford interview; Sabo interview; Bezan interview; Charles Ehrnfelt, interview, March 1, 1996.

18. Sabo interview; Paschke interview; Bezan interview; *Fraternalist* 4 (1936).

19. Ehrnfelt interview; Perry interview; Ford interview; Paschke interview; Sabo interview; Bezan interview; Wendell Taylor, interview, March 10, 1996.

20. *Fraternalist* 4 (1936); Garrett, "Guidance," 79; Taylor interview; Paschke interview.

21. Dean L. Smith, *Nickel a Month*, 45, 121–22; Paschke interview; Ford interview.

22. Sabo interview; Ehrnfelt interview.

23. Paschke interview; Taylor interview; Ford interview.

24. Ehrnfelt interview; Taylor interview; Ford interview.

25. Sabo interview; Ford interview; Taylor interview.

26. Dean L. Smith, *Nickel a Month*, 123.

27. Harley and Orrisa Garrett, interview, July 13, 1996.
When asked whether children could complain to Sutherland-Kirkpatrick, a former

resident who spent more than a decade in the home lamented, "You could never, never reach her. She was on a different planet" (Taylor interview).

28. Taylor interview; Harley and Orrisa Garrett interview; Ehrnfelt interview; Taylor interview; Ford interview; Security Benefit Home and Hospital Association, minutes, June 12, 1935, and November 30, 1938, SBG; Garrett, "Guidance," 92.

The information from the minutes of the board about the small number of permanent runaways accords with the memories of former residents. See Paschke interview; Taylor interview; Sabo interview; Julia Peebles Kulscar and Alex Kulscar, interview, May 9, 1995.

29. Dean L. Smith, *Nickel a Month*, 98–99; Security Benefit Association, National Council, *Proceedings* (1928), 38–39; "Interest Centers in Home and Hospital," *Security News* 40 (October 1934): 19; *Security News* (Home and Hospital Section) (ca. 1930), SBG; Bezan interview; Paschke interview; Ford interview; Ehrnfelt interview; "Can You Imagine . . .," *Fraternalist* 4 (1936).

30. Dean L. Smith, *Nickel a Month*, 116–17; Garrett, "Guidance," 32–33; Bezan interview; Paschke interview; Ford interview; Ehrnfelt interview.

31. Garrett, "Guidance," 4–5, 33–66; William Martin Proctor, *Educational and Vocational Guidance: A Consideration of Guidance as It Relates to All of the Essential Activities of Life* (Boston: Houghton Mifflin, 1925), 221.

32. Garrett, "Guidance," 92; Ehrnfelt interview; Harley and Orrisa Garrett interview; Sabo interview.

33. Garrett, "Guidance," 32–33, 36.

34. Ibid., 37–38. Garrett also suggested, "We must play square. We must explain the nature, purpose, and necessity of every rule and law which the nature of the home makes it necessary for us to enforce" (38).

35. Ibid., 41–43.

36. "The Student Council," *Fraternalist* 4 (1936); Garrett, "Guidance," 46–47, 51–52; Bezan interview.

37. Garrett, "Guidance," 78; Harley and Orrisa Garrett interview.

38. Harley and Orrisa Garrett interview; Security Benefit Home and Hospital Association, minutes, November 6, 1940, SBG; Security Benefit Association, "Report of the National President" (1944), 6–7, SBAP.

39. Security Benefit Clinic and Hospital, superintendent's report (1946), 6, SBG; Security Benefit Association, "Report of the National President" (1944), 7, SBAP.

On the reasons for rejection, see, for example, Security Benefit Home and Hospital Association, minutes, September 23, 1936, November 4, 1937, and August 23 and October 11, 1939, SBG.

40. Richard B. McKenzie, "Orphanage Alumni: How They Have Done and How They Evaluate Their Experience," in *Rethinking Orphanages for the Twenty-first Century*, ed. Richard B. McKenzie (Thousand Oaks, Calif.: Sage Publications, 1999), 103–26.

To conduct my research of SBA alumni, I relied on several sources for names and addresses: the Security Benefit Group of Companies, which has sponsored reunions during the last two decades; Harley and Orrisa Garrett; and former students who have kept track of alumni. Alumni also gave valuable help in providing addresses for siblings who had been residents. I sent the questionnaire to twenty-eight individuals; twenty responded.

41. McKenzie, "Orphanage Alumni," 107–8; SBA Survey Results.

42. McKenzie, "Orphanage Alumni," 108, 116–17; SBA Survey Results.

There was a choice of categories: physical abuse (excessive use of force and unwarranted corporal punishment); mental abuse (serious emotional deprivation or depreciation of self-worth); and sexual abuse (inappropriate sexual activity, from fondling to intercourse). Again, some respondents selected select more than one category.

43. Security Benefit Home and Hospital Association, minutes, 1924–35, SBG; SBA Survey Results.

44. SBA Survey Results; McKenzie, "Orphanage Alumni," 119.

45. SBA Survey Results; McKenzie, "Orphanage Alumni," 119.

46. SBA Survey Results.

47. Ibid.

48. Ibid.

49. Ibid.

50. Ehrnfelt interview; Bezan interview; Sabo interview.

51. SBA Survey Results.

52. Ibid. A respondent called for "closer screening of Matrons/Patrons, accepting only those qualified to govern and/or supervise grown children. . . . Example: The Nelson's were college grads youth oriented—truly a gift from heaven."

53. Eve P. Smith, "Bring Back the Orphanages? What Policymakers of Today Can Learn from the Past," *Child Welfare* 74 (January–February 1995): 138; McKenzie, "Orphanage Alumni," 109–10.

54. SBA Survey Results; McKenzie, "Orphanage Alumni," 110–13; conversation with Richard McKenzie, February 15, 1999.

55. SBA Survey Results; McKenzie, "Orphanage Alumni," 112–14; conversation with McKenzie.

56. SBA Survey Results; McKenzie, "Orphanage Alumni," 111–12.

57. Eve P. Smith, "Bring Back the Orphanages?," 138; SBA Survey Results; McKenzie, "Orphanage Alumni," 115.

58. Garrett, "Guidance," 63–64.

For a description of the test, see John G. Darley and Dwight J. Ingle, "An Analysis of the Bernreuter Personality Inventory in Occupational Guidance," in *Research Studies in Individual Diagnosis*, ed. Donald G. Paterson (Minneapolis: University of Minnesota Press, 1934), 32–41.

Chapter Six

1. John S. Haller Jr., *American Medicine in Transition, 1840–1910* (Urbana: University of Illinois Press, 1981), 245–47; Jerome L. Schwartz, "Early History of Prepaid Medical Care Plans," *Bulletin of the History of Medicine* 39 (September–October 1965): 455–63; Stuart D. Brandes, *American Welfare Capitalism, 1880–1940* (Chicago: University of Chicago Press, 1976), 92–102; Alan Derickson, *Workers' Health, Workers' Democracy: The Western Miners' Struggle, 1891–1925* (Ithaca: Cornell University Press, 1988), 88–154.

2. John Duffy, ed., *History of Medicine in Louisiana* (Baton Rouge: Louisiana State University Press, 1962), 2:399–400; Gary R. Mormino and George E. Pozzetta, *The Immigrant World of Ybor City: Italians and Their Latin Neighbors in Tampa, 1885–1985* (Urbana: University of Illinois Press, 1987), 197–98; Durward Long, "An Immigrant Cooperative Medicine Program in the South, 1887–1963," *Journal of Southern History* 31 (November 1965): 423–24.

3. David G. Green, *Working-Class Patients and the Medical Establishment: Self-Help in*

Britain from the Mid-Nineteenth Century to 1948 (New York: St. Martin's Press, 1985), 93; David G. Green and Lawrence G. Cromwell, *Mutual Aid or Welfare State: Australia's Friendly Societies* (Sydney: Allen and Unwin, 1984), xv, 94; Susan Keen, "Associations in Australian History: Their Contribution to Social Capital," *Journal of Interdisciplinary History* 29 (Spring 1999): 639–59.

4. "Discussion, Dr. Henry B. Hemenway, Evanston, Ill.," *Bulletin of the American Academy of Medicine* 10 (December 1909): 635; John V. Woodruff, "Contract Practice," *New York State Journal of Medicine* 15 (October 1916): 509; S. S. Goldwater, "Dispensaries: A Growing Factor in Curative and Preventive Medicine," *Boston Medical and Surgical Journal* 172 (April 29, 1915): 614.

5. Illinois Health Insurance Commission, *Report* (Springfield, 1919), 125–26; Anna Kalet, "Voluntary Health Insurance in New York City," *American Labor Legislation Review* 6 (June 1916): 149–50; Michael M. Davis Jr., *Immigrant Health and the Community* (New York: Harper and Brothers, 1921), 100–101; Edgar Sydenstricker, "Existing Agencies for Health Insurance in the United States," in U.S. Department of Labor, Bureau of Labor Statistics, *Bulletin* 212 (Washington, D.C.: Government Printing Office, 1917), 465–67.

6. George E. Holtzapple, "Lodge Practice," *Pennsylvania Medical Journal* 11 (April 1908): 530–33.

7. Ibid.; Horace M. Alleman, "Lodge Practice," *Pennsylvania Medical Journal* 15 (December 1911): 225.

To estimate the number of adult males in each locality in 1907, I subtracted three years' worth of increase from the 1910 census figure using 1900 as my base. See U.S. Census Office, *Twelfth Census of the United States Taken in the Year 1900: Population* (Washington, D.C.: Government Printing Office, 1902), 2 (pt. 2): 240–44; U.S. Department of Commerce, Bureau of the Census, *Thirteenth Census of the United States Taken in the Year 1910: Population* (Washington, D.C.: Government Printing Office, 1913), 3:586–611.

The medical fees paid by fraternal society members in Pennsylvania were comparable to those in the rest of the country. See James G. Burrow, *Organized Medicine in the Progressive Era: The Move toward Monopoly* (Baltimore: Johns Hopkins University Press, 1977), 123; Kalet, "Voluntary Health Insurance," 150–51; W. F. Zierath, "Contract Practice," *Wisconsin Medical Journal* 6 (August 1907): 151; Illinois Health Insurance Commission, *Report*, 478, 529; California Social Insurance Commission, *Report* (Sacramento, 1917), 109; George S. Mathews, "Contract Practice in Rhode Island," *Bulletin of the American Academy of Medicine* 10 (December 1909): 601; "Contract Practice," *West Virginia Medical Journal* 4 (June 1910): 425; J. W. Bolton, "Lodge Practice," *Journal of the Missouri State Medical Association* 12 (April 1915): 158–59.

8. "The Iniquitous Contract and Lodge Practice," *Northwest Medicine* 4 (April 1906): 133–34.

I used the methodology described in the preceding note. See U.S. Census Office, *Twelfth Census*, 247–48; U.S. Department of Commerce, *Thirteenth Census*, 1007–8. Societies with lodge practice in Seattle were the IOF, Foresters of America, the Fraternal Brotherhood, the Order of Buffalo, the Improved Order of Red Men, and the FOE.

As late as 1914 a survey of local family budgets, which appeared in the University of Pennsylvania Studies, stated that as a general rule "the adult members of the textile-mill workers' families of Kensington belong to lodges, the dues for which entitle the members . . . to the services of the lodge physicians" (Bureau of Applied Economics, Inc., "Standards of Living: A Compilation of Budgetary Studies," *Bulletin* 7 [1920]: 153).

9. David Rosner, *A Once Charitable Enterprise: Hospitals and Health Care in Brooklyn and New York, 1885–1915* (Cambridge: Cambridge University Press, 1982), 125–26, 146–48; American Medical Association, *Data on Social Insurance* (Chicago: American Medical Association, 1919), 45–47.

10. Fraternal Order of Eagles, *Journal of Proceedings* (1910), 379; Loyal Order of Moose, *Minutes* (1914), 89, 101; "The Supreme Chief Greeted in Hamilton," *Forester* 12 (December 1902): 359; Albert C. Stevens, *The Cyclopedia of Fraternities* (New York: E. B. Treat, 1907), 113.

11. Stevens, *Cyclopedia*, 113, 139–40, 222–23; Independent Order of Foresters, *Minutes* (1902), 3.

12. Independent Order of Foresters, *Minutes* (1905), 124–25.

13. Alvin J. Schmidt, *Fraternal Organizations* (Westport, Conn.: Greenwood, 1980), 94; Fraternal Order of Eagles, *Journal of Proceedings* (1908), 110; Arthur Preuss, comp., *A Dictionary of Secret and Other Societies* (St. Louis: B. Herder, 1924), 133; *Eagle Magazine* 17 (May 1929): 1–43, 45.

14. Fraternal Order of Eagles, *Journal of Proceedings* (1910), 379, and (1927), 217; "Medical Economics," *Journal of the American Medical Association* 54 (March 19, 1910): 988.

15. Loyal Order of Moose, *Proceedings* (1913), 161–64, and (1914), 151–53; *Helena Independent*, August 4, 1911.

16. Harry J. Walker, "Negro Benevolent Societies in New Orleans: A Study of Their Structure, Function, and Membership" (M.A. thesis, Fisk University, 1937), 21, 47, 332–35. See also Claude F. Jacobs, "Strategies of Neighborhood Health-Care among New Orleans Blacks: From Voluntary Association to Public Policy" (Ph.D. diss., Tulane University, 1980), and "Benevolent Societies of New Orleans Blacks during the Late Nineteenth and Early Twentieth Centuries," *Louisiana History* 29 (Winter 1988): 21–33.

17. Harry J. Walker, "Negro Benevolent Societies," 22; Jacobs, "Benevolent Societies," 23; Duffy, *History of Medicine*, 101–2.

18. Harry J. Walker, "Negro Benevolent Societies," 35–38; Emily Clark, "'By All the Conduct of Their Lives': A Laywoman's Confraternity in New Orleans, 1730–1744," *William and Mary Quarterly*, 3d ser., 54 (October 1997): 769–94.

19. Harry J. Walker, "Negro Benevolent Societies," 23–27, 43; "Tuberculosis and New Orleans," *New Orleans Medical and Surgical Journal* 83 (March 1931): 651; Evelyn Campbell Beven, *City Subsidies to Private Charitable Agencies in New Orleans: The History and Present Status, 1824–1933* (New Orleans: Tulane University Press, 1934), v, 6–9; Robert E. Moran Sr., "Public Relief in Louisiana from 1928 to 1960," *Louisiana History* 14 (Fall 1973): 369–70.

20. Harry J. Walker, "Negro Benevolent Societies," 47, 59–62, 119.

21. Duffy, *History of Medicine*, 399–400; U.S. Census Office, *Abstract of the Twelfth Census of the United States, 1900* (Washington, D.C.: Government Printing Office, 1904), 140–58.

22. Harry J. Walker, "Negro Benevolent Societies," 186, 193–94; Jacobs, "Benevolent Societies," 26. Contracts between lodges and drugstores existed in other parts of the country. See Rexwald Brown, "Evils of the Lodge Practice System," *California State Journal of Medicine* 6 (April 1908): 126.

23. Jacobs, "Strategies," 101–2.

24. Ladies Friends of Faith Benevolent Association, minutes, August 2, 1914–October 1, 1916, Amistad Research Center, Tulane University, New Orleans, La.

25. Ibid.

26. "An Example That Should Be Followed," *Pennsylvania Medical Journal* 8 (November 1904): 107.

27. Zierath, "Contract Practice," 150; "Contract Practice," *West Virginia Medical Journal*, 426; Burrow, *Organized Medicine*, 126.

28. John McMahon, "The Ethical versus the Commercial Side of Medical Practice—Which Will We Serve?," *California State Journal of Medicine* 8 (July 1910): 243; John B. Donaldson, "Contract Practice," *Pennsylvania Medical Journal* 12 (December 1908): 212–14; "A New Shame," *California State Journal of Medicine* 7 (June 1909): 194; "Discussion, Dr. F. F. Lawrence, of Columbus," *Bulletin of the American Academy of Medicine* 10 (December 1909): 637; Holtzapple, "Lodge Practice," 536.

29. A. B. Hirsh, "Is Lodge Practice a Preventable Evil?," *Pennsylvania Medical Journal* 12 (December 1908): 215; "Discussion, Albert M. Eaton," *Pennsylvania Medical Journal* 11 (April 1908): 538.

30. "Discussion, Dr. F. T. Rogers, Providence," *Bulletin of the American Academy of Medicine* 10 (December 1909): 629; "Lodge Practice and Its After Effects," *Journal of the Medical Society of New Jersey* 9 (February 1913): 474; "Discussion, Dr. H. A. Tomlinson, St. Peter, Minn.," *Bulletin of the American Academy of Medicine* 10 (December 1909): 638; Morris J. Clurman, "The Lodge Practice Evil of the Lower East Side," *Medical Record* 78 (October 22, 1910): 718.

"The idea of coercion [exerted by a lodge] to any physician," Dr. Bolton argued, "is certainly one of the most repugnant that the lodge doctor must submit to. It is only natural for any physician having this feeling to neglect his duty to his patients" (Bolton, "Lodge Practice," 159).

31. Clurman, "Lodge Practice Evil," 718; "Discussion, Eaton," 538; Bolton, "Lodge Practice," 158; Zierath, "Contract Practice," 151.

32. "Contract Practice," *West Virginia Medical Journal*, 425; Straub Sherrer, "The Contract Physician: His Use and Abuse," *Pennsylvania Medical Journal* 8 (November 1904): 106; "No Contract Practice for Meadville," *Pennsylvania Medical Journal* 13 (November 1909): 148; George Rosen, *The Structure of American Medical Practice, 1875–1941* (Philadelphia: University of Pennsylvania Press, 1983), 99; Goldwater, "Dispensaries," 614–15.

"We cannot escape from the fact that these poor people are not able to pay the most modest fee where continuous treatment is necessary" ("The Vexed Question—Lodge Practice," *New York State Journal of Medicine* 13 (November 1913): 562).

33. Charles S. Sheldon, "Contract Practice," *Bulletin of the American Academy of Medicine* 10 (December 1909): 590.

Referring to competition from the lodge doctor, an editorial in the *Illinois Medical Journal* warned that "where rate cuts begin there is no limit to the depth of the cut and finally all practitioners and the community suffer" ("Contract Practice," *Illinois Medical Journal* 22 [November 1907]: 505).

34. Burrow, *Organized Medicine*, 127; Harry J. Walker, "Negro Benevolent Societies," 256.

35. Harry J. Walker, "Negro Benevolent Societies," 263; Maximilian Hurwitz, *The Workmen's Circle: Its History, Ideals, Organization, and Institutions* (New York: Workmen's Circle, 1936), 179–80.

36. John C. McManemin, "A Defence of Contract Practice," *Bulletin of the American Academy of Medicine* 10 (December 1909): 615.

37. Mathews, "Contract Practice," 604; Loyal Order of Moose, *Minutes* (1921), 205.

38. Hirsh, "Is Lodge Practice a Preventable Evil?," 215; Goldwater, "Dispensaries," 614; Holtzapple, "Lodge Practice," 537.

39. E. Richard Brown, *Rockefeller Medicine Men: Medicine and Capitalism in America* (Berkeley: University of California Press, 1979), 64–65, 82; Gerald E. Markowitz and David Karl Rosner, "Doctors in Crisis: A Study of the Use of Medical Education Reform to Establish Modern Professional Elitism in Medicine," *American Quarterly* 25 (March 1973): 95–96; Ronald Hamowy, "The Early Development of Medical Licensing Laws in the United States, 1875–1900," *Journal of Libertarian Studies* 3 (1979): 102–3; Paul Starr, *The Social Transformation of American Medicine* (New York: Basic Books, 1982), 117–18.

40. A. Ravogli, "Physicians in Contract Practice with Mutual Benevolent Societies," *Bulletin of the American Academy of Medicine* 10 (December 1909): 611.

41. "Facts That Every Member Should Know and Remember," *Forester* 23 (August 1902): 239; "200,000 Independent Foresters Will See the Old Year Out," *Independent Forester* 21 (October 15, 1900): 103; Independent Order of Foresters, Supreme Court, *Minutes* (1902), 3–4, and (1908), 3, 51–59.

42. Kalet, "Voluntary Health Insurance," 147.

43. "Medical Economics," 988; "Contract Practice," *West Virginia Medical Journal*, 425; "Ruling of the Grand Worthy President," *Eagle Magazine* 2 (September 1914): 12; Independent Order of Foresters, Supreme Court, *Constitution and Laws* (1912), 152.

44. "Discussion, Lawrence," 637; Clurman, "Lodge Practice Evil," 718; "Discussion, Hemenway," 635; Bolton, "Lodge Practice," 159.

45. Clurman, "Lodge Practice Evil," 717–18; Mathews, "Contract Practice," 604.

46. Rexwald Brown, "Evils of the Lodge Practice System," 126; Zierath, "Contract Practice," 154–55.

47. "The Lodge Doctor," *Western Medical Times* 36 (October 1916): 126, 173–74.

48. "Shall We Have the Community Doctor?," *Eagle Magazine* 5 (December 1916): 28, 4; "Supreme Chief Greeted in Hamilton," 359.

49. "Contract Practice," *Maine Medical Society Journal*, as reprinted in *Journal of the Medical Society of New Jersey* 13 (June 1916): 336; Fraternal Order of Eagles, *Journal of Proceedings* (1910), 380; Harry J. Walker, "Negro Benevolent Societies," 70.

50. Harry J. Walker, "Negro Benevolent Societies," 72, 75, 79.

51. Holtzapple, "Lodge Practice," 534.

52. Harry J. Walker, "Negro Benevolent Societies," 221, 227, 229; Loyal Order of Moose, *Proceedings* (1914), 152.

53. "Lodge Practice in Its Relation to Qualifications for Membership," *New York State Journal of Medicine* 13 (June 1913): 299; Ravogli, "Physicians in Contract Practice," 608–9.

54. Rosen, *Structure*, 106; Ravogli, "Physicians in Contract Practice," 609.

55. "Vexed Question," 562–63. The author of the editorial asked, "When sickness enters the home of the poor, who is there to give them succor, who is to respond to their midnight calls but these lodge doctors?" (562).

56. Rosen, *Structure*, 104; Burrow, *Organized Medicine*, 128–31; Schwartz, "Early History," 460–63.

57. Rosner, *Once Charitable Enterprise*, 107, 147–51; Odin W. Anderson, *The Uneasy Equilibrium: Private and Public Financing of Health Services in the United States, 1875–1965* (New Haven: College and University Press, 1968), 33–36.

58. Michael M. Davis Jr. and Andrew R. Warner, *Dispensaries: Their Management*

and Development (New York: Macmillan, 1918), 353; David Rosner, "Health Care for the 'Truly Needy': Nineteenth-Century Origins of the Concept," *Milbank Memorial Fund Quarterly* 60 (Summer 1982): 377–80; Rosner, *Once Charitable Enterprise*, 127; "Shall We Have the Community Doctor?," 4; Hurwitz, *Workmen's Circle*, 178.

59. Burrow, *Organized Medicine*, 131; "Contract Practice," *Journal of the Medical Society of New Jersey*, 336; *Pennsylvania Medical Journal* 14 (November 1910): 152; Editorial, *Journal of the Michigan State Medical Society* 8 (December 1909): 596; "Contract Practice," *West Virginia Medical Journal*, 426; "Contract Practice," *Illinois Medical Journal*, 504.

60. Zierath, "Contract Practice," 162; W. H. Haughy, "A Proposed Solution for Certain Phases of Contract Practice," *Journal of the Michigan State Medical Society* 10 (January 1911): 29–30.

61. Donaldson, "Contract Practice," 212; "Shall We Have the Community Doctor?," 4.

62. "Vexed Question," 561–63; Albert T. Lytle, "Contract Medical Practice: An Economic Study," *New York State Journal of Medicine* 15 (March 1915): 106.

On the pressures exerted by various local societies against lodge doctors, see Burrow, *Organized Medicine*, 126–32; "Medical Ethics and County By-Laws," *Texas State Journal of Medicine* 8 (February 1913): 257–58; "Contract Practice," *Journal of the Medical Society of New Jersey*, 336; "Contract Practice," *West Virginia Medical Journal*, 426; "Discussion, Dr. J. K. Weaver, Norristown," *Bulletin of the American Academy of Medicine* 10 (December 1909): 631–32; "Contract Practice," *California State Journal of Medicine* 4 (February 1906): 44–45; Rene Bine, "Contract Practice," *California State Journal of Medicine* 10 (February 1912): 52; "Contract Practice," *Medical Council* 19 (October 1914): 398; "An Example That Should Be Followed," 107; "No Contract Practice for Meadville," 148; "Report of the Committee on Lodge Practice," *Pennsylvania Medical Journal* 15 (October 1911): 57; Fraternal Order of Eagles, *Journal of Proceedings* (1912), 204–5.

63. Howard Pursell, letter, "Lodge Practice," *Pennsylvania Medical Journal* 14 (December 1910): 237; Loyal Order of Moose, *Minutes* (1913), 164.

64. Holtzapple, "Lodge Practice," 536; "Contract Practice," *West Virginia Medical Journal*, 426; Zierath, "Contract Practice," 163.

Hirsh pointed to the irony that workers "do not hesitate through their 'beneficial orders' . . . to apply to medical practitioners the very 'sweating' methods they so vehemently condemn in the case of their employers" (Hirsh, "Is Lodge Practice a Preventable Evil?," 216).

65. Fraternal Order of Eagles, *Journal of Proceedings* (1910), 185; "Report of the Supreme Dictator," *Call of the Moose* 4 (September 1912): 4.

66. Fraternal Order of Eagles, *Journal of Proceedings* (1905), 106, and (1911), 152; Loyal Order of Moose, *Minutes* (1913), 164; "Report of the Supreme Dictator," 4.

67. *Helena Independent*, August 3, 4, 1911.

68. Ibid., August 4, 10, 13, 15, 1911; *State of Montana, ex rel. John G. Thompson v. St. Mary's Female Academy*, in the District Court of the First Judicial District of the State of Montana, in and for the County of Lewis and Clark, Petition for Writ of Mandate, August 2, 1911, Lewis and Clark County Courthouse, Helena, Mont.

69. *Helena Independent*, August 17, 1911.

70. Fraternal Order of Eagles, *Journal of Proceedings* (1912), 204–5.

71. Thomas J. E. Walker, *Pluralistic Fraternity: The History of the International Worker's Order* (New York: Garland, 1991), 18–20.

During the depression, massive unemployment severely weakened the membership base of the black lodges in New Orleans, and the numbers of societies fell by nearly half. The decline did not abate in subsequent decades. See Harry J. Walker, "Negro Benevolent Societies," 20–21, 114.

72. Starr, *Social Transformation*, 120–21, 126; Markowitz and Rosner, "Doctors in Crisis," 95–107; Todd L. Savitt, "Abraham Flexner and the Black Medical Schools," in *Beyond Flexner: Medical Education in the Twentieth Century*, ed. Barbara Barzansky and Norman Gevitz (New York: Greenwood, 1992), 73–79.

Chapter Seven

1. Abb Landis, *Life Insurance* (Nashville, Tenn.: Abb Landis, 1914), 16–19; Olaf H. Johnson, *Conversion of the Fraternal Society into an Old Line Company: Advisability, Tendency, Objections* (Madison, Wis.: Democrat Printing, 1928), 5–6; Walter Basye, *History and Operation of Fraternal Insurance* (Rochester, N.Y.: Fraternal Monitor, 1919), 115–16.

2. Basye, *History and Operation* 113–16; "The Law-Making Mania," *Fraternal Monitor* 2 (August 1, 1891): 11.

3. Basye, *History and Operation*, 118–21.

4. Ibid., 51, 57; Keith L. Yates, *The Fogarty Years: A History of the A.O.U.W., America's First Fraternal Life Insurance Society* (Seattle: Evergreen, 1972), 255–58.

5. Edward J. Dunn, *Builders of Fraternalism in America* (Chicago: Fraternal Book Concern, 1924), bk. 1, 55, 58, 187; Miles M. Dawson, "Fraternal Life Insurance," *Fraternal Monitor* 15 (March 1, 1905): 17; Nathan S. Boynton, "Let Us Paddle Our Own Canoe," *Review, Ladies of the Maccabees* 5 (February 1, 1899): 2.

6. "The Dilemma of Fraternal Orders," *Spectator* 56 (August 27, 1896): 92; *Spectator* 55 (August 15, 1895): 78.

7. "The National Fraternal Congress," *Spectator* 56 (November 26, 1896): 251; B. H. Meyer, "Fraternal Insurance in the United States," *Annals of the American Academy of Political and Social Science* 17 (March 1901): 262–63, 272; Walter S. Nichols, "Fraternal Insurance: Its Character, Virtues, and Defects," in *Yale Insurance Lectures; Being the Lectures on Life Insurance Delivered in the Insurance Course at Yale University* (New Haven: Tuttle, Morehouse and Taylor, 1904), 1:171–73.

8. J. Owen Stalson, *Marketing Life Insurance: Its History in America* (1942; reprint, Bryn Mawr, Pa.: McCahan Foundation, 1969), 450; Henry Moir, *Life Assurance Primer: A Textbook* (New York: Spectator, 1930), 4–6.

9. John Charles Herbert Emery, "The Rise and Fall of Fraternal Methods of Social Insurance: A Case Study of the Independent Order of Oddfellows of British Columbia Sickness Insurance, 1874–1951" (Ph.D. diss., University of British Columbia, 1993), 5–6, 19–20, 129–33. One successful assessment plan was the New York Stock Exchange. At the turn of the century each broker belonged to an association that guaranteed a death benefit of $10,000. This association, upon the death of a broker, levied an equal assessment on all brokers to pay the policy. The key to the success of this system was that the death benefit was an incidental feature of membership. This also meant that the association always enjoyed a constant infusion of new lives. See "The Cheapest Insurance," *World's Work* 11 (April 1906): 7397–98.

10. Stalson, *Marketing Life Insurance*, 460–61; Dunn, *Builders of Fraternalism*, bk. 1, 169–71.

11. Dunn, *Builders of Fraternalism*, bk. 1, 65–67, 169; Terence O'Donnell, *History of Life*

Insurance in Its Formative Years (Chicago: American Conservation Company, 1936), 641; Stalson, *Marketing Life Insurance*, 450–52; Basye, *History and Operation*, 193–94.

12. William Francis Barnard, "After Readjustment, What?," *Fraternal Monitor* 14 (December 1, 1903): 15–16; Abb Landis, Notes and Comments, *Fraternal Monitor* 16 (March 1, 1906): 13; Basye, *History and Operation*, 297–98.

13. Nichols, "Fraternal Insurance," 173–75; Stalson, *Marketing Life Insurance*, 452.

14. Dunn, *Builders of Fraternalism*, bk. 1, 54–55.

15. Ibid., 58–59, 231–33; Basye, *History and Operation*, 63.

16. "Cheapest Insurance," 7400.

17. Dunn, *Builders of Fraternalism*, bk. 1, 68–75, 186, 337, and bk. 2, 10, 216, 239, 251–56, 304, 387–88.

18. "National Fraternal Congress," 252.

19. Dunn, *Builders of Fraternalism*, bk. 1, 72–75, and bk. 2, 8–12; George E. West, "Concerning Valuation," *Fraternal Monitor* 16 (November 1, 1905): 6.

20. Katherine Coles Clay, "'Home Sweet Home': A Maccabee Playlet," *Ladies Review* 14 (December 1908): 254.

21. Landis, Notes and Comments, *Fraternal Monitor* 16 (November 1, 1905): 14; Basye, *History and Operation*, 185–86.

"Real mutuality," the *Fraternal Monitor* editorialized, "was not a characteristic of membership of the early societies with their inequitable plan of insufficient rates for a few. Real mutuality is contained in level premium certificates . . . because all members are on a just and equitable basis" ("Level Premium and Reserve Accumulation," *Fraternal Monitor* 29 [March 1, 1919]: 7).

22. Basye, *History and Operation*, 197; Lester W. Zartman, ed., *Life Insurance* (New Haven: Yale University Press, 1914), 375.

23. Basye, *History and Operation*, 33; P. H. J. H. Gosden, *The Friendly Societies in England, 1815–1875* (New York: A. M. Kelley, 1967), 105–14; Abb Landis, *Friendly Societies and Fraternal Orders* (Winchester, Tenn.: Abb Landis, 1900), 14–15, 31.

24. Landis, *Friendly Societies*, 16.

25. Landis, Notes and Comments, *Fraternal Monitor* 17 (February 1, 1907): 13; "British Friendly Societies and Fraternal Orders," *Life Insurance Independent* 16 (October 1904): 235; C. H. Robinson, "English Fraternals," *Fraternal Monitor* 19 (September 1, 1908): 19.

26. Dunn, *Builders of Fraternalism*, bk. 2, 251; Edwin M. Johnson, "The Old Orders and 'Competition,'" *Fraternal Monitor* 11 (April 1, 1901): 18; William Francis Barnard, "Ave, Caesar Imperator, Morituri (?) Salutamus," *Fraternal Monitor* 12 (January 1, 1903): 16–17.

27. C. H. Robinson, "The Associated Fraternities of America," *Fraternal Monitor* 11 (April 1, 1901): 13–15; Basye, *History and Operation*, 124–25; Dunn, *Builders of Fraternalism*, bk. 2, 80–82, 250–52.

28. *Fraternal Monitor* 10 (September 1, 1900): 15; "Bureaucratic Control," *Fraternal Monitor* 7 (November 1, 1906): 5, 7.

29. Abb Landis, "Too Much Legislation and Regulation," *Fraternal Monitor* 15 (March 1, 1905): 23. Landis was indignant: "Members are neither children nor imbeciles, and do not need the fatherly care of insurance commissioners or State legislators" (Landis, "Life Insurance and Fraternal Orders," *Annals of the American Academy of Political and Social Science* 24 [November 1904]: 56).

30. Gosden, *Friendly Societies*, 184–87; William Henry Beveridge, *Voluntary Action:*

. *A Report on Methods of Social Advance* (London: Allen and Unwin, 1949), 57; Landis, *Friendly Societies*, 16, 21–27; Landis, Notes and Comments, *Fraternal Monitor* 15 (May 1, 1905): 13.

31. Robinson, "English Fraternals," 19; Landis, Notes and Comments, *Fraternal Monitor* 15 (May 1, 1905): 12; *Fraternal Monitor* 10 (September 1, 1900): 12.

32. Dunn, *Builders of Fraternalism*, bk. 1, 342–43, and bk. 2, 81–83.

33. Yates, *Fogarty Years*, 82.

34. "An Actual Condition," *Fraternal Monitor* 13 (December 1, 1902): 5–6; Dunn, *Builders of Fraternalism*, bk. 2, 82; Barnard, "Ave, Caesar," 15–16; Charles Richmond Henderson, "Industrial Insurance," *American Journal of Sociology* 22 (January 1907): 42–44; National Convention of Insurance Commissioners of the United States, *Proceedings* (1909), 43.

35. Basye, *History and Operation*, 126–29; George Dyre Eldridge, "The Mobile Agreement," *Fraternal Monitor* 21 (December 1, 1910): 18–21; Z. H. Austin, "Objections to the Proposed Law," *Fraternal Monitor* 21 (December 1, 1910): 19–21.

36. Joseph B. Maclean, *Life Insurance* (New York: McGraw-Hill, 1962), 480–81; Eldridge, "Mobile Agreement," 18–19; Basye, *History and Operation*, 127–29, 135–36, 140–41, 147, 159, 163; Carlos S. Hardy, *Fraternal Insurance Law* (Los Angeles: Carlos S. Hardy, 1916), 29–31.

Another unintended consequence of the Mobile Law and subsequent legislation was to preclude societies from providing unemployment insurance. There is little evidence, however, that they wanted to sell such policies (at least in a formal sense), although many (see Chapters 3 and 12) followed the practice of carrying the unemployed on the rolls.

Similar laws prevented the commercial companies from offering unemployment insurance, though some, such as the Metropolitan, expressed interest in doing so. See Michael B. Rappaport, "The Private Provision of Unemployment Insurance," *Wisconsin Law Review*, no. 1 (1992): 61–129.

37. Austin, "Objections to the Proposed Law," 19–21.

38. Carl W. Kimpton, "Untrammeled Development of the Fraternal System," *Fraternal Monitor* 22 (November 1, 1911): 18–19.

39. National Convention of Insurance Commissioners, *Proceedings* (1912), 193–95.

40. Dunn, *Builders of Fraternalism*, bk. 1, 346–49, and bk. 2, 11; National Convention of Insurance Commissioners, *Proceedings* (1907), 249–50, and (1912), 190–91.

41. Basye, *History and Operation*, 82–87, 129–30.

42. Dunn, *Builders of Fraternalism*, bk. 2, 175, 304–5.

43. Richard de Raismes Kip, *Fraternal Life Insurance in America* (Philadelphia: College Offset Press, 1953), 15, 169.

Chapter Eight

1. Theda Skocpol, *Protecting Soldiers and Mothers: The Political Origins of Social Policy in the United States* (Cambridge: Harvard University Press, Belknap Press, 1992), 177–85; Ronald L. Numbers, *Almost Persuaded: American Physicians and Compulsory Health Insurance, 1912–1920* (Baltimore: Johns Hopkins University Press, 1978), 15.

2. Numbers, *Almost Persuaded*, 25–26; "Health Insurance: Tentative Draft of an Act," *American Labor Legislation Review* 6 (June 1916): 255–59.

3. Numbers, *Almost Persuaded*, 27, 42–43; "Health Insurance," 244–45. According to

the AALL, the "capitation payment, of so much per person per year, common now in lodge practice, has in it elements which bring about an undue amount of work, and in turn forces neglectful, hurried service to the patients" (244).

4. "Industrial Accident Insurance," *California State Journal of Medicine* 14 (December 1916): 469; "Report of Committee on Social Insurance," *American Medical Association Bulletin* 11 (March 15, 1916): 320; "Meeting of the Committee on Medical Economics, New York Academy of Medicine," *New York State Journal of Medicine* 16 (December 1916): 607, 611; Numbers, *Almost Persuaded*, 32, 42, 47.

5. Skocpol, *Protecting Soldiers*, 207–10.

6. Topics of the Month, *Fraternal Monitor* 18 (December 1, 1907): 13; Editorial and Personal, *Ladies Review* 15 (April 1909).

7. "The Government Pension and Insurance Schemes," *Fraternal Monitor* 21 (April 1, 1912): 12–13; National Fraternal Congress and Associated Fraternities of America, *Proceedings* (1913), 494. For other fraternal critiques, see Randolph J. Brodsky, "Social and Fraternal Insurance," *Fraternal Monitor* 21 (January 1, 1911): 21; "Compulsory Insurance in Denmark," *Fraternal Monitor* 22 (December 1, 1911): 16.

8. John B. Andrews to James N. Lynch, April 19, 1917, reel 17, AALL Papers, Kheel Center for Labor-Management Documentation and Archives, Cornell University, Ithaca, N.Y.; David G. Green, *Working-Class Patients and the Medical Establishment: Self-Help in Britain from the Mid-Nineteenth Century to 1948* (New York: St. Martin's Press, 1985), 159–63.

9. *Eagle Magazine* 2 (August 1914): 33.

10. John J. Lentz, "Fraternal Societies under Universal Health Insurance," *American Labor Legislation Review* 7 (March 1917): 80–81, 105. In 1917 the American Insurance Union had 60,394 members. See Edward J. Dunn, *Builders of Fraternalism in America* (Chicago: Fraternal Book Concern, 1924), bk. 2, 437, 462–65.

11. "Health Insurance," 258, 262–63; Andrews to Lynch, reel 17, AALL Papers; Numbers, *Almost Persuaded*, 25; California Social Insurance Commission, *Report* (Sacramento, 1917), 82, 89–95, 310; Illinois Health Insurance Commission, *Report* (Springfield, 1919), 477.

12. "State Insurance and Foreign Fraternals," *Western Review* 21 (August 1915): 25; Andrews to the editor of *Western Review*, December 23, 1915, reel 15, AALL Papers.

13. Andrews to the editor, AALL Papers.

14. Andrews to L. J. Harris, December 24, 1915, reel 15, AALL Papers.

15. Isaac M. Rubinow, *Standards of Health Insurance* (New York: Henry Holt, 1916), 25–26; John R. Commons, "A Reconstruction Health Program," *Survey* 42 (September 6, 1919): 801.

16. Committee on Social and Industrial Justice, Progressive National Service, *Sickness Insurance* (New York, ca. 1914), 5, box 4, Health Insurance, AALL Papers.

17. Arthur J. Viseltear, "Compulsory Health Insurance in California, 1915–18," *Journal of the History of Medicine and Allied Sciences* 29 (April 1969): 152–56; J. Lee Kreader, "Isaac Max Rubinow: Pioneer Specialist in Social Insurance," *Social Service Review* 50 (September 1976): 402, 411.

18. Viseltear, "Compulsory Health Insurance," 158–59.

19. Ibid., 157–58; *San Francisco Chronicle*, November 21, 1916; I. M. Rubinow, "20,000 Miles over the Land: A Survey of the Spreading Health Insurance Movement," *Survey* 37 (March 3, 1917): 634.

20. National Fraternal Congress of America, *Proceedings* (1916), 62; (1917), 119; (1919),

22; Thomas R. Wendell, "Strong Opposition to Compulsory Health Insurance," *Western Review* 24 (December 1918): 11.

21. Numbers, *Almost Persuaded*, 113.

22. Ibid., 56, 67; Legislative Notes, *New York State Journal of Medicine* 16 (March 1916): 158; "Report of Committee on Compulsory Health Insurance," *California State Journal of Medicine* 15 (June 1917): 195; I. M. Rubinow, *The Quest for Security* (New York: Henry Holt, 1934), 213.

23. Alice B. Locke, "Compulsory Insurance Opposed by Women's Benefit Societies," *National Civic Federation Review* 5 (July 10, 1920): 14; Numbers, *Almost Persuaded*, 97.

24. John Sullivan, *Social Insurance* (Philadelphia: National Fraternal Congress of America, 1918), 19; "Menace of Social Insurance," *Fraternal Monitor* 30 (November 1, 1919): 7.

25. Minnie W. Aydelotte, "Social Insurance," *Ladies Review* 23 (April 1918): 40; National Fraternal Congress of America, *Proceedings* (1918), 90.

26. Aydelotte, "Social Insurance," 40, and "The Fallacy of Social Insurance," *Ladies Review* 24 (May 1918): 56.

27. "Menace of Social Insurance," 5; Mary MacEachern Baird, Editorial Comment, *Ladies Review* 25 (March 1919).

28. "Menace of Social Insurance," 5.

29. National Fraternal Congress of America, *Proceedings* (1920), 100; Roy Lubove, *The Struggle for Social Security, 1900–1935* (Cambridge: Harvard University Press, 1968), 34–41, 148–49, 158.

30. Sullivan, *Social Insurance*, 16, 20; Abb Landis, *Life Insurance* (Nashville, Tenn.: Abb Landis, 1914), 252.

31. Sullivan, *Social Insurance*, 16; Woman's Benefit Association of the Maccabees, Supreme Review, *Regular Session* (1919), 50; Locke, "Compulsory Insurance," 16.

32. Editorial Comment, *Ladies Review* 25 (March 1919); "Menace of Social Insurance," 8.

33. Sullivan, *Social Insurance*, 8, 38–39; Woman's Benefit Association of the Maccabees, *Regular Session* (1919), 50, 53.

34. Sullivan, *Social Insurance*, 39; National Fraternal Congress of America, *Proceedings* (1917), 153–55, and (1918), 70.

35. Sullivan, *Social Insurance*, 26–27; "Menace of Social Insurance," 7–8; New York City Conference of Charities and Correction, *Proceedings* (1918), 73; New York State Conference of Charities and Correction, *Proceedings* (1919), 194.

36. Skocpol, *Protecting Soldiers*, 430.

37. Molly Ladd-Taylor, *Mother-Work: Women, Child Welfare, and the State, 1890–1930* (Urbana: University of Illinois Press, 1994), 135, 146–47; Linda Gordon, *Pitied but Not Entitled: Single Mothers and the History of Welfare, 1890–1935* (New York: Free Press, 1994), 62–64; Mark H. Leff, "Consensus for Reform: The Mothers-Pension Movement in the Progressive Era," *Social Service Review* 47 (September 1973): 400–401.

38. Skocpol, *Protecting Soldiers*, 286–93; Lubove, *Struggle for Social Security*, 45–65.

39. S. H. Wolfe, "The Blight of Social Insurance," *Fraternal Monitor* 31 (November 1920): 21.

40. Wolfe, "Blight," 21; National Fraternal Congress of America, *Proceedings* (1918), 66.

41. National Fraternal Congress of America, *Proceedings* (1917), 114–15.

42. "Standard Constitution for Federations," *Weekly Underwriter* 93 (August 28, 1915): 271; "New York Federation," *Weekly Underwriter* 99 (December 7, 1918): 815; "Fraternals

Endorse Federation," *Weekly Underwriter* 95 (September 9, 1916): 251; "Radicalism Condemned: Insurance Federations Strong against Visionaries," *Weekly Underwriter* 101 (September 20, 1919): 437; *Fraternal Monitor* 29 (March 1, 1919): 12−13.

43. Facts and Opinion, *Weekly Underwriter* 97 (December 22, 1917): 798; Viseltear, "Compulsory Health Insurance," 178.

For a sample of IESA's argumentative approach, see William Gale Curtis, "Social Insurance," Insurance Economics Society of America, *Bulletin* 3 (1917).

For a highly critical account of the IESA, see New York State League of Women Voters, "Report and Protest to the Governor, the Legislature, and the People of New York," *American Labor Legislation Review* 10 (March 1920): 81−104.

44. James Weinstein, *The Corporate Ideal in the Liberal State, 1900−1918* (1969; reprint, Westport, Conn.: Greenwood, 1981), 7, 27−61, 120−38.

45. Numbers, *Almost Persuaded*, 62−63; "Menace of Social Insurance," 8.

46. Beatrix Hoffman, "Health Insurance and the Making of the American Welfare State" (Ph.D. diss., Rutgers University, 1996), 57−64; Numbers, *Almost Persuaded*, 17−19.

47. Numbers, *Almost Persuaded*, 18−22.

48. Frederick L. Hoffman to Irving Fisher, December 11, 1916, reel 17, AALL Papers.

49. "If Not Compulsory Insurance—What?," *National Civic Federation Review* 4 (June 5, 1919): 1−2.

50. Ibid., 16−17; "Compulsory Sickness Insurance," *National Civic Federation Review* 5 (April 1, 1920): 6−7.

51. "Menace of Social Insurance," 9; "Casualty and Surety Convention," *Weekly Underwriter* 99 (December 7, 1918): 846. On the devotion of Gompers to Freemasonry, see Lynn Dumenil, *Freemasonry and American Culture, 1880−1930* (Princeton: Princeton University Press, 1984), 21.

52. Numbers, *Almost Persuaded*, 79−82, 152; Rubinow, "20,000 Miles," 631, 634; Frederick L. Hoffman, *Failure of German Compulsory Health Insurance: A War Revelation* (Newark, N.J.: Prudential Life Insurance, 1918), 10−11.

53. *San Francisco Chronicle*, January 17, 1917.

54. Viseltear, "Compulsory Health Insurance," 178; New York State League of Women Voters, "Report and Protest," 95−96; Facts and Opinions, *Weekly Underwriter* 97 (December 22, 1917): 798; National Fraternal Congress of America, *Proceedings* (1919), 22; *San Francisco Examiner*, October 3, 1918.

55. Andrews to Lynch, April 19, 1917, reel 17, AALL Papers.

56. Numbers, *Almost Persuaded*, 81.

Buoyed by the victory in California, the AOUW helped to derail state-mandated insurance in Arkansas. John R. Frazer, grand master of the state grand lodge and a member of the Arkansas Insurance Federation, called the proposal "paternalism carried to an extreme." See L. H. Moore to John B. Andrews, January 28, 1919, reel 19, AALL Papers.

57. Numbers, *Almost Persuaded*, 85−86, 91.

58. "Insurance Federation of New York," *Weekly Underwriter* 96 (November 3, 1917): 585−86; "New York Federation," 815; *New York Times*, March 20, 1919; New York State League of Women Voters, "Report and Protest," 95−96; National Fraternal Congress of America, *Proceedings* (1919), 22; C. D. Babcock, "Mystery and the Menace of Compulsory Health Insurance in the United States," in *Selected Articles on Social Insurance*, ed. Julia E. Johnsen (New York: W. W. Wilson, 1922), 230.

59. New York State League of Women Voters, "Report and Protest," 86−87, 94−97; Rubinow, "20,000 Miles," 635.

60. Numbers, *Almost Persuaded*, 91; "Notes on the Hearing of the Davenport Health Insurance Bill," 2, file: Health Insurance, box 4, AALL Papers.

61. Numbers, *Almost Persuaded*, 90–91; Frederick MacKenzie, "The Legislative Campaign in New York for the 'Welfare Bills,'" *American Labor Legislation Review* 10 (March 1920): 136.

62. Numbers, *Almost Persuaded*, 95–96; Locke, "Compulsory Insurance," 14; National Fraternal Congress of America, *Proceedings* (1920), 99.

63. Rubinow, *Quest for Security*, 214.

Chapter Nine

1. For more information on the hospitalization plans of other societies and specific lodges, see Jerome L. Schwartz, "Early History of Prepaid Medical Care Plans," *Bulletin of the History of Medicine* 39 (September–October 1965): 451–52; Arthur J. Sabin, *Red Scare in Court: New York versus the International Workers Order* (Philadelphia: University of Pennsylvania Press, 1993), 240; Julius Rosenwald Fund, *New Plans of Medical Service* (Chicago: Julius Rosenwald Fund, 1936), 19–20, 50–51, 61; "Free Medical Service of Detroit Members of Columbian Circle," *National Economist* 32 (August 1924): 5; "Ward in Mount Sinai Hospital," in Independent Order, Free Sons of Israel, Grand Lodge of the United States, *Convention* (1907), 16; National Fraternal Congress of America, *Proceedings* (1929), 196; Anna Kalet, "Voluntary Health Insurance in New York City," *American Labor Legislation Review* 6 (June 1916): 149–50.

2. Charles K. Knight, "Fraternal Life Insurance," *Annals of the American Academy of Political and Social Science* 80 (March 1927): 100–101.

3. "Report of the Committee on General Welfare," in National Fraternal Congress of America, *Proceedings* (1929), 196–97; Judah J. Shapiro, *The Friendly Society: A History of the Workmen's Circle* (New York: Media Judaica, 1970), 131–32; Independent Order of Foresters, Rainbow Sanitarium for Tuberculosis, *Annual Report* (1925), 5–34; Edward J. Dunn, *Builders of Fraternalism in America* (Chicago: Fraternal Book Concern, 1924), bk. 2, 395, 397, 401, 427; David L. Ellison, *Healing Tuberculosis in the Woods: Medicine and Science at the End of the Nineteenth Century* (Westport, Conn.: Greenwood, 1994), 183–84; Barbara Bates, *Bargaining for Life: A Social History of Tuberculosis, 1876–1938* (Philadelphia: University of Pennsylvania Press, 1992), 183–85.

4. Este Erwood Buffum, *Modern Woodmen of America: A History* (Rock Island, Ill.: Modern Woodmen of America, 1927), 1:34–36; "Report on Fraternal National Sanitarium," in Knights and Ladies of Security, National Council, *Proceedings* (1906), 159–65; Dean L. Smith, *A Nickel a Month* (St. Louis: MidAmerica Publishing, 1979), 7–9.

5. Dean L. Smith, *Nickel a Month*, 9; Buffum, *Modern Woodmen*, 1:35; National Fraternal Congress of America, *Proceedings* (1929), 196.

6. Buffum, *Modern Woodmen*, 1:45, 125, 295; Jeanne E. Abrams, *Blazing the Tuberculosis Trail: The Religio-Ethnic Role of Four Sanatoria in Early Denver* (Denver: Colorado Historical Society, 1990), 1–5.

7. Buffum, *Modern Woodmen*, 1:30, 37–39.

8. Ibid., 30, 51, 47–58.

9. Ibid., 30, 32–33, 55–56, 60.

10. Ibid., 28, 55–56.

11. Ibid., 29, 31–33.

12. Ibid., 61–62.

13. Ellison, *Healing Tuberculosis*, 184; Bates, *Bargaining*, 116, 318–27; Mark Caldwell, *The Last Crusade: The War on Consumption, 1862–1954* (New York: Atheneum, 1988), 116–17; Buffum, *Modern Woodmen*, 1:54–56. Also, see J. A. Rutledge and John B. Crouch, "The Ultimate Results in 1654 Cases of Tuberculosis Treated at the Modern Woodmen of America Sanatorium," *American Review of Tuberculosis* 2 (February 1919): 762.

14. Maximilian Hurwitz, *The Workmen's Circle: Its History, Ideals, Organization, and Institutions* (New York: Workmen's Circle, 1936), 179–80; Shapiro, *Friendly Society*, 132–33.

15. Sol Kliger, "15 Years of Medicine in the Workmen's Circle," *Call of Youth* 2 (June 1934): 18; Hurwitz, *Workmen's Circle*, 184–86; Shapiro, *Friendly Society*, 132–33.

16. "The Medical Department of the Workmen's Circle," *Call of Youth* 1 (May 1933); Workmen's Circle, minutes, October 1927, Workmen's Circle Papers, YIVO Institute, New York, N.Y.; Phil Dauber, "The Workmen's Circle Serves," *Call of Youth* 8 (May–June 1940): 28; Shapiro, *Friendly Society*, 133; I. S. Falk, C. Rufus Rorem, and Martha D. Ring, *The Costs of Medical Care: A Summary of Investigations on the Economic Aspects of the Prevention and Care of Illness* (Chicago: University of Chicago Press, 1933), 463.

17. Independent Order of Foresters, *Minutes* (1929), 36–38, and (1933), 15, 41–43; National Fraternal Congress of America, *Proceedings* (1940), 150–51.

18. C. D. Parker, "Physician Appraises Fraternal Benefits," *Fraternal Age* 12 (June 1936): 18.

19. "Is Your Hive Actively Fraternal," *Ladies Review* 11 (December 1905): 281; Ida M. Bandy, "A Hospital Room in Arkansas," *Ladies Review* 14 (March 1908): 61; "The Lillian M. Hollister Hospital Service," *Ladies Review* 16 (October 1912): 179; "Our Illinois Hospital Service Committee," *Ladies Review* 19 (October 1913): 165; "Our Hospital Service Interests," *Ladies Review* 10 (July 1914): 116; Ladies of the Maccabees of the World, Supreme Hive, *Regular Review* (1915), 62–67; Woman's Benefit Association of the Maccabees, *Regular Session* (1919), 33–35; "Hospital and Home Department," *Ladies Review* 21 (March 1915): 52.

20. "The Object of Our Hospital Service," *Ladies Review* 24 (November–December 1918): 124; Elizabeth M. Hooper, M.D., "Benefits of the Hospital Service," *Ladies Review* 24 (September 1918): 102.

21. "Women Who Are Eminent Physicians," *Ladies Review* 11 (July 1905): 152–53; "Our Watchful Guardians," *Ladies Review* 12 (May 1906): 105; "The Medical Department," *Ladies Review* 15 (November 1909): 242.

22. "Hospital Service Directory," *Ladies Review* 25 (January 1919): 11; Woman's Benefit Association of the Maccabees, Supreme Review, *Regular Session* (1923), 55–57.

23. Ella J. Fifield, M.D., "The Visiting Nurse," *Ladies Review* 30 (May 1924): 56; "Object of Our Hospital Service," 124.

24. Editorial Comment, *Ladies Review* 28 (January–February 1922).

25. Woman's Benefit Association of the Maccabees, *Regular Session* (1923), 24, 56; "Report of Supreme Health Supervisor," *Ladies Review* 37 (September 1931): 136.

26. "Watching the Health of Our Juniors," *Ladies Review* 31 (July–August 1925): 79.

27. "Rules Governing W.B.A. Visiting Nurse Service," *Ladies Review* 31 (April 1925): 43.

28. Woman's Benefit Association, Supreme Review, *Regular Session* (1935), 118; "Report of the Supreme Record Keeper," *Ladies Review* 29 (August 1923): 101; "Notes from Our Health Centers," *Ladies Review* 29 (October 1923): 129.

29. Woman's Benefit Association, Supreme Review, *Regular Session* (1934), 83; "Forty

Second Annual Report of the Supreme President," *W.B.A. Review* 41 (April 1935); "Note-worthy Health Center Record," *W.B.A. Review* 41 (April 1935): 8.

30. "Our Hospital Service," *Ladies Review* 24 (August 1918): 88; Annie E. Reynolds, M.D., "Health Service Reviewed in Report," *W.B.A. Review* 41 (October 1935): 8; Woman's Benefit Association, Supreme Review, *Reports of Officers* (1950), 44, and (1958), 39–40.

31. Joan Burton Trauner, "From Benevolence to Negotiation: Prepaid Health Care in San Francisco, 1850–1950" (Ph.D. diss., University of California, San Francisco, 1977), 12–26; Gary R. Mormino and George E. Pozzetta, *The Immigrant World of Ybor City: Italians and Their Latin Neighbors in Tampa, 1885–1985* (Urbana: University of Illinois Press, 1987), 197–99; Harold S. Stevens, "Cuba's Health Trusts," *Medical Economics* 8 (December 1930): 9–12, 123–33; Commission on Cuban Affairs, *Problems of the New Cuba* (New York: Foreign Policy Association, 1935), 38–39, 119–22; Aline Helg, *Our Rightful Share: The Afro-Cuban Struggle for Equality, 1886–1912* (Chapel Hill: University of North Carolina Press, 1995), 132–33.

32. Mormino and Pozzetta, *Immigrant World*, 198–99; Durward Long, "An Immigrant Co-operative Medicine Program in the South, 1887–1963," *Journal of Southern History* 31 (November 1965): 428–29.

33. Edgar Sydenstricker, "Existing Agencies for Health Insurance in the United States," in U.S. Department of Labor, Bureau of Labor Statistics, *Bulletin* 212 (Washington, D.C.: Government Printing Office, 1917), 452; Angus Laird, "Cooperative Health Plans in Tampa," *Medical Care* 2 (July 1942): 235, 238.

One of the effects of the membership rule of Centro Asturiano was to keep out Afro-Cubans. In response Afro-Cubans also organized societies in Tampa to provide sick benefits, although none of them established hospitals. See Susan D. Greenbaum, "Economic Cooperation among Urban Industrial Workers: Rationality and Community in an Afro-Cuban Mutual Aid Society, 1904–1927," *Social Science History* 17 (Summer 1993): 179–80.

34. Dean L. Smith, *Nickel a Month*, 7–9.

35. Ibid., 13–14.

36. Ibid., 20, 22–25; Security Benefit Association, National Council, *Proceedings* (1920), 166, and (1924) 36–37; "Sidelights on the H & H," *Knights and Ladies of Security* 25 (February 1919): 10.

37. "Our Dreams Have All Come True," *Security News* 31 (January 1925): 2; Security Benefit Association, National Council, *Proceedings* (1928), 28–30; and Dean L. Smith, *Nickel a Month*, 131–33.

38. "Attractive Plans of Protection," *Security News* 31 (August 1925): 32; "Juvenile Whole Life Certificate," *Security News* 33 (September 1927): 31; Security Benefit Association, National Council, *Proceedings* (1928), 49.

39. "Our Dreams Have All Come True," 2; Helen Hershfield Avnet, *Voluntary Medical Insurance in the United States: Major Trends and Current Problems* (New York: Medical Administration Service, 1944), 77, 84; "Free Urinalysis to All Members of Order," *Security News* 31 (April 1925); John C. Goodman and Gerald L. Musgrave, *Patient Power: Solving America's Health Care Crisis* (Washington, D.C.: Cato Institute, 1992), 233.

40. "Summary of Work Done in Our Hospital during the Year 1928" and "Clinical Laboratory Report," Security Benefit Life Insurance Company, Record Department, General Correspondence, reel B-8, SBG; "National President's Report," *Security News* 34 (August 1928): 5.

To estimate the number of women, I sampled 1,200 individuals who used the hospital between 1925 and 1930 from patient lists of Council 1 (Topeka), Council 4 (North Topeka), Council 32 (Kansas City), and Council 282 (Kansas City). See Security Benefit Life Insurance Company, Record Department, General Correspondence, reel B-8, SBG.

41. Kansas Superintendent of Insurance, *Report* (1925), 159, and (1928), 102–3; Security Benefit Association, National Council, *Proceedings* (1928), 30, 34; "National President's Report," 5.

42. Stella Dixon to J. M. Kirkpatrick, *Security News* 32 (March 1926): 22; Gus Lading to Kirkpatrick and Mrs. E. R. Gunnerson to Kirkpatrick, *Security News* 33 (March 1927): 22.

43. "National President's Report," 5.

44. "Enroll in the Hall of Fame," *Security News* 35 (June 1929): 1; "Assignment of Rooms in Addition to Hospital," June 21, 1929, Security Benefit Life Insurance Company, Record Department, General Correspondence, reel B-8, SBG.

45. "New $800,000 Hospital to Be Occupied," *Security News* 36 (May 1930): 3; Dean L. Smith, *Nickel a Month*, 138–40.

46. Kirkpatrick to the officers and members of the Security Benefit Association, March 19, 1930, Minutes of the Board of Trustees, SBAP.

47. Kirkpatrick to the officers and members of the Security Benefit Association, and minutes of the meeting to the Board of Trustees of the Security Benefit Home and Hospital Association, July 25, 1933, SBAP.

48. "The S.B.A. Hospital Leads," *Security News* 27 (May 1931): 1, 4; Falk, Rorem, and Ring, *Costs of Medical Care*, 110.

49. Dean L. Smith, *Eleven Men and Eleven Dollars* (Topeka: Security Benefit Life Insurance, 1976), 82, 85–86; Kansas Commissioner of Insurance, *Report* (1929), 119–20; Michigan Commissioner of Insurance, *Report* (1936), 140–41.

50. Kansas Superintendent of Insurance, *Report* (1925), 159, 161; General Superintendent, Security Benefit Clinic and Hospital, Annual Report (1950), 61–62, Security Benefit Life Insurance Company, General Correspondence, reel B-15, SBG.

51. Security Benefit Association, National Council, *Proceedings* (1928), 33; General Superintendent, Security Benefit Home and Hospital Association, Annual Report (1945), 15, SBG. Also, in Security Benefit Life Insurance Company, Record Department, General Correspondence, SBG, see [Summary of work in the SBA Hospital, 1928–31], 1932, reel B-9; "Copy made up for the 1936 Report of J. M. K. for National Convention," reel B-11; [Summary of work in the SBA Hospital, 1936–39], reel B-13; "Summary of Work done in S.B.A. Hospital," [1940–44], reel B-14; General Superintendent, Security Benefit Clinic and Hospital, Annual Report (1948) and (1950), reel B-15.

52. "Members Admitted to the Security Benefit Association Hospital, 1925–1936," Security Benefit Life Insurance Company, Record Department, Correspondence, 1937–1939, reel B-12; "Members in the Security Benefit Association Hospital, 1936, 1937, 1938, and 1939," Security Benefit Life Insurance Company, Record Department, General Correspondence, reel B-13; General Superintendent, Security Benefit Clinic and Hospital, Annual Report (1945), 10; (1948), v, 48; (1950), iii, all in SBG.

53. Security Benefit Association, National Council, *Proceedings* (1928), 33; [Summary of work in the SBA Hospital, 1928–31], Security Benefit Life Insurance Company, Record Department, General Correspondence, 1932, reel B-9, SBG.

54. Security Benefit Association, National Council, *Proceedings* (1928), 257.

55. S. R. Boykin to Kirkpatrick, December 27, 1934, Security Benefit Life Insurance Company, Record Department, General Correspondence, 1932, reel B-9, SBG.

56. Kirkpatrick to Boykin, June 30, 1934, ibid.; Boykin to Kirkpatrick, January 6, 1943, Security Benefit Life Insurance Company, General Correspondence, reel B-15, SBG.

57. William D. Cutter to Kirkpatrick, March 7, 1938, and Kirkpatrick to Cutter, March 12, 1938, Security Benefit Life Insurance Company, General Correspondence, reel B-15, SBG.

58. H. G. Weiskotten to J. F. Sheen, June 5, 1943; Weiskotten to Kirkpatrick, June 10, 1942; F. H. Arestad to D. F. Joslin, October 19, 1946; Kirkpatrick to Arestad, October 30, 1946, all in ibid.

The SBA relied on direct advertising and urged patients to turn in lists of membership prospects. In 1947, for example, 14 percent of the patients who were discharged recommended 6,374 prospects. See General Superintendent, Security Benefit Clinic and Hospital, Annual Report (1948), iv, SBG.

59. Paul Starr, *The Social Transformation of American Medicine* (New York: Basic Books, 1982), 295–98, 306–7.

60. Ibid. 311–15; Hugh Holleman Macaulay Jr., *Fringe Benefits and Their Federal Tax Treatment* (New York: Columbia University Press, 1959), 58–59, 151–57.

61. Nathan Sinai, Odin W. Anderson, and Melvin L. Dollar, *Health Insurance in the United States* (New York: Commonwealth Fund, 1946), 43–44; Starr, *Social Transformation*, 308.

62. Starr, *Social Transformation*, 308–10.

63. Dean L. Smith, *Nickel a Month*, 147, 169; "Members in the Security Benefit Association Hospital, 1936, 1937, 1938, and 1939," Security Benefit Life Insurance Company, Record Department, General Correspondence, reel B-13, SBG; General Superintendent, Security Benefit Clinic and Hospital, Annual Report (1947), x; (1948), v, 48; (1950), iii, SBG; Commission on Hospital Care, *Hospital Care in the United States* (New York: Commonwealth Fund, 1947), 545; U.S. Department of Commerce, *Historical Statistics of the United States: Colonial Times to 1970*, pt. 1 (Washington, D.C.: Government Printing Office, 1975), 81.

64. Starr, *Social Transformation*, 384–85; Minutes of the Board of Trustees, Security Benefit Home and Hospital Association, June 23, 1944, SBG.

65. General Superintendent, Security Benefit Home and Hospital Association, Annual Report (1945), 10, and (1946), x, SBG; Dean L. Smith, *Nickel a Month*, 168–69; "Members Admitted to the Security Benefit Association Hospital, 1925–1936," Security Benefit Life Insurance Company, Record Department, Correspondence, 1937–39, reel B-12, and General Superintendent, Security Benefit Clinic and Hospital, Annual Report (1950), iii, SBG.

66. Dean L. Smith, *Nickel a Month*, 166–67, 173–74.

67. General Superintendent, Security Benefit Clinic and Hospital, Annual Report (1950), iv, SBG; Dean L. Smith, *Nickel a Month*, 174–77, and *Eleven Men*, 101–2; Security Benefit Life Insurance Company, *Security Benefit Life Insurance Company, 1892–1956* (Topeka: Security Benefit Life Insurance, 1956), 46–47.

68. John Abendroth, M.D., interview, February 6, 1997; Trauner, "From Benevolence to Negotiation," 133, 138.

Chapter Ten

1. C. J. Carson, "Formal Opening of Taborian Hospital," *Taborian Star* 18 (March 1942); International Order of Twelve Knights and Daughters of Tabor, Mississippi Juris-

diction, *Souvenir Edition: Celebrating the Opening of the Hospital of the Knights and Daughters of Tabor* [ca. 1942], 13, Milburn Crowe Collection, City Hall, Mound Bayou, Miss.; Jessie L. Dobbins, interview, September 29, 1995.

For black hospitals in general, see Vanessa Northington Gamble, *Making a Place for Ourselves: The Black Hospital Movement, 1920–1945* (New York: Oxford University Press, 1995); Mitchell F. Rice and Woodrow Jones Jr., *Public Policy and the Black Hospital: From Slavery to Segregation to Integration* (Westport, Conn.: Greenwood, 1994).

2. Earline Rae Ferguson, "Sisterhood and Community: The Sisters of Charity and African American Women's Health Care in Indianapolis, 1876–1920," in *Midwestern Women: Work, Community, and Leadership at the Crossroads*, ed. Wendy Hamand Venet and Lucy Eldersveld Murphy (Bloomington: Indiana University Press, 1997), 166; Julius Rosenwald Fund, *Negro Hospitals: A Compilation of Available Statistics* (Chicago: Julius Rosenwald Fund, 1931), 12, 14, 48–49, app. 1.

3. Rice and Jones, *Public Policy*, 50–51, 64; Julius Rosenwald Fund, *Negro Hospitals*, 14, 46; Edwina Walls, "Some Extinct Black Hospitals of Little Rock and Pulaski County," *Pulaski County Historical Review* 34 (Spring 1986): 4–8; A. E. Bush and P. L. Dorman, *History of the Mosaic Templars of America: Its Founders and Officials* (Little Rock: Central Printing, 1924), 192–94, 260; United Friends of America, *Hospital and Nursing Home: Open House and Dedication* [Little Rock, 1965], 1, courtesy of the Reverend Thomas Banks, Little Rock; Sutton E. Griggs, *Triumph of the Simple Virtues, or, the Life Story of John L. Webb* (Hot Springs, Ark.: Messenger Publishing, 1926), 11–13, 23–24; R. L. Polk and Company, *Polk's Hot Springs City Directory* (Kansas City, 1926), 61.

4. The most accessible source on the Lily White Hospital (which opened in 1950) is the *Florida Sentinel*, the black newspaper for Tampa. The publisher, C. Blythe Andrews, was the grand president of the Lily White Security Benefit Association.

T. J. Huddleston Jr., with Mrs. Henry [Willie Jean] Espy, interview with Barbara Allen, March 5, 1980, Special Collections, B. S. Ricks Memorial Library, Yazoo City, Miss.; "Delta Doctor Performs 34,000 Operations," *Ebony*, March 1950, 27–29; Maurice Elizabeth Jackson, "Mound Bayou: A Study in Social Development" (M.A. thesis, University of Alabama, 1937), 75; "The Afro-American Sons and Daughters Hospital," *Afro-American Courier*, November 1, 1927, 1; "Afros Still Growing at a Marvelous Rate," *Afro-American Courier*, May 1, 1929, 5.

5. Janice Coleman, "The Open Door of That Little Hospital at Mound Bayou" (unpublished manuscript, University of Mississippi, Oxford, 1995), 2 (copy in Beito's possession); International Order of Twelve Knights and Daughters of Tabor, Mississippi Jurisdiction, *The Mission of Tabor* [ca. 1964], 6, Crowe Collection; International Order, *Souvenir Edition*, 4.

6. Albert B. Britton Jr., M.D., interview, August 20, 1997. Of the eleven top officials in the Mississippi Jurisdiction in 1942, three were women. See International Order, *Souvenir Edition*, 7–8.

L. C. Dorsey, a former executive director of the Delta Health Center, speculates that the higher percentage of women was due in part to gender-based employment differences. She notes that men were often absent from the plantation on various jobs or seeking work and thus had fewer opportunities to participate in fraternal societies. In addition, they were more likely to run afoul of whites who feared the consequences of allowing black men to meet in large groups. See L. C. Dorsey, interview, January 10, 1996.

7. "Outstanding Leader Passes," *The Voice* (Mound Bayou) 3 (August 31–September 15,

1970): 1; International Order, *Souvenir Edition*, 13; Perry A. Smith III, interview, July 5, 1996.

8. International Order, *Souvenir Edition*, 7; International Order of Twelve Knights and Daughters of Tabor, Mississippi Jurisdiction, *Proceedings* (1928), 43, and (1929), 14, folder 14, box 64, Kelly Miller Smith Papers, Jean and Alexander Heard Library, Vanderbilt University, Nashville, Tenn.; "In the Fullness of Time" [1950], folder 4, box 65, Smith Papers; "Chief Grand Mentor's Message to Extra Grand Session, Knights and Daughters of Tabor," May 31, 1938, folder 17, box 64, Smith Papers; Dickson Hartwell and Carol Weld, "Mississippi's Miracle Town," *Coronet*, September 1951, 126; Jackson, "Mound Bayou," 37.

9. Coleman, "Open Door," 5–6, 17; Mississippi State Board of Health, Study of Midwife Activities in Mississippi, July 1, 1921–July 30, 1929, folder 8, box 222, Julius Rosenwald Papers, Fisk University, Nashville, Tenn.

A major service offered by the county and state public health departments was to train and license midwives. For more information, see Laura D. S. Harrell, "Medical Services in Mississippi, 1890–1970," in *History of Mississippi*, ed. Richard Aubrey McLemore (Hattiesburg: University and College Press of Mississippi, 1973), 2:554–59; David L. Cohn, *Where I Was Born and Raised* (Boston: Houghton Mifflin, 1948), 348–50; Aaron Shirley, M.D., interview, July 17, 1997.

10. Eugene P. Booze to Michael M. Davis, April 5, 1929, and "Memorandum Regarding Request for Assistance in Mound Bayou, Miss.," September 14, 1929, folder 5, box 240, and J. H. Snider to ——, April 30, 1940, folder 7, box 233, all in Rosenwald Papers; Coleman, "Open Door," 6; Matthew Walker, "Mound Bayou—Meharry's Neighbor," *Journal of the National Medical Association* 65 (July 1973): 309.

For more on medical care for blacks in the South during this period, see Edward H. Beardsley, *A History of Neglect: Health Care for Blacks and Mill Workers in the Twentieth Century South* (Knoxville: University of Tennessee Press, 1987), 35–39. In 1970, 69 percent of black families in Bolivar County lived below the poverty line. See U.S. Department of Commerce, Social and Economic Statistics Administration, Bureau of the Census, *Social and Health Indicators System*, pt. 2, *Rural, Mound Bayou, Mississippi* (Washington, D.C.: Government Printing Office, 1973), 33.

11. Vera Pigee, *The Struggle of Struggles*, pt. 2 (Detroit: Harlo, 1979), 75. For more on hospital segregation, see Lynn Pohl, "Treating Racism: Hospital Desegregation and Medical Interaction in a Mississippi Community" (paper presented at the annual conference of the Association for Research on Nonprofit Organizations and Voluntary Action, Indianapolis, Ind., December 1997).

12. Janet Sharp Hermann, *The Pursuit of a Dream* (New York: Oxford University Press, 1981), 20, 221–23, 233, 240–43; Coleman, "Open Door," 9–11.

13. Coleman, "Open Door," 11; International Order, *Souvenir Edition*, 7; "Chief Grand Mentor's Message."

14. *Taborian Star* 18 (March 1942). Four local white doctors also delivered favorable remarks at the dedication ceremony.

In 1938 the Grand Session of the Knights and Daughters of Tabor, probably with Smith's support, named Huddleston as the "South's greatest Negro Fraternal Head." See *Afro-American Courier*, November 1938.

15. Matthew Walker, "Mound Bayou," 310; Eugene P. Booze to Michael M. Davis, April 5, 1929, folder 5, box 240, Rosenwald Papers.

16. Robert J. Smith, "Managed Health Care: The Taborian Hospital Experience, 1942–1983" (an address to Alpha Omicron Boule, Seattle, Washington, October 22, 1994).

17. "Baccalaureate and Commencement," *Medical Evangelist* 21 (June 20, 1935): 1–3, Department of Archives and Special Collections, Loma Linda University, Loma Linda, Calif.; "The President Elect," *Journal of the National Medical Association* 47 (November 1955): 406, 428; Edward M. Boyd, interview, October 27, 1995. The development of Howard's educational background and early political views can be seen in his letters to Joseph A. Tucker, the president of Oakwood between 1924 and 1931, in Archives, Eva B. Dyke Library, Oakwood College, Huntsville, Ala.

18. International Order, *Souvenir Edition*, 9; International Order of Twelve Knights and Daughters of Tabor, *The Taborian Hospital, Mound Bayou, Mississippi* [ca. 1957], Bolivar County Public Library, Cleveland, Miss.; "Tabor Leads Them All," *Century Voice* 3 (August 1944).

The hospital did not provide ambulances, although a few patients secured them from commercial burial insurance companies and funeral homes. See Asa G. Yancey, M.D., interview, December 12, 1995.

19. P. M. Smith, "Monthly Message and Rulings," *Taborian Star* 18 (April 1942); "The Fifty-sixth Annual Grand Session Knights and Daughters of Tabor Passes into History," *Taborian Star* 20 (November–December 1945); *Taborian Star* 18 (June 1942) and (July 1942); *Taborian Star* 20 (January–February 1945) and (March–April 1945).

The population estimate for 1945 represented an average of the 1940 and 1950 census figures for the nonwhite population of the fifteen Mississippi counties that are either entirely or partly in the Delta. See U.S. Department of Commerce, Bureau of the Census, *Sixteenth Census (1940)*, vol. 2, *Characteristics of the Population*, pt. 4 (Washington, D.C.: Government Printing Office, 1943), 232–36, and *Seventeenth Census* (1950), vol. 2, *Characteristics of the Population*, pt. 24, *Mississippi* (Washington, D.C.: Government Printing Office, 1951), table 44, 90–94.

In 1945 the Knights and Daughters of Tabor had 47,450 members in Mississippi. At the same time, 49.6 percent of the men, women, and children who were patients were from Bolivar County. Based on this information, it was assumed that 49.6 percent of the members (about 23,578) lived in the county. If true, this would mean that 51 percent of all 46,228 blacks in Bolivar County were members and thus entitled to care. These calculations, of course, rest on the dubious assumption that the patient rolls reflected the geographical distribution of the membership. While it is probable that a disproportionate percentage of members would *tend* to cluster in the county over time, exact estimates are impossible. The true percentage may have been lower or, for that matter, higher.

20. Matthew Walker, "Mound Bayou," 311; Robert J. Smith, "Managed Health Care," 8; Edward Verner, M.D., interview, December 30, 1995.

21. Virtually all sources describe ordinary members as coming from the ranks of the rural poor, who even by the standards of the time qualified for indigent care. The top leadership, on the other hand, often worked in middle-class occupations, such as teaching and the ministry, and sometimes owned small businesses and farms. See John W. Hatch, interview, December 5, 1995; H. Jack Geiger, M.D., interview, August 10, 1995; Yancey interview; Louella Thurmond, interview, October 2, 1995; Verner interview, December 30, 1995; "Some Hospital Rules, Regulations, and Rates," *Taborian Star* 19 (March–April 1944).

In 1958 a urinalysis, complete blood count, blood sugar, and EKG were routine upon admission to the Taborian Hospital. See Mavis Phillips to Foster L. Fowler, memorandum: "The Taborian Hospital Incorporated, Mound Bayou, Mississippi," July 10, 1958, folder: Taborian Hospital, Facilities Licensure and Certification Division, Mississippi Department of Health, Jackson.

22. P. M. Smith, "Monthly Message and Rulings," *Taborian Star* 18 (February 1942); Yancey interview; Earlee Thompson, interview, October 11, 1995; Thurmond interview.

23. Hartwell and Weld, "Mississippi's Miracle Town," 125–28; Hodding Carter, "He's Doing Something about the Race Problem," *Saturday Evening Post*, February 23, 1946, 31. The rules provided that a new member be no older than age fifty and have a physician's certificate showing that he or she was "sound and healthy." They also prohibited lodges from admitting people "who have served a time in prison, or habitual drunkards. A man, to be received, must have both of his arms and legs" (International Order of Twelve Knights and Daughters of Tabor, *Manual . . . General Laws, Regulations, Ceremonies, Drill, and Landmarks* [Mound Bayou, 1951], 123, folder: Knights and Daughters of Tabor, Mississippi Insurance Department, Jackson).

24. Hartwell and Weld, "Mississippi's Miracle Town," 127; "Some Hospital Rates, Rules, and Regulations," *Taborian Star* 18 (February 1943); "Recommendations," 1946, folder 20, box 64, Smith Papers.

25. Annyce Campbell, interview, October 12, 1995; "Notice, P. M. Smith Must Go!" and "Flash News: P. M. Smith Must Go," 1946, folder 16, box 64, Smith Papers; "Hospital Information, Taborian Hospital, Mound Bayou, Miss.," January 31, 1947, and untitled account of the dispute by an official of the Knights and Daughters of Tabor [ca. 1947], folder 6, box 65, Smith Papers.

26. "Applicants for the $1,000 Policy," 1948, folder: United Order of Friendship of America, Mississippi Insurance Department; Hartwell and Weld, "Mississippi's Miracle Town," 127; United Order of Friendship of America, *Constitution and By-Laws* (1949), 1, 18–21, folder: Affiliation of Taborian Hospital with Meharry Medical College and the Development of the OEO Planning Grant, Matthew L. Walker Papers, Meharry Medical College, Nashville, Tenn.

27. "Examination Report: United Order of Friendship of America," December 31, 1960, folder: "Hearing before a Committee of the Mississippi Commission on Hospital Care, in the Matter of Licensing Friendship Clinic, Mound Bayou" [1961], Facilities Licensure and Certification Division, Mississippi Department of Health; Campbell interview, October 12, 1995; Esther Burton, interview, November 2, 1995.

28. John Dittmer, *Local People: The Struggle for Civil Rights in Mississippi* (Urbana: University of Illinois Press, 1994), 32–33; "Mound Bayou: Biggest Building Boom Hits All-Negro Town," *Ebony*, September 1946, 19–24; George F. David, "Deep in the Delta," *Journal of Human Relations* 2 (Spring 1954): 72–75; *Jackson Daily News*, December 14, 1955; Luther McKaskill, M.D., interview, January 18, 1996; Boyd interview.

29. James Summerville, *Educating Black Doctors: A History of Meharry Medical College* (Tuscaloosa: University of Alabama Press, 1983), 93–96, 124; Robert J. Smith, "Managed Health Care," 6–8; Matthew Walker, "Mound Bayou," 310–11.

30. For more on the role of Jim Crow in the Delta and the rise of civil rights, see Dittmer, *Local People*; Charles M. Payne, *I've Got the Light of Freedom: The Organizing Tradition and the Mississippi Freedom Struggle* (Berkeley: University of California Press, 1995); Neil R. McMillen, *Dark Journey: Black Mississippians in the Age of Jim Crow* (Urbana: University of Illinois Press, 1989).

31. A notable example was the Reverend Kelly Miller Smith, a son of P. M. Smith. As a minister in Nashville during the early 1960s, he was an organizer of the sit-down demon-

strations in the city. Peter J. Paris, a professor at the Princeton Theological Seminary, states that the Knights and Daughters of Tabor "prepared Smith for the black consciousness movement of the late sixties" and reflected an "abhorrence of racial discrimination and segregation as paramount evils" (Marcia Riggs, *The Kelly Miller Smith Papers* [Nashville: Jean and Alexander Heard Library, Vanderbilt University, 1989], viii).

32. *Mound Bayou Sentinel*, October 11, 1952; Dittmer, *Local People*, 32–33, 38–40, 53; Payne, *I've Got the Light*, 31–32; "National Council of Negro Leadership, Voters Rally," December 8, 1957, folder 2, box 7, Amzie Moore Papers, State Historical Society of Wisconsin, Madison.

Howard also organized "Mound Bayou Days," which brought together activists from groups such as the RCNL and the NAACP. The participants included Fannie Lou Hamer, Charles Evers, Aaron Henry, and Amzie Moore. See Payne, *I've Got the Light*, 154–55; Kay Mills, *This Little Light of Mine: The Life of Fannie Lou Hamer* (New York: Dutton, 1993), 40–41.

33. *Mound Bayou Sentinel*, October 3, 1953; Mrs. Medgar [Myrlie] Evers (with William Peters), *For Us the Living* (Garden City: Doubleday, 1967), 76–79, 89–90, 94, 116–17, 132–34; Maryanne Vollers, *Ghosts of Mississippi: The Murder of Medgar Evers and the Trials of Byron de la Beckwith and the Haunting of the New South* (Boston: Little, Brown, 1995), 40–44, 56.

34. Burton interview; Evers, *For Us the Living*, 90; Simeon Booker, *Black Man's America* (Englewood Cliffs, N.J.: Prentice-Hall, 1964), 167–69; Dittmer, *Local People*, 47; Vera Pigee, *The Struggle of Struggles*, pt. 1 (Detroit: Harlo, 1975), 63, 106. There is no solid evidence that Howard's participation in civil rights resulted in any harassment from the Insurance Department of Mississippi or the Mississippi Commission on Hospital Care. Charles Evers recalls, however, that "rednecks had shot out his clinic so many times that his patients stayed away" (Charles Evers and Andrew Szanton, *Have No Fear: The Charles Evers Story* [New York: Wiley, 1997], 110).

35. Verner interview, December 30, 1995; Hatch interview; Coleman, "Open Door," 26. Smith contributed $100 to the NAACP in 1943. See L. C. Jefferson to P. M. Smith, November 12, 1943, folder 6, box 65, Smith Papers.

The Taborian Hospital cooperated with the Medical Committee for Human Rights. Volunteers for the committee, including doctors and nurses from around the country, gave aid to civil rights protesters. The work of the committee had been preceded by that of the NMA. As members of the state affiliate of the NMA, both Burton at the Friendship Clinic and James L. Lowry, who was George's successor at the Taborian Hospital, had supported this effort. See Albert B. Britton Jr., M.D., interview, July 17, 1997; Shirley interview; Doug McAdam, *Freedom Summer* (New York: Oxford University Press, 1988), 154–55.

36. Verner interview, December 30, 1995; Yancey interview; Charlotte Walker, M.D., interview, January 21, 1996; *Mound Bayou Sentinel*, February 21, 1953. During a hospital expansion campaign Smith advised members that every "friend—white or colored must be called upon for contribution" (P. M. Smith, "Bi-Monthly Message and Rulings," *Taborian Star* 19 [May–June 1944]).

37. International Order, *Mission of Tabor*, 11, 17; Friendship Clinic, Application for Hospital Renewal, Mississippi Commission on Hospital Care, 1958–66, Facilities Licensure and Certification Division, Mississippi Department of Health. The hospitals did not employ midwives. All babies were delivered by doctors, nurses, or medical students from Meharry. See Walker interview; McKaskill interview.

38. *Jackson Daily News*, August 31, 1950. Former employees do not recall that either hospital made use of folk remedies. See Walker interview; Edward Verner, M.D., interview, August 20, 1997; Campbell interview, October 12, 1995.

39. Perry A. Smith interview; Walker interview.

40. International Order, *Taborian Hospital*, and *Mission of Tabor*, 32–33; *Taborian Bulletin* (January 1963), 16th ed., 5, 8, Bolivar County Public Library; Knights and Daughters of Tabor, Jurisdiction of Mississippi, *Taborian Constitution* [1964], 21–22, folder: Taborian Hospital, Mississippi Department of Health; Dobbins interview. The United Order of Friendship adopted virtually the same collection system; see Campbell interview, October 12, 1995. The only source of governmental funds for the Taborian Hospital was reimbursement for the care of indigent patients. In 1962 the county and state paid for seventy-four patients. Occasional contributions came from foundations, other fraternal societies, and legacies of wills. Most notably, the Taborian Hospital obtained $24,100 in 1957 from the Ford Foundation for purchases of new equipment, and in 1963 it received $5,000 from the Prince Hall Masons of Alabama. See *Taborian Bulletin*, 8, 15; International Order, *Taborian Hospital*; Burton interview.

41. *Mound Bayou Sentinel*, November 8, 1952, and February 28, 1953; Letters, *Taborian Star* 18 (February 1943).

42. *Mound Bayou Sentinel*, November 8, 22, 1952.

43. P. M. Smith, "Monthly Message and Rulings," *Taborian Star* 18 (May 1942); "Monthly Message and Rulings," May 1941, folder 18, box 64, Smith Papers; United Order of Friendship of America, *Constitution and By-Laws*, 17; Dobbins interview.

44. Annyce Campbell, interview, August 26, 1996.

45. Thurmond interview; McKaskill interview.

46. D. Tumminello to Mississippi Commission for Hospital Care, March 10, 1961, and O. E. Ringold to Mississippi Hospital Commission, March 11, 1961, both in folder: "Hearing before a Committee," Mississippi Department of Health.

47. Jessie Lowry, interview, December 12, 1995; Thurmond interview; Campbell interview, August 26, 1996.

48. Phillips to Fowler, memorandum, Mississippi Department of Health; Matthew Walker, "Mound Bayou," 310–11; Louis Bernard, unpublished "Presentation," Archives, Meharry Medical College; Verner interview, August 20, 1997. When Earlee Thompson started her career at the Taborian Hospital at age fourteen, she earned $12 per month as a nurse's aide. Later, the Knights and Daughters of Tabor paid for her to take courses at Meharry Medical College. She resumed work at the hospital as a certified operating room technician.

49. Yancey interview; Verner interview, December 30, 1995; McKaskill interview; Hatch interview.

50. George N. Sadka to James L. Lowry, June 28, 1965, and Sadka to L. B. Griffin, January 26, 1965, folder: Taborian Hospital, Mississippi Department of Health. After nearly closing the Friendship Clinic an official from the commission complained that "no visible progress is being made toward correcting the deficiencies found in your institution, and which you promised faithfully would be corrected approximately one year ago" (Fowler to R. L. Drew, March 13, 1962, folder: Friendship Clinic, Mississippi Department of Health). The files of the Mississippi hospital commission on both hospitals contain numerous other letters that discuss regulatory matters. Dr. Luther McKaskill, a surgeon at the Friendship Clinic in the late 1950s and early 1960s, expressed a common view among the staff of both hospitals when he complained that "a lot of it [the regulation]

was nit-picking. I don't think it was necessary to save lives. It put pressure. A lot of the good people got disheartened and left" (McKaskill interview).

51. Cyril A. Walwyn, M.D., interview with Barbara Allen, March 26, 1980, Special Collections, Ricks Memorial Library; Emma L. Barnes, interview, September 9, 1995; Walls, "Some Extinct Black Hospitals," 7–8.

52. Paul Starr, *The Social Transformation of American Medicine* (New York: Basic Books, 1982), 384–85; Hatch interview; Geiger interview; and Robert J. Smith, interview, April 17, 1996.

53. Beardsley, *History of Neglect*, 176–78; Starr, *Social Transformation*, 348–51.

McKaskill states that by the late 1950s some local blacks had begun to chastise their friends who joined the two societies on the grounds that "'you're just paying those nickels and dimes that don't mean nothing anyway. If you get real sick, you got to go somewhere—Jackson or Memphis or somewhere like that.' I suspect that permeated a lot of the people" (McKaskill interview).

54. U.S. Department of Health, Education, and Welfare, Public Health Service, *Hill-Burton Project Register, July 1, 1947–June 30, 1970* (Washington, D.C.: Government Printing Office, 1970), 150–58; Ringold to Mississippi Hospital Commission, folder: "Hearing before a Committee," Mississippi Department of Health.

55. Thurmond interview; McKaskill interview; Hatch interview.

56. James C. Cobb, *The Most Southern Place on Earth: The Mississippi Delta and the Roots of Regional Identity* (New York: Oxford University Press, 1992), 253–55; Nicholas Lemann, *The Promised Land: The Great Black Migration and How It Changed America* (New York: Vintage, 1991), 309, 319; "The Fifty-sixth Annual Grand Session"; Mississippi Insurance Department, *Biennial Report*, 1959–1961 (Jackson, 1961), 723; "Examination Report," 6; Geiger interview; Dobbins interview; Hatch interview; Campbell interview, August 26, 1996.

57. International Order, *Mission of Tabor*, 29–30; *Taborian Bulletin*, 18; "Increased Assessments Mortuary and Hospital Rider," folder: "Hearing before a Committee," Mississippi Department of Health.

58. Summerville, *Educating*, 124–26; Matthew Walker, "Mound Bayou," 312; Background Data, Mound Bayou Community Hospital, 1967, folder: Mound Bayou Community Hospital, Facilities Licensure and Certification Division, Mississippi Department of Health; L. C. Dorsey, "Health Care in the Delta," *Western Wire*, Spring 1994, 22–23.

59. P. M. Smith et al. to Walter Dell Davis [ca. 1967], folder: Knights and Daughters of Tabor, Mississippi Insurance Department.

60. Louis Bernard, interview, December 19, 1995; Thurmond interview; Campbell interview, August 26, 1996.

61. Geiger interview; Hatch interview. Dr. Count D. Gibson Jr., a pioneer with the Delta Health Center, commented, "It all depends on from whose perspective. Here were our doctors trained in northern hospitals coming down to look at this. How many other rural little hospitals, black or white, mainly white, might not have been all that different?" (Count D. Gibson Jr., interview, October 2, 1995).

Geiger, Hatch, and Gibson had become acquainted with the Taborian Hospital and the Friendship Clinic through their work in the Medical Committee for Human Rights. See Richard A. Couto, *Ain't Gonna Let Nobody Turn Me 'Round: The Pursuit of Racial Justice in the Rural South* (Philadelphia: Temple University Press, 1991), 270–71.

62. Dorsey interview. She adds that "most people loved those doctors [at the fraternal hospitals] because they were kind to their patients and they did listen."

63. Milburn Crowe, interview, August 10, 1995; Willie T. Woodley, interview, September 9, 1995; Dorothy R. Grady, interview, September 30, 1995; Rosetta Barntley, interview, November 21, 1995; Minnie Mabrey, interview, September 9, 1995; Thurmond interview; Lowry interview; Campbell interview, October 12, 1995; Thompson interview; Dobbins interview; Burton interview. The above were either patients or staff at the Taborian Hospital or the Friendship Clinic. McKaskill recalls that the hospitals "weren't in such good financial shape but I thought they were fairly well run. . . . Of course, everything then was dirt cheap. . . . People were given good quality care" (McKaskill interview).

64. Yancey interview; Robert J. Smith interview; Bernard interview.

65. Robert J. Smith interview; Bernard interview.

66. Robert J. Smith interview.

67. Bernard interview; Robert J. Smith interview; Verner interview, August 20, 1997; Yancey interview.

68. Friendship Clinic, Application for Hospital Renewal, Mississippi Commission on Hospital Care, 1958–66, folder: Friendship Clinic, Mississippi Department of Health; Application for Hospital Renewal, Mississippi Commission on Hospital Care, 1961–66, folder: Taborian Hospital; Duke Endowment, Hospital and Orphan Section, *Annual Report* [1958–62].

69. The statistics from South Carolina hospitals deserve several caveats as measures for comparison. First, while there is some overlap, the years of comparison (1961–66 vs. 1958–62) differ somewhat. Moreover, the figures for South Carolina include little information about demographics.

70. The statistics on newborns as a percentage of patients were 8.9 percent for the Taborian Hospital, 8.2 percent for the Friendship Clinic, 16.3 percent for blacks in South Carolina, and 10.1 percent for whites in South Carolina.

71. Individual patient records of the Taborian Hospital and the Friendship Clinic, which are now in the possession of the Delta Health Center, are closed to public scrutiny under state law.

Geiger interview; Robert J. Smith interview; Walker interview; Verner interview; Yancey interview. Bernard recalls that "every now and then, people would come into the clinic with their bags packed and say, 'Doctor, I've come to stay.' . . . Depending on what the transportation situation was like we might say, 'Okay, we will let you sleep here tonight and you can go home in the morning'" (Bernard interview).

72. Bernard interview; *Black Enterprise*, December 1972, 38–39; *Time*, November 25, 1974, 107.

73. *Clarion-Ledger* (Jackson), July 17, 1983.

Chapter Eleven

1. U.S. President's Research Committee on Social Trends, *Recent Social Trends in the United States: Report of the President's Research Committee on Social Trends* (New York: McGraw-Hill, 1933), 2:935–36.

2. Ibid.; Jesse Frederick Steiner, *Americans at Play: Recent Trends in Recreation and Leisure Time Activities* (New York: McGraw Hill, 1933), 129; Richard de Raismes Kip, *Fra-*

ternal Life Insurance in America (Philadelphia: College Offset Press, 1953), 15; "Progress," *Mooseheart Magazine* 6 (September 1920): 1; Loyal Order of Moose, *Proceedings* (1930), 160; Lynn Dumenil, *Freemasonry and American Culture, 1880–1930* (Princeton: Princeton University Press, 1984), 225.

3. Monroe N. Work, *Negro Year Book: Annual Encyclopedia of the Negro* (Tuskegee: Tuskegee Institute, Alabama, Negro Year Book Pub. Co., 1916–17), 395–400; (1925–26), 462–65; (1931–32), 523–25.

4. Merah S. Stuart, *An Economic Detour: A History of Insurance in the Lives of American Negroes* (New York: Wendell Malliet, 1940), 11–34; David M. Fahey, *The Black Lodge in White America: "True Reformer" Browne and His Economic Strategy* (Dayton, Ohio: Wright State University Press, 1994), 33–38; John Sibley Butler, *Entrepreneurship and Self-Help among Black Americans: A Reconsideration of Race and Economics* (Albany: State University of New York Press, 1991), 141–42.

5. Terence O'Donnell, *History of Life Insurance in Its Formative Years* (Chicago: American Conservation Company, 1936), 552–53; Kip, *Fraternal Life Insurance*, 30–31; Stuart, *Economic Detour*, 33–34.

For the best account of the UOTR, see Fahey, *Black Lodge*, 4–40. On black societies during this period, see J. G. De Roulhac Hamilton, "The Sons and Daughters of I Will Arise," *Scribner's Magazine*, September 1926, 325–31; Sadie Tanner Mossell, "The Standard of Living among One Hundred Negro Migrant Families in Philadelphia," *Annals of the American Academy of Political and Social Science* 98 (November 1921): 200–201; Joe William Trotter Jr., *Coal, Class, and Color: Blacks in Southern West Virginia, 1915–32* (Urbana: University of Illinois Press, 1990), 198–213; New Jersey Conference of Social Work, Interracial Committee, *The Negro in New Jersey* (1932; reprint, New York: Negro Universities Press, 1969), 62–63, 88–89; William A. Muraskin, *Middle-Class Blacks in a White Society: Prince Hall Freemasonry in America* (Berkeley: University of California Press, 1975), 29–31; Charles Edward Dickerson II, "The Benevolent and Protective Order of Elks and the Improved Benevolent and Protective Order of Elks of the World: A Comparative Study, Euro-American and Afro-American Secret Societies" (Ph.D. diss., University of Rochester, 1981), 275–81.

6. Loyal Order of Moose, *Minutes* (1929), 300; Steiner, *Americans at Play*, 127–30; Mary Ann Clawson, *Constructing Brotherhood: Class, Gender, and Fraternalism* (Princeton: Princeton University Press, 1989), 259–63; Lizabeth Cohen, *Making a New Deal: Industrial Workers in Chicago, 1919–1939* (New York: Cambridge University Press, 1990), 96–97; Seth M. Scheiner, *Negro Mecca: A History of the Negro in New York City, 1865–1920* (New York: New York University Press, 1965), 95; Kip, *Fraternal Life Insurance*, 182; "The Recommendation of the Grand Aerie Commission," *Eagle Magazine* 5 (April 1917): 4.

7. Workmen's Circle, National Executive Committee, minutes, May 1928, Workmen's Circle Papers, YIVO Institute for Jewish Research, New York, N.Y.

8. Humbert S. Nelli, *Italians in Chicago, 1880–1930: A Study in Ethnic Mobility* (New York: Oxford University Press, 1970), 238; William E. Mitchell, *Mishpokhe: A Study of New York City Jewish Family Clubs* (The Hague: Mouton, 1978), 47–48, 178.

9. "Taxable Status of Fraternal Insurance," *Yale Law Journal* 47, no. 944 (1938): 967–68; Walter Basye, *History and Operation of Fraternal Insurance* (Rochester, N.Y.: Fraternal Monitor, 1919), 44–45, 67–68; Carlos S. Hardy, *Fraternal Insurance Law* (Los Angeles: Carlos S. Hardy, 1916), 31; Kip, *Fraternal Life Insurance*, 112–13, 116–17.

10. Alexa Benson Henderson, *Atlanta Life Insurance Company: Guardian of Black Eco-*

nomic Dignity (Tuscaloosa: University of Alabama Press, 1990), 14–17, 44, 49–58, 64–68; Sutton E. Griggs, *Triumph of the Simple Virtues, or, the Life Story of John L. Webb* (Hot Springs, Ark.: Messenger Publishing, 1926), 20–21; Mississippi Insurance Department, *Biennial Report* (Jackson, 1913–15), 9; *History and Manual of the Colored Knights of Pythias* (Nashville, Tenn.: National Baptist Publishing Board, 1917), 281–82; John Dittmer, *Black Georgia in the Progressive Era, 1900–1920* (Urbana: University of Illinois Press, 1977), 56.

Referring to the impact of insurance and banking regulation, Maggie L. Walker of the IOSL declared that the "white man doesn't intend to wait until the Negro becomes a financial giant, he intends to attack him and fetter him now, while he is an infant in his swaddling cloths, helpless in his cradle" (Maggie L. Walker, "Benaiah's Valour," 6, Addresses, Maggie L. Walker, 1909, Maggie L. Walker Papers, Maggie L. Walker National Historical Site, Richmond, Va.).

11. Hardy, *Fraternal Insurance Law*, 30; National Fraternal Congress of America, *Proceedings* (1915), 644–46; Basye, *History and Operation*, 116–17, 159; Robert W. Cooper, *An Historical Analysis of the Tontine Principle, with Emphasis on Tontine and Semi-Tontine Life Insurance Policies* (Homewood, Ill.: R. D. Unwin, 1972), 2–7.

12. R. Carlyle Buley, *The American Life Convention, 1906–1952: A Study in the History of Life Insurance* (New York: Appleton-Century Crofts, 1953), 1:120–21; Edward J. Dunn, *Builders of Fraternalism in America* (Chicago: Fraternal Book Concern, 1924), bk. 1, 128, 145–49, 239, 275, and bk. 2, 210–11, 413; Kip, *Fraternal Life Insurance*, 37–38.

13. Abb Landis, *Life Insurance* (Nashville, Tenn.: Abb Landis, 1914), 30, 53; William Francis Barnard, "Respectable Confidence Game," *Fraternal Monitor* 13 (March 1, 1903): 17.

These fraternal objections to endowments hardened during the next two decades. In 1904 Abb Landis called them "an excellent refuge for the man who cannot trust himself to make provision for his old age." He approvingly quoted a longtime critic of endowments who had argued that "the union of insurance and investment is unsanctioned by nature" (Landis, "Life Insurance and Fraternal Orders," *Annals of the American Academy of Political and Social Science* 24 [November 1904]: 53).

14. O'Donnell, *History of Life Insurance*, 637; Dunn, *Builders of Fraternalism*, bk. 1, 128, 148–49.

15. Dunn, *Builders of Fraternalism*, bk. 1, 150, 153, 157; Landis, *Life Insurance*, 30, 35–36, 50–53; Hardy, *Fraternal Insurance Law*, 30; Basye, *History and Operation*, 159; Joseph Stipanovich, "Collective Economic Activity among Serb, Croat, and Slovene Immigrants in the United States," in *Self-Help in Urban America: Patterns of Minority Business Enterprise*, ed. Scott Cummings (Port Washington, N.Y.: Kennikat Press, 1980).

The court rulings against fraternal endowments include *Walker v. Giddings*, 61 N.W. 512 (1894); *Calkins v. Bump*, 79 N.W. 491 (1899); *State ex rel. Supreme Lodge K. P. v. Vandiver*, 111 S.W. 911 (1908); *Kirk v. Fraternal Aid Association*, 149 Pacific 400 (1915).

16. Roger L. Ransom and Richard Sutch, "Tontine Insurance and the Armstrong Investigation: A Case of Stifled Innovation, 1868–1905," *Journal of Economic History* 47 (June 1987): 381–82.

17. Ibid., 382, 385–86.

18. Ibid., 388–90.

19. Abb Landis, Notes and Comments, *Fraternal Monitor* 15 (April 1, 1905): 14; "Insurance vs. Investment," *Ladies Review* 13 (May 1907): 106; Basye, *History and Operation*, 159; Stipanovich, "Collective Economic Activity," 168.

20. "Get on to Get Somewhere! This Train Takes You to Success," *Security News* 29

(July 1923): 6; Security Benefit Life Insurance Company, *Security Benefit Life Insurance Company, 1892–1956* (Topeka: Security Benefit Life Insurance, 1956), 17–18; Dean L. Smith, *Eleven Men and Eleven Dollars* (Topeka: Security Benefit Life Insurance, 1976), 72–73.

21. P. H. J. H. Gosden, *The Friendly Societies in England, 1815–1875* (New York: A. M. Kelley, 1967), 261–67; Eric Hopkins, *Working-Class Self-Help in Nineteenth-Century England: Responses to Industrialization* (London: St. Martin's Press, 1995), 44–45, 59–60; William Henry Beveridge, *Voluntary Action: A Report on Methods of Social Advance* (London: Allen and Unwin, 1949), 52.

22. Basye, *History and Operation*, 135, 197–99; "Fraternals and Annuities," *Weekly Underwriter* 97 (February 2, 1918): 137; U.S. Department of Labor, Bureau of Labor Statistics, "Care of Aged Persons in the United States," *Bulletin* 489 (Washington, D.C.: Government Printing Office, 1929), 158–60.

23. Frank Renkiewicz, "The Profits of Nonprofit Capitalism: Polish Fraternalism and Beneficial Insurance in America," in Cummings, *Self-Help*, 123.

24. Viviana A. Zelizer, *Pricing the Priceless Child: The Changing Social Value of Children* (New York: Basic Books, 1985), 121; R. J. Myers, "The Effect of the Social Security Act on the Life Insurance Needs of Labor," *Journal of Political Economy* 45 (October 1937): 682.

25. "Letter and Circular from the Insurance Commissioner of the State of Virginia," November 27, 1909, file A-1049, Maggie L. Walker Papers; George A. Scott, "What of the Coming Generation," *Knights and Ladies of Security* 21 (November 10, 1915): 1.

26. Security Benefit Association, *Proceedings* (1920), 11, and (1928), 27; Fraternal Monitor, *Statistics of Fraternal Benefit Societies* (Rochester, N.Y., 1930), 2; Cohen, *Making a New Deal*, 72.

27. Louise Wolters Ilse, *Group Insurance and Employee Retirement Plans* (New York: Prentice-Hall, 1953), 30–31, 36.

28. National Fraternal Congress and Associated Fraternities of America, *Proceedings* (1913), 604; Basye, *History and Operation*, 136–37.

29. National Fraternal Congress and Associated Fraternities of America, *Proceedings* (1913), 108, 605–6; National Fraternal Congress of America, *Proceedings* (1916), 125.

30. National Fraternal Congress of America, *Proceedings* (1920), 376; Myers, "Effect of the Social Security Act," 682.

31. National Fraternal Congress of America, *Proceedings* (1915), 179; Casualty Actuarial and Statistical Society of America, *Proceedings* (1920–21), 79–82.

32. National Fraternal Congress of America, *Proceedings* (1926), 140–47. For more on fraternal group insurance and reinsurance of societies on a group basis by commercial companies, see Paul S. Taylor, *Mexican Labor in the United States* (1928–34; reprint, New York: Arno Press, 1970), 2:132, 134; Keith L. Yates, *The Fogarty Years: A History of the A.O.U.W., America's First Fraternal Life Insurance Society* (Seattle: Evergreen, 1972), 153; James R. Cook and Leland A. Larson, *Fraternity at Work: The Woodmen of the World Life Insurance Society* (Omaha: Woodmen of the World Life Insurance Society, 1985), 77; National Fraternal Congress of America, *Proceedings* (1915), 146–47; National Negro Insurance Association, *Proceedings* (1931), 33–34.

33. National Fraternal Congress of America, *Proceedings* (1926), 142; Arthur Preuss, comp., *A Dictionary of Secret and Other Societies* (St. Louis: B. Herder, 1924), 50.

34. National Industrial Conference Board, *Industrial Pensions in the United States* (New York: National Industrial Conference Board, 1925), 5–6; Murray Webb Latimer,

Industrial Pension Systems in the United States and Canada (New York: Industrial Relations Counselors, 1932), 1:20–26, 44–53; Carolyn L. Weaver, *The Crisis in Social Security: Economic and Political Origins* (Durham: Duke University Press Policy Studies, 1982), 48, 62–63.

35. Morris J. Vogel, *The Invention of the Modern Hospital: Boston, 1870–1930* (Chicago: University of Chicago Press, 1980), 121–22; American Medical Association, Bureau of Medical Economics, *Medical Relations under Workmen's Compensation* (Chicago: American Medical Association, 1933), 37–39; Pierce Williams, *The Purchase of Medical Care through Fixed Periodic Payment* (New York: National Bureau of Economic Research, 1932), 59–80, 128.

36. Latimer, *Industrial Pension Systems*, 2:660–63; Dan M. McGill, *Fundamentals of Private Pensions* (Homewood, Ill.: R. D. Irwin, 1964), 23–26; Hugh Holleman Macaulay Jr., *Fringe Benefits and Their Federal Tax Treatment* (New York: Columbia University Press, 1959), 125–26; Rainard B. Robbins, *Impact of Taxes on Industrial Pension Plans* (New York: Industrial Relations Counselors, 1949), 10.

37. For a sample of the middle-of-the-road fraternal position on legislation, see National Fraternal Congress of America, *Proceedings* (1926), 237–60.

38. Ibid. (1920), 375, 377.

39. Ibid. (1915), 655, and (1920), 379–80. "Fraternal Beneficiary Protection," Harding added, "is no longer a voluntary organization in which the individual member has voice or power. His part is only a fiction. . . . The great educational and spiritual features are lost. The loss is beyond comprehension, and all, or nearly all, is due to the interference of the State in its endeavor to regulate and control" (ibid., [1915], 656).

40. Robert A. Woods and Albert J. Kennedy, *The Settlement Horizon: A National Estimate* (New York: Russell Sage Foundation, 1922), 200–203; David M. Tucker, *The Decline of Thrift in America: Our Cultural Shift from Saving to Spending* (New York: Praeger, 1991), 98, 116.

41. Tucker, *Decline of Thrift*, 110–11, 116; M. L. Hale, Letter to the Editor: "The Widows' Pension Controversy," *Survey* 29 (February 22, 1913): 736; Odin W. Anderson, *Health Services in the United States: A Growth Enterprise since 1875* (Ann Arbor: Health Administration Service Press, 1985), 69; Isaac M. Rubinow, *Social Insurance, with Special Reference to American Conditions* (New York: Henry Holt, 1913), 9; John A. Lapp, "The Insurance of Thrift," *Annals of the American Academy of Political and Social Science* 87 (January 1920): 21; Abraham Epstein, *The Challenge of the Aged* (New York: Vanguard Press, 1928), 47, 83, 151.

42. Daniel Horowitz, *The Morality of Spending: Attitudes toward the Consumer Society in America, 1875–1940* (Baltimore: Johns Hopkins University Press, 1985), 114–21; Clarence W. Taber, *The Business of the Household* (Philadelphia: Lippincott, 1926), 8; Tucker, *Decline of Thrift*, 116–18; T. J. Jackson Lears, "From Salvation to Self-Realization: Advertising and the Therapeutic Roots of the Consumer Culture, 1880–1930," in *The Culture of Consumption: Critical Essays in American History, 1880–1980*, ed. Richard Wightman Fox and T. J. Jackson Lears (New York: Pantheon, 1983), 32.

43. Lears, "From Salvation," 30–36; Gilbert Seldes, "Service," *New Republic* 43 (July 15, 1925): 207; Edward W. Bok, "The Greatest Word in the English Language," *World's Work* 41 (November 1924): 59; Clifford Putney, "Service over Secrecy: How Lodge-Style Fraternalism Yielded Popularity to Men's Service Clubs," *Journal of Popular Culture* 27 (Summer 1993): 184; Jeffrey A. Charles, *Service Clubs in American Society: Rotary, Kiwanis, and Lions* (Urbana: University of Illinois Press, 1993), 24–25.

44. Bok, "Greatest Word," 59–60; Putney, "Service over Secrecy," 187; Charles, *Service Clubs*, 25, 29, 50–51.

45. Putney, "Service over Secrecy," 185–87.

46. President's Research Committee, *Recent Social Trends*, 931; Robert S. Lynd and Helen Merrell Lynd, *Middletown: A Study in American Culture* (New York: Harcourt, Brace, 1929), 306.

47. John Chapman Hilder, "Hello, Brother," *Saturday Evening Post*, January 12, 1929, 18; Loyal Order of Moose, *Proceedings* (1928), 278–79; (1930), 286–89; and (1931), 33.

48. Charles, *Service Clubs*, 22–24; Loyal Order of Moose, *Proceedings* (1931), 32–33, and (1935), 38.

49. Loyal Order of Moose, *Proceedings* (1929), 19.

50. Cohen, *Making a New Deal*, 64.

51. "Societies Paying Claims for Sickness," *Fraternal Monitor* 21 (August 1, 1910): 24; "Societies Paying Claims for Sickness," *Fraternal Monitor* 21 (March 1, 1911): 25.

The fourteen leading orders paying sick and funeral benefits were the AOF, the IOOF, the Foresters of America, the Knights of Pythias, the Ancient Order of Hibernians, the Improved Order of Red Men, the Independent Order of Rechabites, the Junior Order of American Mechanics, the FOE, the Patriotic Order of Sons of America, the American Mechanics, the Benevolent and Protective Order of Elks, the Irish Catholic Benevolent Union, and the Daughters of Liberty.

52. An exception was Walter Basye, the editor of the *Fraternal Age*. He described fraternal benefits as "better than charity," adding that the "keeping of people above charity is a greater public service than the giving of alms" (Walter Basye, "Responsibility a Qualification," *Fraternal Age* 12 [May 1936]: 10).

More politically radical societies also struggled with this question. A dissident faction of the WC objected to the creation of a Social Service Department because of a "socialist antagonism to all forms of charity, which some members equated with the term social service" (Judah J. Shapiro, *The Friendly Society: A History of the Workmen's Circle* [New York: Media Judaica, 1970], 134).

Chapter Twelve

1. Robert S. Lynd and Helen Merrell Lynd, *Middletown: A Study in American Culture* (New York: Harcourt, Brace, 1929), 308.

2. Noel P. Gist, "Secret Societies: A Cultural Study of Fraternalism in the United States," *University of Missouri Studies* 15 (October 1, 1940): 42–43; Loyal Order of Moose, *Proceedings* (1930), 160; (1935), 210; (1941), 181; Richard de Raismes Kip, *Fraternal Life Insurance in America* (Philadelphia: College Offset Press, 1953), 15.

My earlier discussion of membership from 1920 to 1930 included data from eleven orders and secret societies that concentrated on sick and funeral benefits. By contrast, I was not able to find complete figures from 1930 to 1940 for five of these organizations: the Benevolent and Protective Order of Elks, the Foresters of America, the FOE, the Independent Order of Good Templars, and the Independent Order of Rechabites.

3. J. G. St. Clair Drake, "The Negro Church and Associations in Chicago," 500, A Research Memorandum Prepared by J. G. St. Clair Drake, The Negro in America, June 1, 1940, Carnegie Myrdal Study, box 1, roll 2, Schomburg Center for Research in Black Culture, New York Public Library, New York, N.Y.; Cleo Walter Blackburn, "Five Hundred Negro Families of Chester, Pennsylvania: Statistical Data" (M.A. thesis, Fisk University,

1936), 36; Howard H. Harlan, "Zion Town: A Study in Human Ecology," *Publications of the University of Virginia Phelps-Stokes Fellowship Papers* 13 (1935): 38−39; Harry J. Walker, "Negro Benevolent Societies in New Orleans: A Study of Their Structure, Function, and Membership" (M.A. thesis, Fisk University, 1937), 319−24; Robert Austin Warner, *New Haven Negroes: A Social History* (New Haven: Yale University Press, 1940), 209; Joe William Trotter Jr., *Coal, Class, and Color: Blacks in Southern West Virginia, 1915−32* (Urbana: University of Illinois Press, 1990), 212−13; Darrel E. Bigham, *We Ask Only a Fair Trial: A History of the Black Community of Evansville, Indiana* (Bloomington: Indiana University Press, 1987), 183−85.

4. Lizabeth Cohen, *Making a New Deal: Industrial Workers in Chicago, 1919−1939* (New York: Cambridge University Press, 1990), 229; "The State of the Order," *Moose Docket* 1 (April 1933): 72; Allison Davis, "The Negro Church and Associations in the Lower South," 178, The Negro in America, June 1, 1940, Carnegie Myrdal Study, Schomburg Center; Donald E. Pienkos, *PNA: A Centennial History of the Polish National Alliance of the United States of North America* (New York: Columbia University Press, 1984), 140.

5. Margaret F. Byington, *Homestead: The Households of a Mill Town* (New York: Charities Publication Committee, 1910), 97; Christopher J. Kauffman, *Faith and Fraternalism: The History of the Knights of Columbus, 1882−1982* (New York: Harper and Row, 1982), 127.

6. Charles Wright Ferguson, *Fifty Million Brothers: A Panorama of American Lodges and Clubs* (New York: Farrar and Rinehart, 1937), 130; Ancient Order of United Workmen, Congress, *Proceedings* (1935), 1; "Fraternal Policy-Holder 'On Own,' Editor Asserts" and "Lodges Sound on Insurance," 1935 newspaper articles, scrapbook of Walter Basye, courtesy of Ruth Basye Robinson, Ormond Beach, Fla.; Kip, *Fraternal Life Insurance*, 42, 70−76, 82.

7. Fraternal Monitor, *Statistics of Fraternal Benefit Societies* (Rochester, N.Y., 1930), 2, and (1935), 2; John Charles Herbert Emery, "The Rise and Fall of Fraternal Methods of Social Insurance: A Case Study of the Independent Order of Oddfellows of British Columbia Sickness Insurance, 1874−1951" (Ph.D. diss., University of British Columbia, 1993), 3−6, 129−33, 136−37, 229−30.

8. Cohen, *Making a New Deal*, 227−29.

9. For more details on fraternal sickness, accident, and disability benefits in the 1930s, see Elizabeth L. Otey, "Cash Benefits under Voluntary Disability Insurance in the United States," U.S. Social Security Board, *Bureau Report*, no. 6 (1940): 73−75.

10. Loyal Order of Moose, *Proceedings* (1935), 210.

11. U.S. Department of Commerce, Bureau of the Census, *Benevolent Institutions, 1910* (Washington, D.C.: Government Printing Office, 1913), 43−44.

12. Noel P. Gist, "Fraternal Societies," in *Development of Collective Enterprise: Dynamics of an Emergent Economy*, ed. Seba Eldridge and Associates (Lawrence: University of Kansas Press, 1943), 179.

13. Ibid.; U.S. Senate, Temporary National Economic Committee, Investigation of the Concentration of Economic Power, Monograph No. 2., *Families and Their Life Insurance: A Study of 2132 Massachusetts Families and Their Life Insurance Policies* (Washington, D.C.: Government Printing Office, 1940), 121; Florence M. Hornback, *Survey of the Negro Population of Metropolitan Johnstown, Pennsylvania* (Johnstown, Pa.: Johnstown Tribune, Johnstown Democrat, 1941), 143.

14. Gist, "Fraternal Societies," 179; Martin Wolins and Irving Piliavin, *Institution or Foster Family: A Century of Debate* (New York: Child Welfare League of America, 1964),

37; Tim Hacsi, "From Indenture to Family Foster Care: A Brief History of Child Placing," *Child Welfare* 74 (January–February 1995): 174–75.

15. National Fraternal Congress of America, *Proceedings* (1930), 188–98; (1944), 82–97; (1947), 130–32; Kauffman, *Faith and Fraternalism*, 316; Kip, *Fraternal Life Insurance*, 150; James R. Cook and Leland A. Larson, *Fraternity at Work: The Woodmen of the World Life Insurance Society* (Omaha: Woodmen of the World Life Insurance Society, 1985), 122; Judah J. Shapiro, *The Friendly Society: A History of the Workmen's Circle* (New York: Media Judaica, 1970), 131–32.

16. Gist, "Fraternal Societies," 180; Loyal Order of Moose, *Proceedings* (1939), 122, 289–91.

17. James J. Davis, "What Have Fraternal Societies of America Contributed to the Nation during the Depression?," *Fraternal Monitor* 46 (September 1935): 51; Conrad H. Mann, "The F.O.E. and the 'New Deal,'" *Fraternal Monitor* 46 (October 1935): 31; Frank E. Hering, "Awakening Interest in Old Age Protection," *American Labor Legislation Review* 13 (June 1923): 139–44.

On the weakness of governmental social welfare before the New Deal, see Edwin Amenta, *Bold Relief: Institutional Politics and the Origins of Modern American Social Policy* (Princeton: Princeton University Press, 1998).

18. "Social Security," *Fraternal Age* 12 (October 1935): 12.

Although the NFCA did not take a public position on Social Security, a resolution in 1936 cautioned against adoption of social welfare legislation that would threaten "self-reliance and individual initiative" and "break down our national character as well as to place financial burdens upon those unable to carry more than they are [at] the present time" ("Militant Resolutions Adopted by the N.F.C. of A.," *Fraternal Age* 12 [September 1936]: 13).

19. De Emmett Bradshaw, "Probable Effect of Social Security on Fraternal Insurance," *Woodmen Magazine* 18 (December 1943): 16.

20. "WBA President Broadcasts Plea for Landon," article from unnamed newspaper, Bina West, Press Notices, Woman's Life Insurance Society Papers, Port Huron, Mich.; "Supreme President's Message on Social Security" and "Social Security Act and How It Affects You," *Log* 8 (November 2, 1936).

In reference to the opposition to Social Security, West hoped that most "real American citizens still prefer rugged individualism to ragged regimentation" ("WBA President Broadcasts Plea").

21. Malcolm R. Giles, "The Future of Moose Fraternalism," *Moose Docket* 4 (November 1935): 50–51; "Insuring against Poverty," *Security News* 41 (September 1935): 4.

22. On the state of fraternal membership at the local level during and after World War II, see Frederick A. Bushee, "Social Organizations in a Small City," *American Journal of Sociology* 51 (November 1945): 221–22; W. Lloyd Warner and Paul S. Lunt, *The Social Life of a Modern Community* (1941; reprint, Westport, Conn.: Greenwood, 1973), 318–51; James West, *Plainville, USA* (New York: Columbia University Press, 1945), 81–83.

23. Michael A. Shadid, *A Doctor for the People: The Autobiography of the Founder of America's First Co-operative Hospital* (New York: Vanguard Press, 1939); Bertram B. Fowler, *The Co-operative Challenge* (Boston: Little, Brown, 1947), 184–95; Louis S. Reed, *Blue Cross and Medical Service Plans* (Washington, D.C.: Federal Security Agency, U.S. Public Health Service, 1947); David Rosner and Gerald Markowitz, "Hospitals, Insurance, and the American Labor Movement: The Case of New York in the Postwar Decades," *Journal of Policy History* 9 (1997): 75–91; Joan Burton Trauner, "From Benevolence to

Negotiation: Prepaid Health Care in San Francisco, 1850–1950" (Ph.D. diss., University of California, San Francisco, 1977), 89, 167. Trauner finds evidence that fraternal hospitals were ill equipped to handle medical inflation because members were resistant to raising dues; see "From Benevolence to Negotiation," 121–31.

For examples of the professional, legal, and tax obstacles faced by fraternal and cooperative plans, see *Fisch v. Sivertsen*, 292 N.W. 758 (1940); Gary R. Mormino and George E. Pozzetta, *The Immigrant World of Ybor City: Italians and Their Latin Neighbors in Tampa, 1885–1985* (Urbana: University of Illinois Press, 1987), 201; Joseph Laufer, "Ethical and Legal Restrictions on Contract and Corporate Practice of Medicine," *Law and Contemporary Problems* 6 (Autumn 1939): 516–27; "Notes: Cooperation in Medicine," *Minnesota Law Review* 35 (March 1951): 373–95; Edwin J. Holman and George W. Cooley, "Voluntary Health Insurance in the United States," *Iowa Law Review* 35 (Winter 1950): 183–217; Burke Shartel and Marcus L. Plant, *The Law of Medical Practice* (Springfield, Ill.: Charles C. Thomas, 1959), 265–72; Odin W. Anderson, *The Uneasy Equilibrium: Private and Public Financing of Health Services in the United States, 1875–1965* (New Haven: College and University Press, 1968), 126; *State ex rel. Goodell v. Security Benefit Association*, 87 Pacific 2d 560 (1939); *La Société Française de Bienfaisance Mutuelle v. Kuchel*, 171 Pacific 2d 544 (1946); *re Farmers' Union Hospital Association of Elk City*, 126 Pacific 2d 244.

24. Loyal Order of Moose, *Proceedings* (1930), 160; (1932), 54–59, 90; (1936), 58, 190; Warner Olivier, *Back of the Dream: The Story of the Loyal Order of Moose* (New York: Dutton, 1952), 87–89; Mooseheart, Superintendent, Progress Report, February 25, 1933, James J. Davis Papers, Moose Correspondence, 1930–40, Manuscript Division, Library of Congress, Washington, D.C.

25. Loyal Order of Moose, *Proceedings* (1932), 88–89; (1936), 46; (1942), 37–38; (1943), 26–27; (1946), 76, 176; (1953), 9; Olivier, *Back of the Dream*, 92–106; Malcolm R. Giles, "Three Important Committees," *Moose Docket* 3 (November 1934): 49–50.

26. Loyal Order of Moose, *Minutes* (1925), 4A; (1926), 3A; Loyal Order of Moose, *Proceedings* (1929), 33; (1935), 258–59; 278; (1940), 105; (1942), 36.

27. Loyal Order of Moose, *Proceedings* (1953), 58, 271.

28. Ibid. (1939), 123–24; (1942), 38; (1943), 250; Kurt Wehrmeister, interview, January 23, 1996.

29. Martin L. Reymert, "Report by the Director of the Mooseheart Laboratory for Child Research," January 12–13, 1951, folder: Conferences, etc., box 3, Martin L. Reymert Papers and Collection, Archives of the History of American Psychology, University of Akron, Akron, Ohio; Wehrmeister interview.

30. Robert W. Kleemeier, "Moosehaven: Congregate Living in a Community of the Retired," *American Journal of Sociology* 59 (January 1954): 347–51; Kurt Wehrmeister, "Moosehaven at 70," *Moose* 79 (December 1992–January 1993): 27–28.

31. Kip, *Fraternal Life Insurance*, 182; Mary Ann Clawson, *Constructing Brotherhood: Class, Gender, and Fraternalism* (Princeton: Princeton University Press, 1989), 263–64.

32. National Fraternal Congress of America, *Statistics of Fraternal Benefit Societies* (Naperville, Ill.: National Fraternal Congress of America, 1988), 1, 4, and (1997), 1, 4; Sandra Jaszczak, ed., *Encyclopedia of Associations: An Associations Unlimited Reference* (New York: Gale, 1997), 1:1853–79; John J. Fialka, "The Folks at Lodge 88 Are Trying to Build a Better Moose Trap," *Wall Street Journal*, November 8, 1996.

Although the historical literature on fraternal societies is still thin, there is an abundance of primary sources. Researchers do not always have an easy task, however. With notable exceptions, libraries and historical societies have made only sporadic preservation efforts, and few published guides exist.

Archives and Manuscripts

The national headquarters of the societies often provide the best starting points for research. A few organizations that maintain archives are the Woman's Life Insurance Society (formerly the WBA) in Port Huron, Michigan; Security Benefit Life (formerly the SBA) in Topeka, Kansas; Moose International (formerly the Loyal Order of Moose) in Mooseheart, Illinois; the IOOF in Winston-Salem, North Carolina; the IOF in Toronto, Ontario; the Degree of Honor in Minneapolis, Minnesota; and the MWA in Rock Island, Illinois. These collections tend to be better endowed on published matter, such as periodicals, proceedings, and ritual books, than they are on unpublished sources, such as membership lists or internal correspondence. To locate the phone numbers and addresses of fraternal home offices, see Sandra Jaszczak, ed., *Encyclopedia of Associations: An Associations Unlimited Reference* (New York: Gale, 1997), 1:1853–79.

Uncovering sources on fraternalism at the local level can be far more daunting. Of the thousands of lodges that once existed, only a small fraction left any trace, much less records of consequence. This makes the full story difficult to tell. Often it is only through records maintained at the lodge level, including membership lists, minutes, and account books, that scholars can adequately evaluate sick benefits, lodge practice, and other locally controlled services. The paucity of lodge records even applies to such leading groups as the FOE, the Loyal Order of Moose, the IOF, and the WBA. These local sources are more likely to turn up at historical societies and in the special collections departments of libraries.

Some of the most complete collections, for both lodges and national offices, are for the societies of the new immigrants and their descendants. The Immigration History Research Center at the University of Minnesota has a superb collection. It contains holdings on the Polish National Alliance, the Order of the Sons of Italy, the Slovene National Benefit Society, the First Catholic Slovak Union, and many others. Other good collections are at the Balch Institute of Philadelphia, the YIVO Institute of New York City, and the Western Reserve Historical Society of Cleveland. The *Records of Ethnic Fraternal Benefit Associations in the United States: Essays and Inventories* (St. Paul: Immigration History Research Center, 1981) is an outstanding research guide.

The challenges of finding primary sources on black societies can be even greater. Only recently have libraries and special collections departments made sustained efforts to incorporate them into their collections. The Schomburg Center for Research in Black Culture at the New York Public Library is especially good on the Prince Hall Masons as well as the GUOOF and its auxiliary, the Household of Ruth. The Birmingham Public Library in Alabama has a massive collection on the Knights of Pythias of North America, Asia, and Africa. The contents include dozens of boxes with proceedings, local financial records of lodges, and correspondence. Similar information on the IOSL can be found in the Maggie L. Walker papers at the Maggie Walker National Historical Site in Richmond, Virginia. The collection has a complete listing of policyholders.

Government Publications

Governmental publications, especially after the 1890s, have much to offer researchers. By the 1920s the annual reports of insurance departments generally included data on fraternal life insurance policyholders, reserves, and assets. Many departments also kept extensive files on individual societies. Other key sources are the annual reports of state labor departments. Among the earliest and most comprehensive is Connecticut Bureau of Labor Statistics, *Annual Report* (1892), vol. 1. It has entries on each of the sick benefit and life insurance orders in the state, including membership statistics, organizational structure, and admission requirements.

Many of the state labor department reports featured periodic surveys of wage earner budgets. These covered people in diverse occupations such as coal miners, carpenters, hack drivers, railroad workers, and employees of vehicle manufacturers. It was typical to ask respondents whether they carried life insurance or had fraternal memberships. For examples, see New Hampshire Bureau of Labor, *Annual Report* (1894); Kansas Bureau of Labor and Industry, *Annual Report* (1895, 1896, 1897, 1899); Michigan Bureau of Labor and Industrial Statistics, *Annual Report* (1896, 1897); Colorado Bureau of Labor Statistics, *Annual Report* (1899–1900). The U.S. Bureau of Labor Statistics summarized the results from the state reports in the *Bulletin* and *Monthly Labor Review*. Wage earner surveys that included data on fraternal insurance are less common after the 1920s. A significant exception is U.S. Senate, Temporary National Economic Committee, Investigation of the Concentration of Economic Power, Monograph No. 2, *Families and Their Life Insurance: A Study of 2132 Massachusetts Families and Their Life Insurance Policies* (Washington, D.C.: Government Printing Office, 1940). The results show the diminished importance of fraternal life insurance at the end of the depression.

Also worthwhile are the reports published by temporary state commissions during the 1910s and 1920s to consider the advisability of compulsory insurance: California Social Insurance Commission, *Report* (Sacramento, 1917); Ohio Health and Old Age Insurance Commission, *Report, Recommendations, Dissenting Opinions* (Columbus, 1919); and Pennsylvania Commission on Old Age Pensions, *Report* (Harrisburg, 1919). The most helpful, at least on fraternal insurance, is Illinois Health Insurance Commission, *Report* (Springfield, 1919). The highlight is a detailed block study of the insurance habits of wage earners in Chicago that includes statistics on the type of insurance (fraternal or commercial), the dollar amount of policies, ethnicity, and income. Federal publications on this subject are also of interest: Edgar Sydenstricker, "Existing Agencies for Health Insurance in the United States," in U.S. Department of Labor, Bureau of Labor Statistics, *Bulletin* 212 (June 1917): 430–75.

The federal government issued periodic reports on homes for the aged and orphanages between the 1910s and 1940s. For information on fraternal institutions, see U.S. Department of Commerce, Bureau of the Census, *Benevolent Institutions, 1910* (Washington, D.C.: Government Printing Office, 1913); *Children under Institutional Care, 1923* (Washington, D.C.: Government Printing Office, 1927); and *Children under Institutional Care and in Foster Homes, 1933* (Washington, D.C.: Government Printing Office, 1935). On fraternal homes for the aged, see U.S. Department of Labor, Bureau of Labor Statistics, "Care of Aged Persons in the United States," *Bulletin* 489 (October 1929): 13–191, and "Homes for Aged in the United States," *Bulletin* 677 (1941): 1–21. It was standard practice to record the name of the sponsoring society, the number of residents, financial budgets, and entrance requirements.

The social science literature relating to fraternalism is vast. During the golden age of research between the 1890s and the 1920s, the main concern was insurance ownership by wage earners, as in Louise Bolard More, *Wage-Earners' Budgets: A Study of Standards and Cost of Living in New York City* (New York: Henry Holt, 1907); Robert Coit Chapin, *The Standard of Living among Workingmen's Families in New York City* (New York: Charities Publication Committee, 1909); Margaret F. Byington, *Homestead: The Households of a Mill Town* (New York: Charities Publication Committee, 1910); Bureau of Applied Economics, Inc., "Standards of Living: A Compilation of Budgetary Studies," *Bulletin* 7 (1920); Esther Louise Little and William Joseph Henry Cotton, *Budgets of Families and Individuals of Kensington, Philadelphia* (Lancaster, Pa.: New Era Printing, 1920); and Theresa S. McMahon, *Social and Economic Standards of Living* (Boston: D. C. Heath, 1925).

By the end of the 1920s the focus of research had shifted toward the social, class, and community aspects of lodges. A landmark study was Robert S. Lynd and Helen Merrell Lynd, *Middletown: A Study in American Culture* (New York: Harcourt, Brace, 1929). Measures of fraternal membership in subsequent decades are in Frederick A. Bushee, "Social Organizations in a Small City," *American Journal of Sociology* 51 (November 1945): 217–26; W. Lloyd Warner and Paul S. Lunt, *The Social Life of a Modern Community* (New Haven: Yale University Press, 1941); James West, *Plainville, USA* (New York: Columbia University Press, 1945); George A. Lundberg, Mirra Komarovsky, and Mary Alice McInerny, *Leisure: A Suburban Study* (New York: Columbia University Press, 1934); and J. Allen Williams Jr., Nicholas Babchuk, and David R. Johnson, "Voluntary Associations and Minority Status: A Comparative Analysis of Anglo, Black, and Mexican Americans," *American Sociological Review* 38 (October 1973): 637–45.

Statistical compilations prepared by the fraternal societies and their clearinghouses are extremely useful. For the life insurance orders, see *Statistics of Fraternal Benefit Societies*, which was published by the *Fraternal Monitor*. It has entries on each constituent society, the number and size of policies, assets, reserves, and social welfare services. For many decades, the *Fraternal Monitor* also published the *Consolidated Chart of Insurance Organizations* on fraternal life, sickness, and disability insurance.

Reference Guides and General Surveys

Until the 1980s the definitive reference guide was Albert C. Stevens, *The Cyclopedia of Fraternities* (New York: E. B. Treat, 1907). Unlike many of his contemporaries, Stevens incorporated black societies into his study. No one can afford to ignore Alvin J. Schmidt's *Fraternal Organizations* (Westport, Conn.: Greenwood, 1980), the modern counterpart to Stevens. Edward J. Dunn, *Builders of Fraternalism in America* (Chicago: Fraternal

Book Concern, 1924), is a comprehensive, balanced, and incisive biographical guide to key leaders of the life insurance societies. Just as importantly, Dunn writes with the credibility of a battle-scarred insider.

The critics of ritualistic "secret societies" during the period should not be neglected. In the vanguard of the opposition was the National Christian Association. Organized in 1869 by evangelical Protestants, it sought to "expose" fraternal rituals as unchristian and elitist. Jonathan Blanchard, the president of Wheaton College, was the founder, and his son Charles carried on the fight in the twentieth century. During its long history the National Christian Association reprinted the rituals of the Masons, the Odd Fellows, the Knights of Pythias, and many other societies. Ironically, many fraternal members regarded these exposés as so reliable that they used them when memorizing their assigned lines in ritualistic ceremonies. The National Christian Association filled its journal, the *Christian Cynosure* (Chicago), with both rituals and jeremiads against secret societies. Catholic critics raised many of the same concerns. A leading example was Arthur Preuss, the compiler of *A Dictionary of Secret and Other Societies* (St. Louis: B. Herder, 1924). Despite his biases, Preuss was generally an accurate reporter and drew heavily on the *Fraternal Monitor* and the *Christian Cynosure* as sources.

Many of the earliest general studies of fraternalism were by insiders. Abb Landis, a fraternal actuary, was a key figure at the turn of the century. His writings, though somewhat technical and dry, give rare insights into the origin of the life insurance societies and their struggles with readjustment: *Friendly Societies and Fraternal Orders* (Winchester, Tenn.: Abb Landis, 1900); *Analysis of Fraternal Societies and Illustrations of Premium Computations* (Nashville, Tenn.: Abb Landis, 1906). Walter Basye, *History and Operation of Fraternal Insurance* (Rochester, N.Y.: Fraternal Monitor, 1919), is a succinct introduction to the background of the life insurance orders and the intricacies of legislation. Charles Wright Ferguson, *Fifty Million Brothers: A Panorama of American Lodges and Clubs* (New York: Farrar and Rinehart, 1937), is a colorful and informative popular account.

The overall record of academic scholarship on fraternalism is woefully deficient. Despite the vast influence of societies in American history, most textbooks (at least when discussing the era after anti-Masonry) virtually ignore them. Some exceptions are Noel P. Gist, "Secret Societies: A Cultural Study of Fraternalism in the United States," *University of Missouri Studies* 15 (October 1, 1940); Richard de Raismes Kip, *Fraternal Life Insurance in America* (Philadelphia: College Offset Press, 1953); and Alvin J. Schmidt, *Oligarchy in Fraternal Organizations: A Study in Organizational Leadership* (Detroit: Gale Research, 1973).

Interest picked up a bit in the 1980s. A turning point was the near-simultaneous appearance of Mark C. Carnes, *Secret Ritual and Manhood in Victorian America* (New Haven: Yale University Press, 1989), and Mary Ann Clawson, *Constructing Brotherhood: Class, Gender, and Fraternalism* (Princeton: Princeton University Press, 1989). Both authors concentrate on the gender and class components of fraternalism. For Clawson the fraternal order was "a cultural institution that maintained and idealized solidarity among white men, [and] it offered gender and race as the most logical and legitimate categories for the organization of collective identity" (255). Carnes and Clawson generally skirt the social welfare services of societies or their influence among blacks and immigrants. Another study that emphasizes both class and mutual aid is James R. Orr and Scott G. McNall, "Fraternal Orders and Working-Class Formation in Nineteenth-Century Kansas," in *Bringing Class Back In: Contemporary and Historical Perspectives*, ed. Scott G. McNall,

Rhonda F. Levine, and Rick Fantasia (Boulder: Westview Press, 1991), 101–17. Robert Whaples and David Buffum, in their "Fraternalism, Paternalism, the Family, and the Market: Insurance a Century Ago," *Social Science History* 15 (1991): 97–122, explore some reasons why wage earners purchased fraternal life insurance and sick benefits.

Fraternal societies often appear as sidelights in historical surveys on voluntary associations. A key work on the antebellum era is Richard D. Brown, "The Emergence of Voluntary Associations in Massachusetts, 1760–1830," *Journal of Voluntary Action* 2 (April 1973): 64–73. Conrad Edick Wright, in *The Transformation of Charity in Postrevolutionary New England* (Boston: Northeastern University Press, 1992), carries the research to a higher level. Wright contributes a valuable typology of voluntary associations, and he ably documents the kinds of people who were members. Don Harrison Doyle, *The Social Order of a Frontier Community: Jacksonville, Illinois, 1825–1870* (Urbana: University of Illinois Press, 1978), is a classic. According to Doyle, voluntary associations, such as fraternal orders, represented a common bond for diverse social and political groups and served as imprimaturs of "good credit risk" (186).

Other works in social history for the nineteenth and early twentieth centuries examine fraternalism more peripherally, such as Brian Greenberg, *Worker and Community: Response to Industrialization in a Nineteenth-Century American City, Albany, New York, 1850–1884* (Albany: State University of New York Press, 1985); David P. Thelen, *Paths of Resistance: Tradition and Dignity in Industrializing Missouri* (New York: Oxford University Press, 1986); John S. Gilkeson Jr., *Middle-Class Providence, 1820–1940* (Princeton: Princeton University Press, 1986); Eric Arnesen, *Waterfront Workers of New Orleans: Race, Class, and Politics, 1863–1923* (New York: Oxford University Press, 1991); Gunther Peck, "Manly Gambles: The Politics of Risk on the Comstock Lode, 1860–1880," *Journal of Social History* 26 (Summer 1993): 701–21; Robert H. Wiebe, *Self-Rule: A Cultural History of American Democracy* (Chicago: University of Chicago Press, 1995); Keith E. Whittington, "Revisiting Tocqueville's America: Society, Politics, and Association in the Nineteenth Century," *American Behavioral Scientist* 42 (September 1998): 21–32; Gerald Gamm and Robert D. Putnam, "The Growth of Voluntary Associations in America, 1840–1940," *Journal of Interdisciplinary History* 29 (Spring 1999): 511–57; Elizabeth Jameson, *All That Glitters: Class, Conflict, and Community in Cripple Creek* (Urbana: University of Illinois Press, 1998); and Peter Dobkin Hall, "Vital Signs: Organizational Population Trends and Civic Engagement in New Haven, Connecticut, 1850–1998," in *Civic Engagement in American Democracy*, ed. Theda Skocpol and Morris Fiorina (Washington, D.C.: Brookings Institution Press, forthcoming).

A key service of fraternal societies was recreation. Because of this book's focus on social welfare, I have generally steered clear of this topic. There is no single book on the recreation services of societies, but Kathy Lee Peiss, *Cheap Amusements: Working Women and Leisure in Turn of the Century New York* (Philadelphia: Temple University Press, 1986), reveals some research possibilities. Although Peiss primarily focuses on reformer-organized working girls clubs, she notes that thousands of women participated in fraternal activities such as balls and annual picnics.

The ritual itself was at the center of fraternal recreation, especially during the nineteenth century. Mark Carnes describes how members often devoted hours at a single time to performing their roles in well-scripted ceremonies. James Davis of the Loyal Order of Moose touched on some of this entertainment appeal when he compared the ritual to "reading a novel or seeing a 'movie.' It teaches certain lessons by means of drama . . . in a way that relaxes the men by its contrast to everyday life" ("James J. Davis

Gives a Full and Complete Answer When a Magazine Writer Questions Fraternalism and Its Need for Existence in Affairs of Life," *Fraternal Monitor* 38 [August 1927]: 8).

To gain a fuller understanding of the British variants of mutual aid, see J. M. Baernreither, *English Associations of Working Men* (1889; reprint, Detroit: Gale Research, 1966); William Henry Beveridge, *Voluntary Action: A Report on Methods of Social Advance* (London: Allen and Unwin, 1949); E. P. Thompson, *The Making of the English Working Class* (New York: Vintage, 1966); P. H. J. H. Gosden, *The Friendly Societies in England, 1815–1875* (New York: A. M. Kelley, 1967), and *Self-Help: Voluntary Associations in the Nineteenth Century* (London: Batsford, 1973); David G. Green, *Working-Class Patients and the Medical Establishment: Self-Help in Britain from the Mid-Nineteenth Century to 1948* (New York: St. Martin's Press, 1985); and Eric Hopkins, *Working-Class Self-Help in Nineteenth-Century England: Responses to Industrialization* (London: St. Martin's Press, 1995).

Histories of Specific Societies

It would be difficult to exaggerate the tremendous influence of Freemasonry as a model for American societies. Some key works on the history of this premier fraternal order during the colonial and antebellum periods are Dorothy Ann Lipson, *Freemasonry in Federalist Connecticut* (Princeton: Princeton University Press, 1977); Wayne A. Huss, *The Master Builders: A History of the Grand Lodge of Free and Accepted Masons of Pennsylvania*, vol. 1, *1731–1873* (Philadelphia: Grand Lodge, 1986), 286–91; and Steven C. Bullock, *Revolutionary Brotherhood: Freemasonry and the Transformation of the American Social Order, 1730–1840* (Chapel Hill: University of North Carolina Press, 1996). For more on Freemasonry in the late nineteenth and early twentieth centuries, see Roy Rosenzsweig, "Boston Masons, 1900–1935: The Lower Middle Class in a Divided Society," *Journal of Voluntary Action Research* 6 (July–October 1977): 119–26; Lynn Dumenil, *Freemasonry and American Culture, 1880–1930* (Princeton: Princeton University Press, 1984); and Anthony D. Fels, "The Square and Compass: San Francisco's Freemasons and American Religion, 1870–1900" (Ph.D. diss., Stanford University, 1987).

Professional historians have produced only a few accounts dealing with specific societies, other than Freemasonry. Among these are Christopher J. Kauffman, *Faith and Fraternalism: The History of the Knights of Columbus, 1882–1982* (New York: Harper and Row, 1982), and John Charles Herbert Emery, "The Rise and Fall of Fraternal Methods of Social Insurance: A Case Study of the Independent Order of Oddfellows of British Columbia Sickness Insurance, 1874–1951" (Ph.D. diss., University of British Columbia, 1993). Emery's analysis of fraternal sick benefits is cogent and original.

Books on particular societies authored or commissioned by fraternalists are James L. Ridgely, *History of American Odd Fellowship: The First Decade* (Baltimore: James L. Ridgely, 1878); Myron W. Sackett, *Early History of Fraternal Beneficiary Societies in America: Origin and Growth, 1868–1880* (Meadville, Pa.: Tribune Publishing, 1914); Este Erwood Buffum and Charles E. Whelan, *Modern Woodmen of America: A History*, 2 vols. (Rock Island, Ill.: Modern Woodmen of America, 1927–35); Warren Potter and Robert Oliver, *Fraternally Yours: A History of the Independent Order of Foresters* (London: Queen Anne Press, 1967); Keith L. Yates, *The Fogarty Years: A History of the A.O.U.W., America's First Fraternal Life Insurance Society* (Seattle: Evergreen, 1972); Dean L. Smith, *Eleven Men and Eleven Dollars* (Topeka: Security Benefit Life Insurance, 1976); James R. Cook and Leland A. Larson, *Fraternity at Work: The Woodmen of the World Life Insurance Society* (Omaha: Woodmen of the World Life Insurance Society, 1985); and Victor C. Wood,

Thoughtful for Our Future: A History of the Gleaners (Adrian, Mich.: Gleaner Life Insurance Society, 1993). On fraternal orphanages, see Warner Olivier, *Back of the Dream: The Story of the Loyal Order of Moose* (New York: Dutton, 1952), and Dean L. Smith, *A Nickel a Month* (St. Louis: MidAmerica Publishing, 1979).

Although they were not among the larger societies, the WC and the International Worker's Order have inspired several books: Maximilian Hurwitz, *The Workmen's Circle: Its History, Ideals, Organization, and Institutions* (New York: Workmen's Circle, 1936); Judah J. Shapiro, *The Friendly Society: A History of the Workmen's Circle* (New York: Media Judaica, 1970); Thomas J. E. Walker, *Pluralistic Fraternity: The History of the International Worker's Order* (New York: Garland, 1991); and Arthur J. Sabin, *Red Scare in Court: New York versus the International Workers Order* (Philadelphia: University of Pennsylvania Press, 1993).

Ethnic Groups, Immigrants, and Women

A partial list of case studies on ethnic societies, by both academics and others, includes John O'Dea, *History of the Ancient Order of Hibernians and Ladies' Auxiliary*, 4 vols. (Philadelphia: Keystone Printing, 1923); Christopher Sverre Norborg, *An American Saga* (Minneapolis: Sons of Norway, 1970); Deborah Dash Moore, *B'nai B'rith and the Challenge of Ethnic Leadership* (Albany: State University of New York Press, 1981); Donald E. Pienkos, *PNA: A Centennial History of the Polish National Alliance of the United States of North America* (New York: Columbia University Press, 1984); and R. Valdimer Baumgarten and Joseph Stefka, *The National Slovak Society: 100 Year History, 1890–1990* (Pittsburgh: National Slovak Society, 1990).

Fraternalism among distinct ethnic groups is covered in Marta Weigle, *Brothers of Light, Brothers of Blood: The Penitentes of the Southwest* (Albuquerque: University of New Mexico Press, 1976); Margaret E. Galey, "Ethnicity, Fraternalism, Social and Mental Health," *Ethnicity* 4 (March 1977): 19–53; William E. Mitchell, *Mishpokhe: A Study of New York City Jewish Family Clubs* (The Hague: Mouton, 1978); Frank Renkiewicz, "The Profits of Nonprofit Capitalism: Polish Fraternalism and Beneficial Insurance in the United States," in *Self-Help in Urban America: Patterns of Minority Business Enterprise*, ed. Scott Cummings (Port Washington, N.Y.: Kennikat Press, 1980), 113–29; M. Mark Stolarik, "A Place for Everyone: Slovak Fraternal-Benefit Societies," in Cummings, *Self-Help*, 130–41; Joseph Stipanovich, "Collective Economic Activity among Serb, Croat, and Slovene Immigrants in the United States," in Cummings, *Self-Help*, 160–76; Michael F. Funchion, ed., *Irish American Voluntary Associations* (Westport, Conn.: Greenwood, 1983); Jose Amaro Hernandez, *Mutual Aid for Survival: The Case of the Mexican American* (Malabar, Fla.: Robert F. Krieger Publishing, 1983); Michael R. Weisser, *A Brotherhood of Memory: Jewish Landsmanshaftn in the New World* (New York: Basic Books, 1985); Hannah Kliger, ed., *Jewish Hometown Associations and Family Circles in New York: The WPA Yiddish Writers' Group Study* (Bloomington: Indiana University Press, 1992); Susan D. Greenbaum, "Economic Cooperation among Urban Industrial Workers: Rationality and Community in an Afro-Cuban Mutual Aid Society, 1904–1927," *Social Science History* 17 (Summer 1993): 173–93; and Daniel Soyer, *Jewish Immigrant Associations and American Identity in New York, 1880–1939* (Cambridge: Harvard University Press, 1997).

On fraternal health care among Cubans, the Spanish, and Italians in Florida, see Durward Long, "An Immigrant Co-operative Medicine Program in the South, 1887–1963,"

Journal of Southern History 31 (November 1965): 417–34, and Gary R. Mormino and George E. Pozzetta, *The Immigrant World of Ybor City: Italians and Their Latin Neighbors in Tampa, 1885–1985* (Urbana: University of Illinois Press, 1987).

Works on immigrant social life that mention fraternal societies include Paul S. Taylor, *Mexican Labor in the United States* (1928–34; reprint, New York: Arno Press, 1970); Humbert S. Nelli, *Italians in Chicago, 1880–1930: A Study in Ethnic Mobility* (New York: Oxford University Press, 1970); Irving Howe, *World of Our Fathers* (New York: Harcourt Brace Jovanovich, 1976); William Toll, *The Making of an Ethnic Middle Class: Portland Jewry over Four Generations* (Albany: State University of New York Press, 1982); John E. Bodnar, *The Transplanted: A History of Immigrants in Urban America* (Bloomington: Indiana University Press, 1985); David M. Emmons, *The Butte Irish: Class and Ethnicity in an American Mining Town, 1875–1925* (Urbana: University of Illinois Press, 1989); and Claire E. Nolte, "Our Brothers across the Ocean: The Czech Sokol in America to 1914," *Czechoslovak and Central European Journal* 11 (Winter 1993): 15–37.

Ivan H. Light, *Ethnic Enterprise in America: Business and Welfare among Chinese, Japanese, and Blacks* (Berkeley: University of California Press, 1972), is still essential reading on mutual aid and self-help among immigrants and blacks. Although written from a very different perspective, the same can be said for Lizabeth Cohen, *Making a New Deal: Industrial Workers in Chicago, 1919–1939* (New York: Cambridge University Press, 1990).

Historians have greatly slighted women's involvement in fraternal societies. A few writers, notably Clawson and Carnes, have dealt with auxiliaries, such as the Eastern Star, but these are exceptions. Nevertheless, several historians underscore the importance of female voluntarism as a more general phenomenon: Karen J. Blair, *The Clubwoman as Feminist: True Womanhood Redefined, 1868–1914* (New York: Holmes and Meier, 1980); Mary P. Ryan, *Cradle of the Middle Class: The Family in Oneida County, New York, 1790–1865* (New York: Cambridge University Press, 1981); and Anne Firor Scott, *Natural Allies: Women's Associations in American History* (Urbana: University of Illinois Press, 1991). Much of what we know about women in lodges comes from the writings of fraternalists. See Keith L. Yates, *An Enduring Heritage: The First One Hundred Years of North American Benefit Association (Formerly Woman's Benefit Association)* (Port Huron, Mich.: North American Benefit Association, 1992).

Blacks

When compared with the number of accounts of fraternalism among women, the literature on black fraternal societies is plentiful: Harry J. Walker, "Negro Benevolent Societies in New Orleans: A Study of Their Structure, Function, and Membership" (M.A. thesis, Fisk University, 1937); Betty M. Kuyk, "The African Derivation of Black Fraternal Orders in the United States," *Comparative Studies in Society and History* 25 (October 1983): 559–92; Joel Walker, "The Social Welfare Policies, Strategies, and Programs of Black Fraternal Organizations in the Northeast United States, 1896–1920" (Ph.D. diss., Columbia University, 1985); and Harold S. Forsythe, "Fraternity in the Service of Liberty and Equality: The Social and Political Functions of African-American Fraternal and Mutual-Aid Societies in Virginia, 1865–1890" (paper presented at the Southern History Association, Atlanta, 1997). Prince Hall Freemasonry has received the greatest emphasis. See William A. Muraskin, *Middle-Class Blacks in a White Society: Prince Hall Freemasonry in America* (Berkeley: University of California Press, 1975); Loretta J. Williams, *Black Freemasonry and Middle-Class Realities* (Columbia: University of Missouri Press, 1980);

and Dennis N. Mihelich, "A Socioeconomic Portrait of Prince Hall Masonry in Nebraska, 1900–1920," *Great Plains Quarterly* 17 (Winter 1997): 35–47.

Although the GUOOF was the largest society among blacks for many years, a scholarly case study on it does not exist. The story is somewhat better for the Elks, the True Reformers, and the IOSL: Charles Edward Dickerson II, "The Benevolent and Protective Order of Elks and the Improved Benevolent and Protective Order of Elks of the World: A Comparative Study, Euro-American and Afro-American Secret Societies" (Ph.D. diss., University of Rochester, 1981), and David M. Fahey, *The Black Lodge in White America: "True Reformer" Browne and His Economic Strategy* (Dayton, Ohio: Wright State University Press, 1994). Also see Elsa Barkley Brown, "Womanist Consciousness: Maggie Lena Walker and the Independent Order of Saint Luke," *Signs* 14 (Spring 1989): 610–33.

As with white societies, the key secondary accounts for black societies are still the official histories. A few are Charles H. Brooks, *The Official History and Manual of the Grand United Order of Odd Fellows in America* (1902; reprint, Freeport, N.Y.: Books for Libraries Press, 1971); William P. Burrell and D. E. Johnson, *Twenty-five Years History of the Grand Fountain of the United Order of True Reformers, 1881–1905* (1909; reprint, Westport, Conn.: Negro Universities Press, 1970); *History and Manual of the Colored Knights of Pythias* (Nashville, Tenn.: National Baptist Publishing Board, 1917); A. E. Bush and P. L. Dorman, *History of the Mosaic Templars of America: Its Founders and Officials* (Little Rock: Central Printing, 1924); Sutton E. Griggs, *Triumph of the Simple Virtues, or, the Life Story of John L. Webb* (Hot Springs, Ark.: Messenger Publishing, 1926); and Wendell P. Dabney, *Maggie L. Walker and the I.O. of Saint Luke: The Woman and Her Work* (Cincinnati: Dabney Publishing, 1927).

Fraternal health care among blacks has turned into an exciting research field. See, for example, Claude F. Jacobs, "Strategies of Neighborhood Health-Care among New Orleans Blacks: From Voluntary Association to Public Policy" (Ph.D. diss., Tulane University, 1980), and "Benevolent Societies of New Orleans Blacks during the Late Nineteenth and Early Twentieth Centuries," *Louisiana History* 29 (Winter 1988): 21–33, and Earline Rae Ferguson, "Sisterhood and Community: The Sisters of Charity and African American Women's Health Care in Indianapolis, 1876–1920," in *Midwestern Women: Work, Community, and Leadership at the Crossroads,* ed. Wendy Hamand Venet and Lucy Eldersveld Murphy (Bloomington: Indiana University Press, 1997), 158–77.

A sampling of books and articles on other aspects of black social life that discuss fraternal societies includes William L. Pollard, *A Study of Black Self-Help* (San Francisco: R and E Research, 1978); Leonard P. Curry, *The Free Black in Urban America, 1800–1850: The Shadow of the Dream* (Chicago: University of Chicago Press, 1981); James Borchert, *Alley Life in Washington: Family, Community, Religion, and Folklife in the City, 1850–1970* (Urbana: University of Illinois Press, 1982); Peter J. Rachleff, *Black Labor in Richmond, 1865–1890* (Urbana: University of Illinois Press, 1984); Darrel E. Bigham, *We Ask Only a Fair Trial: A History of the Black Community of Evansville, Indiana* (Bloomington: Indiana University Press, 1989); Ralph Watkins, "A Reappraisal of the Role of Voluntary Associations in the African American Community," *Afro-Americans in New York Life and History* 14 (July 1990): 51–60; Joe William Trotter Jr., *Coal, Class, and Color: Blacks in Southern West Virginia, 1915–32* (Urbana: University of Illinois Press, 1990); John Sibley Butler, *Entrepreneurship and Self-Help among Black Americans: A Reconsideration of Race and Economics* (Albany: State University of New York Press, 1991); Elsa Barkley Brown, "Uncle Ned's Children: Negotiating Community and Freedom in Postemancipation Richmond, Virginia" (Ph.D. diss., Kent State University, 1994); Nick Salvatore, *We All*

Got History: The Memory Books of Amos Webber (New York: Times Books, 1996); Anne Meis Knupfer, *Toward a Tenderer Humanity and a Nobler Womanhood: African American Women's Clubs in Turn-of-the-Century Chicago* (New York: New York University Press, 1996); and Daniel Levine, "A Single Standard of Civilization: Black Private Social Welfare Institutions in the South, 1880s–1920s," *Georgia Historical Quarterly* (Spring 1997): 1–26.

Since the early twentieth century, social scientists have occasionally delved into black fraternalism, notably W. E. B. Du Bois, *Economic Cooperation among Negro Americans* (Atlanta: Atlanta University Press, 1907); Howard W. Odum, "Social and Mental Traits of the Negro: Research into the Conditions of the Negro Race in Southern Towns," *Studies in History, Economics, and Public Law* 37 (1910); Asa E. Martin, *Our Negro Population: A Sociological Study of the Negroes of Kansas City, Missouri* (1913; reprint, New York: Negro Universities Press, 1969); Sadie Tanner Mossell, "The Standard of Living among One Hundred Negro Migrant Families in Philadelphia," *Annals of the American Academy of Political and Social Science* 98 (November 1921): 173–201; Howard H. Harlan, "Zion Town: A Study in Human Ecology," *Publications of the University of Virginia Phelps-Stokes Fellowship Papers* 13 (1935); Cleo Walter Blackburn, "Five Hundred Negro Families of Chester, Pennsylvania: Statistical Data" (M.A. thesis, Fisk University, 1936); Hortense Powdermaker, *After Freedom: A Cultural Study in the Deep South* (1939; reprint, New York: Russell and Russell, 1966); J. G. St. Clair Drake, "The Negro Church and Associations in Chicago," 500, A Research Memorandum Prepared by J. G. St. Clair Drake, The Negro in America, June 1, 1940, Carnegie Myrdal Study, box 1, roll 2 (Schomburg Center for Research in Black Culture, New York Public Library, New York, N.Y.); Robert Austin Warner, *New Haven Negroes: A Social History* (New Haven: Yale University Press, 1940); Florence M. Hornback, *Survey of the Negro Population of Metropolitan Johnstown, Pennsylvania* (Johnstown, Pa.: Johnstown Tribune, Johnstown Democrat, 1941); S. John Dackawich, "Voluntary Association of Central Area Negroes," *Pacific Sociological Review* 9 (Fall 1966): 74–78; and Jack C. Ross and Raymond H. Wheeler, *Black Belonging: A Study of the Social Correlates of Work Relations among Negroes* (Westport, Conn.: Greenwood, 1971).

Health Care

An adequate understanding of fraternal medical services, such as lodge practice and hospitalization, requires some knowledge of broader historical trends in health care. Paul Starr, *The Social Transformation of American Medicine* (New York: Basic Books, 1982), remains the best overview. Also important are Gerald E. Markowitz and David Karl Rosner, "Doctors in Crisis: A Study of the Use of Medical Education Reform to Establish Modern Professional Elitism in Medicine," *American Quarterly* 25 (March 1973): 83–107; Ronald Hamowy, "The Early Development of Medical Licensing Laws in the United States, 1875–1900," *Journal of Libertarian Studies* 3 (1979): 73–119; David Rosner, *A Once Charitable Enterprise: Hospitals and Health Care in Brooklyn and New York, 1885–1915* (Cambridge: Cambridge University Press, 1982); George Rosen, *The Structure of American Medical Practice, 1875–1941* (Philadelphia: University of Pennsylvania Press, 1983); and Todd L. Savitt, "Abraham Flexner and the Black Medical Schools," in *Beyond Flexner: Medical Education in the Twentieth Century*, ed. Barbara Barzansky and Norman Gevitz (New York: Greenwood, 1992), 65–81.

On health care for blacks, see James Summerville, *Educating Black Doctors: A History of Meharry Medical College* (Tuscaloosa: University of Alabama Press, 1983); Edwina Walls, "Some Extinct Black Hospitals of Little Rock and Pulaski County," *Pulaski County Historical Review* 34 (Spring 1986): 3–13; Mitchell F. Rice and Woodrow Jones Jr., *Public Policy and the Black Hospital: From Slavery to Segregation to Integration* (Westport, Conn., Greenwood, 1994); and Vanessa Northington Gamble, *Making a Place for Ourselves: The Black Hospital Movement, 1920–1945* (New York: Oxford University Press, 1995).

Many cooperative medical plans shared common features with lodge practice and fraternal hospitalization and faced similar challenges. On union health care, see Alan Derickson, *Workers' Health, Workers' Democracy: The Western Miners' Struggle, 1891–1925* (Ithaca: Cornell University Press, 1988), and David Rosner and Gerald Markowitz, "Hospitals, Insurance, and the American Labor Movement: The Case of New York in the Postwar Decades," *Journal of Policy History* 9 (1997): 74–95. Both Bertram B. Fowler, *The Co-operative Challenge* (Boston: Little, Brown, 1947), and Michael A. Shadid, *Crusading Doctor: My Fight for Cooperative Medicine* (1956; reprint, Norman: University of Oklahoma Press, 1992), relate the story of the Community Hospital of Elk City, Oklahoma. For overviews of these and other cooperative medical arrangements, see Franz Goldmann, *Voluntary Medical Care Insurance in the United States* (New York: Columbia University Press, 1948); Jerome L. Schwartz, "Early History of Prepaid Medical Care Plans," *Bulletin of the History of Medicine* 39 (September–October 1965): 450–75; and Joan Burton Trauner, "From Benevolence to Negotiation: Prepaid Health Care in San Francisco, 1850–1950" (Ph.D. diss., University of California, San Francisco, 1977).

The professional, legal, and tax obstacles confronted by fraternal and cooperative medical plans are discussed in Joseph Laufer, "Ethical and Legal Restrictions on Contract and Corporate Practice of Medicine," *Law and Contemporary Problems* 6 (Autumn 1939): 516–27; *State ex rel. Goodell v. Security Benefit Association*, 87 Pacific 2d 560 (1939); *Fisch v. Sivertsen*, 292 N.W. 758 (1940); *La Société Française de Bienfaisance Mutuelle v. Kuchel*, 171 Pacific 2d 544 (1946); Frank R. Kennedy, "The American Medical Association: Power, Purpose, and Politics in Organized Medicine," *Yale Law Journal* 63 (May 1954): 938–1023; and Burke Shartel and Marcus L. Plant, *The Law of Medical Practice* (Springfield, Ill.: Charles C. Thomas, 1959).

For more on the rise of third-party payment systems, see Louis S. Reed, *Blue Cross and Medical Service Plans* (Washington, D.C.: Federal Security Agency, U.S. Public Health Service, 1947); George W. Cooley, "Voluntary Health Insurance in the United States," *Iowa Law Review* 35 (Winter 1950): 183–217; and Ronald L. Numbers, "The Third Party: Health Insurance in America," in *Sickness and Health in America: Readings in the History of Medicine and Public Health*, by Judith Walzer Leavitt and Ronald L. Numbers (Madison: University of Wisconsin Press, 1985), 233–45. Morris J. Vogel, *The Invention of the Modern Hospital: Boston, 1870–1930* (Chicago: University of Chicago Press, 1980), argues persuasively that workmen's compensation was a precursor to the third-party payment system.

Commercial Insurance, Pensions, and Industrial Welfare

In addition to fraternal societies, the pre–New Deal safety net included commercial insurance, company pensions, and industrial welfare programs. Carolyn L. Weaver, *The*

Crisis in Social Security: Economic and Political Origins (Durham: Duke University Press Policy Studies, 1982), has not received the attention it deserves. Other relevant works are Stuart D. Brandes, *American Welfare Capitalism, 1880–1940* (Chicago: University of Chicago Press, 1976); Andrea Tone, *The Business of Benevolence: Industrial Paternalism in Progressive America* (Ithaca: Cornell University Press, 1997); and Steven A. Sass, *The Promise of Private Pensions: The First One Hundred Years* (Cambridge: Harvard University Press, 1997). For some modern implications, see Daniel Shapiro, "Can Old-Age Insurance Be Justified?," in *The Welfare State*, ed. Ellen Frankel Paul, Fred D. Miller Jr., and Jeffrey Paul (Cambridge: Cambridge University Press, 1997), 116–44.

On tontine insurance, a ubiquitous form of old-age protection at the turn of the century, see Robert W. Cooper, *An Historical Analysis of the Tontine Principle, with Emphasis on Tontine and Semi-Tontine Life Insurance Policies* (Homewood, Ill.: R. D. Unwin, 1972). Roger L. Ransom and Richard Sutch, "Tontine Insurance and the Armstrong Investigation: A Case of Stifled Innovation, 1868–1905," *Journal of Economic History* 47 (June 1987): 379–90, is a provocative contribution. Unfortunately, social welfare historians have rarely cited it.

On industrial insurance, a chief competitor to fraternal insurance among the working class, see Charles Richmond Henderson, *Industrial Insurance in the United States* (Chicago: University of Chicago Press, 1911); Marquis James, *The Metropolitan Life: A Study in Business Growth* (New York: Viking, 1947); Earl Chapin May and Will Oursler, *The Prudential: A Story of Human Security* (Garden City: Doubleday, 1950), 36–37; William H. A. Carr, *From Three Cents a Week: The Story of the Prudential Insurance Company of America* (Englewood Cliffs, N.J.: Prentice-Hall, 1975); and Diane Hamilton, "The Cost of Caring: The Metropolitan Life Insurance Company's Visiting Nurse Service, 1909–1953," *Bulletin of the History of Medicine* 63 (Fall 1989): 414–34.

Industrial policies were the bread and butter of the leading black commercial insurance companies, many of which were founded by former fraternalists: Merah S. Stuart, *An Economic Detour: A History of Insurance in the Lives of American Negroes* (New York: Wendell Malliet, 1940); Jesse Edward Gloster, *North Carolina Mutual Life: Its Historical Development and Current Operations* (New York: Arno Press, 1976); Alexa Benson Henderson, *Atlanta Life Insurance Company: Guardian of Black Economic Dignity* (Tuscaloosa: University of Alabama Press, 1990); and Robert E. Weems Jr., *Black Business in the Black Metropolis: The Chicago Metropolitan Assurance Company, 1925–1985* (Bloomington: Indiana University Press, 1996).

Governmental Welfare

Theda Skocpol, *Protecting Soldiers and Mothers: The Political Origins of Social Policy in the United States* (Cambridge: Harvard University Press, Belknap Press, 1992), explores major issues in the history of the early welfare state. For more on the debates over compulsory health insurance in the 1910s, see Ronald L. Numbers, *Almost Persuaded: American Physicians and Compulsory Health Insurance, 1912–1920* (Baltimore: Johns Hopkins University Press, 1978), and Beatrix R. Hoffman, "Health Insurance and the Making of the American Welfare State" (Ph.D. diss., Rutgers University, 1996). Other recent works on the development of the early welfare state include Molly Ladd-Taylor, *Mother-Work: Women, Child Welfare, and the State, 1890–1930* (Urbana: University of Illinois Press, 1994); David A. Moss, *Socializing Security: Progressive-Era Economists and the Origins of American Social Policy* (Cambridge: Harvard University Press, 1996); and Joanne L.

Goodwin, *Gender and the Politics of Welfare Reform: Mothers' Pensions in Chicago, 1911–1929* (Chicago: University of Chicago Press, 1997).

The impact of unemployment on workers and unemployment insurance is covered in Daniel Nelson, *Unemployment Insurance: The American Experience, 1915–1935* (Madison: University of Wisconsin Press, 1969); Alexander Keyssar, *Out of Work: The First Century of Unemployment in Massachusetts* (Cambridge: Cambridge University Press, 1986); Udo Sautter, *Three Cheers for the Unemployed: Government and Unemployment before the New Deal* (New York: Cambridge University Press, 1991); Michael B. Rappaport, "The Private Provision of Unemployment Insurance," *Wisconsin Law Review*, no. 1 (1992): 61–129; and Richard K. Vedder and Lowell E. Gallaway, *Out of Work: Unemployment and Government in Twentieth-Century America* (New York: Holmes and Meier, 1993).

The relationship between the federal tax code and fringe benefits is examined in Edwin Amenta, *Bold Relief: Institutional Politics and the Origins of Modern American Social Policy* (Princeton: Princeton University Press, 1998). Earlier works on this subject are Murray Webb Latimer, *Industrial Pension Systems in the United States and Canada*, vol. 1 (New York: Industrial Relations Counselors, 1932); Rainard B. Robbins, *Impact of Taxes on Industrial Pension Plans* (New York: Industrial Relations Counselors, 1949); Hugh Holleman Macaulay Jr., *Fringe Benefits and Their Federal Tax Treatment* (New York: Columbia University Press, 1959); and Dan M. McGill, *Fundamentals of Private Pensions* (Homewood, Ill.: R. D. Irwin, 1964).

Nonfraternal Voluntarism and Philanthropy

Beginning in the 1910s, fraternal orders of all stripes faced stiff competition from the Rotary, the Kiwanis, and other service organizations. Jeffrey A. Charles, *Service Clubs in American Society: Rotary, Kiwanis, and Lions* (Urbana: University of Illinois Press, 1993), and Clifford Putney, "Service over Secrecy: How Lodge-Style Fraternalism Yielded Popularity to Men's Service Clubs," *Journal of Popular Culture* 27 (Summer 1993): 179–90, argue that fraternal mutual aid during the 1920s gave way to the new ethic of service to society as a whole.

Meanwhile, the old values of thrift, self-reliance, and self-sacrifice lost some of their luster. A few works on this transformation are T. J. Jackson Lears, "From Salvation to Self-Realization: Advertising and the Therapeutic Roots of the Consumer Culture, 1880–1930," in *The Culture of Consumption: Critical Essays in American History, 1880–1980*, ed. Richard Wightman Fox and T. J. Jackson Lears (New York: Pantheon, 1983), 3–38; Daniel Horowitz, *The Morality of Spending: Attitudes toward the Consumer Society in America, 1875–1940* (Baltimore: Johns Hopkins University Press, 1985); and David M. Tucker, *The Decline of Thrift in America: Our Cultural Shift from Saving to Spending* (New York: Praeger, 1991).

The literature on orphanages, albeit largely dealing with nonfraternal institutions, is rapidly growing. See Peter C. Holloran, *Boston's Wayward Children: Social Services for Homeless Children, 1830–1930* (Rutherford, N.J.: Fairleigh Dickinson University Press, 1989); Gary Edward Polster, *Inside Looking Out: The Cleveland Jewish Orphan Asylum, 1868–1924* (Kent, Ohio: Kent State University Press, 1990); Hyman Bogen, *The Luckiest Orphans: A History of the Hebrew Orphan Asylum of New York* (Urbana: University of Illinois Press, 1992); Reena Sigman Friedman, *These Are Our Children: Jewish Orphanages in the United States, 1880–1925* (Hanover, N.H.: University Press of New England for Brandeis University Press, 1994); Nurith Zmora, *Orphanages Reconsidered: Child Care*

Institutions in Progressive Era Baltimore (Philadelphia: Temple University Press, 1994); Eve P. Smith, "Bring Back the Orphanages? What Policymakers of Today Can Learn from the Past," *Child Welfare* 74 (January–February 1995): 115–41; Wilma Peebles-Wilkins, "Jane Porter Barrett and the Virginia Industrial School for Colored Girls: Community Response to the Needs of African American Children," *Child Welfare* 74 (January–February 1995): 143–61; Kenneth Cmiel, *A Home of Another Kind: One Chicago Orphanage and the Tangle of Child Welfare* (Chicago: University of Chicago Press, 1995); Matthew A. Crenson, *Building the Invisible Orphanage: A Prehistory of the American Welfare System* (Cambridge: Harvard University Press, 1998); and Richard B. McKenzie, ed., *Rethinking Orphanages for the Twenty-first Century* (Thousand Oaks, Calif.: Sage Publications, 1999). The rhetoric, and often the reality, of Mooseheart and other fraternal orphanages strongly resembled the George Junior Republics and related experiments: Jack M. Holl, *Juvenile Reform in the Progressive Era: William R. George and the Junior Republic Movement* (Ithaca: Cornell University Press, 1971), and LeRoy Ashby, *Saving the Waifs: Reformers and Dependent Children, 1890–1917* (Philadelphia: Temple University Press, 1984).

Until, and even after, the depression, public and private social welfare organizations subscribed to the doctrine of the "deserving" and "undeserving." For many years most historians regarded these distinctions as misguided, simplistic, or tinged with class bias. See, in particular, Michael B. Katz, *The Undeserving Poor: From the War on Poverty to the War on Welfare* (New York: Pantheon, 1989), and Linda Gordon, *Pitied but Not Entitled: Single Mothers and the History of Welfare, 1890–1935* (New York: Free Press, 1994). More recently, others have cast this dichotomy in a more positive light: Marvin N. Olasky, *The Tragedy of American Compassion* (Washington, D.C.: Regnery Gateway, 1992), and Gertrude Himmelfarb, *The De-Moralization of Society: From Victorian Virtues to Modern Values* (New York: Knopf, 1995). For a hard-hitting critique of Olasky, see Stephen T. Ziliak, "The End of Welfare and the Contradiction of Compassion," *Independent Review* 1 (Spring 1997): 55–73. For a biography of perhaps the leading charity society proponent of making distinctions between the deserving and the undeserving, see Joan Waugh, *Unsentimental Reformer: The Life of Josephine Shaw Lowell* (Cambridge: Harvard University Press, 1997). The essays in Donald T. Critchlow and Charles H. Parker, eds., *With Us Always: A History of Private Charity and Public Welfare* (Landham, Md.: Rowman and Littlefield, 1998), provide diverse perspectives on a wide range of topics.

There were parallels between the goals of fraternal societies and settlement houses during the late nineteenth and early twentieth centuries. Both movements shared, at least in part, the ideals of breaking down distinctions between classes and different ethnic groups and creating cultural and recreational outlets for the working class. An obvious difference is that the initiative in the settlement house movement came primarily from people who were neither working class nor beneficiaries of the services. Books on this subject include Elisabeth Lasch-Quinn, *Black Neighbors: Race and the Limits of Reform in the American Settlement House Movement, 1890–1945* (Chapel Hill: University of North Carolina Press, 1993); Ruth Hutchinson Crocker, *Social Work and Social Order: The Settlement Movement in Two Industrial Cities, 1889–1930* (Urbana: University of Illinois Press, 1992); Mina Julia Carson, *Settlement Folk: Social Thought and the American Settlement Movement, 1885–1930* (Chicago: University of Chicago Press, 1990); Rivka Shpak Lissak, *Pluralism and Progressives: Hull House and the New Immigrants, 1890–1919* (Chicago: University of Chicago Press, 1989); and Allen F. Davis, *American Heroine: The Life and Legend of Jane Addams* (New York: Oxford University Press, 1973).

Social Capital and Civil Society

The history of fraternal societies has significant implications for recent debates on social capital, networks of trust, and civil society. The term "social capital" is used in Robert D. Putnam, with Roberto Leonardi and Raffaella Y. Nanetti, *Making Democracy Work: Civic Traditions in Modern Italy* (Princeton: Princeton University Press, 1993), to describe the "features of social organization, such as trust, norms, and networks, that can improve the efficiency of society by facilitating coordinated actions" (167). Putnam points to the waning membership of voluntary associations, including fraternal orders, as evidence in his much cited "Bowling Alone: America's Declining Social Capital," *Journal of Democracy* 6 (January 1995): 65–78. Meanwhile, Francis Fukuyama weighs in with *Trust: The Social Virtues and the Creation of Prosperity* (New York: Free Press, 1995). According to Fukuyama, a high level of trust is the best guarantee of economic vibrancy and social stability. Much like Putnam, he associates frayed voluntary and kinship networks in the United States as symptomatic of a "Crisis of Trust" (267). For a more upbeat assessment of the current levels of social capital and trust in the United States, see Everett Carll Ladd, *The Ladd Report* (New York: Free Press, 1999). Two other recent studies on trust as a feature of voluntarism are Daniel B. Klein, "Trust for Hire: Voluntary Remedies for Quality and Safety," and Daniel B. Klein and Jeremy Shearmur, "Good Conduct in the Great Society: Adam Smith and the Role of Reputation." Both are in Daniel Klein, ed., *Reputation: Studies in Voluntary Elicitation of Good Conduct* (Ann Arbor: University of Michigan Press, 1997), 87–133.

Several other works of interest should be mentioned. Although rarely cited, Charles A. Murray, *In Pursuit: Of Happiness and Good Government* (New York: Simon and Shuster, 1988), anticipates many of the arguments of Putnam and Fukuyama. Murray contends that the well-being of a society ultimately depends on the strength (to quote Edmund Burke) of its "little platoons." He stresses that "the little platoons of work, family, and community are the nexus . . . through which the satisfactions that happiness represents are obtained" (261). The modern implications of mutual aid are examined in depth in David Schmidtz and Robert E. Goodin, *Social Welfare and Individual Responsibility* (Cambridge: Cambridge University Press, 1998).

Conclusion

The opportunities for further scholarship are almost endless. A few possible topics immediately come to mind. There is a need, for example, for a fuller comparison of British and American arrangements of mutual aid. Such a study can help answer the question of why Americans embraced the model of the life insurance society while the British did not. The rise and fall of the endowment societies is almost unexplored territory. Historians know very little about who belonged to these societies, their importance as social organizations, or the reasons for their rapid decline. Similar questions can be asked about the quasi-fraternal burial societies, which held sway among blacks in the South and in many northern cities.

The impact of public policy on shaping the character and fate of fraternal societies is another inviting topic. The "crowding out thesis" awaits further exploration. This would entail an assessment of the respective roles played by government regulation, commercial insurance, private corporations, and fraternal internal weaknesses. On a related theme, historians need to dig more deeply into the relationship between the tax code and the rise of third-party payment systems.

The historiography of fraternalism, like that for labor or women's history in the 1950s, is in its infancy. This situation is bound to change as scholars continue to realize that the study of fraternalism offers new insights into such disciplines as the history of medical care, insurance, social welfare, community life, children, blacks, and women. For these and many other reasons, it is safe to predict an improvement in the quantity and quality of research during the coming decades.